Shojo Beat

S·A
Special A

Kei & Midori

Volume 11

Story & Art by
Maki Minami

STORY

★At the tender age of 6, carpenter's daughter Hikari Hanazono suffered her first loss to the wealthy Kei Takishima in a wrestling match. Now the hardworking Hikari has followed Kei to the most elite school for the rich just to beat him! I call this story "Overthrow Takishima! Rise Above Perpetual Second Place!!" It's the story of Hikari's sweat, tears and passion, with a little bit of love thrown in!

★Hikari and Kei finally have their long-awaited first date… But Midori, Kei's mom, comes for a sudden visit and eventually sends them to Australia for Christmas. The two really begin to enjoy their Christmas together when Midori shows up with a surprise…

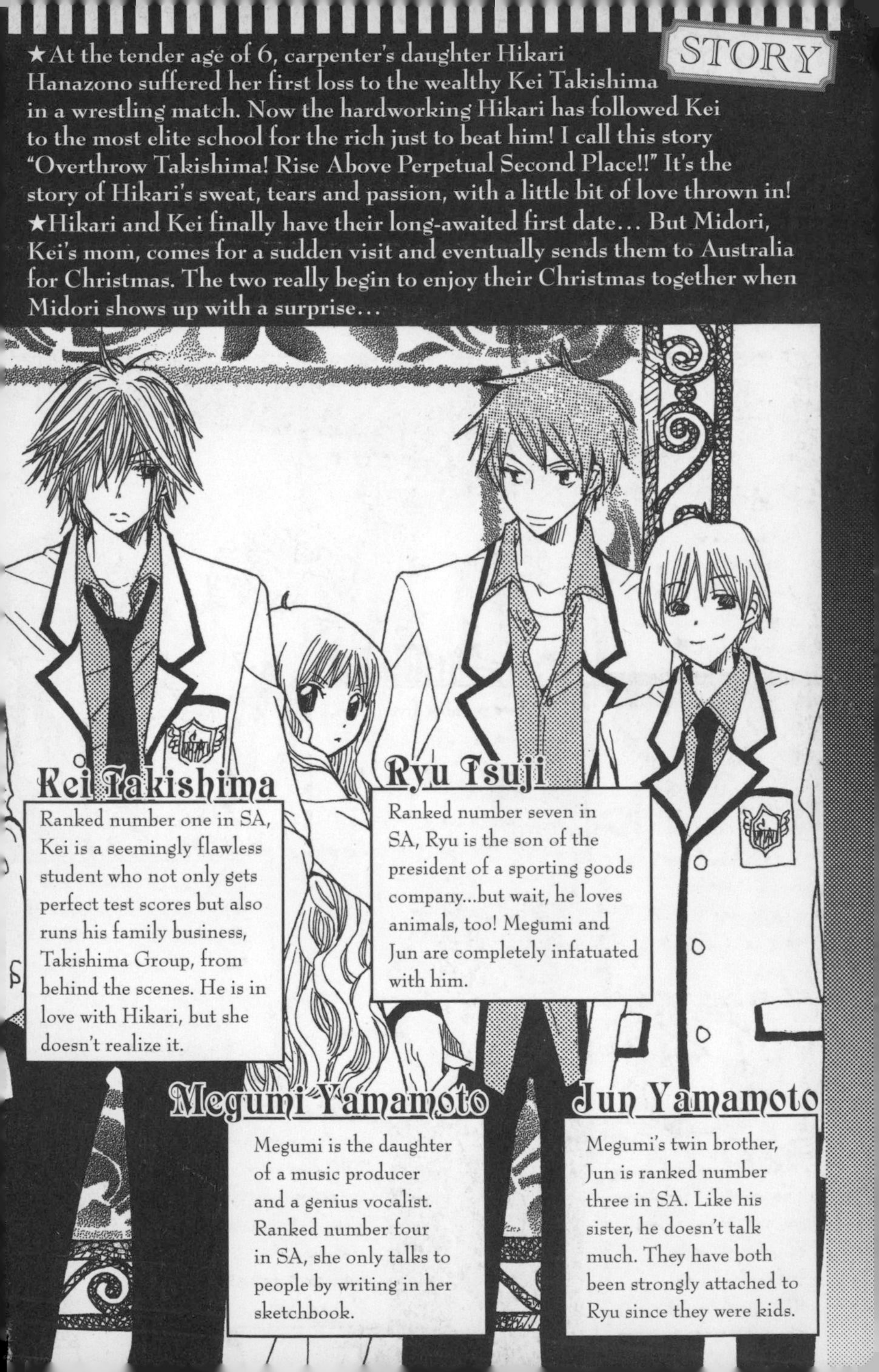

Kei Takishima
Ranked number one in SA, Kei is a seemingly flawless student who not only gets perfect test scores but also runs his family business, Takishima Group, from behind the scenes. He is in love with Hikari, but she doesn't realize it.
Ryu Tsuji
Ranked number seven in SA, Ryu is the son of the president of a sporting goods company...but wait, he loves animals, too! Megumi and Jun are completely infatuated with him.
Megumi Yamamoto
Megumi is the daughter of a music producer and a genius vocalist. Ranked number four in SA, she only talks to people by writing in her sketchbook.
Jun Yamamoto
Megumi's twin brother, Jun is ranked number three in SA. Like his sister, he doesn't talk much. They have both been strongly attached to Ryu since they were kids.

S·A CHARACTERS

Hikari goes to an elite school called Hakusenkan High School. This school divides each grade level into groups A through F, according to the students' test scores. Group A includes only the top seven students in each class. Then the top seven students from all grades' A groups are put into a group called Special A, which is considered much higher than all others. Known as SA, they are "the elite among the elite."

What is "Special A"?

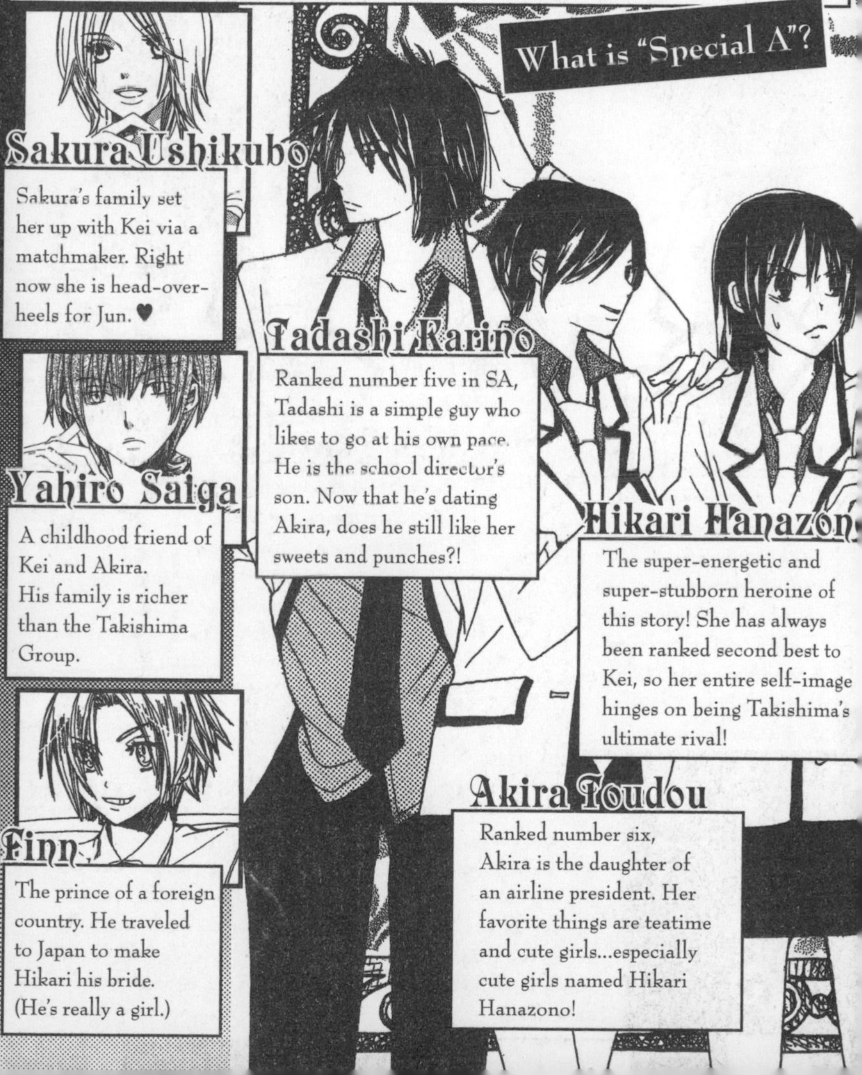

Hikari Hanazono

The super-energetic and super-stubborn heroine of this story! She has always been ranked second best to Kei, so her entire self-image hinges on being Takishima's ultimate rival!

Akira Toudou

Ranked number six, Akira is the daughter of an airline president. Her favorite things are teatime and cute girls...especially cute girls named Hikari Hanazono!

Tadashi Karino

Ranked number five in SA, Tadashi is a simple guy who likes to go at his own pace. He is the school director's son. Now that he's dating Akira, does he still like her sweets and punches?!

Sakura Ushikubo

Sakura's family set her up with Kei via a matchmaker. Right now she is head-over-heels for Jun. ♥

Yahiro Saiga

A childhood friend of Kei and Akira. His family is richer than the Takishima Group.

Finn

The prince of a foreign country. He traveled to Japan to make Hikari his bride. (He's really a girl.)

Contents

Mom and Son

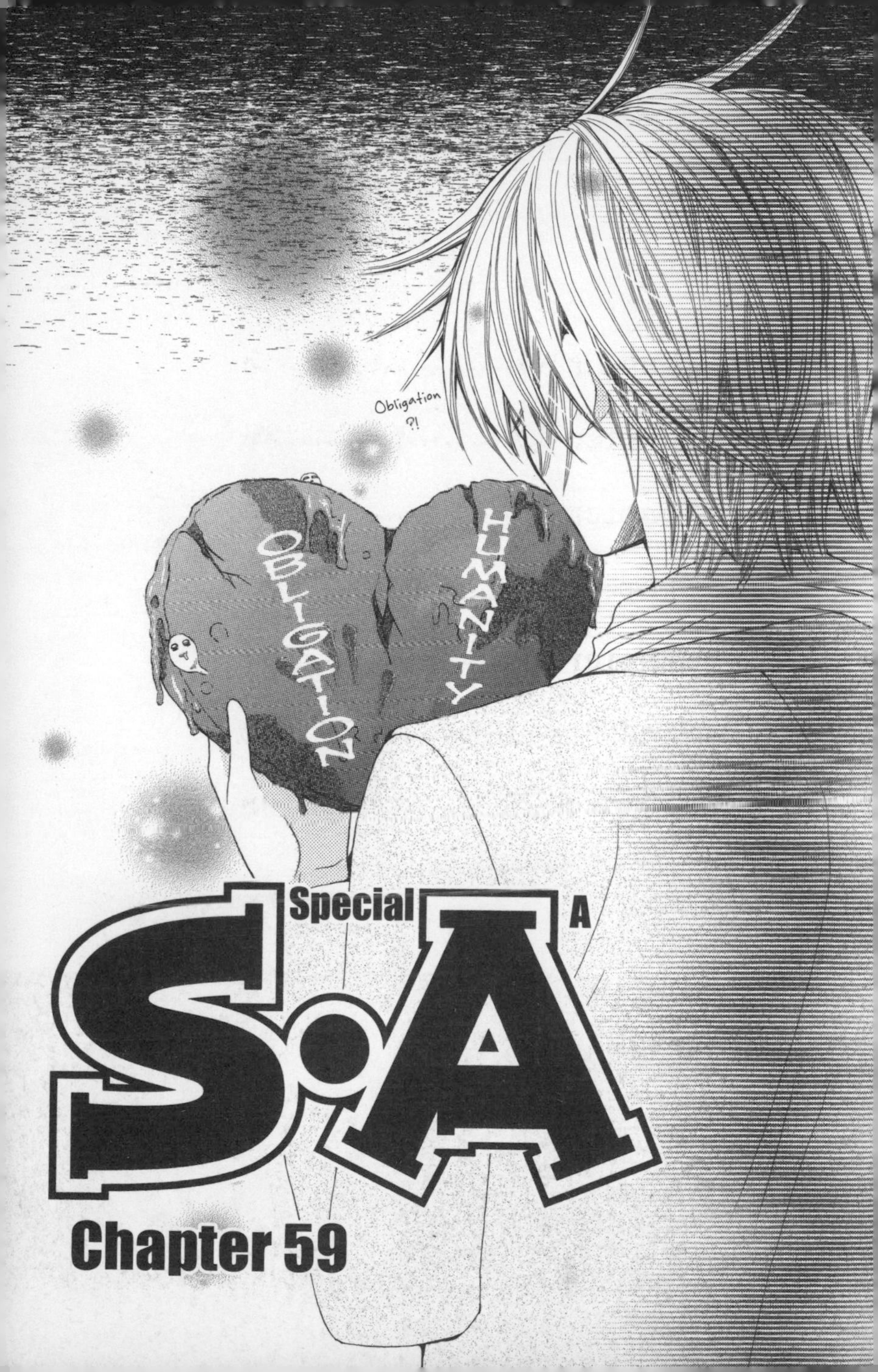
Obligation ?!
HUMANITY
OBLIGATION
Special A
S.A
Chapter 59

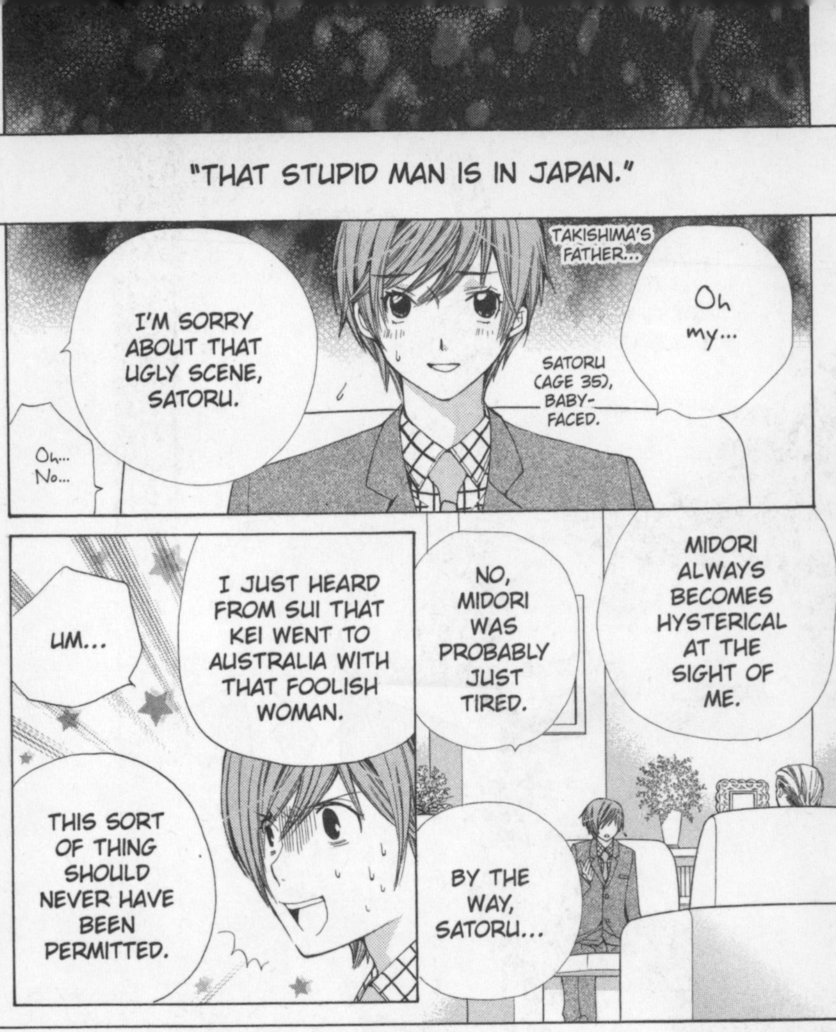
"THAT STUPID MAN IS IN JAPAN."
TAKISHIMA'S FATHER...
Oh my...
SATORU (AGE 35), BABY-FACED.
I'M SORRY ABOUT THAT UGLY SCENE, SATORU.
Oh... No...
MIDORI ALWAYS BECOMES HYSTERICAL AT THE SIGHT OF ME.
NO, MIDORI WAS PROBABLY JUST TIRED.
BY THE WAY, SATORU...
I JUST HEARD FROM SUI THAT KEI WENT TO AUSTRALIA WITH THAT FOOLISH WOMAN.
UM...
THIS SORT OF THING SHOULD NEVER HAVE BEEN PERMITTED.

- COVER PLUS "THIS AND THAT" •
- THIS TIME IT'S KEI WITH HIS MOTHER. VOLUMES 1 THROUGH 3 WERE SA MEMBERS. VOLUME 4 WAS HIKARI AND A GUY, SO I'M MIRRORING THAT WITH KEI AND A WOMAN. DID ANYONE NOTICE? WHAT? WHO CARES? OKAY.
- S.A IS FINALLY IN VOLUME 11. IN THE BEGINNING, I THOUGHT IT WOULD BE GREAT TO DO FOUR OR FIVE, AND BEFORE I NOTICED IT, WE WERE ALREADY IN DOUBLE DIGITS... AND IT REALLY IS ALL THANKS TO YOU!!
- AND CAN YOU BELIEVE IT'S BEING ANIMATED!! WHAT CAN I SAY?!! I'M SO HAPPY I DON'T KNOW WHAT TO DO! HA HA!

I bet she ran out of stock cover art ideas.

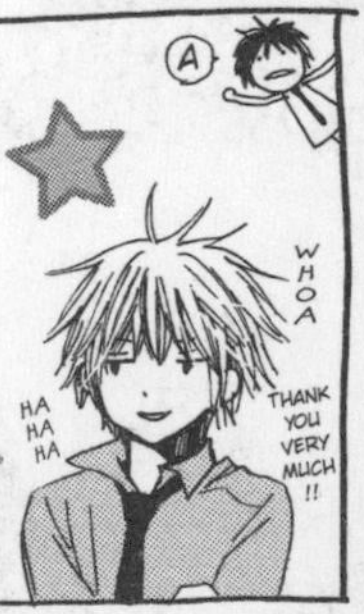
A
WHOA
HA HA HA
THANK YOU VERY MUCH !!

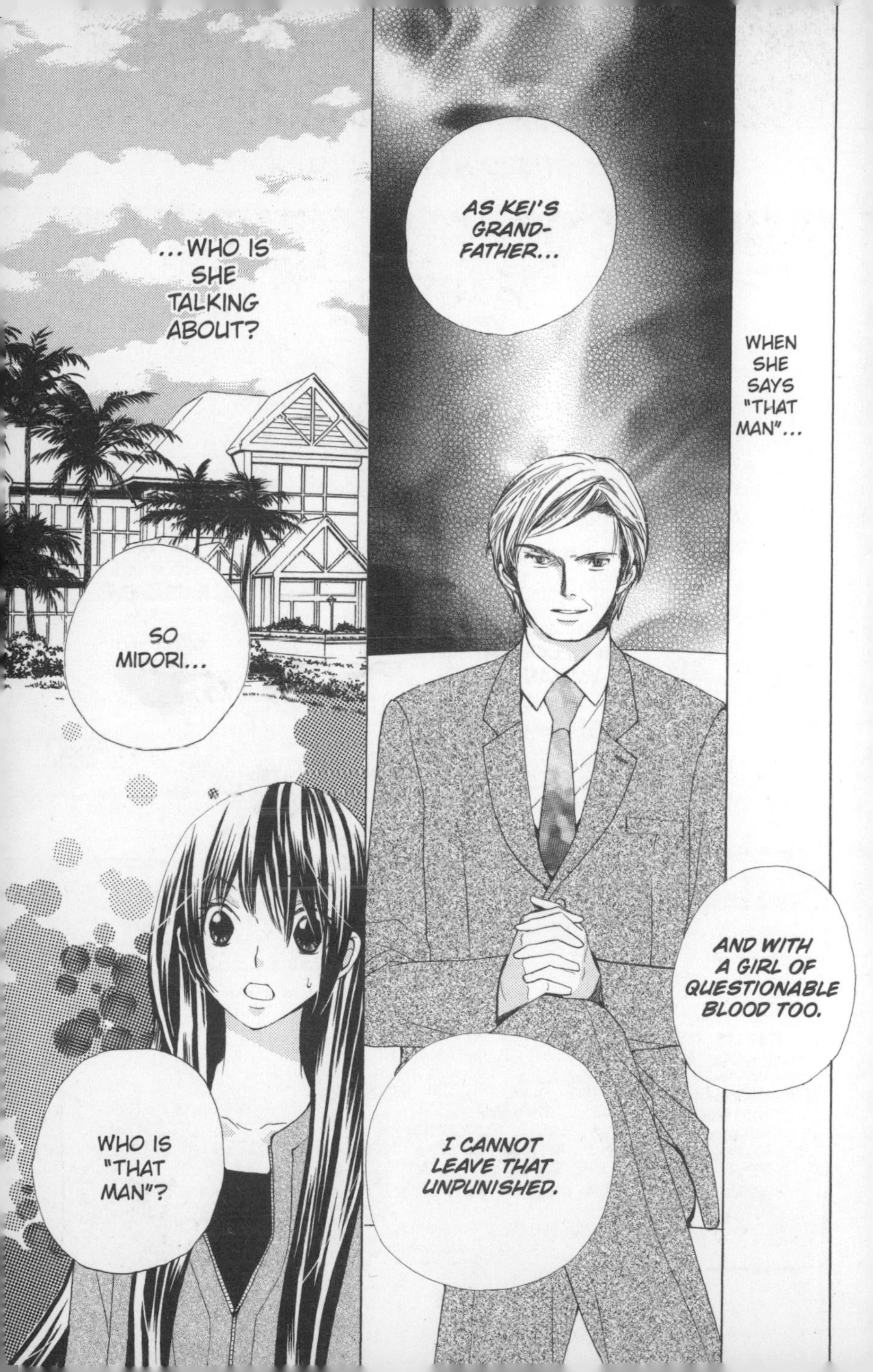
WHEN SHE SAYS "THAT MAN"...
AS KEI'S GRAND-FATHER...
AND WITH A GIRL OF QUESTIONABLE BLOOD TOO.
I CANNOT LEAVE THAT UNPUNISHED.
...WHO IS SHE TALKING ABOUT?
SO MIDORI...
WHO IS "THAT MAN"?

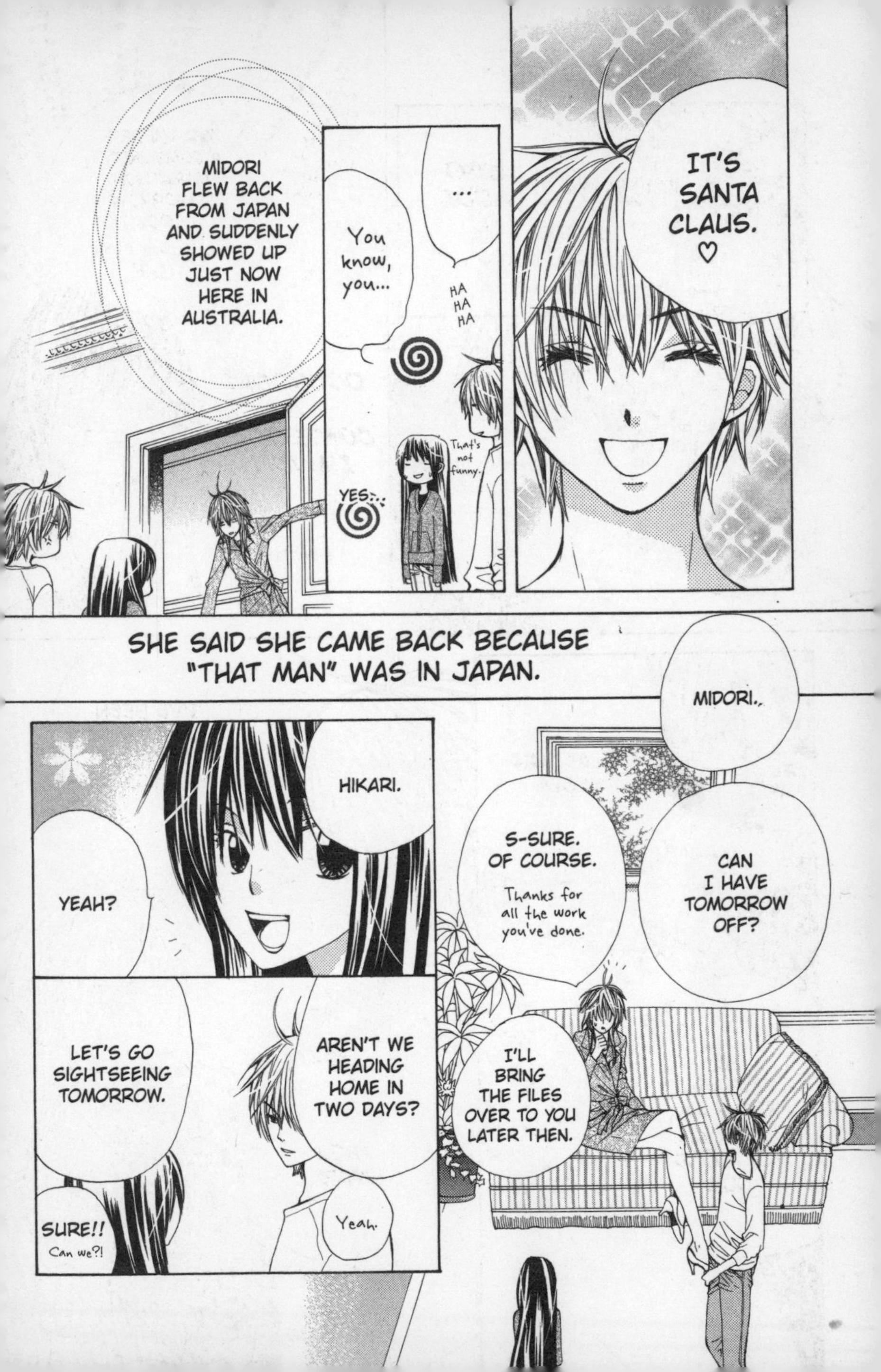
IT'S SANTA CLAUS. ♡
...
You know, you...
HA HA HA
That's not funny..
YES:..
MIDORI FLEW BACK FROM JAPAN AND SUDDENLY SHOWED UP JUST NOW HERE IN AUSTRALIA.
SHE SAID SHE CAME BACK BECAUSE "THAT MAN" WAS IN JAPAN.
MIDORI.,
CAN I HAVE TOMORROW OFF?
S-SURE. OF COURSE.
Thanks for all the work you've done.
I'LL BRING THE FILES OVER TO YOU LATER THEN.
HIKARI.
YEAH?
LET'S GO SIGHTSEEING TOMORROW.
AREN'T WE HEADING HOME IN TWO DAYS?
Yeah.
SURE!!
Can we?!

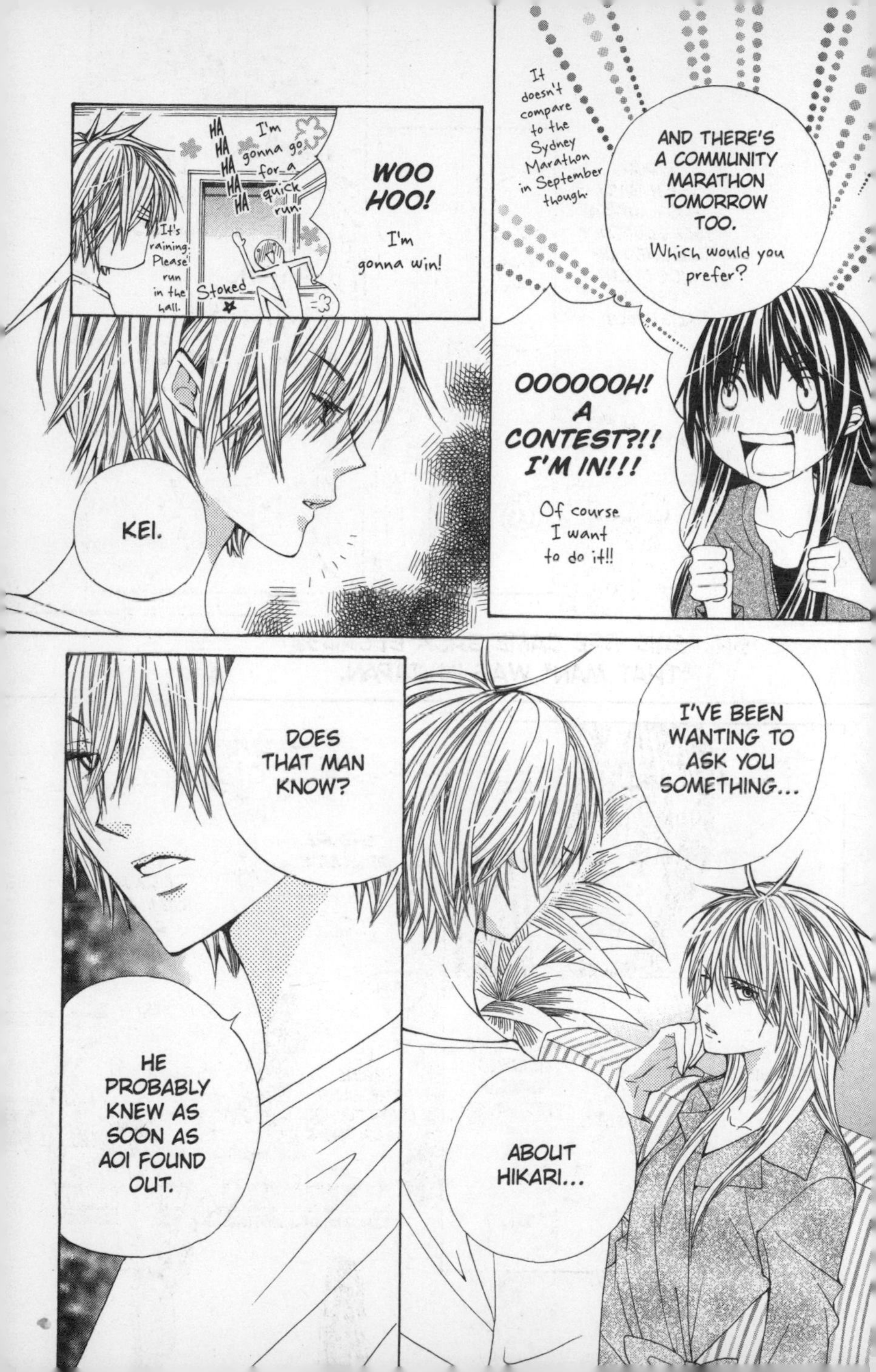
AND THERE'S A COMMUNITY MARATHON TOMORROW TOO.
Which would you prefer?
It doesn't compare to the Sydney Marathon in September though.
OOOOOOH! A CONTEST?!! I'M IN!!!
Of course I want to do it!!
WOO HOO!
I'm gonna win!
I'm gonna go for a quick run.
HA HA HA HA HA
It's raining. Please run in the hall.
Stoked
KEI.
I'VE BEEN WANTING TO ASK YOU SOMETHING...
ABOUT HIKARI...
DOES THAT MAN KNOW?
HE PROBABLY KNEW AS SOON AS AOI FOUND OUT.

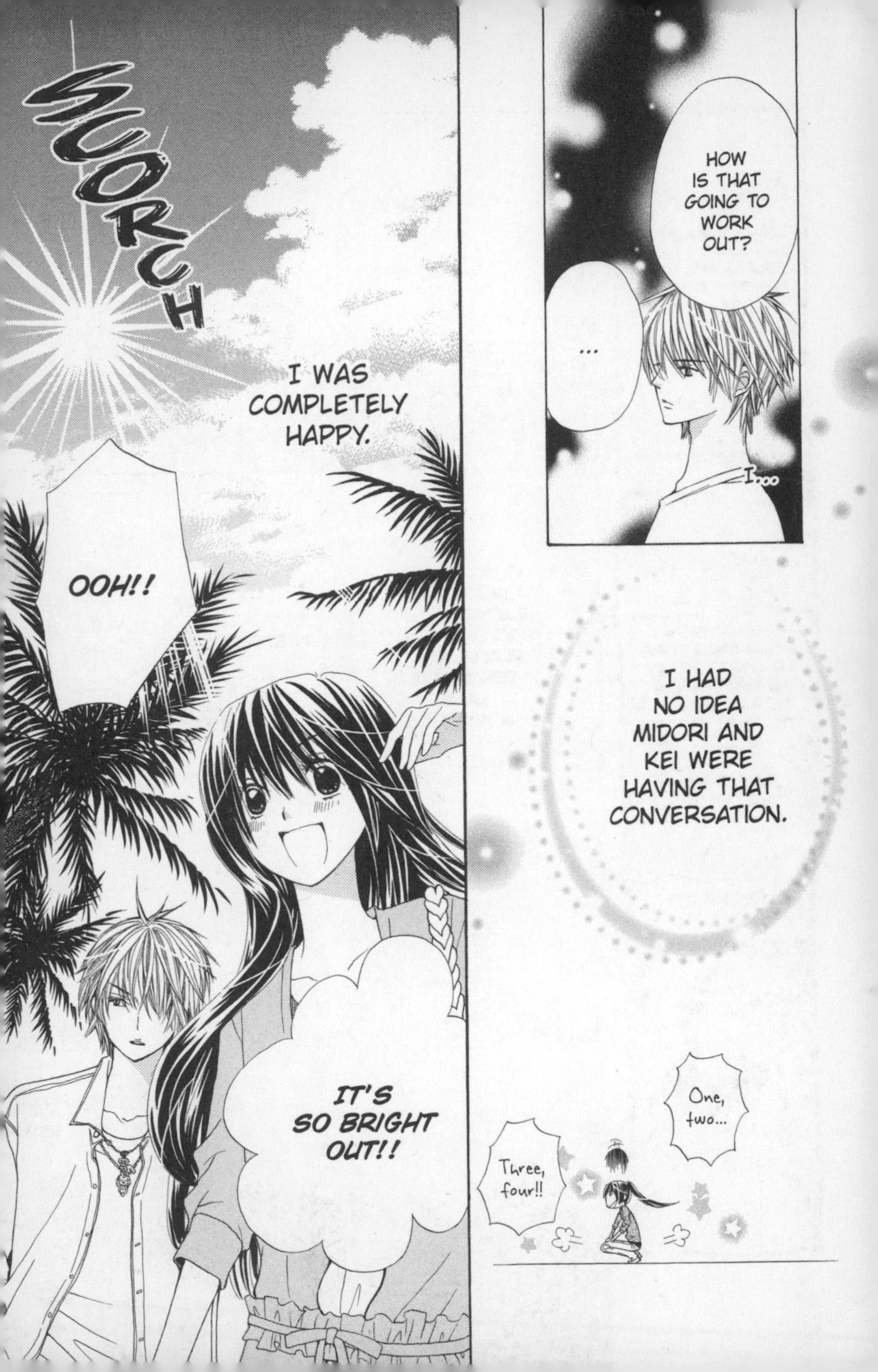
HOW IS THAT GOING TO WORK OUT?
...
I...
I HAD NO IDEA MIDORI AND KEI WERE HAVING THAT CONVERSATION.
One, two...
Three, four!!
SCORCH
I WAS COMPLETELY HAPPY.
OOH!!
IT'S SO BRIGHT OUT!!

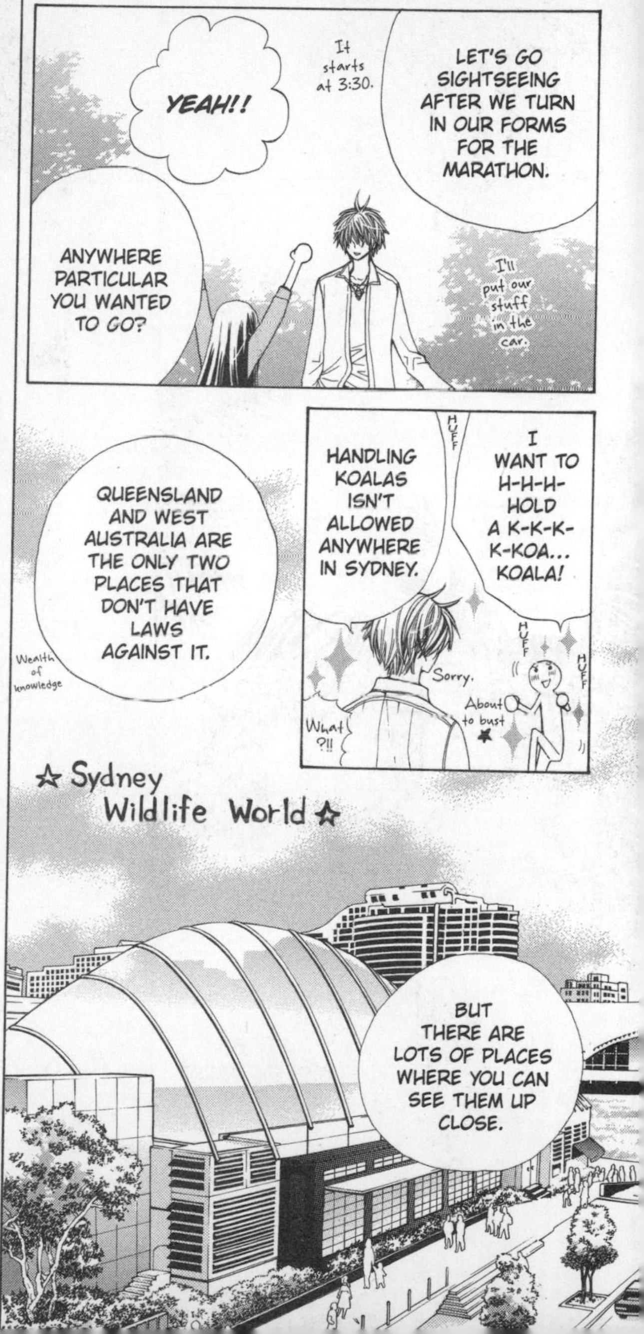
LET'S GO SIGHTSEEING AFTER WE TURN IN OUR FORMS FOR THE MARATHON.
It starts at 3:30.
YEAH!!
I'll put our stuff in the car.
ANYWHERE PARTICULAR YOU WANTED TO GO?
I WANT TO H-H-H-HOLD A K-K-K-K-KOA... KOALA!
HUFF
HUFF
HUFF
HANDLING KOALAS ISN'T ALLOWED ANYWHERE IN SYDNEY.
Sorry.
About to bust
What?!!
QUEENSLAND AND WEST AUSTRALIA ARE THE ONLY TWO PLACES THAT DON'T HAVE LAWS AGAINST IT.
Wealth of knowledge
☆ Sydney Wildlife World ☆
BUT THERE ARE LOTS OF PLACES WHERE YOU CAN SEE THEM UP CLOSE.

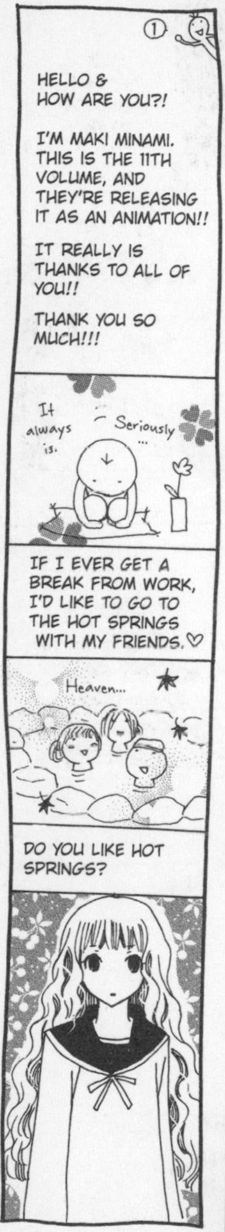
①
HELLO & HOW ARE YOU?!
I'M MAKI MINAMI. THIS IS THE 11TH VOLUME, AND THEY'RE RELEASING IT AS AN ANIMATION!!
IT REALLY IS THANKS TO ALL OF YOU!!
THANK YOU SO MUCH!!!
Seriously...
It always is.
IF I EVER GET A BREAK FROM WORK, I'D LIKE TO GO TO THE HOT SPRINGS WITH MY FRIENDS. ♡
Heaven...
DO YOU LIKE HOT SPRINGS?

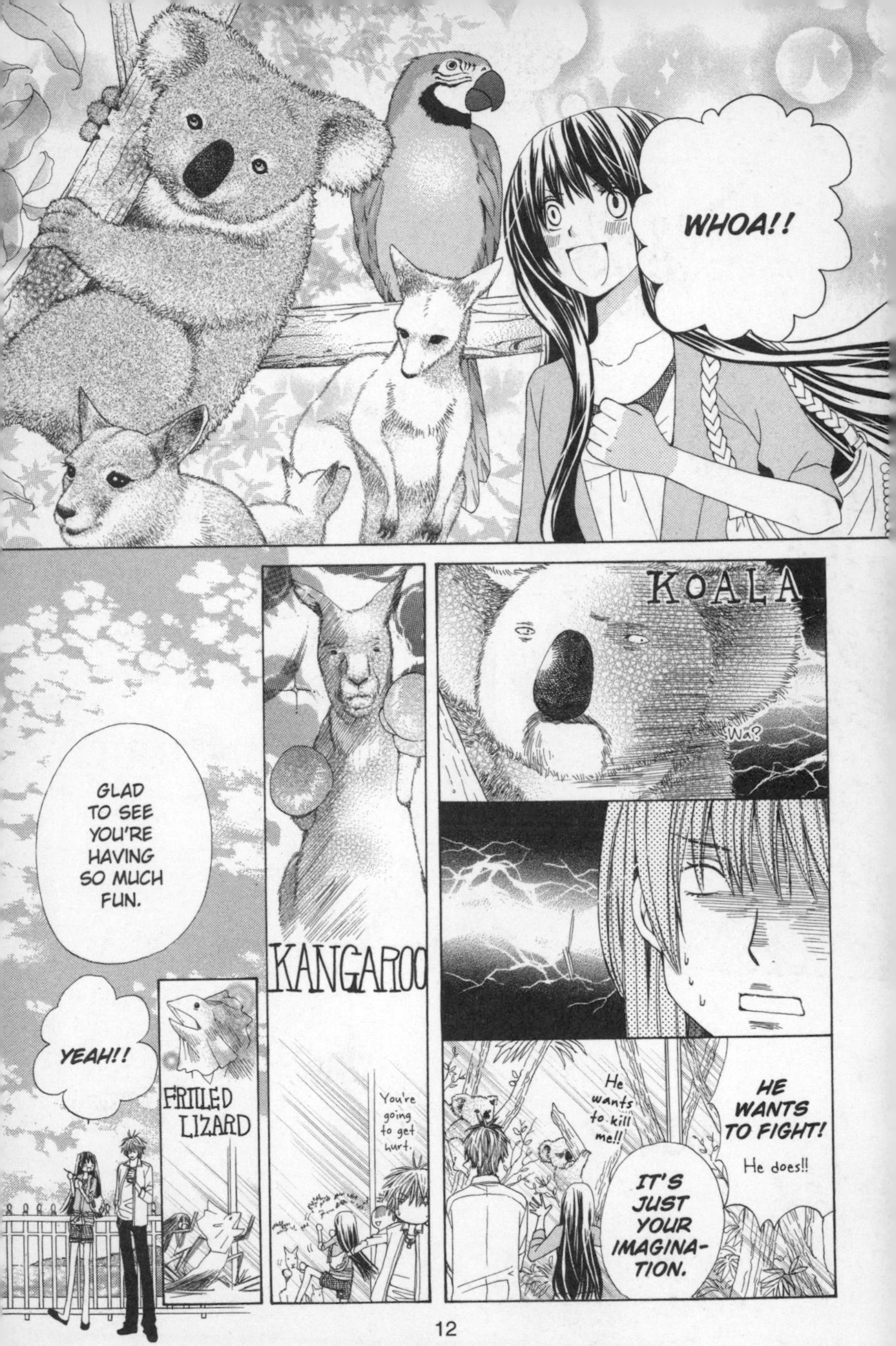
WHOA!!
KOALA
Wa?
KANGAROO
GLAD TO SEE YOU'RE HAVING SO MUCH FUN.
HE WANTS TO FIGHT!
He does!!
He wants to kill me!!
IT'S JUST YOUR IMAGINATION.
You're going to get hurt.
FRILLED LIZARD
YEAH!!

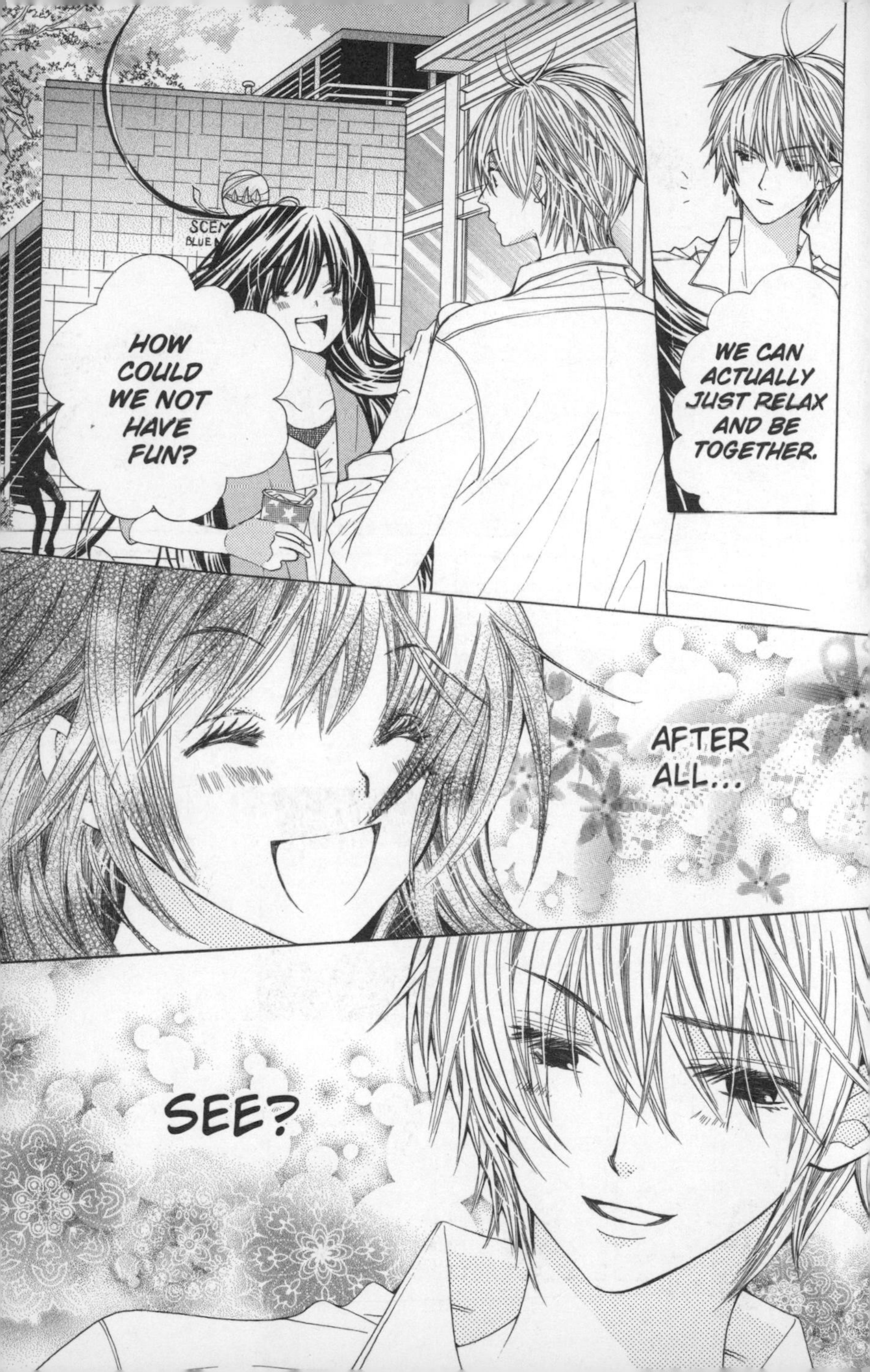
WE CAN ACTUALLY JUST RELAX AND BE TOGETHER.
HOW COULD WE NOT HAVE FUN?
AFTER ALL...
SEE?

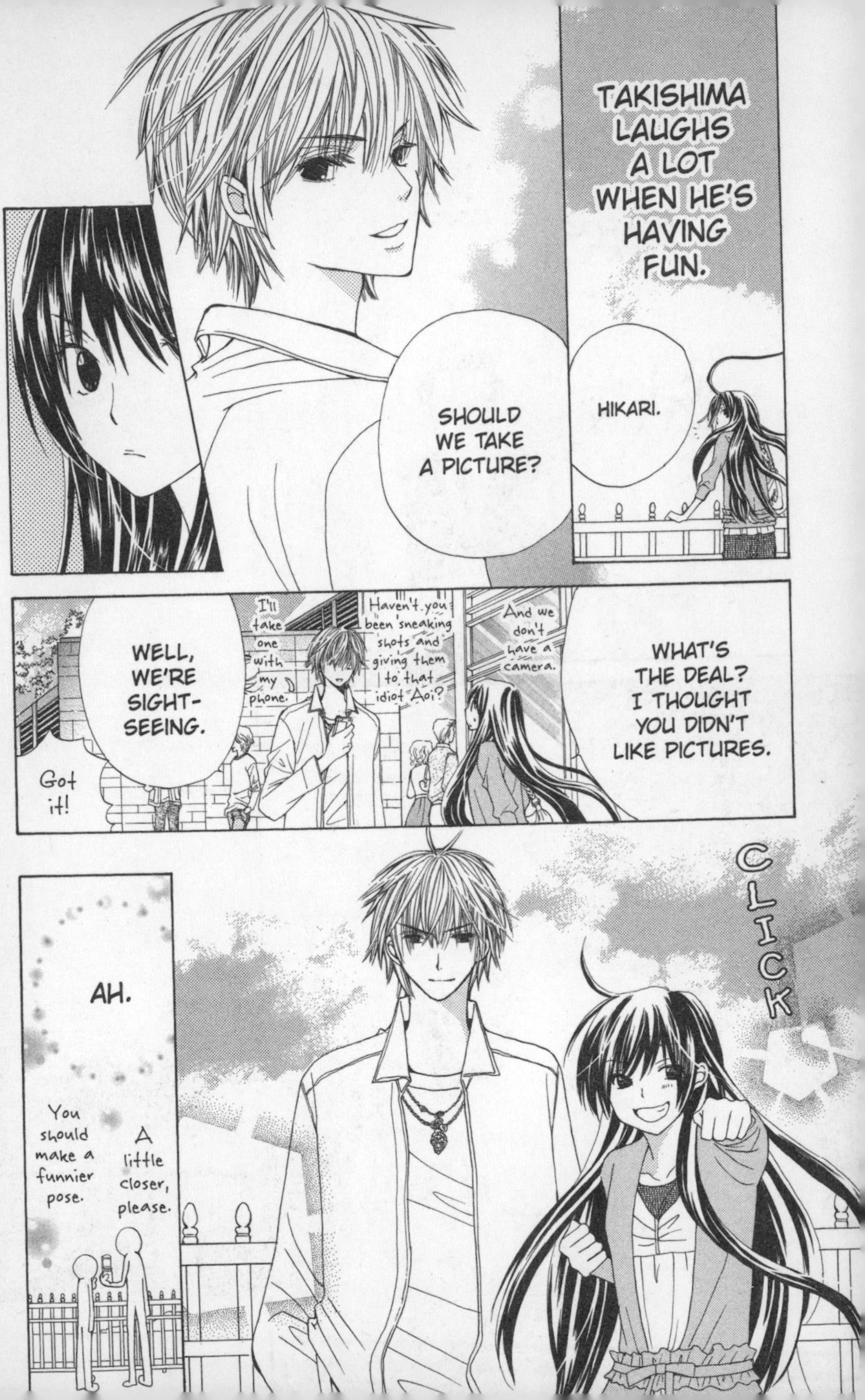
TAKISHIMA LAUGHS A LOT WHEN HE'S HAVING FUN.
HIKARI.
SHOULD WE TAKE A PICTURE?
WHAT'S THE DEAL? I THOUGHT YOU DIDN'T LIKE PICTURES.
And we don't have a camera.
Haven't you been sneaking shots and giving them to that idiot Aoi?
I'll take one with my phone.
WELL, WE'RE SIGHT-SEEING.
Got it!
CLICK
AH.
A little closer, please.
You should make a funnier pose.

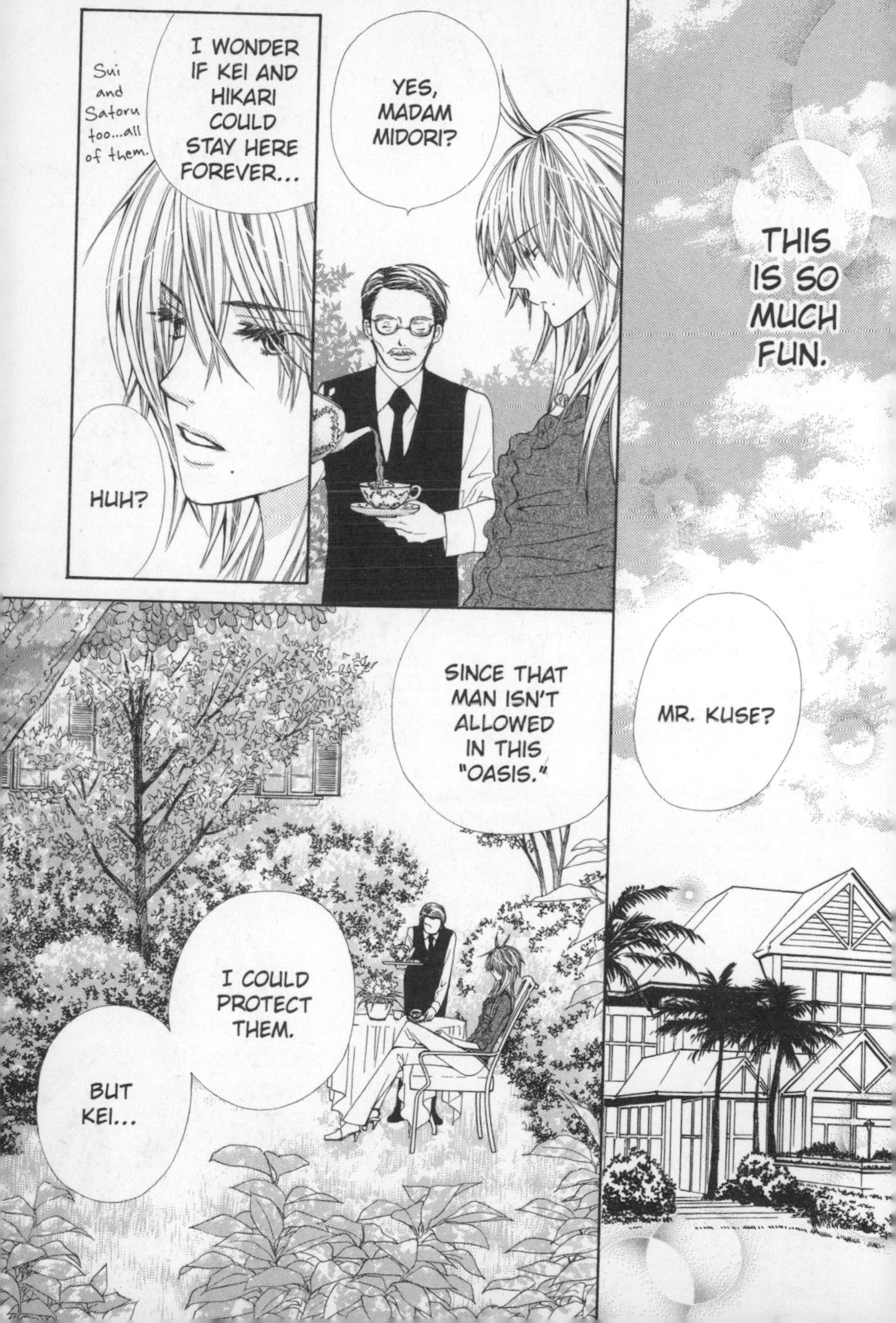
THIS IS SO MUCH FUN.
MR. KUSE?
YES, MADAM MIDORI?
I WONDER IF KEI AND HIKARI COULD STAY HERE FOREVER...
Sui and Satoru too...all of them.
HUH?
SINCE THAT MAN ISN'T ALLOWED IN THIS "OASIS."
I COULD PROTECT THEM.
BUT KEI...

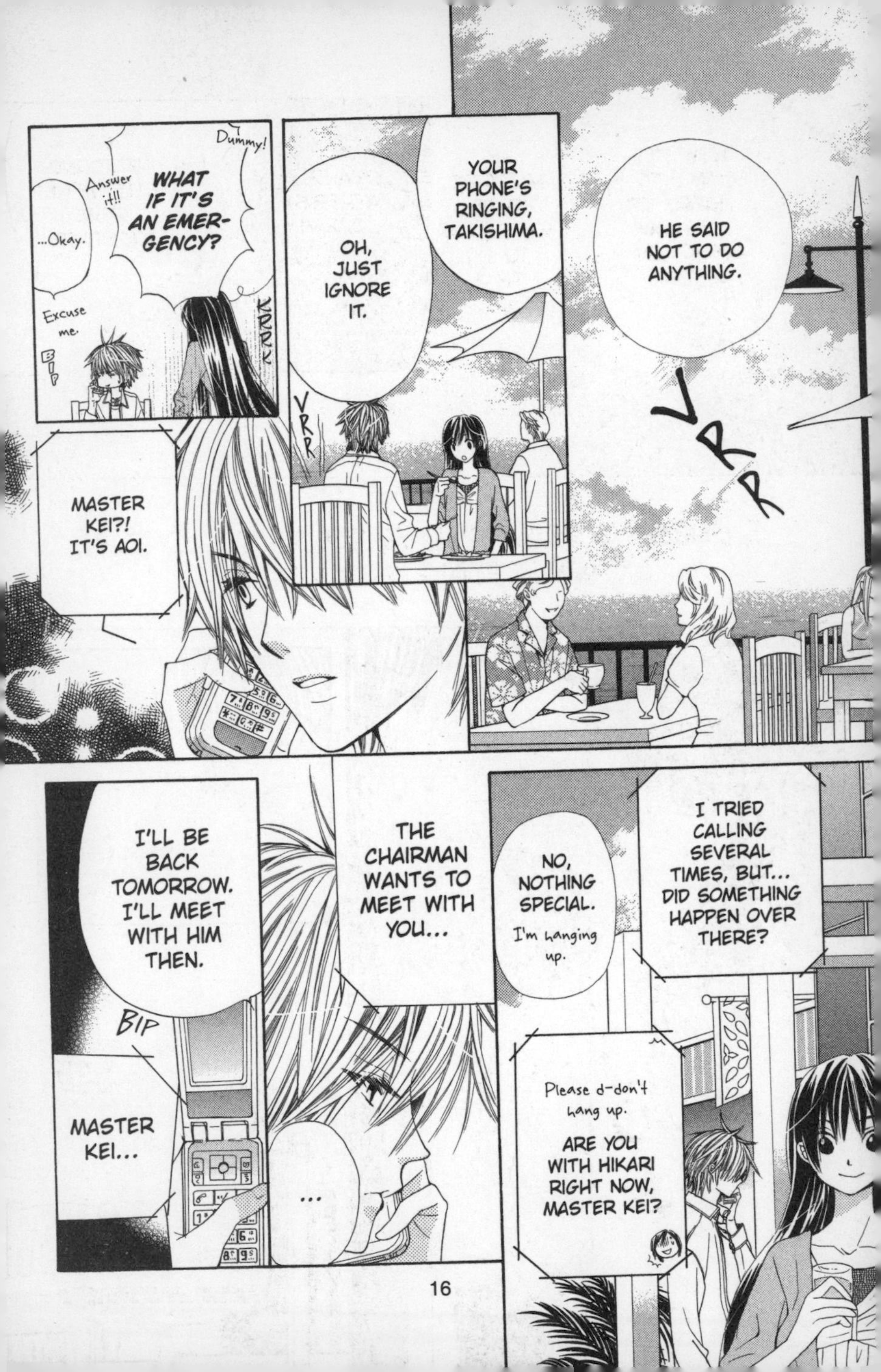

HE SAID NOT TO DO ANYTHING.
VRRR
YOUR PHONE'S RINGING, TAKISHIMA.
OH, JUST IGNORE IT.
VRR
Dummy!
WHAT IF IT'S AN EMERGENCY?
Answer it!!
...Okay.
VRRR
Excuse me.
BIP
MASTER KEI?! IT'S AOI.
I TRIED CALLING SEVERAL TIMES, BUT... DID SOMETHING HAPPEN OVER THERE?
NO, NOTHING SPECIAL.
I'm hanging up.
Please d-don't hang up.
ARE YOU WITH HIKARI RIGHT NOW, MASTER KEI?
THE CHAIRMAN WANTS TO MEET WITH YOU...
...
I'LL BE BACK TOMORROW. I'LL MEET WITH HIM THEN.
BIP
MASTER KEI...

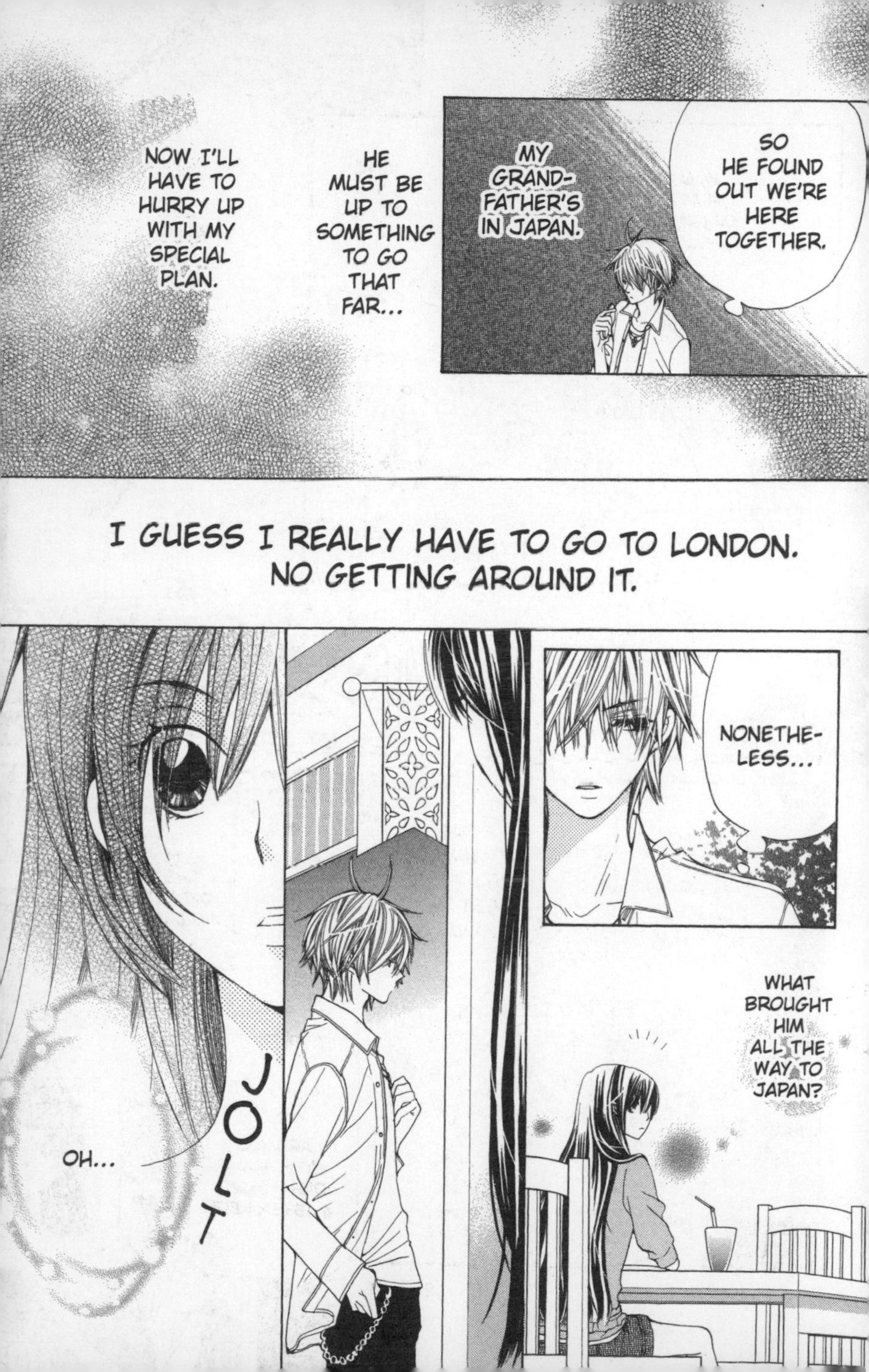
SO HE FOUND OUT WE'RE HERE TOGETHER.
MY GRANDFATHER'S IN JAPAN.
HE MUST BE UP TO SOMETHING TO GO THAT FAR...
NOW I'LL HAVE TO HURRY UP WITH MY SPECIAL PLAN.
I GUESS I REALLY HAVE TO GO TO LONDON. NO GETTING AROUND IT.
NONETHELESS...
WHAT BROUGHT HIM ALL THE WAY TO JAPAN?
JOLT
OH...

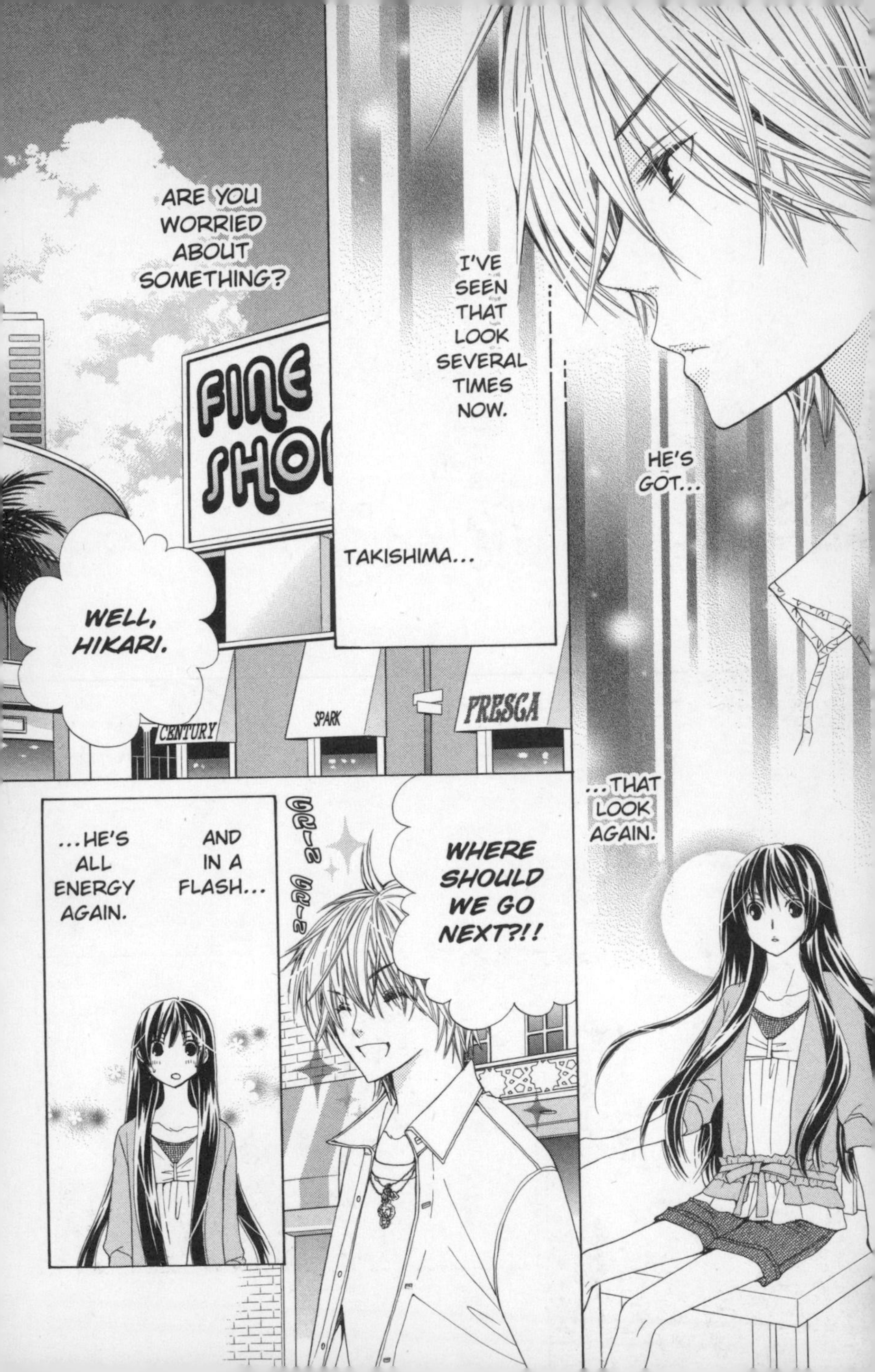
I'VE SEEN THAT LOOK SEVERAL TIMES NOW.
TAKISHIMA...
HE'S GOT...
...THAT LOOK AGAIN.
ARE YOU WORRIED ABOUT SOMETHING?
WELL, HIKARI.
CENTURY
SPARK
PRESCA
WHERE SHOULD WE GO NEXT?!!
GRIN GRIN
AND IN A FLASH...
...HE'S ALL ENERGY AGAIN.

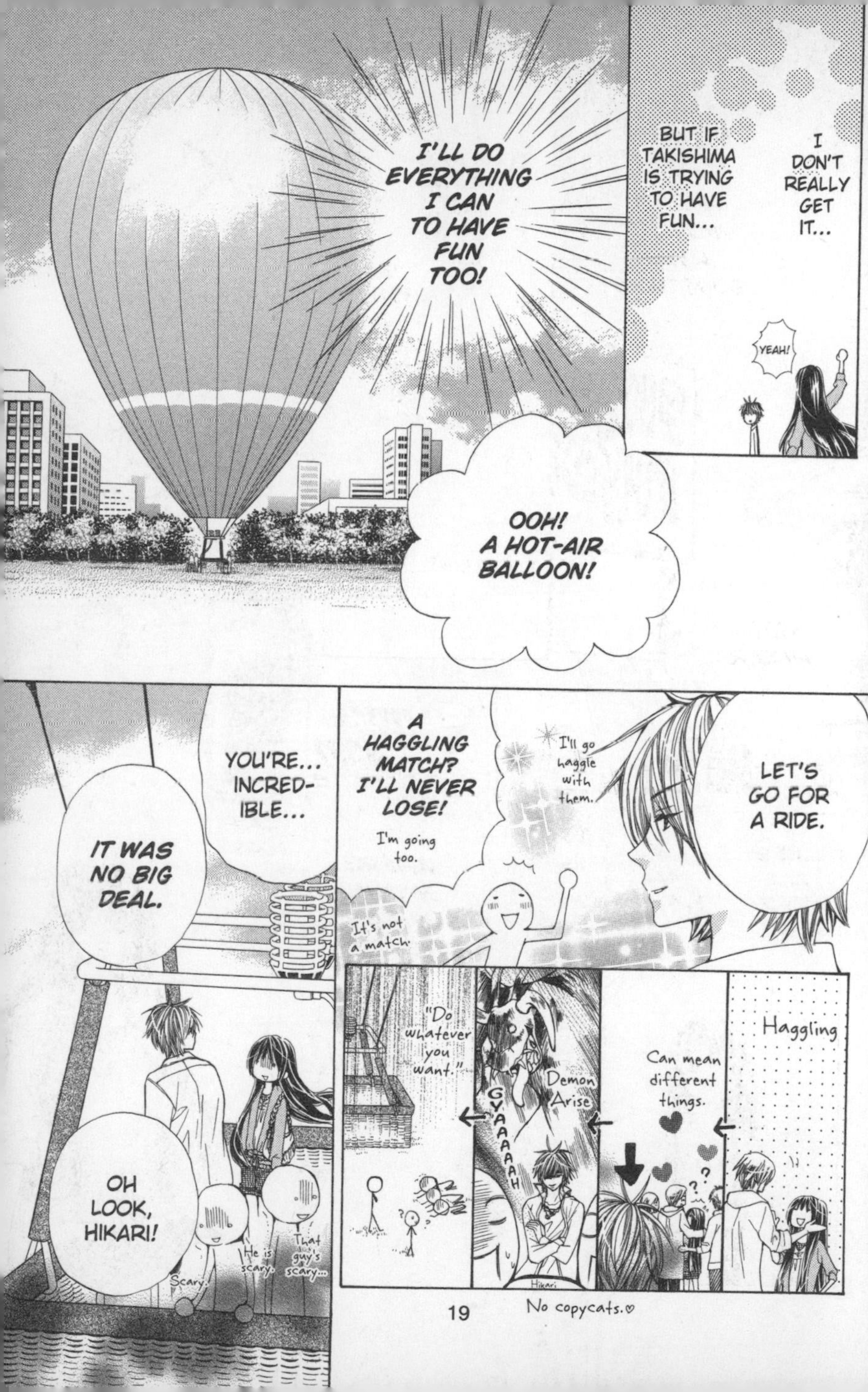
I DON'T REALLY GET IT...
BUT IF TAKISHIMA IS TRYING TO HAVE FUN...
YEAH!
I'LL DO EVERYTHING I CAN TO HAVE FUN TOO!
OOH! A HOT-AIR BALLOON!
LET'S GO FOR A RIDE.
I'll go haggle with them.
A HAGGLING MATCH? I'LL NEVER LOSE!
I'm going too.
It's not a match.
Haggling
Can mean different things.
Demon Arise
GYAAAAAH
Hikari
"Do whatever you want."
No copycats.♡
YOU'RE... INCREDIBLE...
IT WAS NO BIG DEAL.
OH LOOK, HIKARI!
That guy's scary...
He is scary.
Scary.

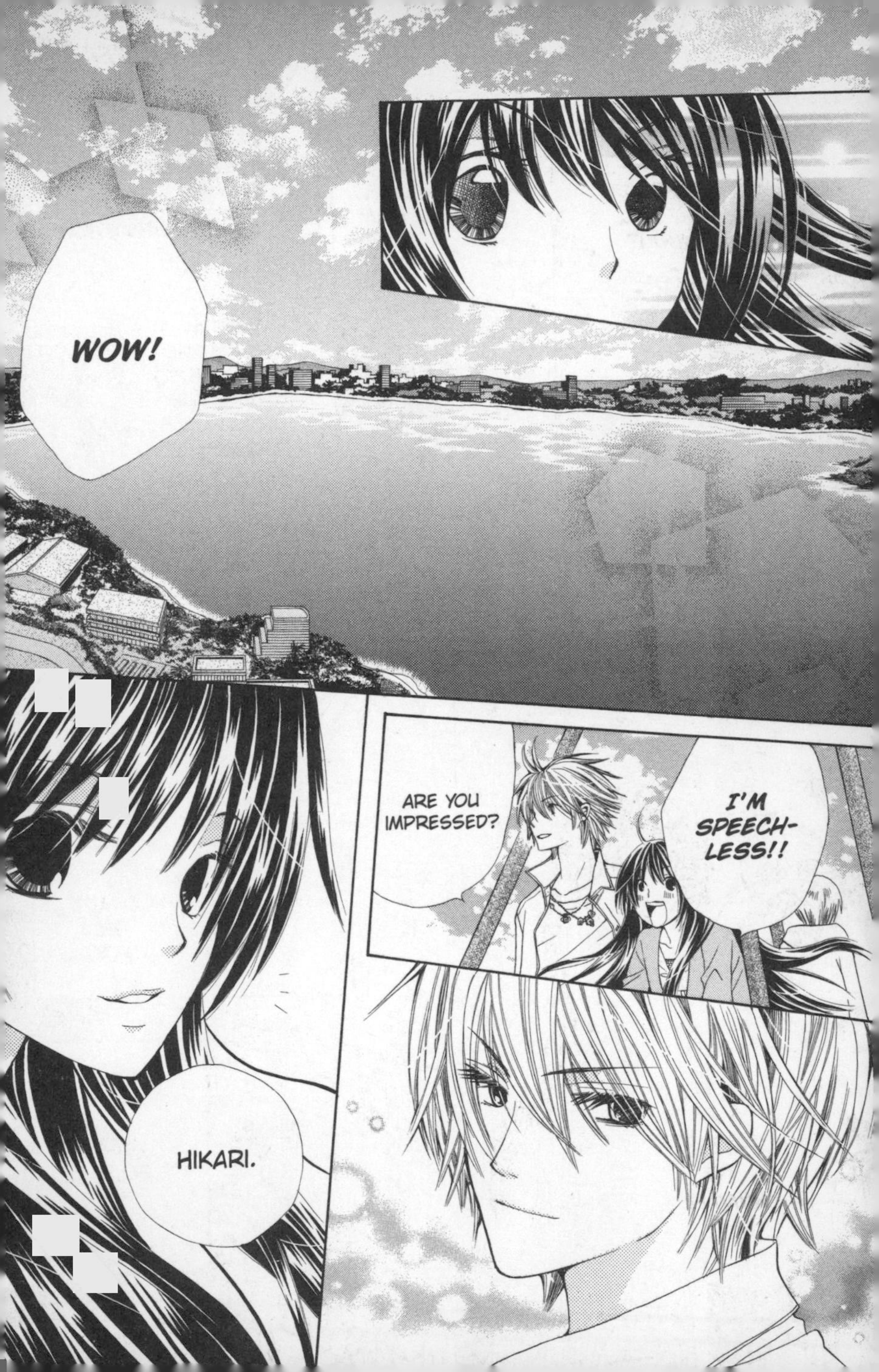
WOW!
I'M SPEECH-LESS!!
ARE YOU IMPRESSED?
HIKARI.

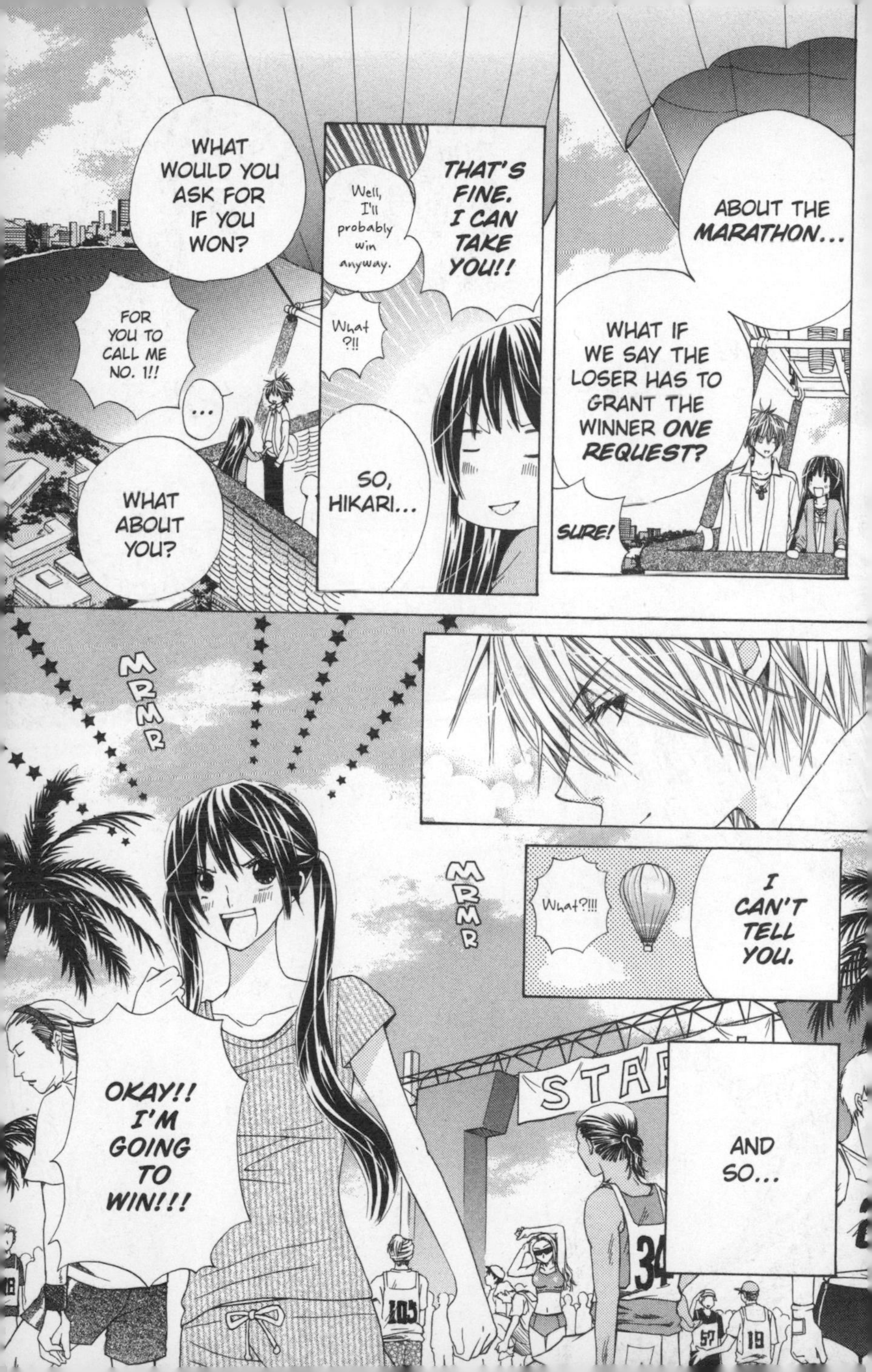
ABOUT THE MARATHON...
WHAT IF WE SAY THE LOSER HAS TO GRANT THE WINNER ONE REQUEST?
SURE!
THAT'S FINE. I CAN TAKE YOU!!
Well, I'll probably win anyway.
What?!!
SO, HIKARI...
WHAT WOULD YOU ASK FOR IF YOU WON?
FOR YOU TO CALL ME NO. 1!!
...
WHAT ABOUT YOU?
I CAN'T TELL YOU.
What?!!!
AND SO...
MRMR
OKAY!! I'M GOING TO WIN!!!
MRMR

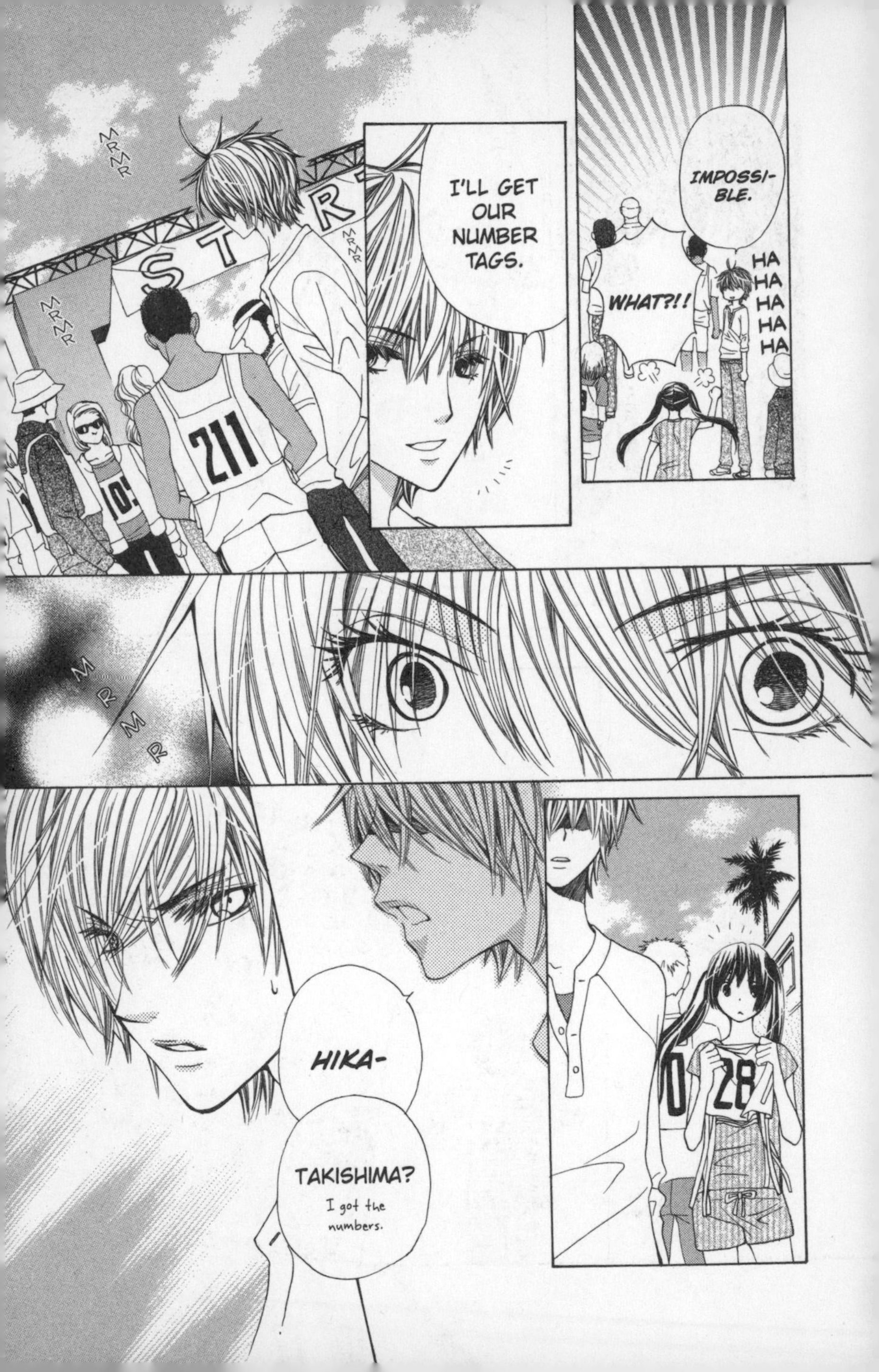
IMPOSSI-BLE.
HA HA HA HA HA
WHAT?!!
I'LL GET OUR NUMBER TAGS.
MRMR
MRMR
MRMR
MRMR
HIKA-
TAKISHIMA?
I got the numbers.

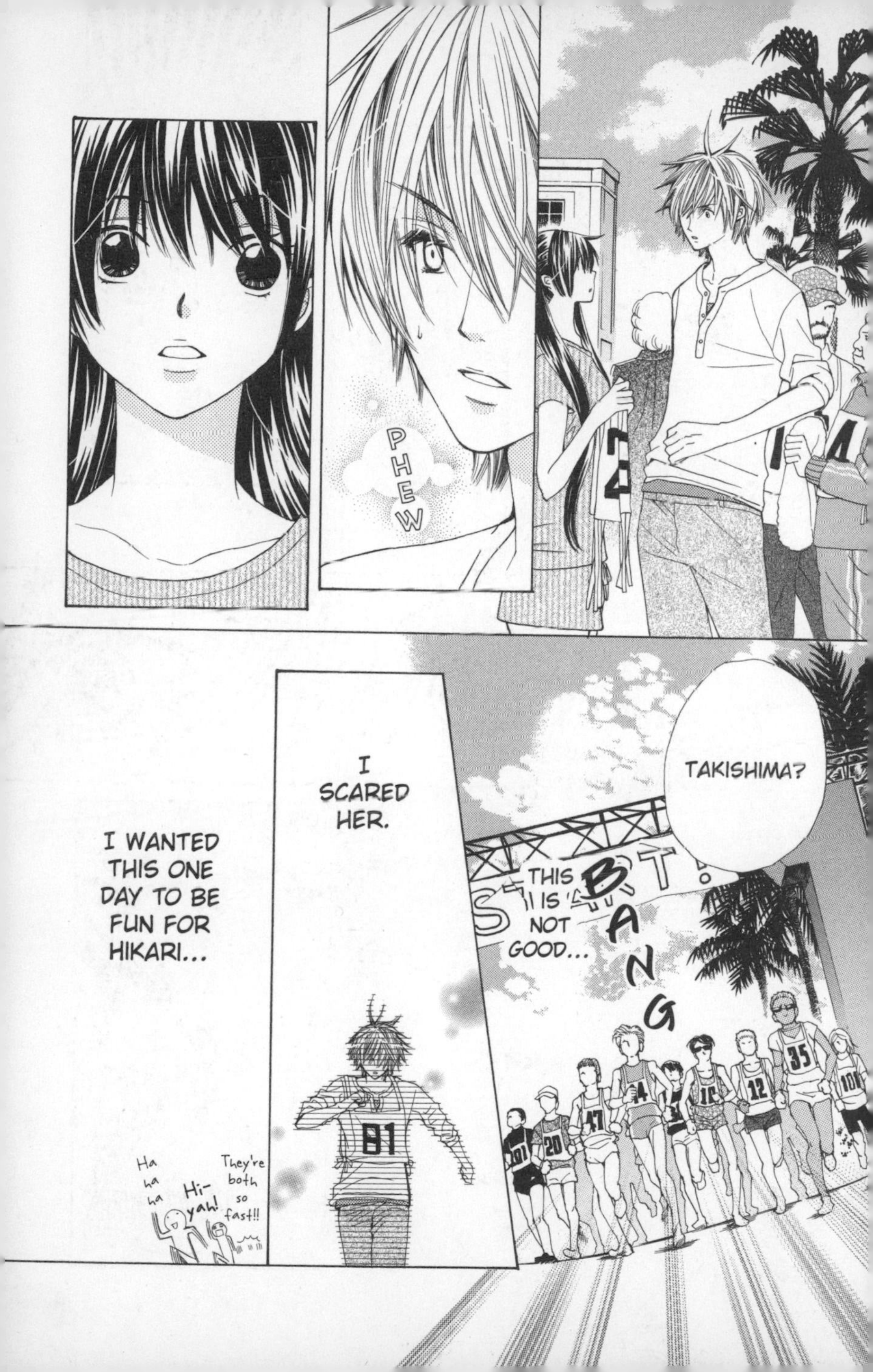
PHEW
TAKISHIMA?
BANG
THIS IS NOT GOOD...
I SCARED HER.
I WANTED THIS ONE DAY TO BE FUN FOR HIKARI...
They're both so fast!!
Hi-yah!
Ha ha ha

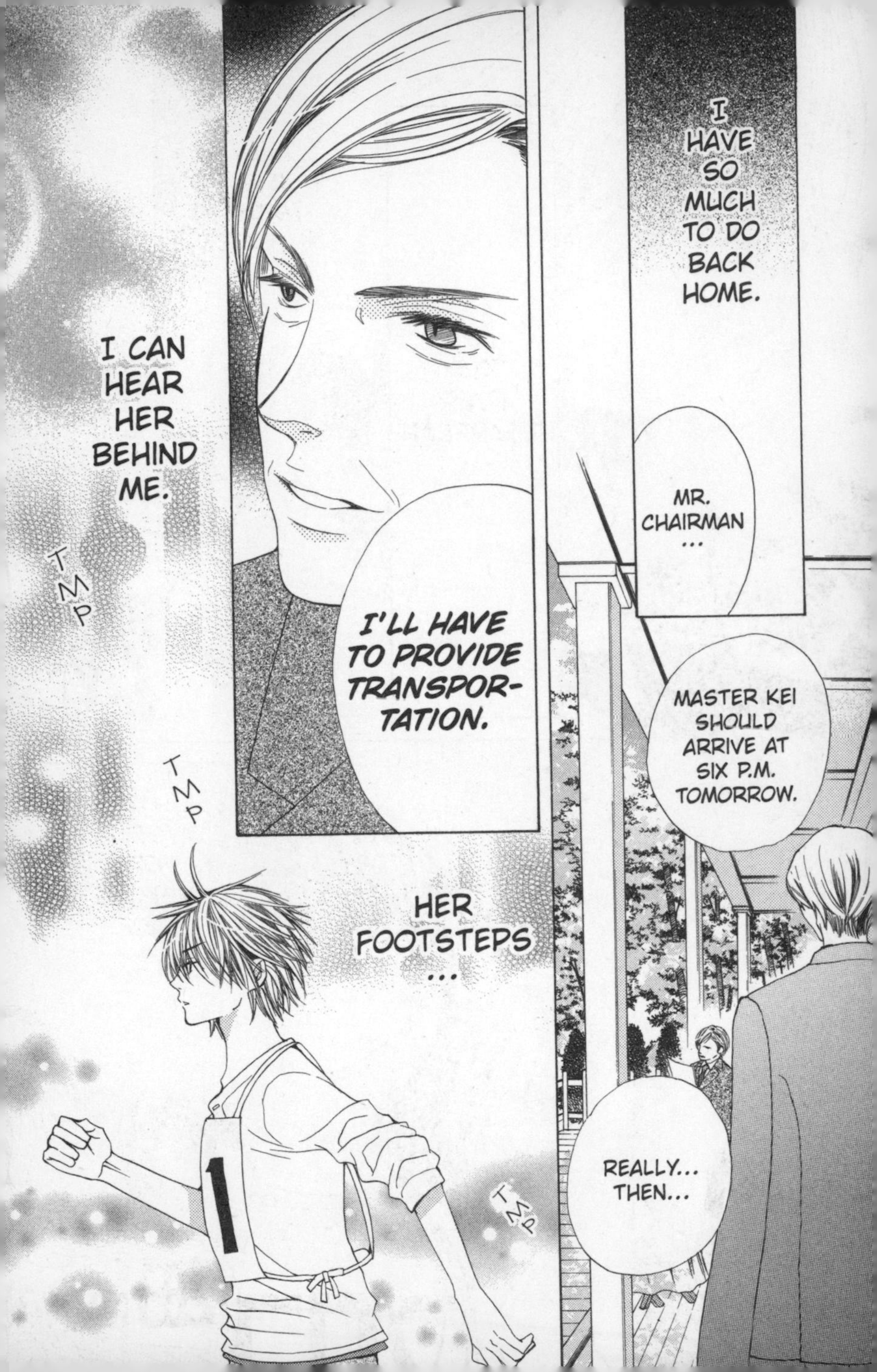
I HAVE SO MUCH TO DO BACK HOME.
MR. CHAIRMAN...
MASTER KEI SHOULD ARRIVE AT SIX P.M. TOMORROW.
REALLY... THEN...
I'LL HAVE TO PROVIDE TRANSPORTATION.
I CAN HEAR HER BEHIND ME.
TMP
TMP
HER FOOTSTEPS...
TMP

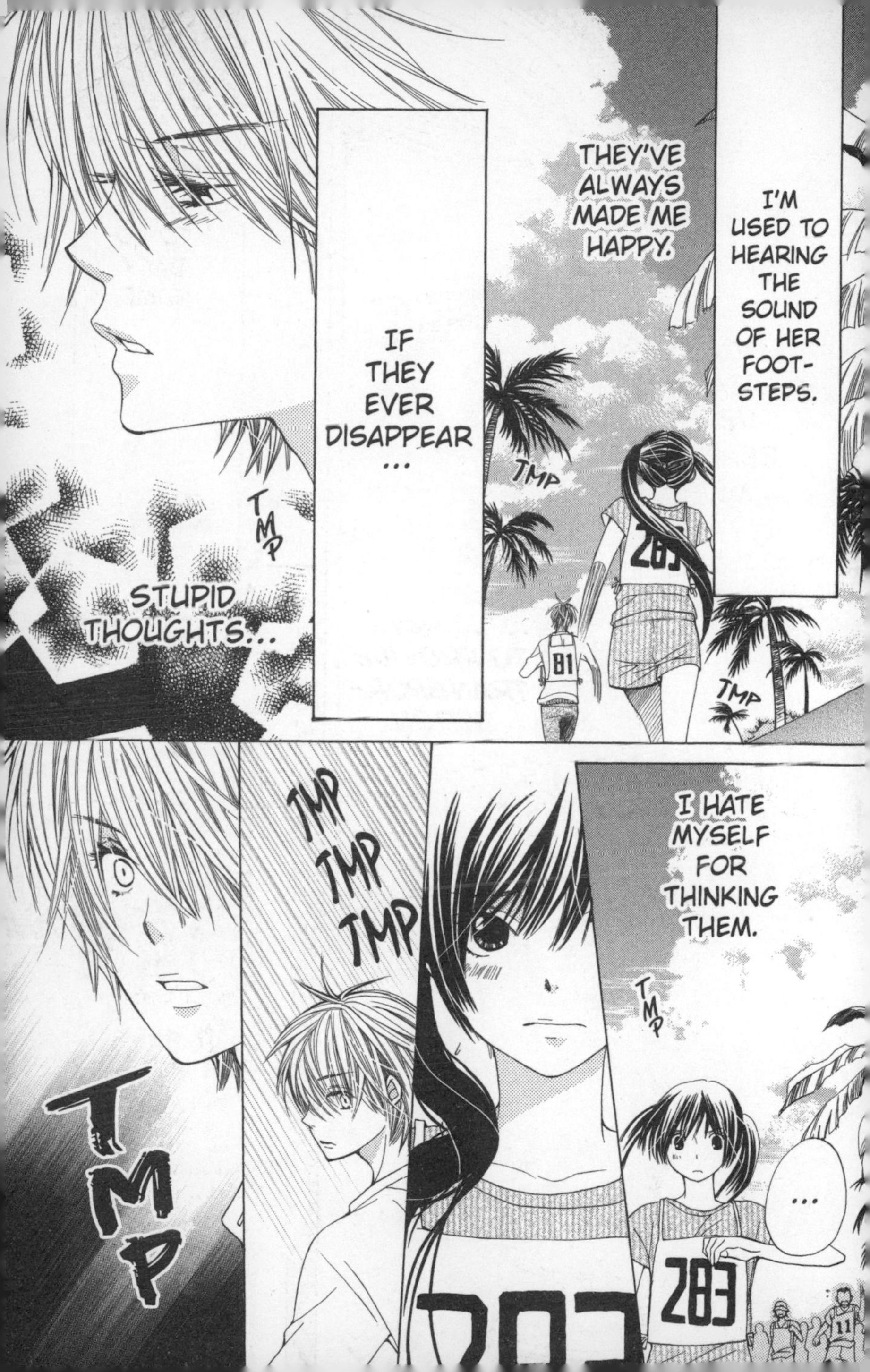
I'M USED TO HEARING THE SOUND OF HER FOOT-STEPS.
THEY'VE ALWAYS MADE ME HAPPY.
TMP
TMP
IF THEY EVER DISAPPEAR...
TMP
STUPID THOUGHTS...
I HATE MYSELF FOR THINKING THEM.
TMP
...
TMP TMP TMP
TMP

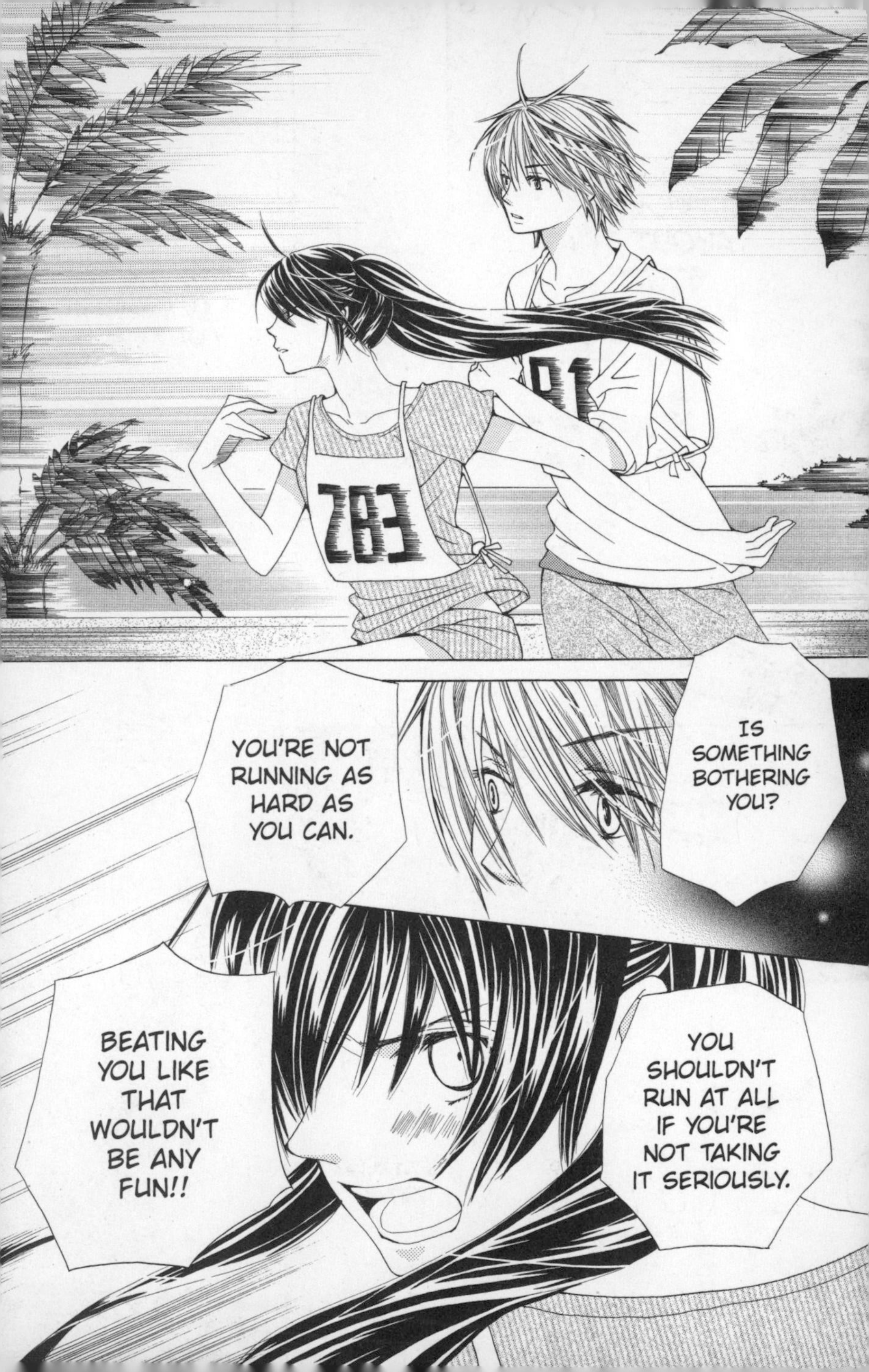
283
IS SOMETHING BOTHERING YOU?
YOU'RE NOT RUNNING AS HARD AS YOU CAN.
YOU SHOULDN'T RUN AT ALL IF YOU'RE NOT TAKING IT SERIOUSLY.
BEATING YOU LIKE THAT WOULDN'T BE ANY FUN!!

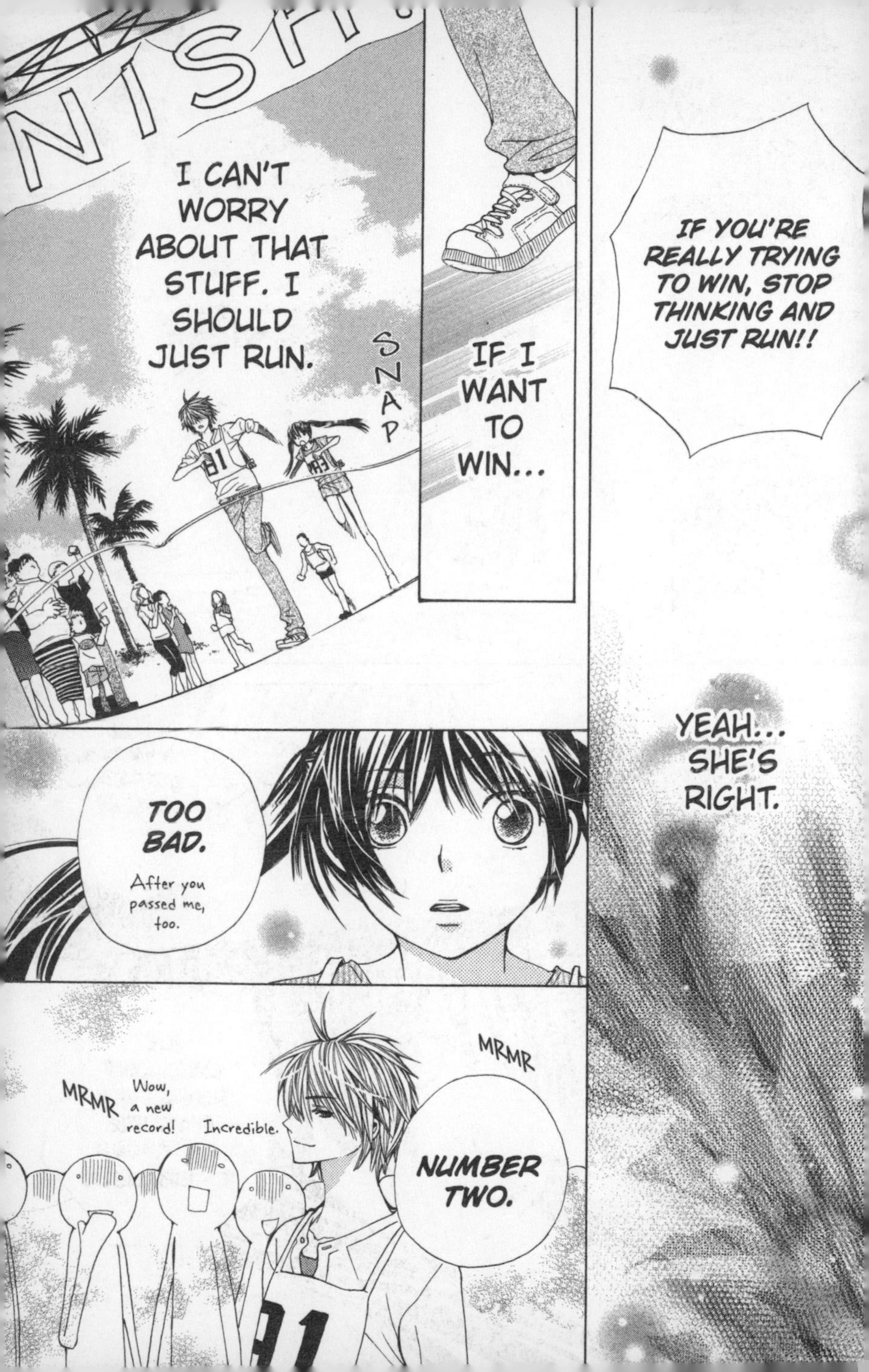
IF YOU'RE REALLY TRYING TO WIN, STOP THINKING AND JUST RUN!!
YEAH... SHE'S RIGHT.
IF I WANT TO WIN...
SNAP
I CAN'T WORRY ABOUT THAT STUFF. I SHOULD JUST RUN.
TOO BAD.
After you passed me, too.
MRMR
NUMBER TWO.
Incredible.
Wow, a new record!
MRMR

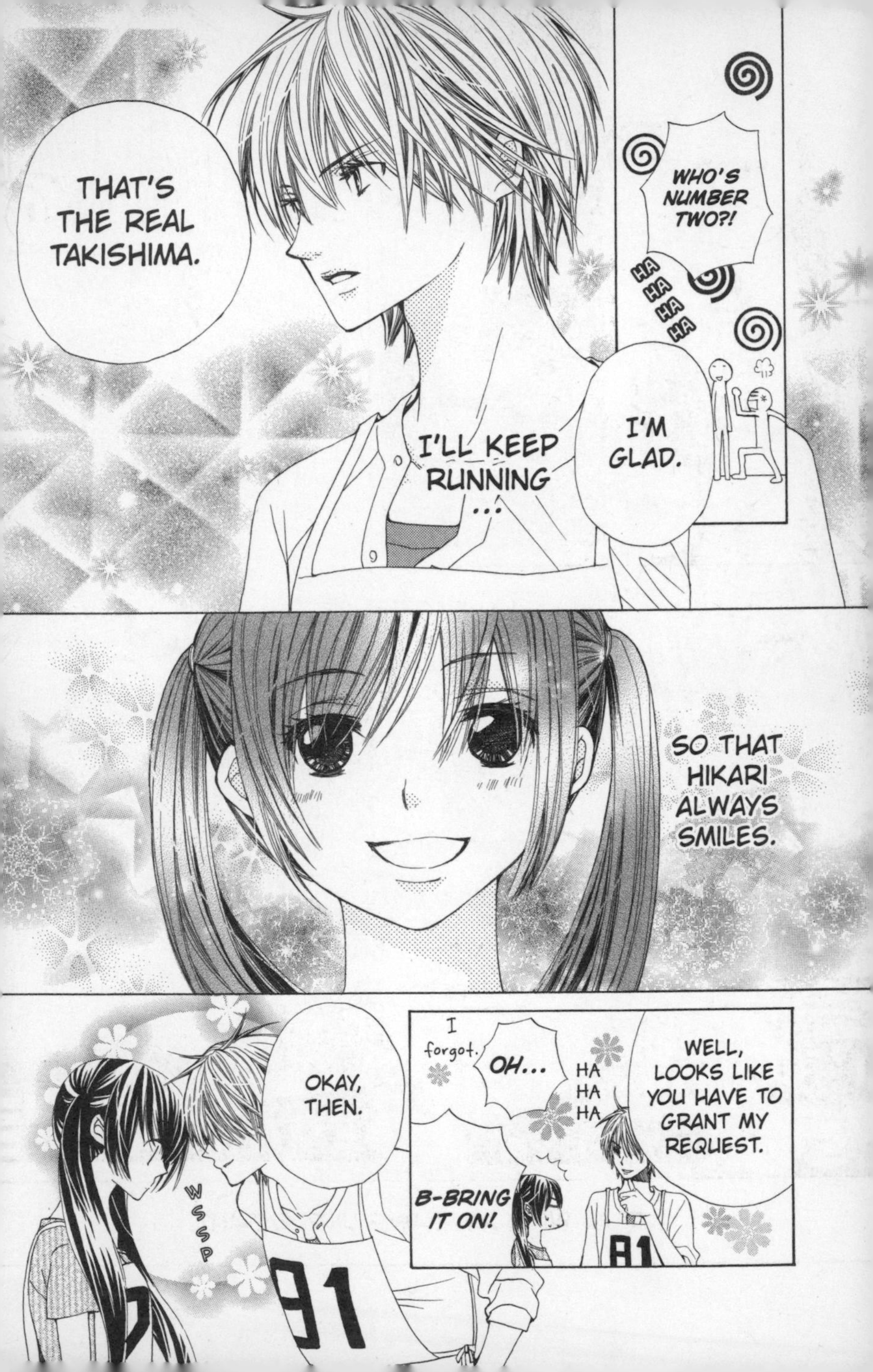
WHO'S NUMBER TWO?!
HA HA HA HA
THAT'S THE REAL TAKISHIMA.
I'M GLAD.
I'LL KEEP RUNNING ...
SO THAT HIKARI ALWAYS SMILES.
WELL, LOOKS LIKE YOU HAVE TO GRANT MY REQUEST.
HA HA HA
OH...
I forgot.
B-BRING IT ON!
OKAY, THEN.
WSSP

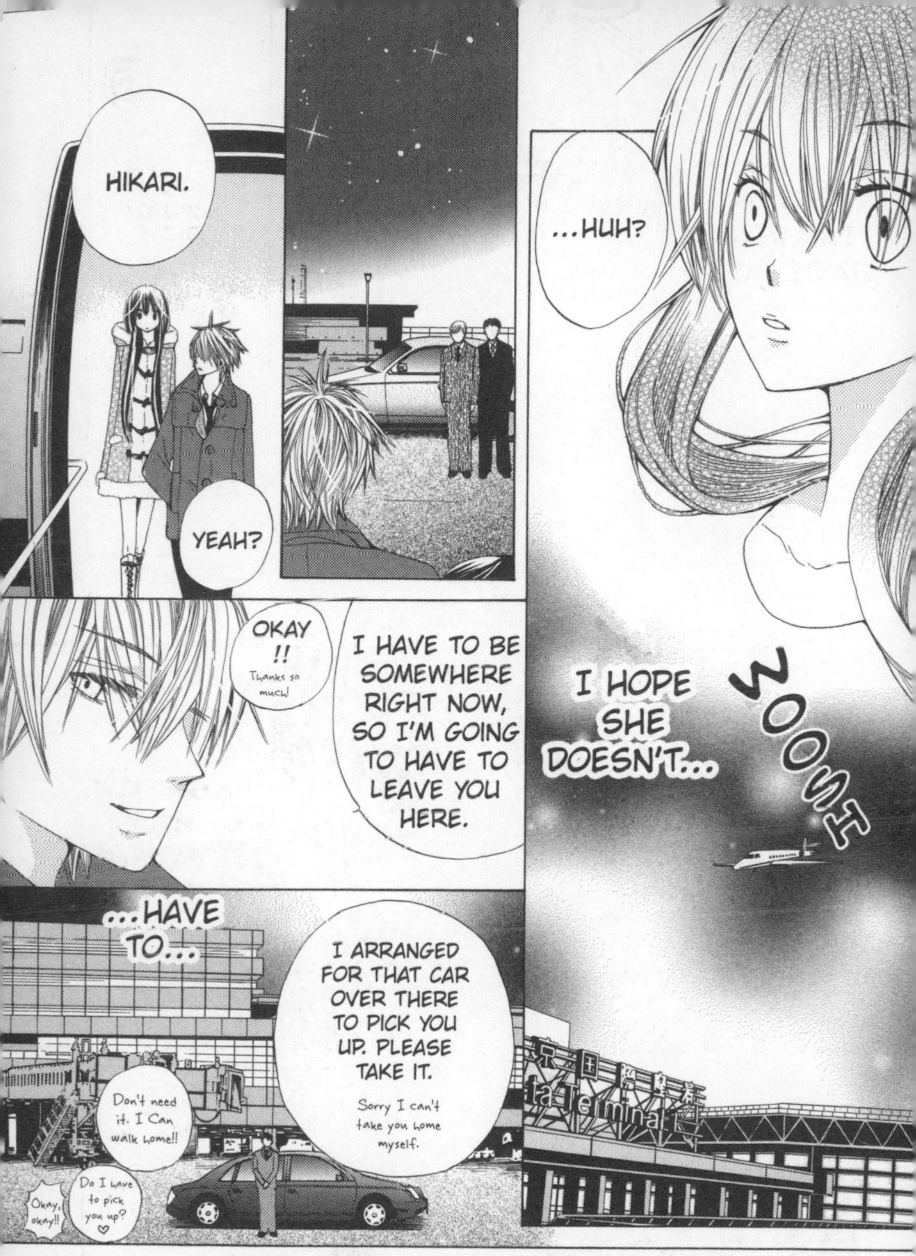
...HUH?
I HOPE SHE DOESN'T...
WOOSH
HIKARI.
YEAH?
I HAVE TO BE SOMEWHERE RIGHT NOW, SO I'M GOING TO HAVE TO LEAVE YOU HERE.
OKAY !! Thanks so much!
I ARRANGED FOR THAT CAR OVER THERE TO PICK YOU UP. PLEASE TAKE IT.
Sorry I can't take you home myself.
...HAVE TO...
Don't need it. I can walk home!!
Do I have to pick you up? ♡
Okay, okay!!

...DEAL WITH ANYTHING UNPLEASANT.

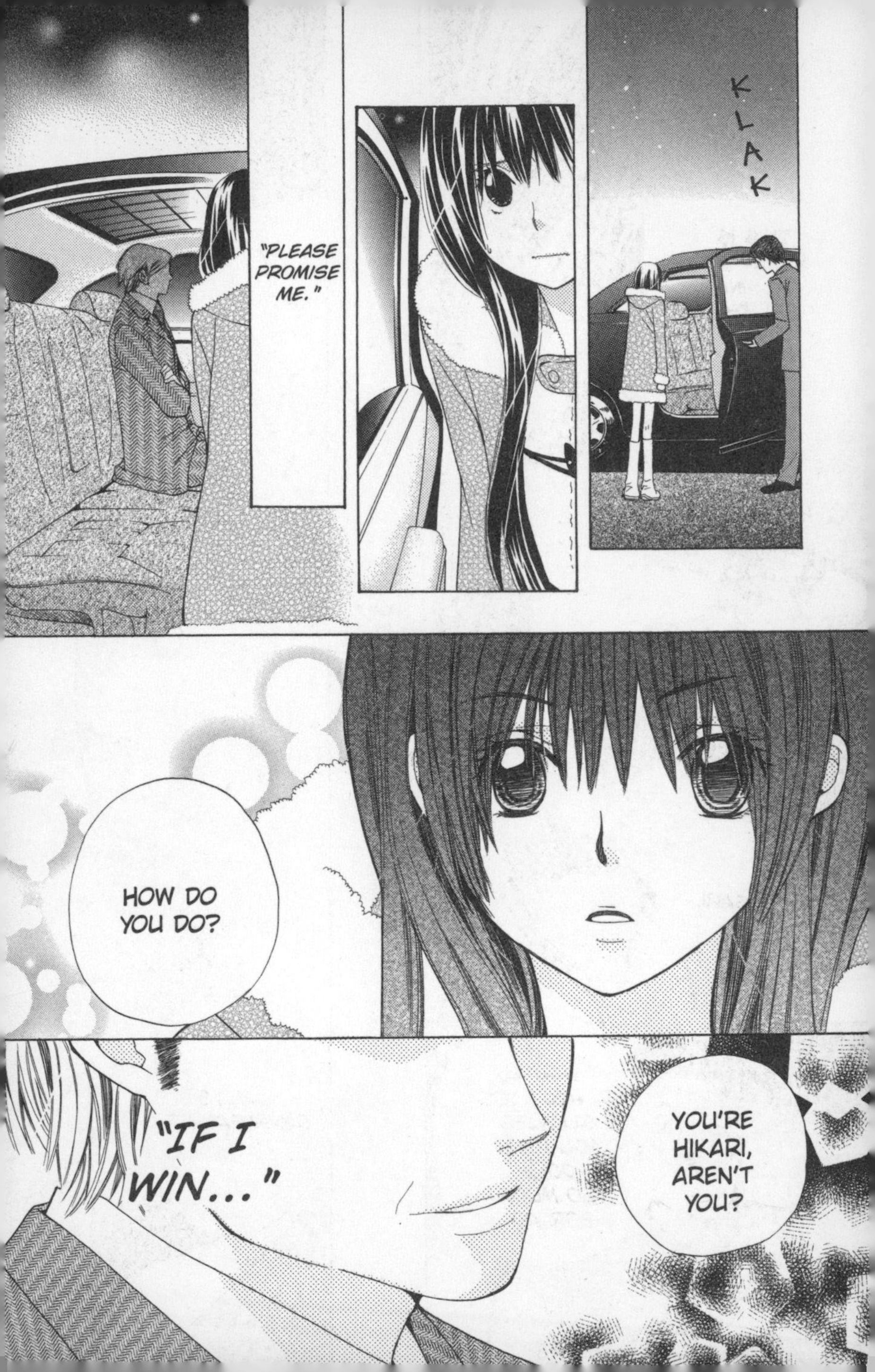
KLAK
"PLEASE PROMISE ME."
HOW DO YOU DO?
YOU'RE HIKARI, AREN'T YOU?
"IF I WIN..."

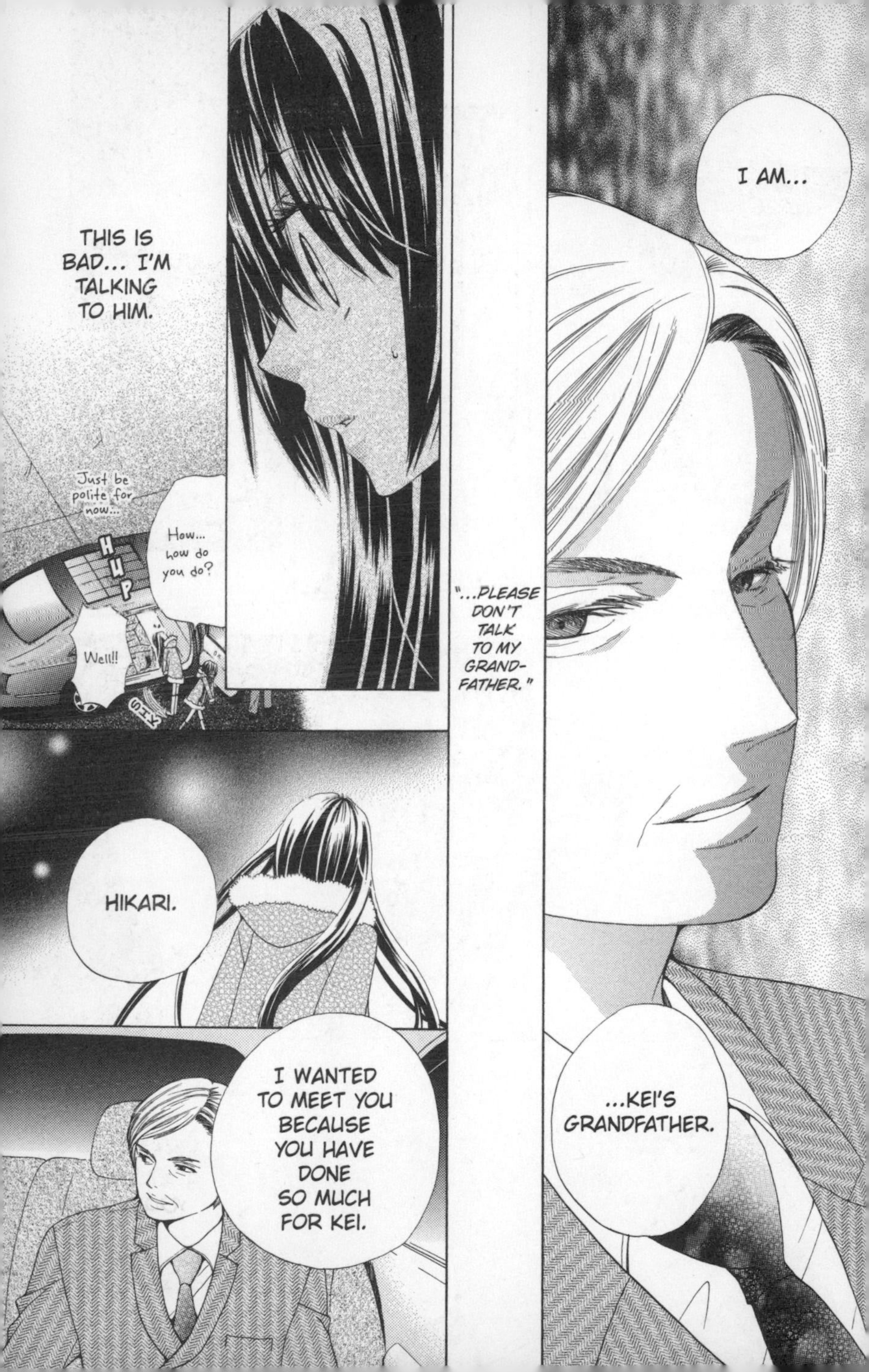
I AM...
...KEI'S GRANDFATHER.
"...PLEASE DON'T TALK TO MY GRANDFATHER."
THIS IS BAD... I'M TALKING TO HIM.
Just be polite for now...
How... how do you do?
HUP
Well!!
HIKARI.
I WANTED TO MEET YOU BECAUSE YOU HAVE DONE SO MUCH FOR KEI.

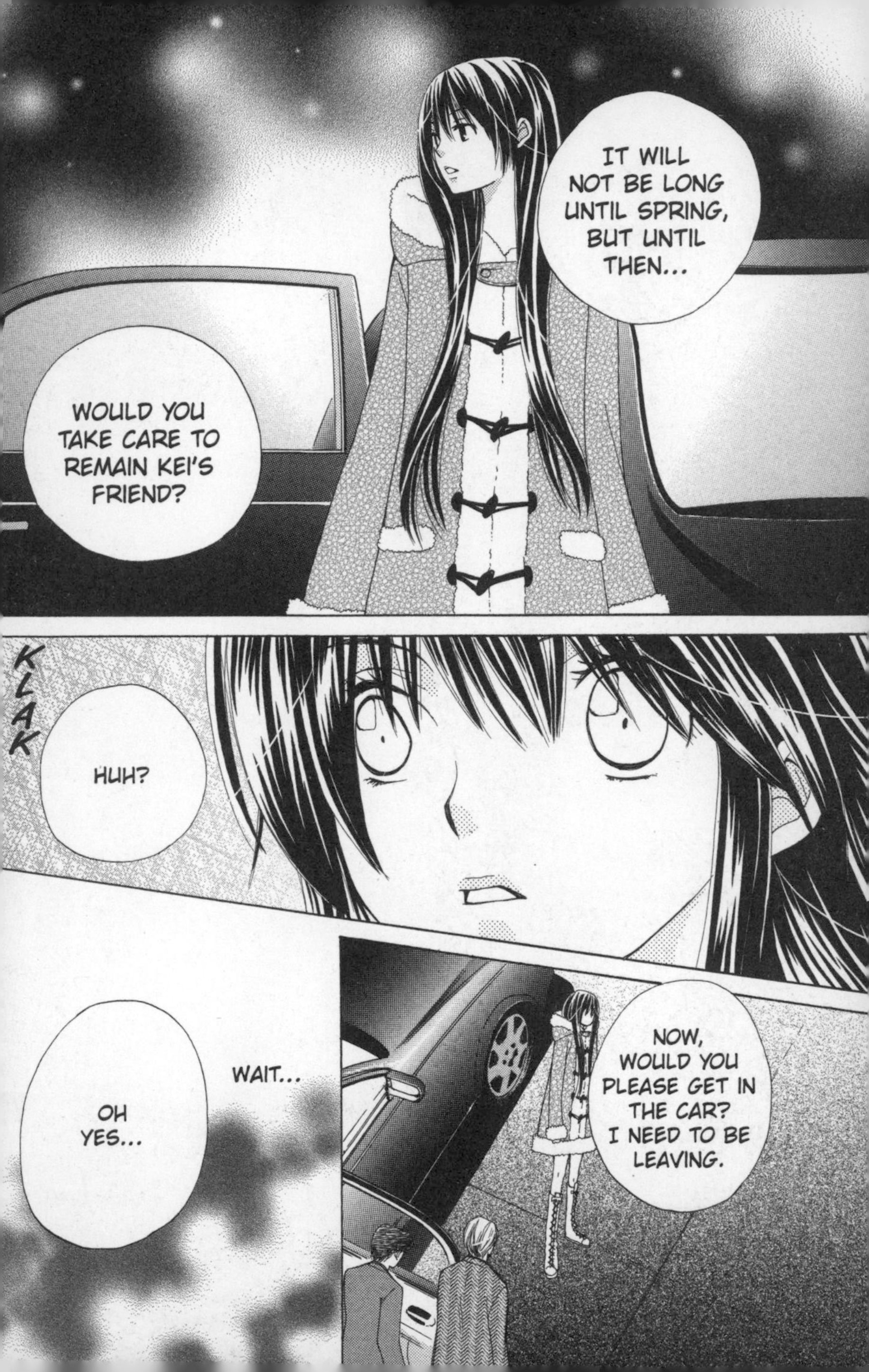
IT WILL NOT BE LONG UNTIL SPRING, BUT UNTIL THEN...
WOULD YOU TAKE CARE TO REMAIN KEI'S FRIEND?
KLAK
HUH?
NOW, WOULD YOU PLEASE GET IN THE CAR? I NEED TO BE LEAVING.
WAIT...
OH YES...

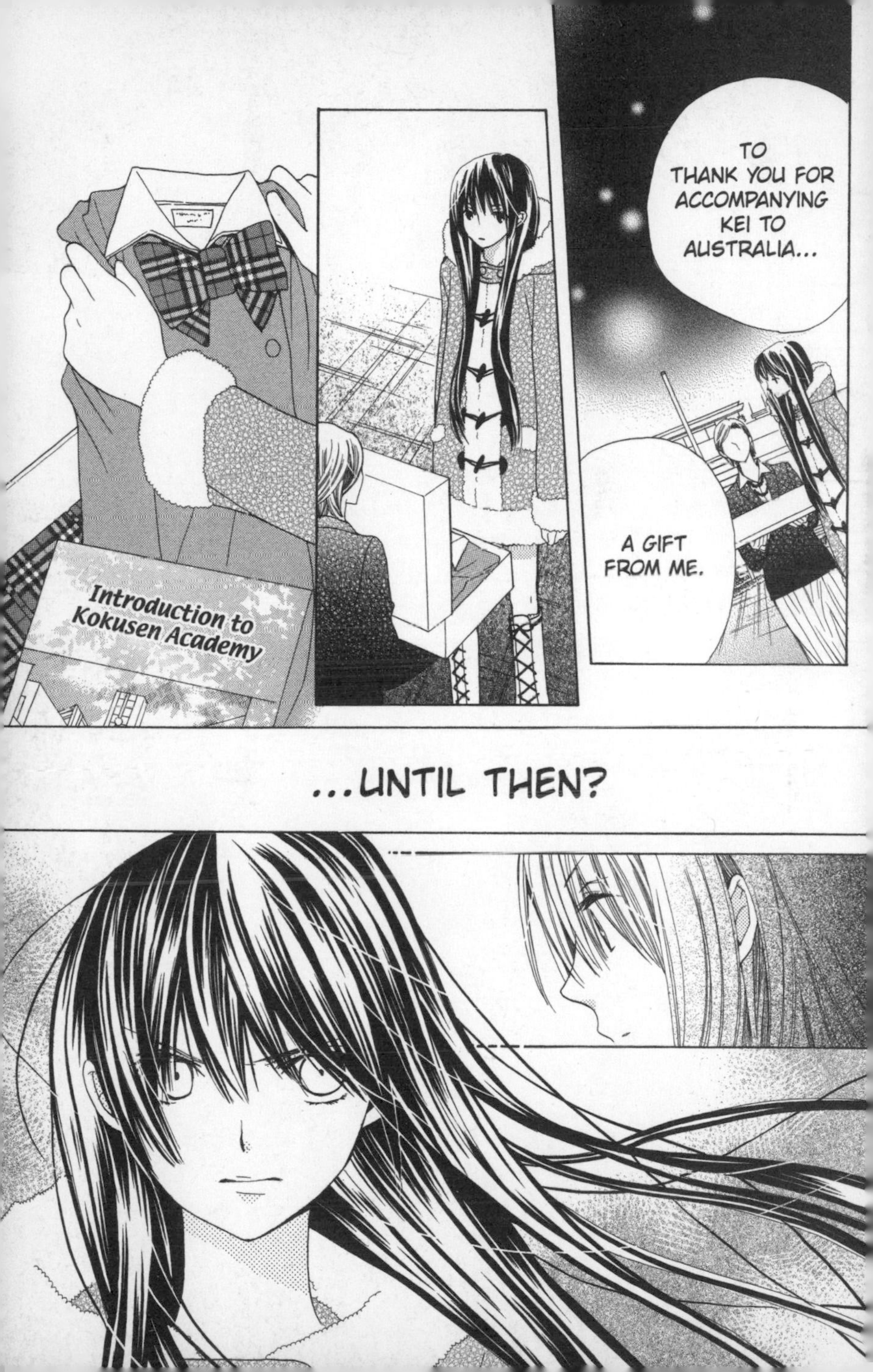
TO THANK YOU FOR ACCOMPANYING KEI TO AUSTRALIA...
A GIFT FROM ME.
Introduction to Kokusen Academy
...UNTIL THEN?

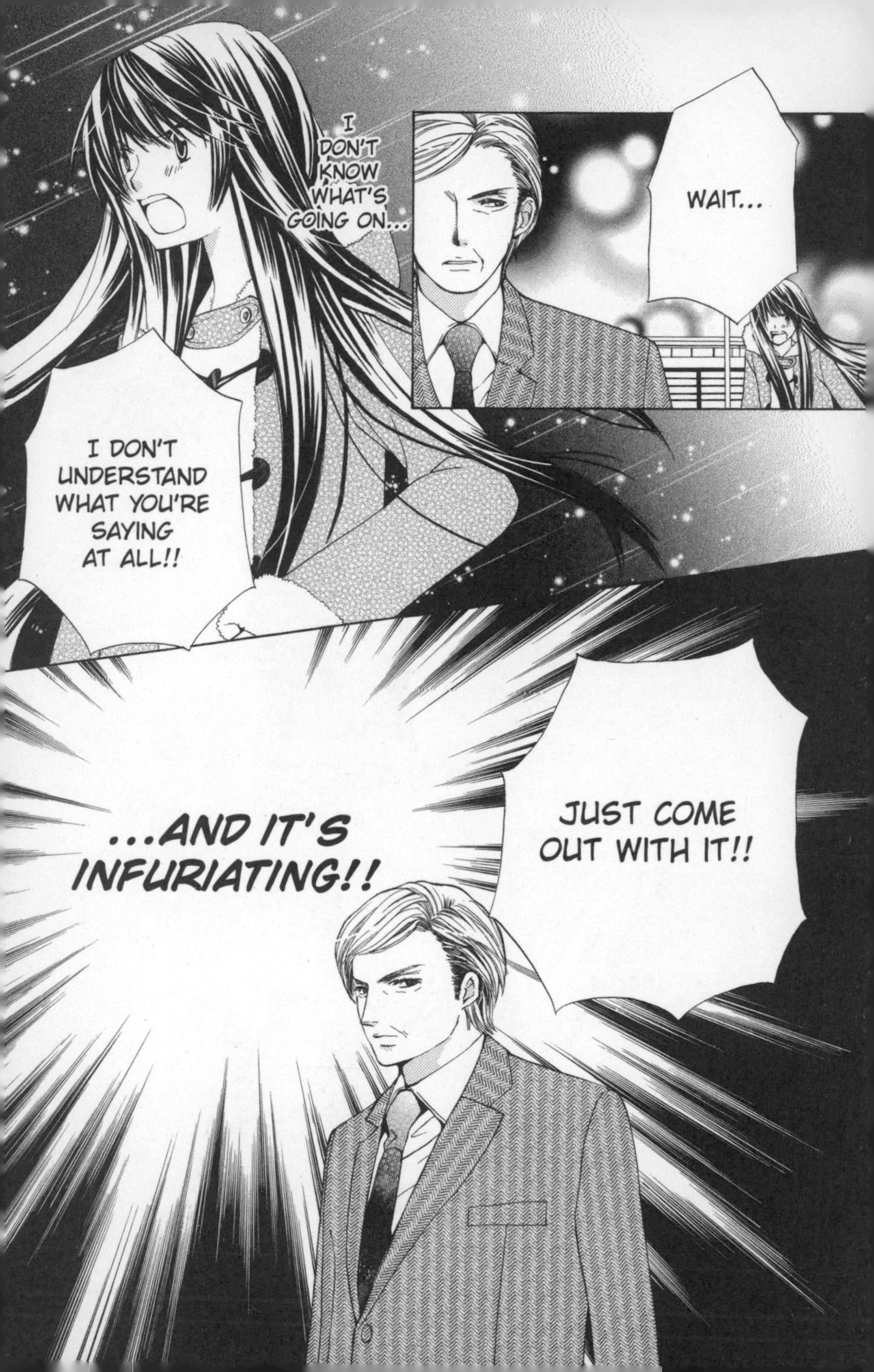
WAIT...
I DON'T KNOW WHAT'S GOING ON...
I DON'T UNDERSTAND WHAT YOU'RE SAYING AT ALL!!
JUST COME OUT WITH IT!!
...AND IT'S INFURIATING!!

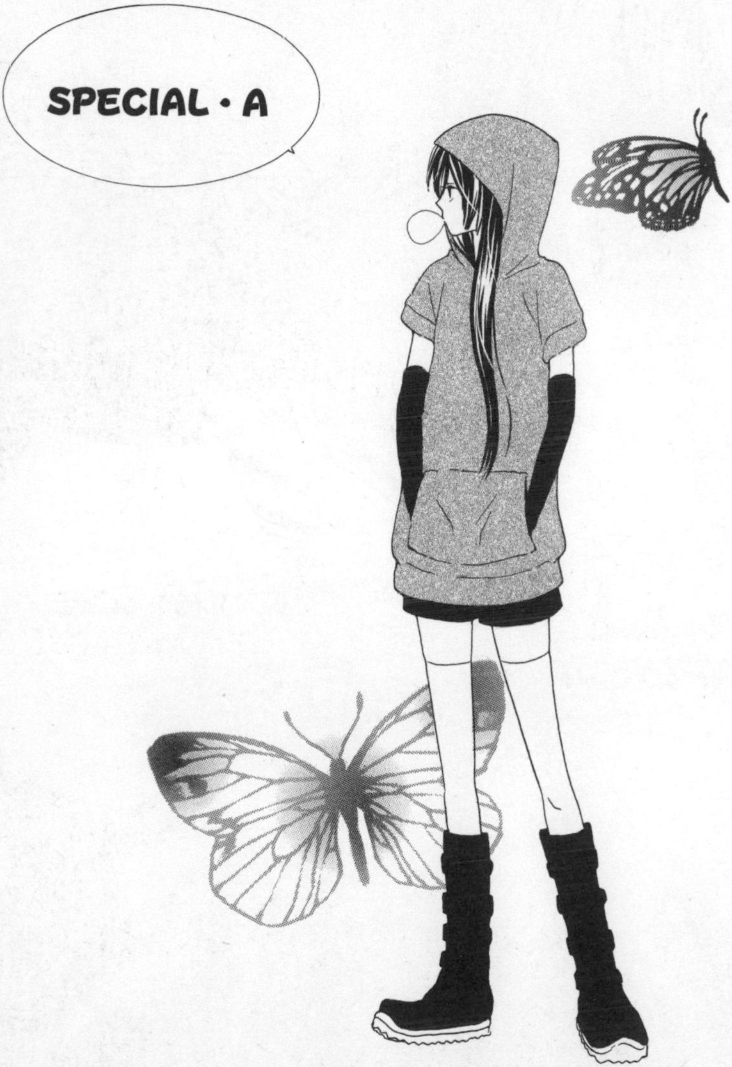
SPECIAL • A

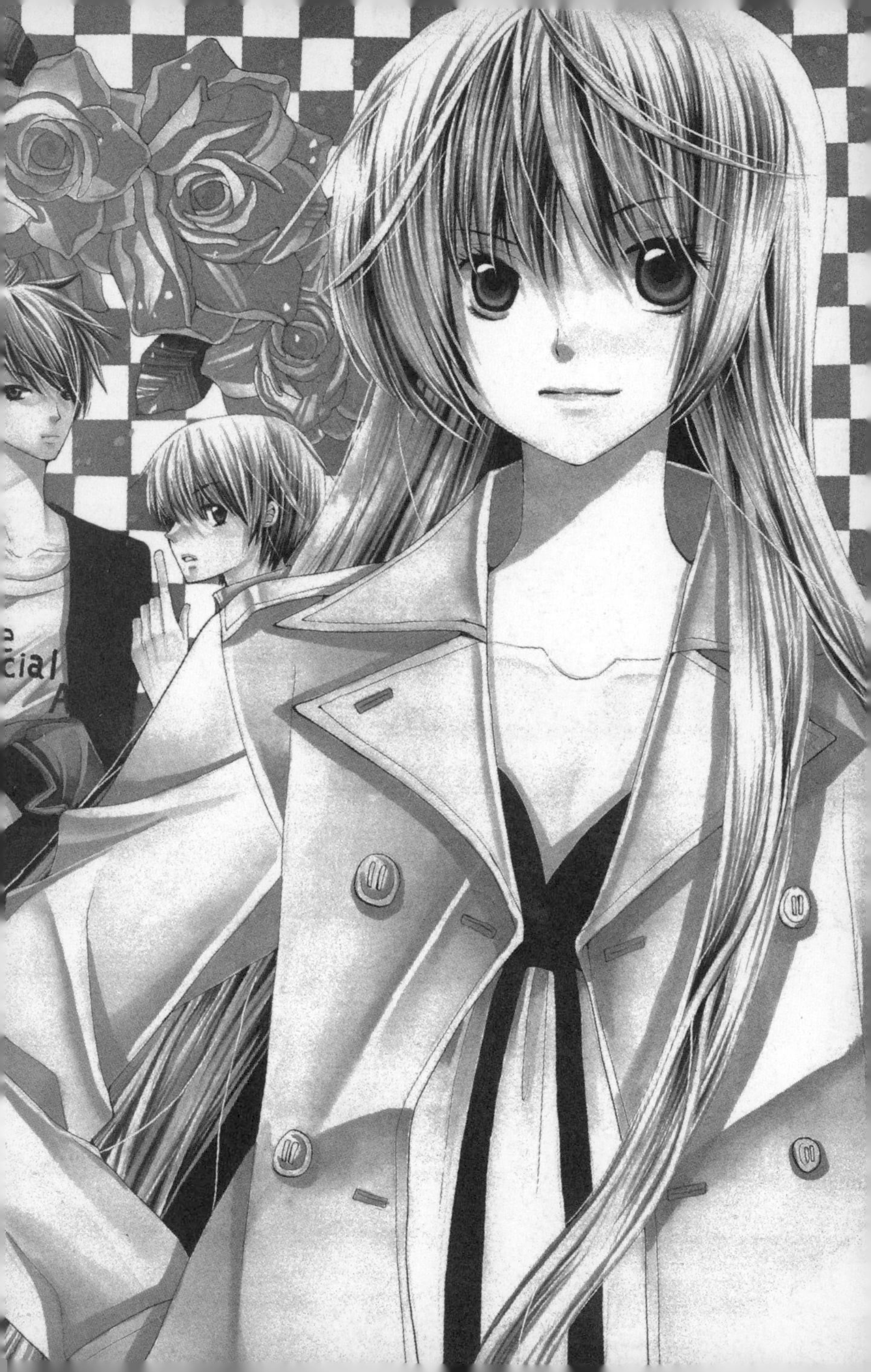

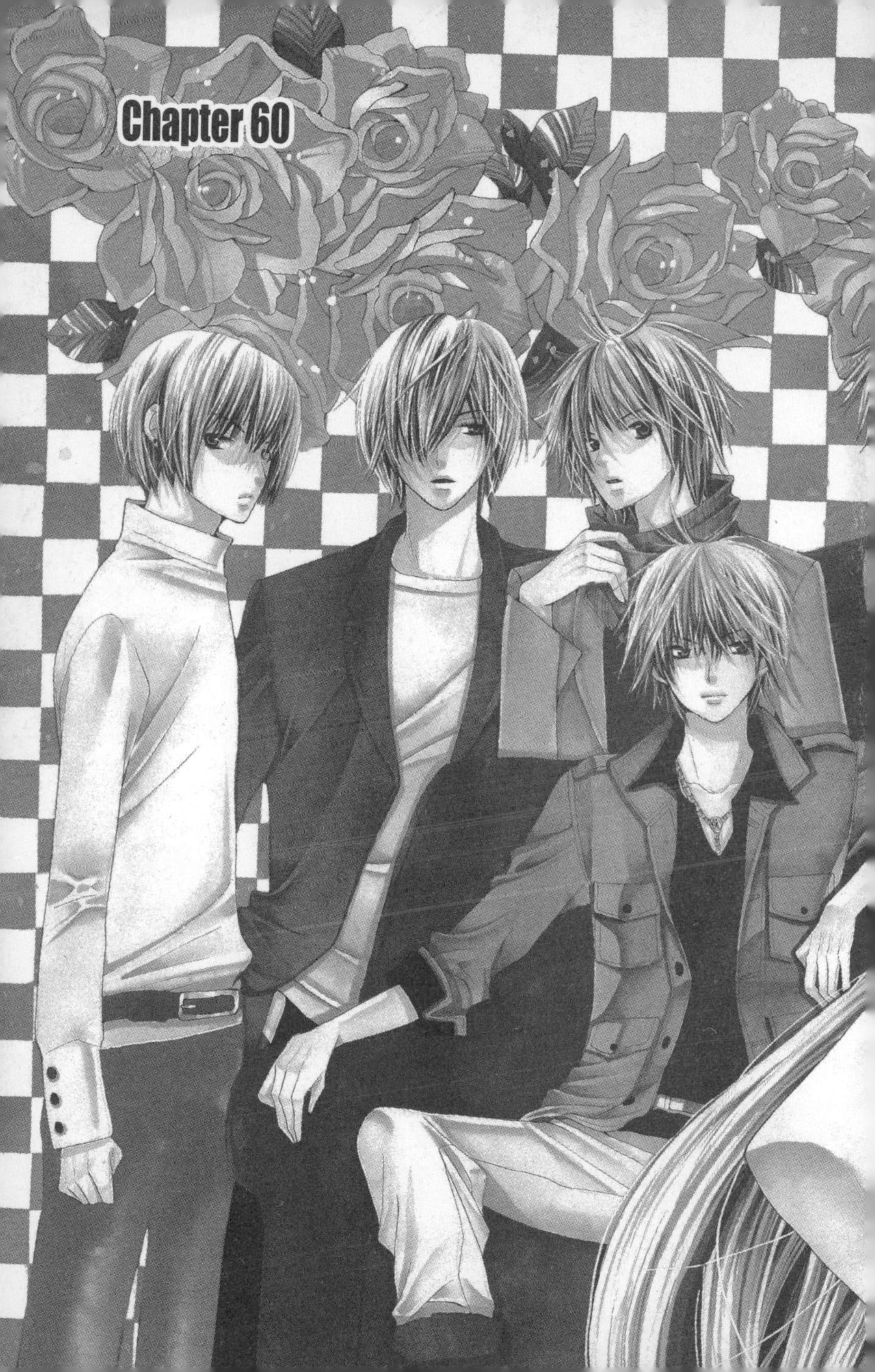
Chapter 60

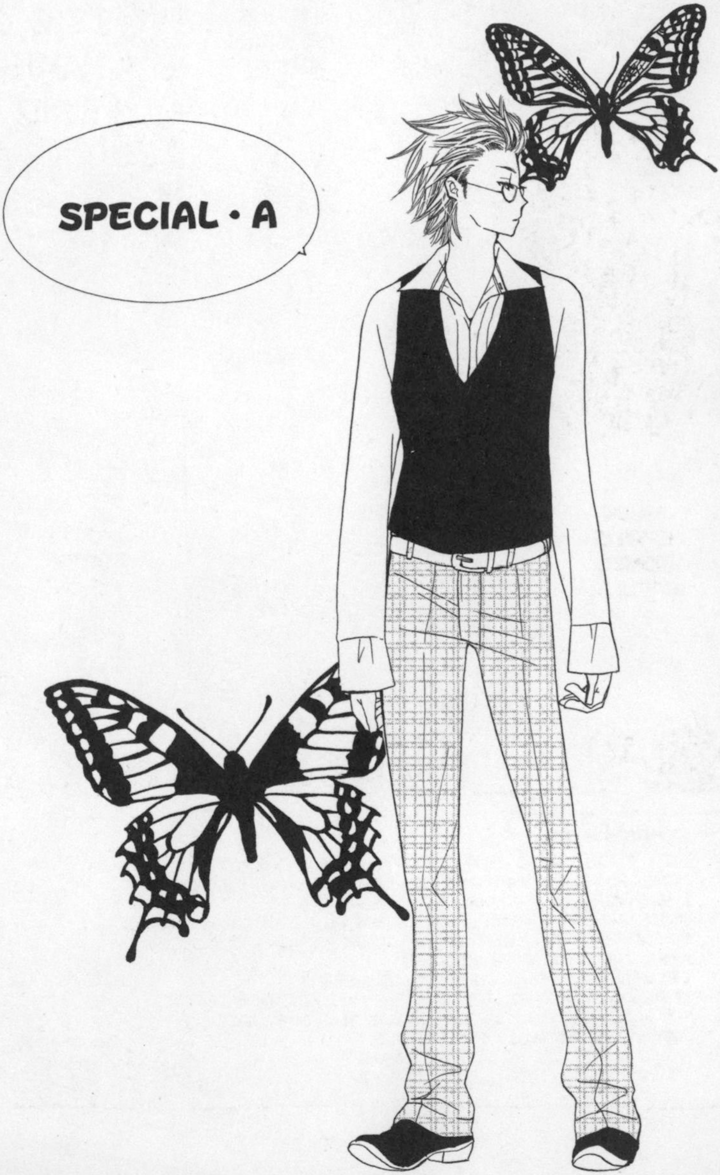
SPECIAL • A

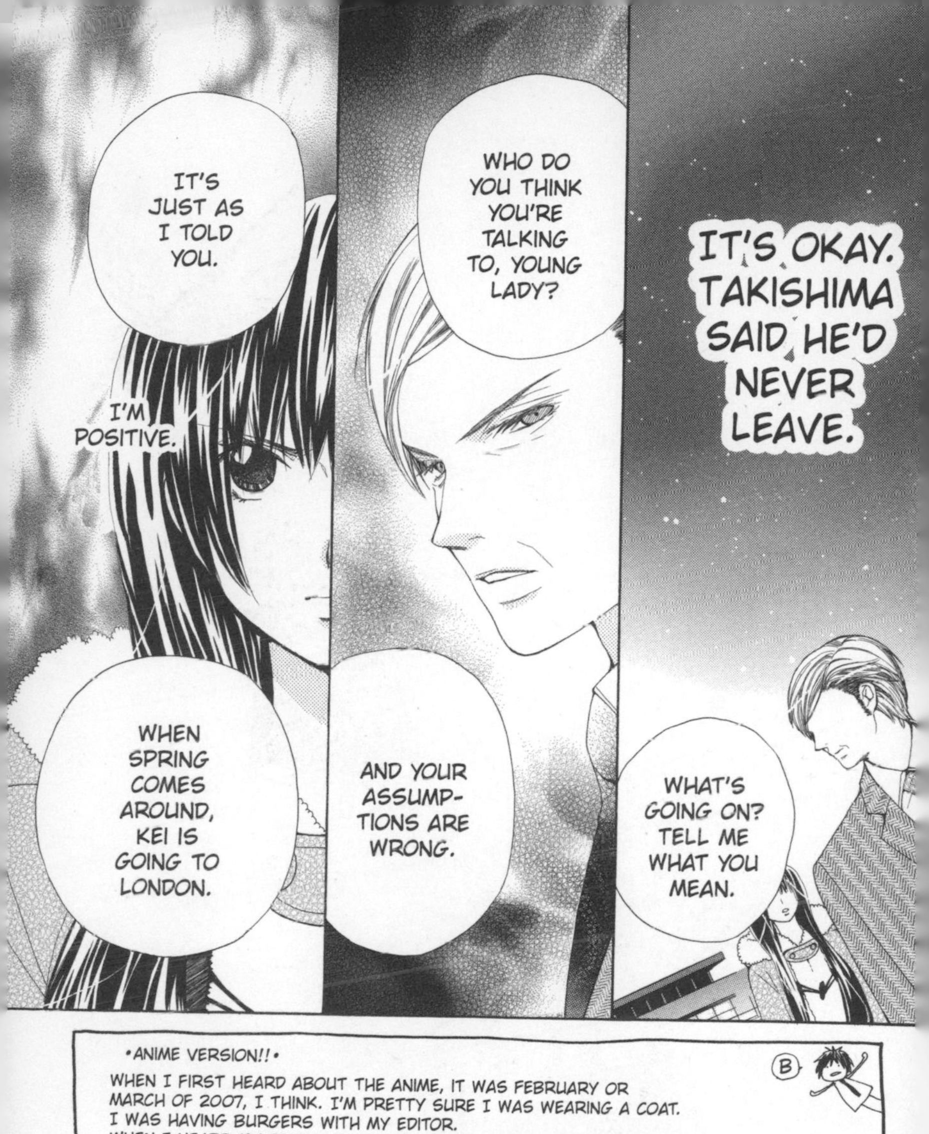
IT'S OKAY. TAKISHIMA SAID HE'D NEVER LEAVE.
WHAT'S GOING ON? TELL ME WHAT YOU MEAN.
WHO DO YOU THINK YOU'RE TALKING TO, YOUNG LADY?
AND YOUR ASSUMPTIONS ARE WRONG.
IT'S JUST AS I TOLD YOU.
I'M POSITIVE.
WHEN SPRING COMES AROUND, KEI IS GOING TO LONDON.

•ANIME VERSION!!•

WHEN I FIRST HEARD ABOUT THE ANIME, IT WAS FEBRUARY OR MARCH OF 2007, I THINK. I'M PRETTY SURE I WAS WEARING A COAT. I WAS HAVING BURGERS WITH MY EDITOR.
WHEN I HEARD MY EDITOR SAY, "THERE'S TALK OF AN ANIME," I WAS SO EXCITED THAT I PICKED UP THE WATER PITCHER AND MADE A BIG MESS, JUST LIKE IN THE COMICS.
I BLURTED OUT, "EH? IS S.A GOOD ENOUGH?!"
IT WAS ONLY A 50-50 CHANCE AT THE TIME, SO I DIDN'T KNOW IF IT WOULD REALLY HAPPEN. I DECIDED TO FORGET ABOUT IT UNTIL IT WAS ACTUALLY DECIDED.

...About it... They might forget... After all...

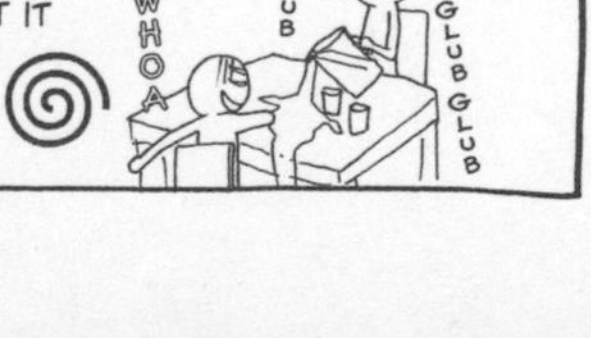
B-BMP
B-BMP
GLUB
WHOA
GLUB GLUB

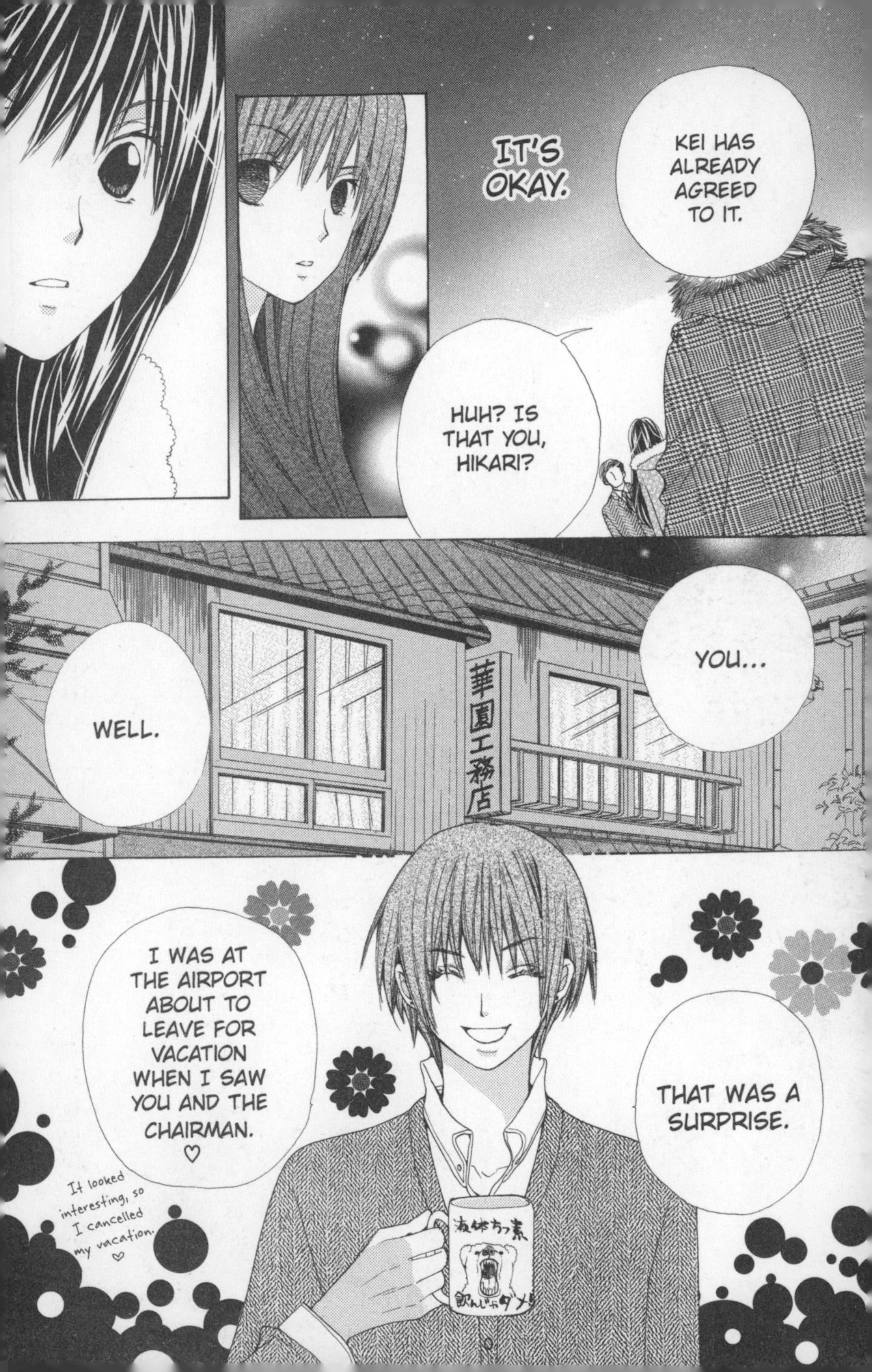
KEI HAS ALREADY AGREED TO IT.
IT'S OKAY.
HUH? IS THAT YOU, HIKARI?
YOU...
華園工務店
WELL.
THAT WAS A SURPRISE.
I WAS AT THE AIRPORT ABOUT TO LEAVE FOR VACATION WHEN I SAW YOU AND THE CHAIRMAN. ♡
It looked interesting, so I cancelled my vacation. ♡

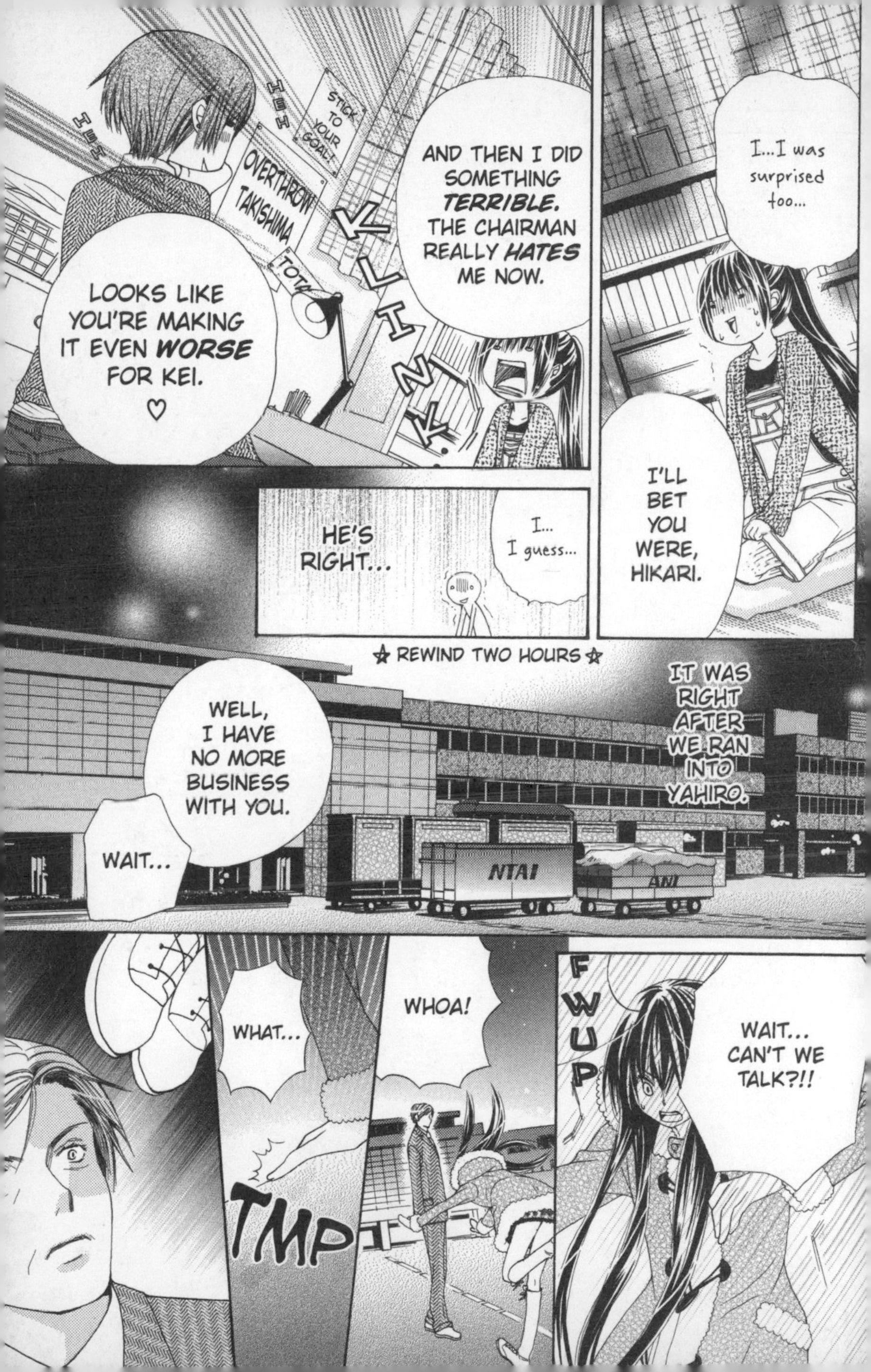
I...I was surprised too...
I'LL BET YOU WERE, HIKARI.
AND THEN I DID SOMETHING TERRIBLE. THE CHAIRMAN REALLY HATES ME NOW.
VLINK
STICK TO YOUR GOAL!
OVERTHROW TAKISHIMA
TOTAL
HEH HEH
LOOKS LIKE YOU'RE MAKING IT EVEN WORSE FOR KEI. ♡
I... I guess...
HE'S RIGHT...
☆ REWIND TWO HOURS ☆
IT WAS RIGHT AFTER WE RAN INTO YAHIRO.
WELL, I HAVE NO MORE BUSINESS WITH YOU.
WAIT...
NTAI
ANI
FWUP
WAIT... CAN'T WE TALK?!!
WHOA!
TMP
WHAT...

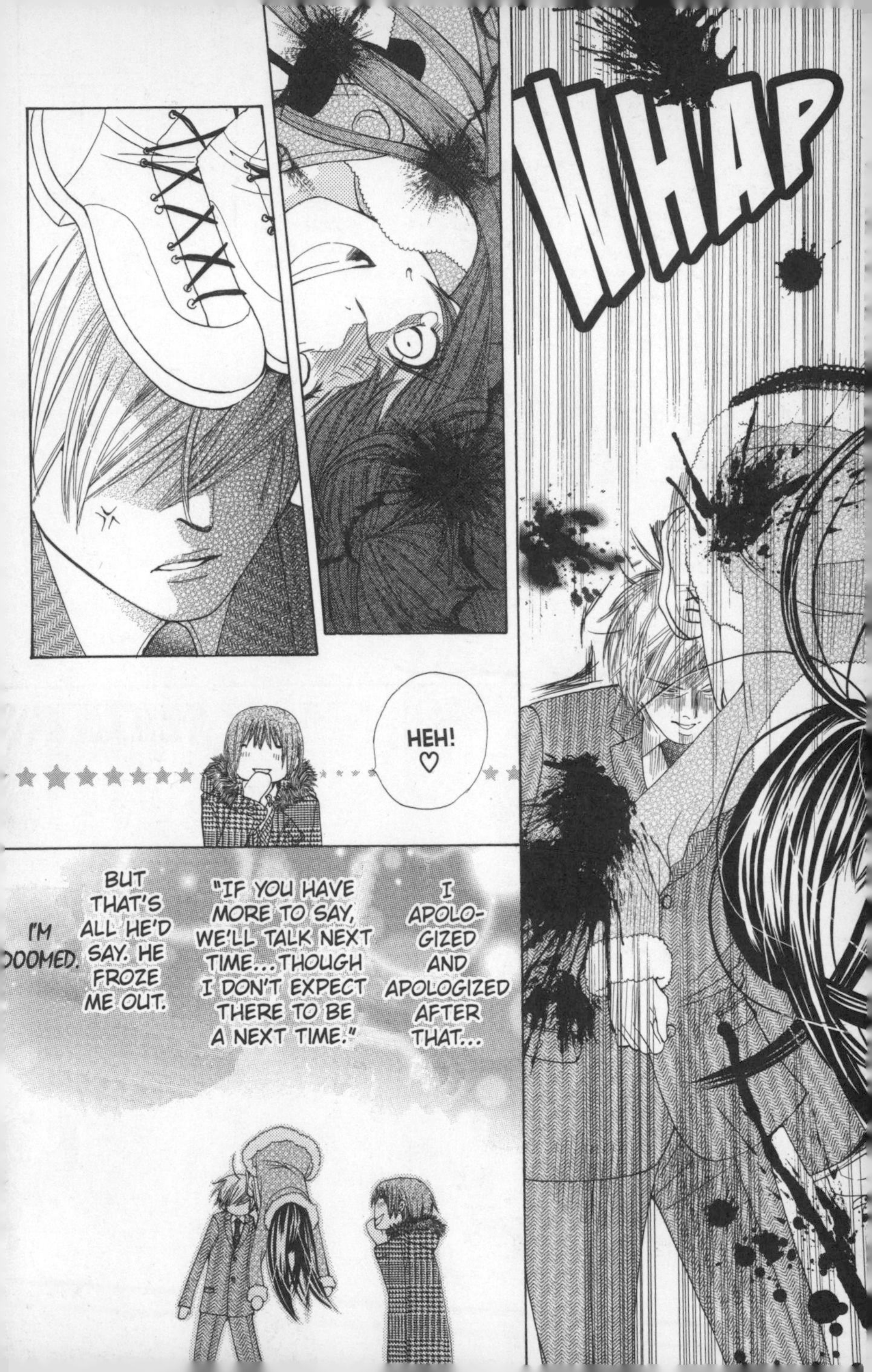
WHAP
HEH! ♡
I APOLOGIZED AND APOLOGIZED AFTER THAT...
"IF YOU HAVE MORE TO SAY, WE'LL TALK NEXT TIME... THOUGH I DON'T EXPECT THERE TO BE A NEXT TIME."
BUT THAT'S ALL HE'D SAY. HE FROZE ME OUT.
I'M DOOMED.

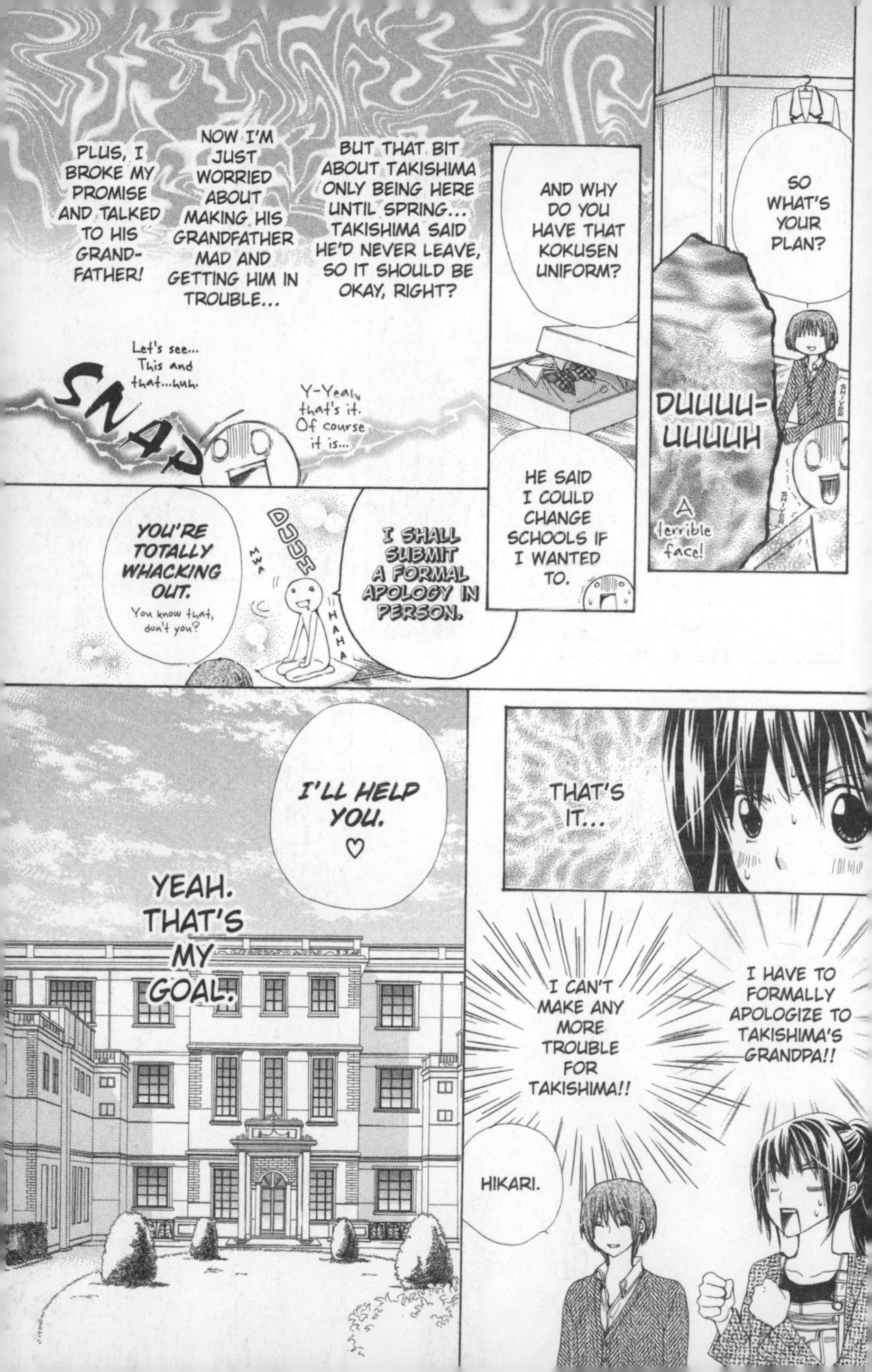
SO WHAT'S YOUR PLAN?
DUUUU-UUUUH
A terrible face!
SHIVER
SHIVER
AND WHY DO YOU HAVE THAT KOKUSEN UNIFORM?
HE SAID I COULD CHANGE SCHOOLS IF I WANTED TO.
BUT THAT BIT ABOUT TAKISHIMA ONLY BEING HERE UNTIL SPRING... TAKISHIMA SAID HE'D NEVER LEAVE, SO IT SHOULD BE OKAY, RIGHT?
NOW I'M JUST WORRIED ABOUT MAKING HIS GRANDFATHER MAD AND GETTING HIM IN TROUBLE...
PLUS, I BROKE MY PROMISE AND TALKED TO HIS GRANDFATHER!
Let's see... This and that...huh.
SNAP
Y-Yeah, that's it. Of course it is...
I SHALL SUBMIT A FORMAL APOLOGY IN PERSON.
HAHA
DUH
YOU'RE TOTALLY WHACKING OUT.
You know that, don't you?
THAT'S IT...
I HAVE TO FORMALLY APOLOGIZE TO TAKISHIMA'S GRANDPA!!
I CAN'T MAKE ANY MORE TROUBLE FOR TAKISHIMA!!
HIKARI.
I'LL HELP YOU. ♡
YEAH. THAT'S MY GOAL.

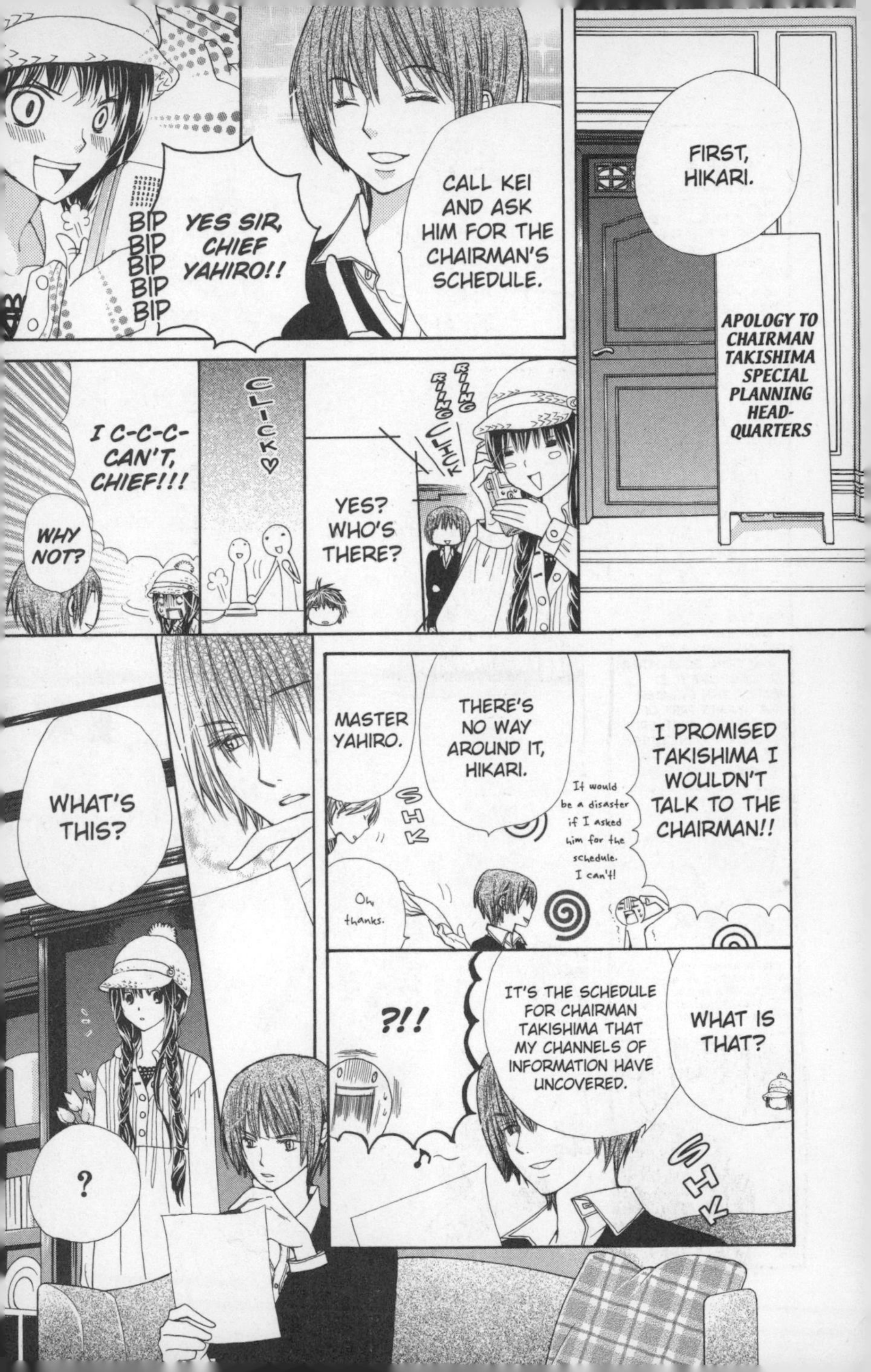
APOLOGY TO CHAIRMAN TAKISHIMA SPECIAL PLANNING HEAD-QUARTERS
FIRST, HIKARI.
CALL KEI AND ASK HIM FOR THE CHAIRMAN'S SCHEDULE.
YES SIR, CHIEF YAHIRO!!
BIP BIP BIP BIP BIP
RING RING
CLICK
YES? WHO'S THERE?
CLICK♥
I C-C-C-CAN'T, CHIEF!!!
WHY NOT?
I PROMISED TAKISHIMA I WOULDN'T TALK TO THE CHAIRMAN!!
It would be a disaster if I asked him for the schedule. I can't!
THERE'S NO WAY AROUND IT, HIKARI.
MASTER YAHIRO.
SHK
Oh thanks.
WHAT IS THAT?
IT'S THE SCHEDULE FOR CHAIRMAN TAKISHIMA THAT MY CHANNELS OF INFORMATION HAVE UNCOVERED.
?!!
SHK
WHAT'S THIS?
?

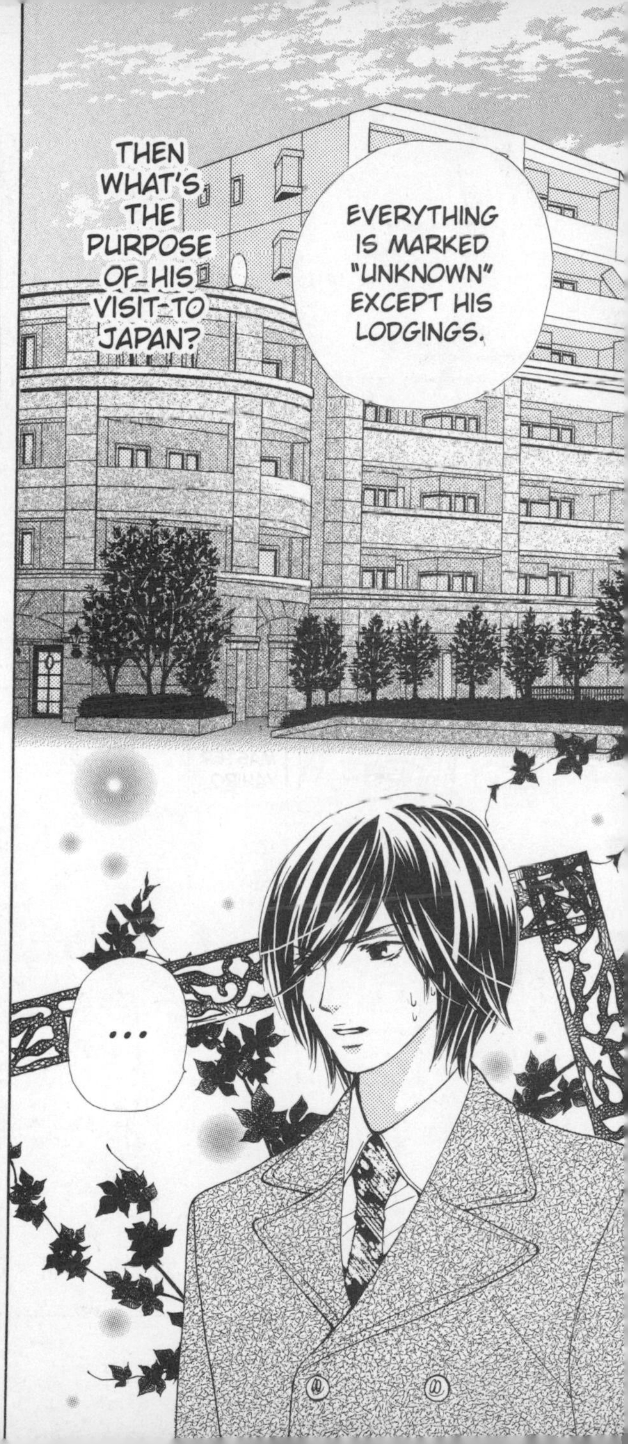
EVERYTHING IS MARKED "UNKNOWN" EXCEPT HIS LODGINGS.
THEN WHAT'S THE PURPOSE OF HIS VISIT TO JAPAN?
...

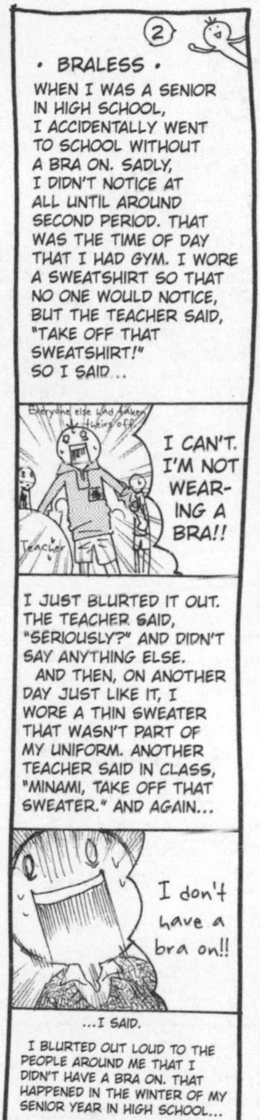
2
• BRALESS •
WHEN I WAS A SENIOR IN HIGH SCHOOL, I ACCIDENTALLY WENT TO SCHOOL WITHOUT A BRA ON. SADLY, I DIDN'T NOTICE AT ALL UNTIL AROUND SECOND PERIOD. THAT WAS THE TIME OF DAY THAT I HAD GYM. I WORE A SWEATSHIRT SO THAT NO ONE WOULD NOTICE, BUT THE TEACHER SAID, "TAKE OFF THAT SWEATSHIRT!" SO I SAID...
Everyone else had taken theirs off.
I CAN'T. I'M NOT WEARING A BRA!!
Teacher
I JUST BLURTED IT OUT. THE TEACHER SAID, "SERIOUSLY?" AND DIDN'T SAY ANYTHING ELSE.
AND THEN, ON ANOTHER DAY JUST LIKE IT, I WORE A THIN SWEATER THAT WASN'T PART OF MY UNIFORM. ANOTHER TEACHER SAID IN CLASS, "MINAMI, TAKE OFF THAT SWEATER." AND AGAIN...
I don't have a bra on!!
...I SAID.
I BLURTED OUT LOUD TO THE PEOPLE AROUND ME THAT I DIDN'T HAVE A BRA ON. THAT HAPPENED IN THE WINTER OF MY SENIOR YEAR IN HIGH SCHOOL...

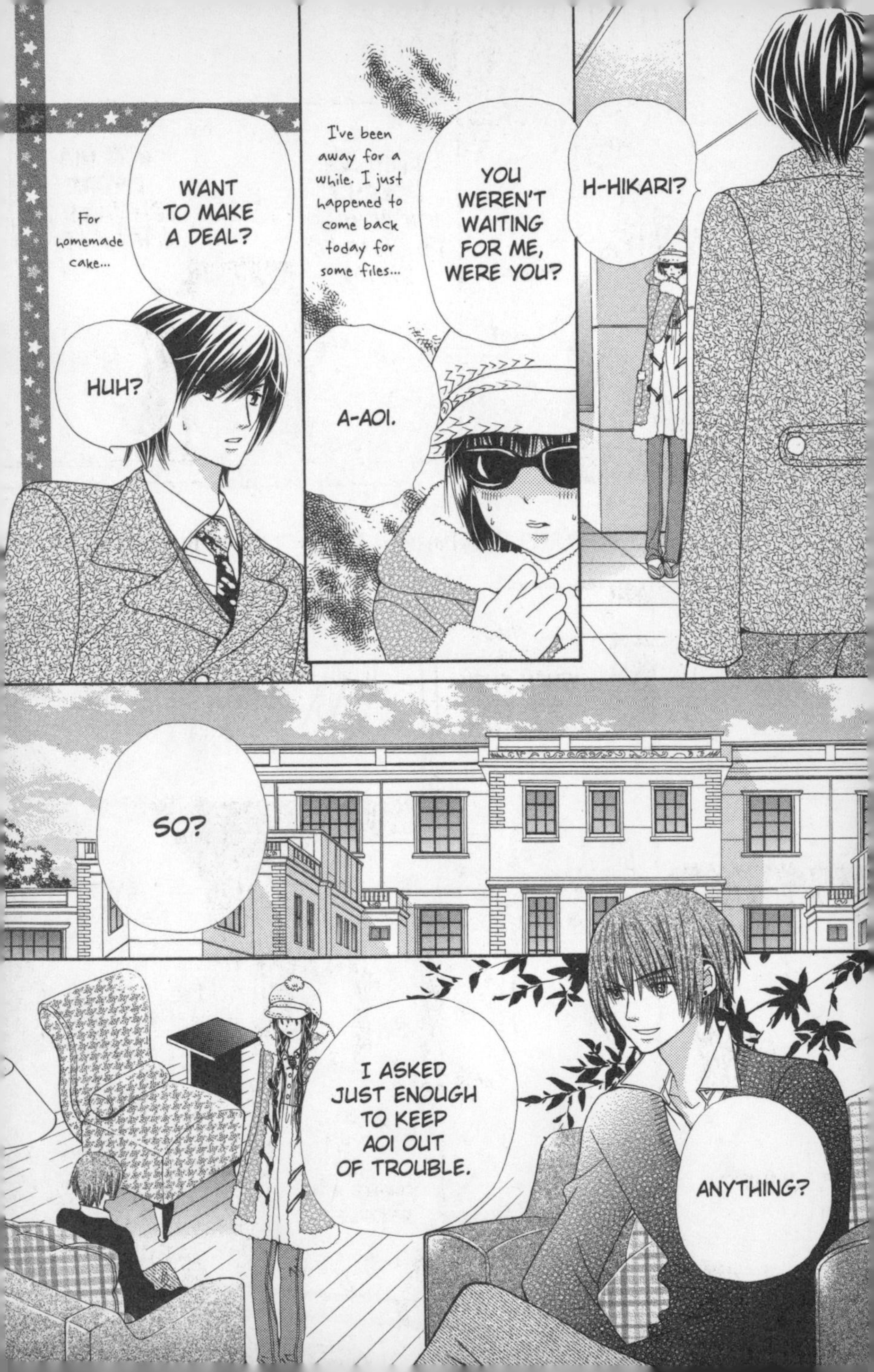
H-HIKARI?
YOU WEREN'T WAITING FOR ME, WERE YOU?
I've been away for a while. I just happened to come back today for some files...
A-AOI.
WANT TO MAKE A DEAL?
For homemade cake...
HUH?
SO?
ANYTHING?
I ASKED JUST ENOUGH TO KEEP AOI OUT OF TROUBLE.

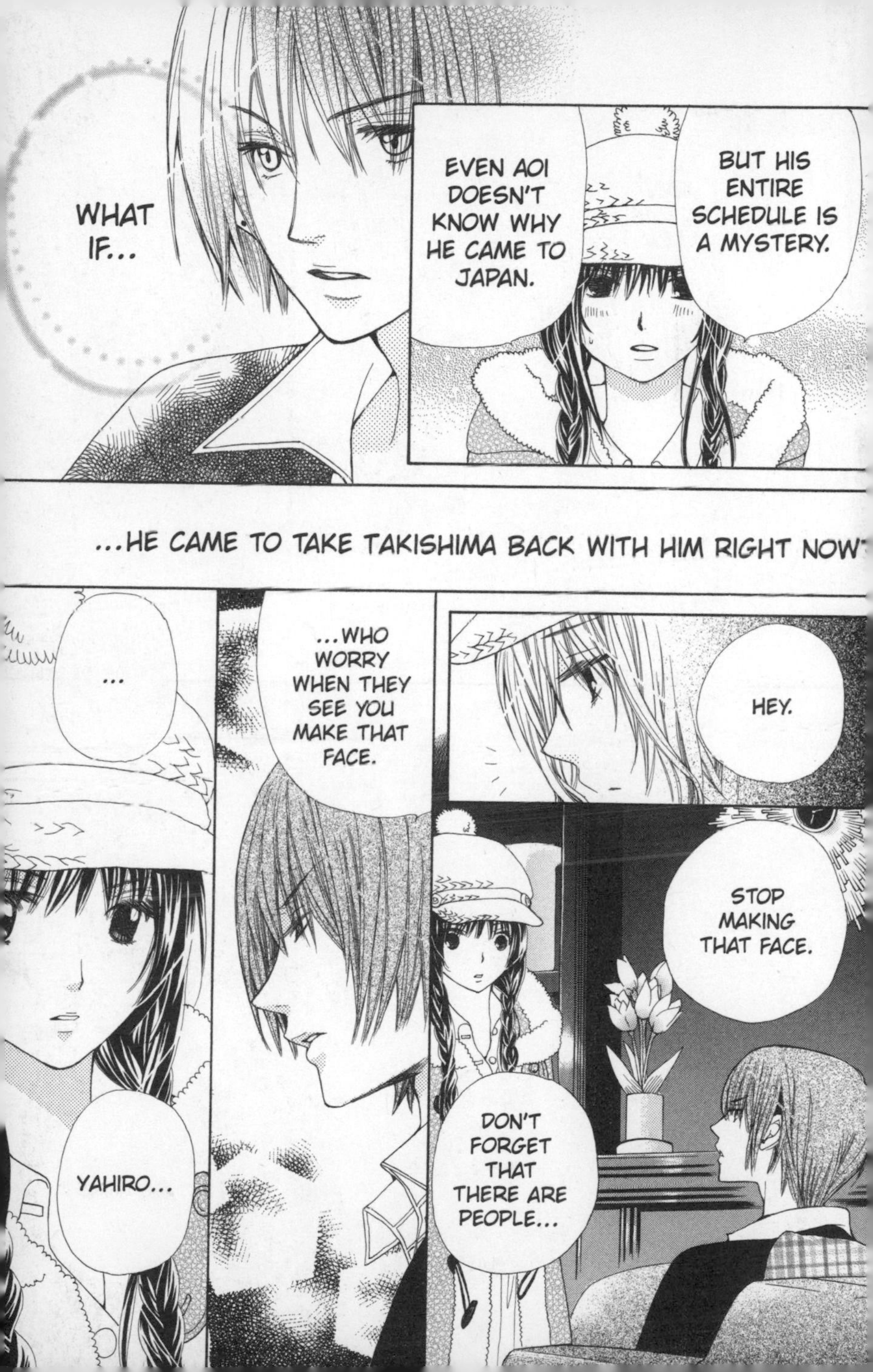
BUT HIS ENTIRE SCHEDULE IS A MYSTERY.
EVEN AOI DOESN'T KNOW WHY HE CAME TO JAPAN.
WHAT IF...
...HE CAME TO TAKE TAKISHIMA BACK WITH HIM RIGHT NOW
HEY.
STOP MAKING THAT FACE.
DON'T FORGET THAT THERE ARE PEOPLE...
...WHO WORRY WHEN THEY SEE YOU MAKE THAT FACE.
...
YAHIRO...

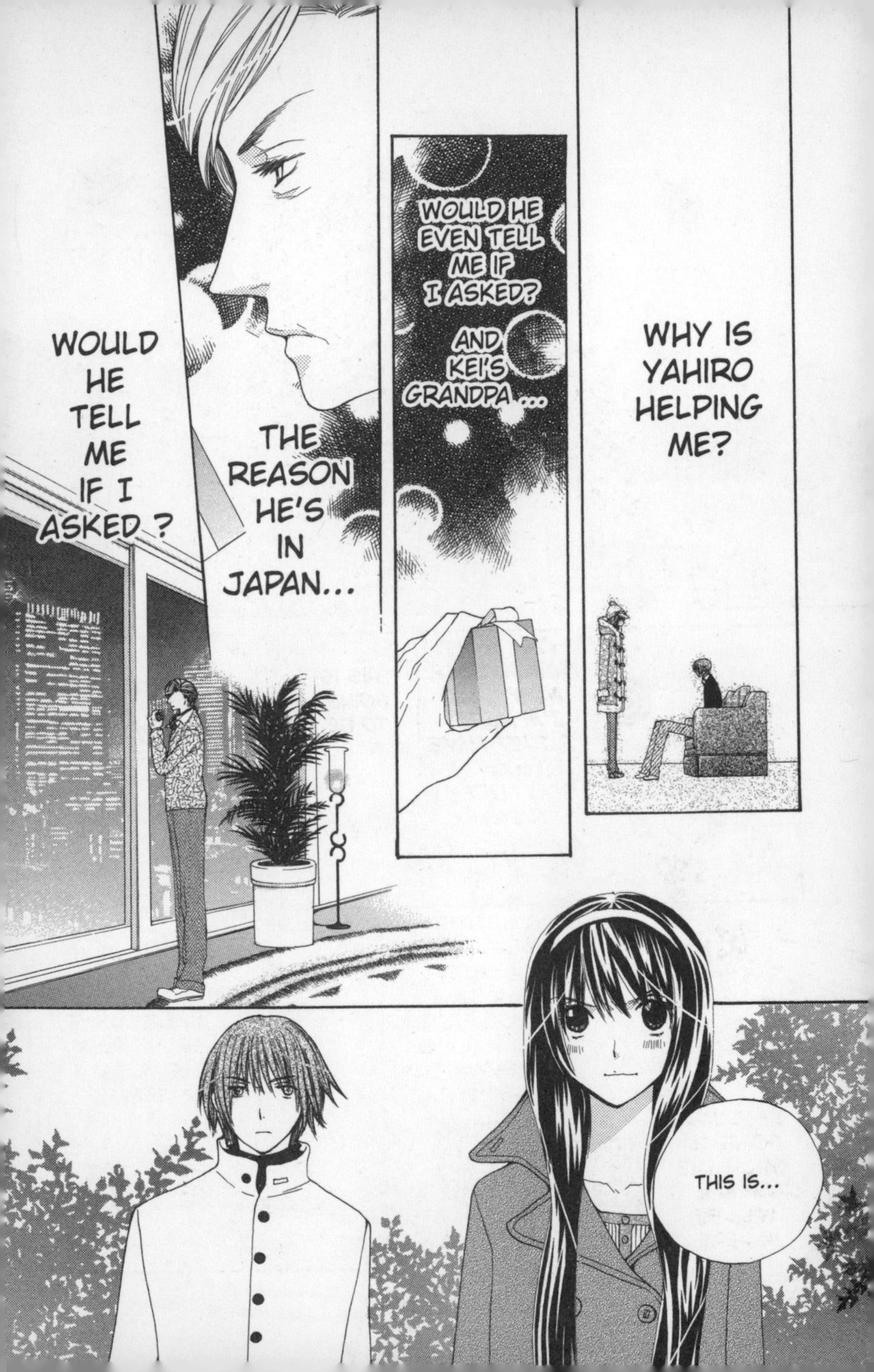
WHY IS YAHIRO HELPING ME?
WOULD HE EVEN TELL ME IF I ASKED?
AND KEI'S GRANDPA...
THE REASON HE'S IN JAPAN...
WOULD HE TELL ME IF I ASKED ?
THIS IS...

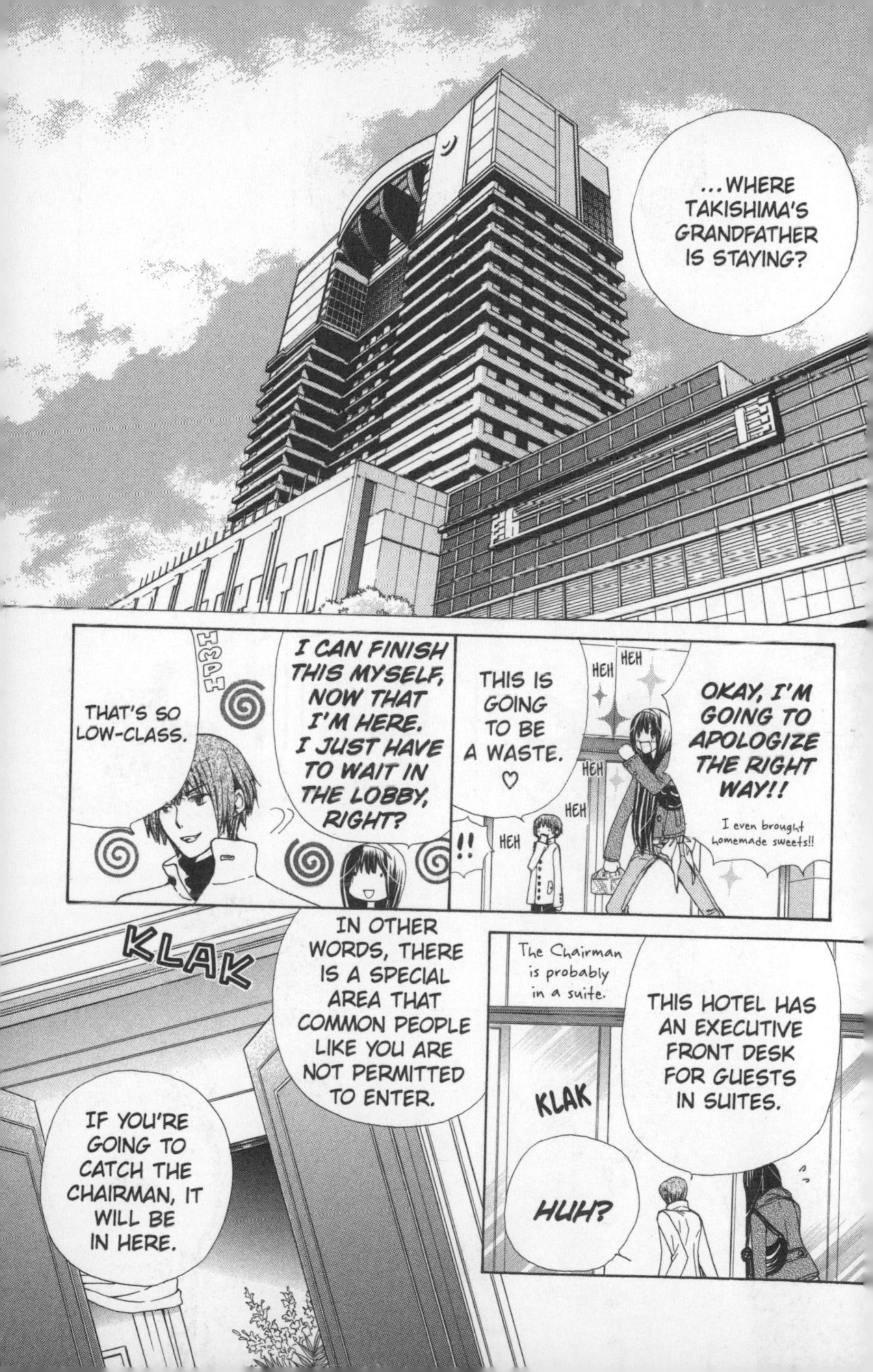
...WHERE TAKISHIMA'S GRANDFATHER IS STAYING?
OKAY, I'M GOING TO APOLOGIZE THE RIGHT WAY!!
I even brought homemade sweets!!
HEH HEH
HEH
HEH
HEH
THIS IS GOING TO BE A WASTE. ♡
!!
I CAN FINISH THIS MYSELF, NOW THAT I'M HERE. I JUST HAVE TO WAIT IN THE LOBBY, RIGHT?
HMPH
THAT'S SO LOW-CLASS.
The Chairman is probably in a suite.
THIS HOTEL HAS AN EXECUTIVE FRONT DESK FOR GUESTS IN SUITES.
KLAK
HUH?
IN OTHER WORDS, THERE IS A SPECIAL AREA THAT COMMON PEOPLE LIKE YOU ARE NOT PERMITTED TO ENTER.
KLAK
IF YOU'RE GOING TO CATCH THE CHAIRMAN, IT WILL BE IN HERE.

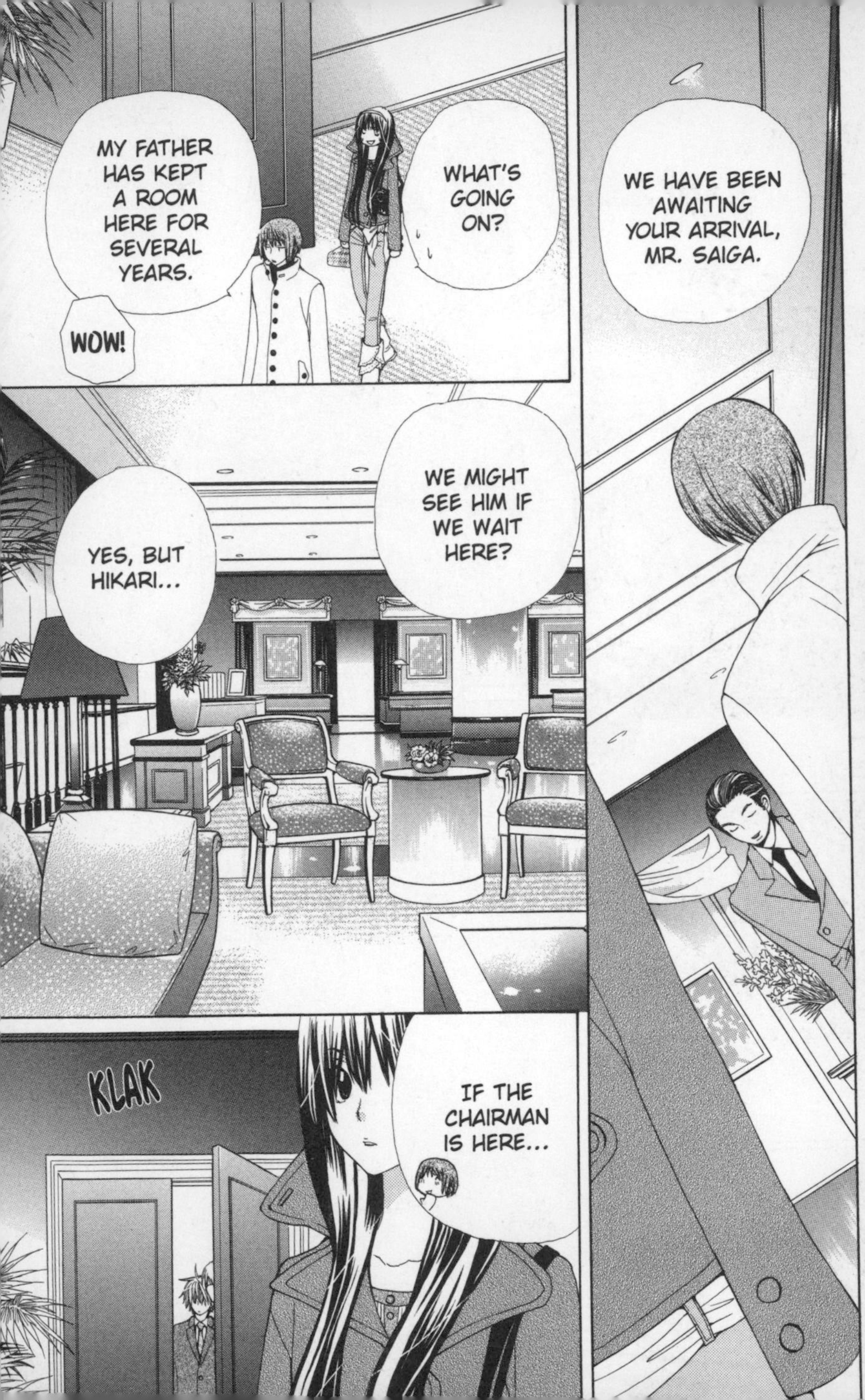
WE HAVE BEEN AWAITING YOUR ARRIVAL, MR. SAIGA.
WHAT'S GOING ON?
MY FATHER HAS KEPT A ROOM HERE FOR SEVERAL YEARS.
WOW!
WE MIGHT SEE HIM IF WE WAIT HERE?
YES, BUT HIKARI...
IF THE CHAIRMAN IS HERE...
KLAK

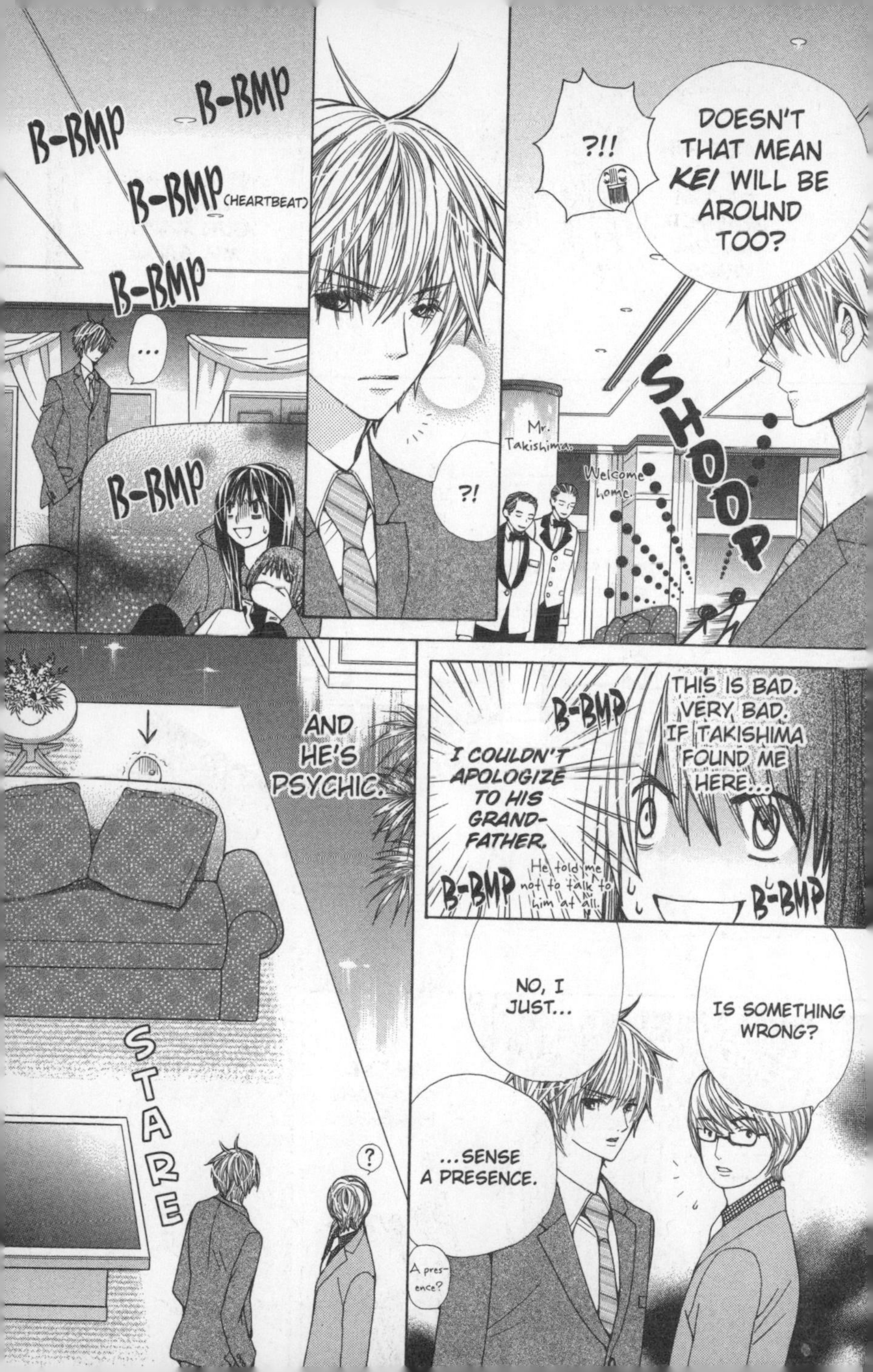

DOESN'T THAT MEAN KEI WILL BE AROUND TOO?
?!!
SHOOP
Mr. Takishima.
Welcome home.
?!
B-BMP
B-BMP
B-BMP (HEARTBEAT)
B-BMP
...
B-BMP
THIS IS BAD. VERY BAD. IF TAKISHIMA FOUND ME HERE...
B-BMP
I COULDN'T APOLOGIZE TO HIS GRANDFATHER.
He told me not to talk to him at all.
B-BMP
B-BMP
AND HE'S PSYCHIC.
IS SOMETHING WRONG?
NO, I JUST...
...SENSE A PRESENCE.
A presence?
STARE
?

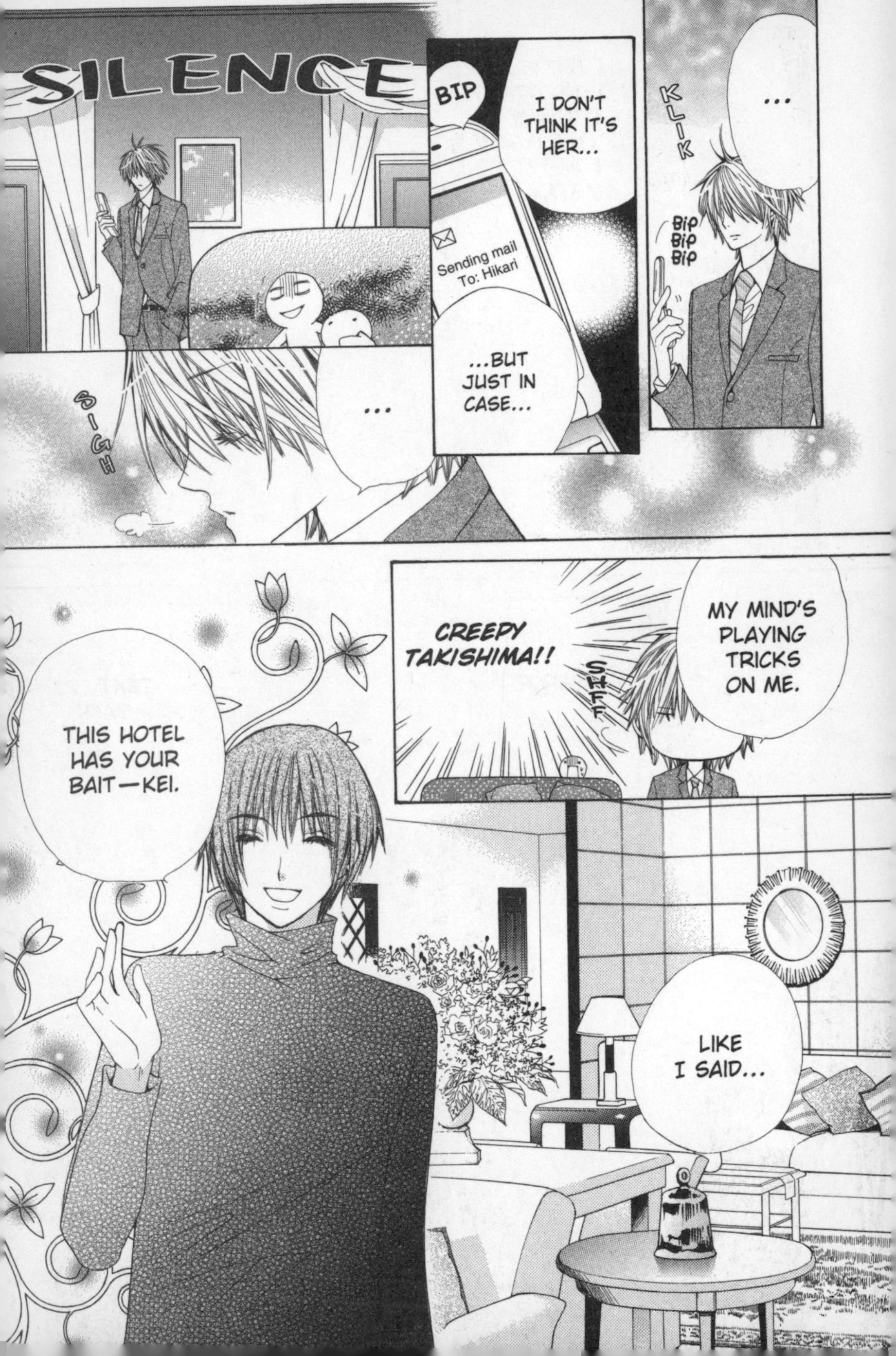
KLIK
...
BIP
BIP
BIP
BIP
I DON'T THINK IT'S HER...
Sending mail
To: Hikari
...BUT JUST IN CASE...
SILENCE
SIGH
...
MY MIND'S PLAYING TRICKS ON ME.
SHFF
CREEPY TAKISHIMA!!
LIKE I SAID...
THIS HOTEL HAS YOUR BAIT—KEI.

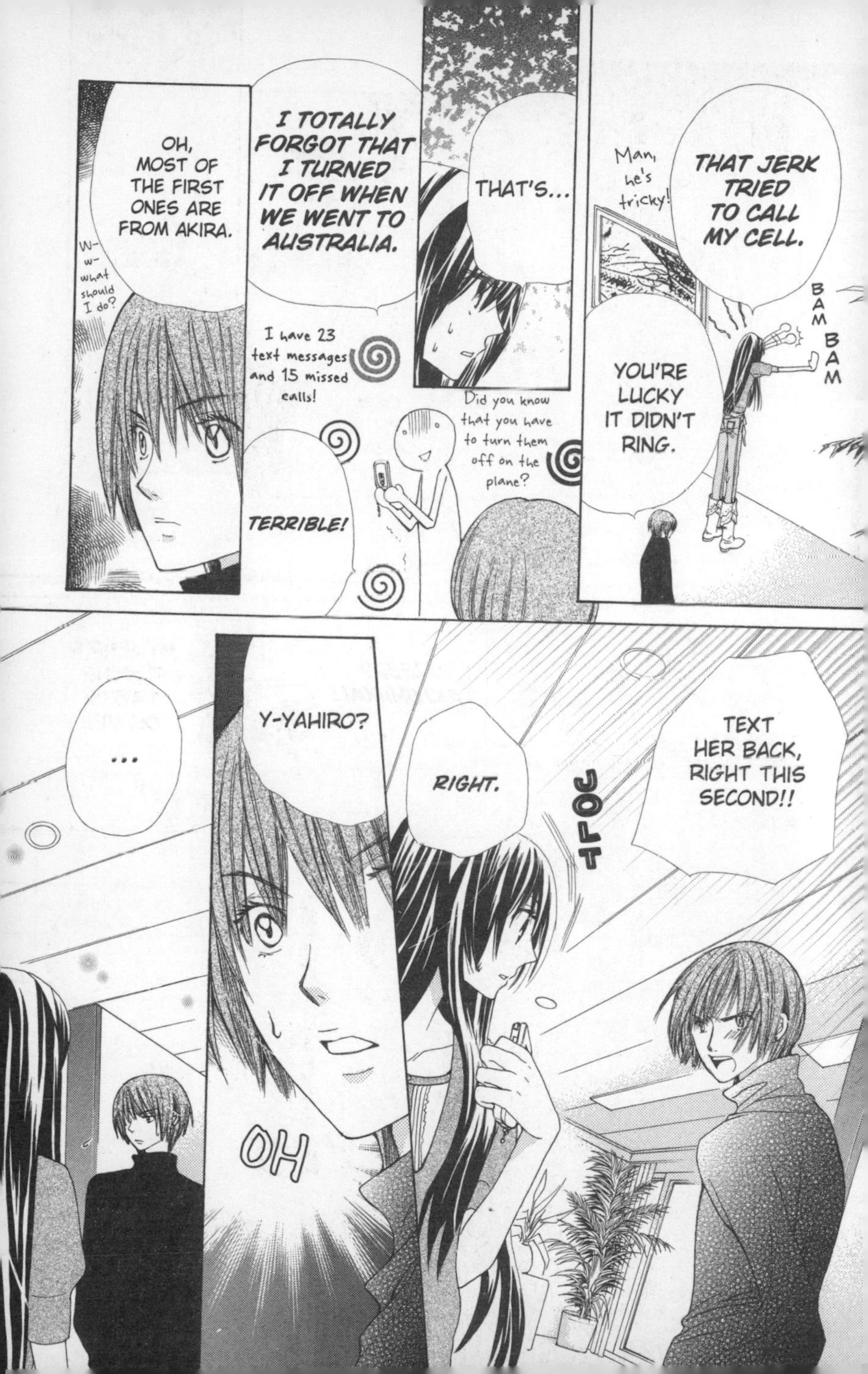
THAT JERK TRIED TO CALL MY CELL.
Man, he's tricky!
BAM BAM BAM
YOU'RE LUCKY IT DIDN'T RING.
THAT'S...
I TOTALLY FORGOT THAT I TURNED IT OFF WHEN WE WENT TO AUSTRALIA.
Did you know that you have to turn them off on the plane?
I have 23 text messages and 15 missed calls!
TERRIBLE!
OH, MOST OF THE FIRST ONES ARE FROM AKIRA.
W-w-what should I do?
TEXT HER BACK, RIGHT THIS SECOND!!
JOLT
RIGHT.
Y-YAHIRO?
OH
...

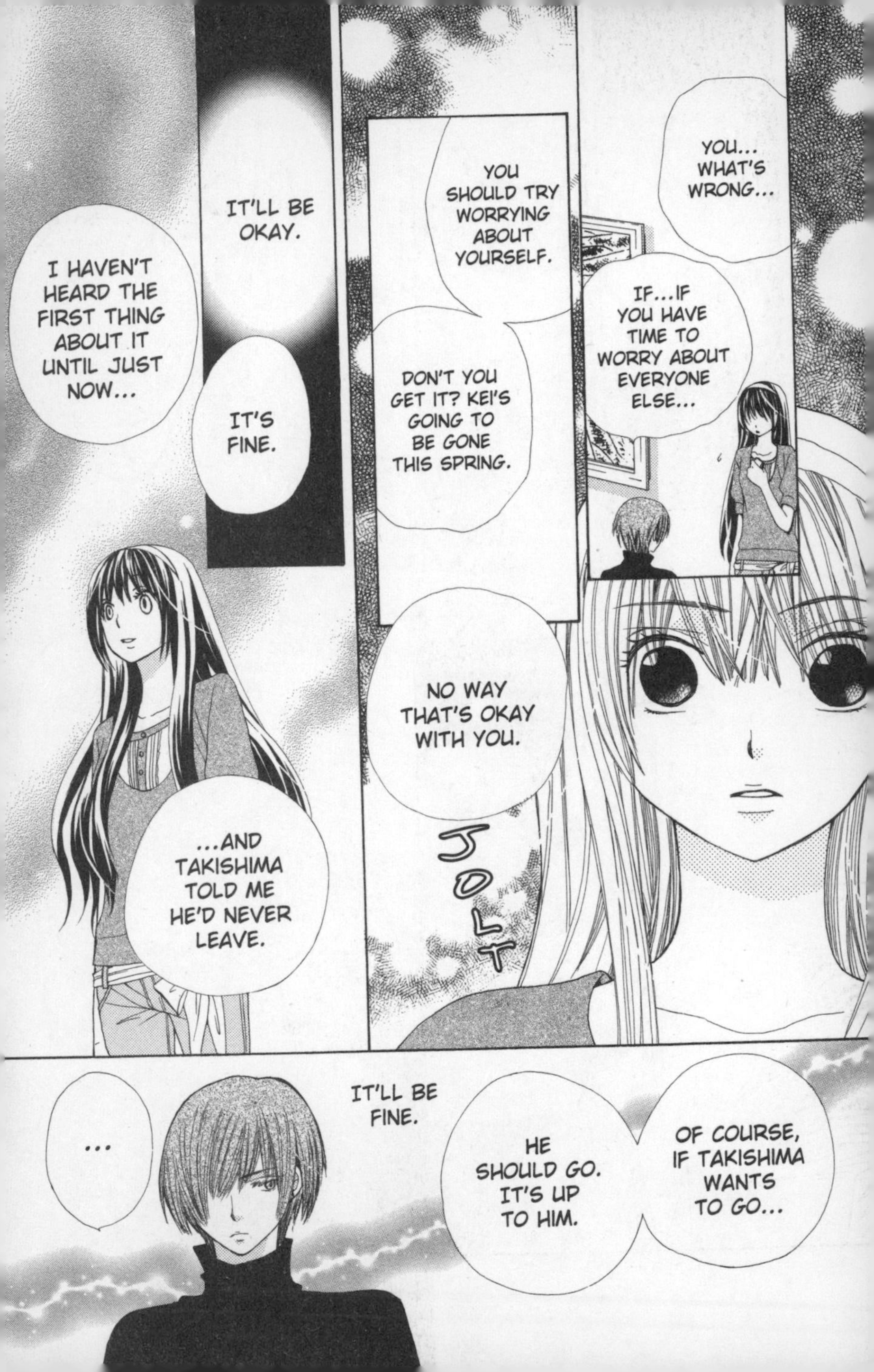
YOU... WHAT'S WRONG...
IF...IF YOU HAVE TIME TO WORRY ABOUT EVERYONE ELSE...
YOU SHOULD TRY WORRYING ABOUT YOURSELF.
DON'T YOU GET IT? KEI'S GOING TO BE GONE THIS SPRING.
NO WAY THAT'S OKAY WITH YOU.
JOLT
IT'LL BE OKAY.
IT'S FINE.
I HAVEN'T HEARD THE FIRST THING ABOUT IT UNTIL JUST NOW...
...AND TAKISHIMA TOLD ME HE'D NEVER LEAVE.
OF COURSE, IF TAKISHIMA WANTS TO GO...
HE SHOULD GO. IT'S UP TO HIM.
IT'LL BE FINE.
...

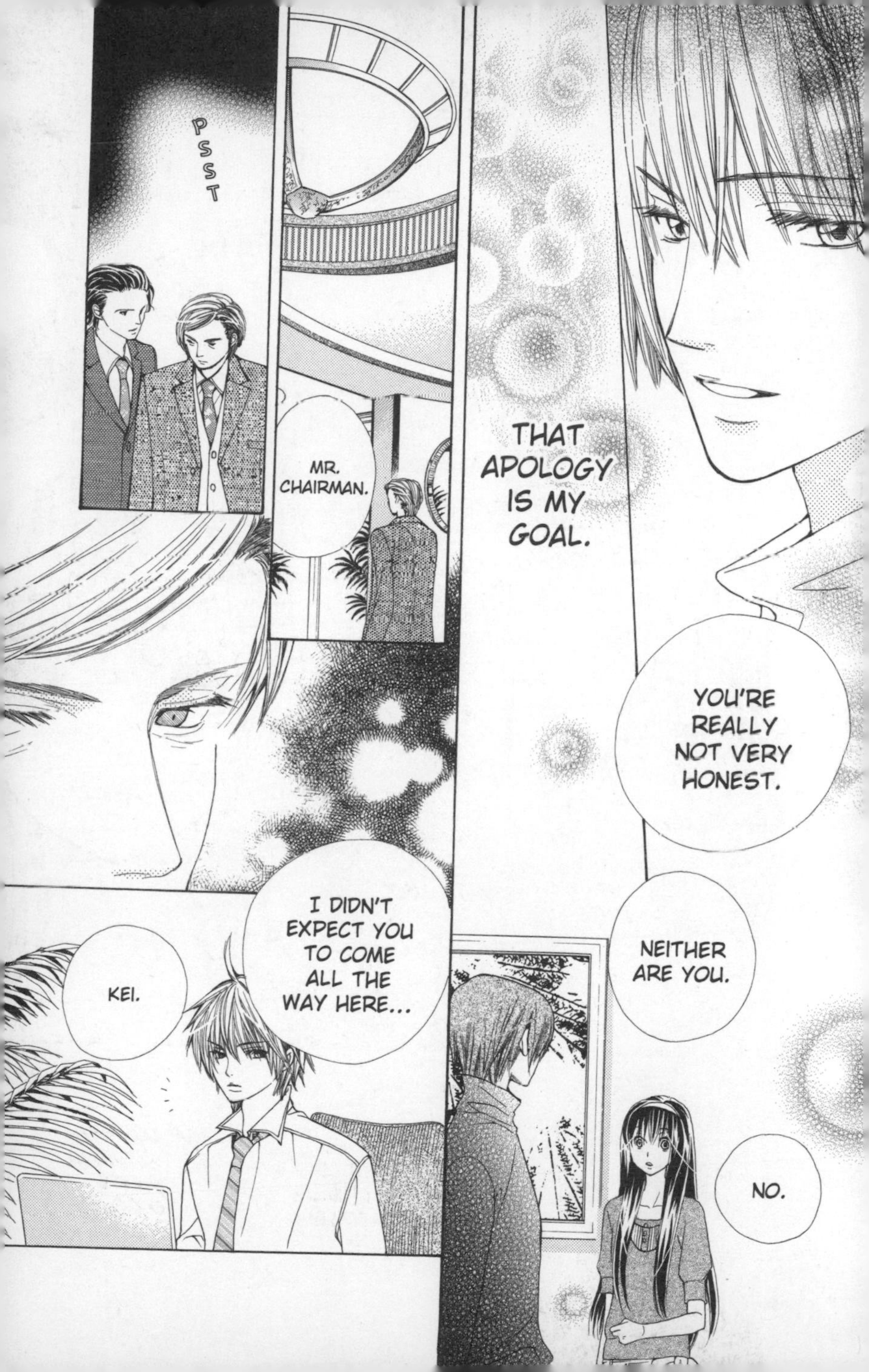
THAT APOLOGY IS MY GOAL.
YOU'RE REALLY NOT VERY HONEST.
NEITHER ARE YOU.
NO.
MR. CHAIRMAN.
PSST
I DIDN'T EXPECT YOU TO COME ALL THE WAY HERE...
KEI.

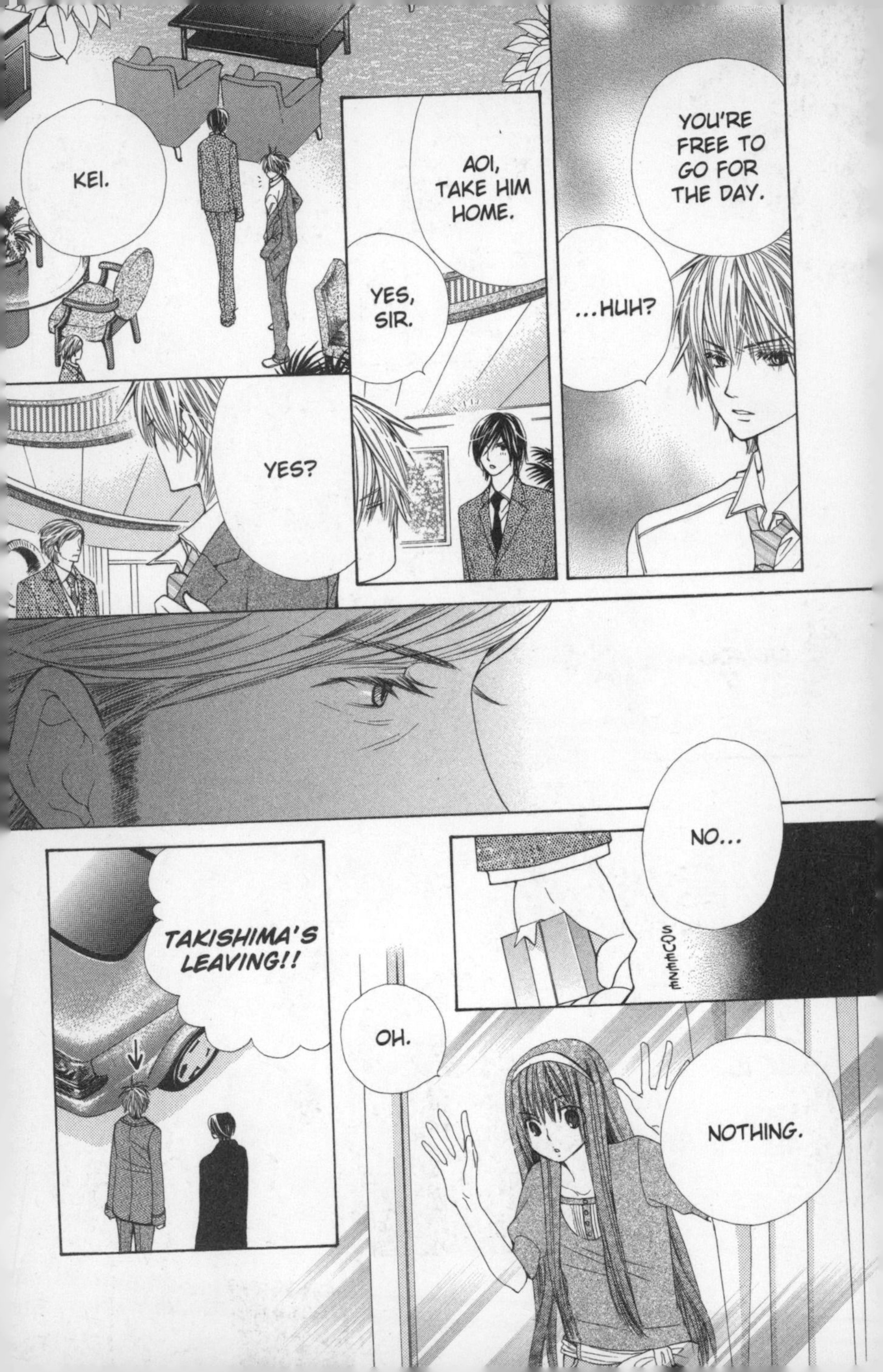
YOU'RE FREE TO GO FOR THE DAY.
...HUH?
AOI, TAKE HIM HOME.
YES, SIR.
KEI.
YES?
NO...
SQUEEZE
TAKISHIMA'S LEAVING!!
OH.
NOTHING.

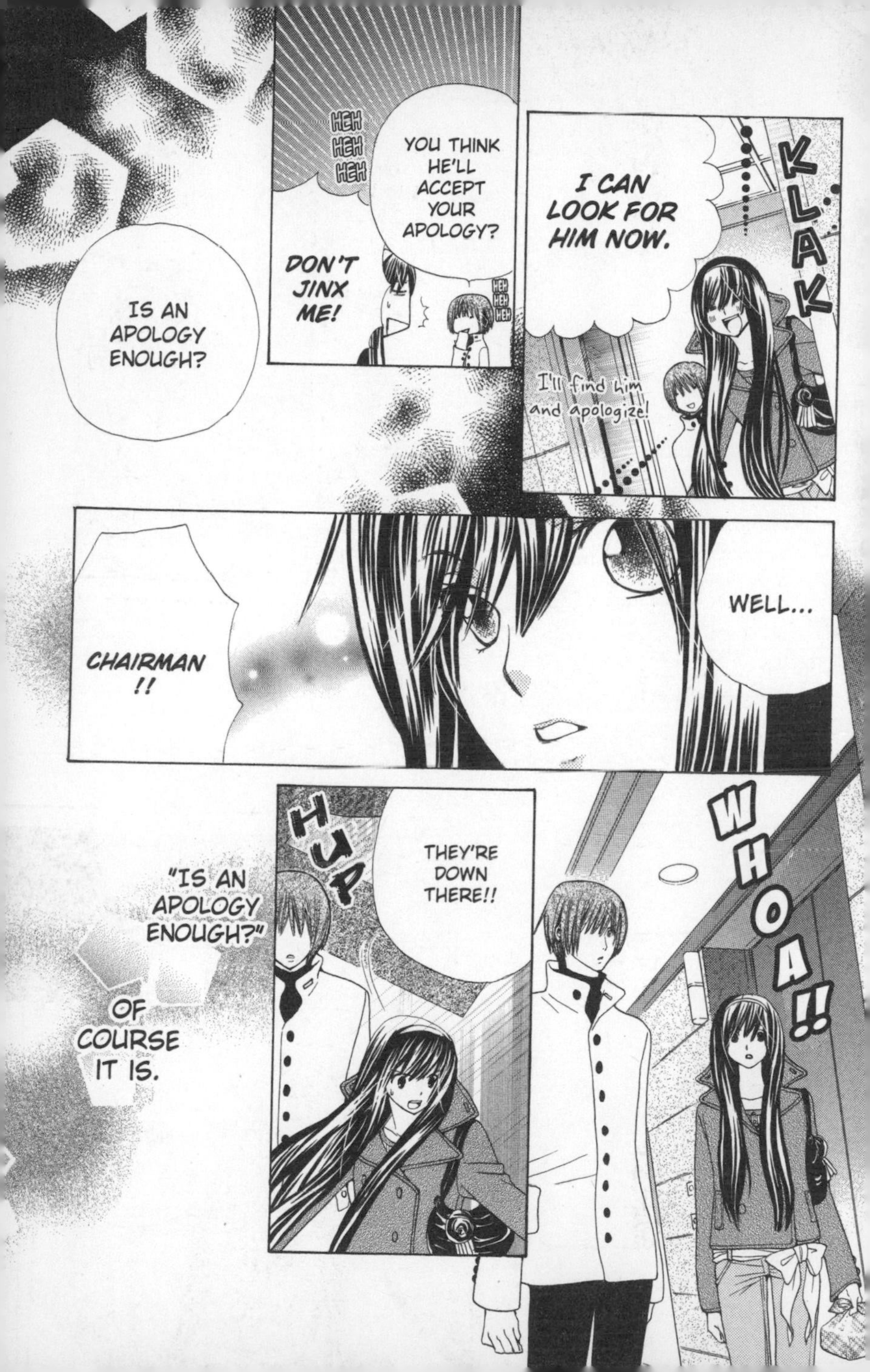

KLAK
I CAN LOOK FOR HIM NOW.
I'll find him and apologize!
HEH HEH HEH
YOU THINK HE'LL ACCEPT YOUR APOLOGY?
HEH HEH HEH
DON'T JINX ME!
IS AN APOLOGY ENOUGH?
WELL...
CHAIRMAN !!
WHOA!!
THEY'RE DOWN THERE!!
HUP
"IS AN APOLOGY ENOUGH?"
OF COURSE IT IS.

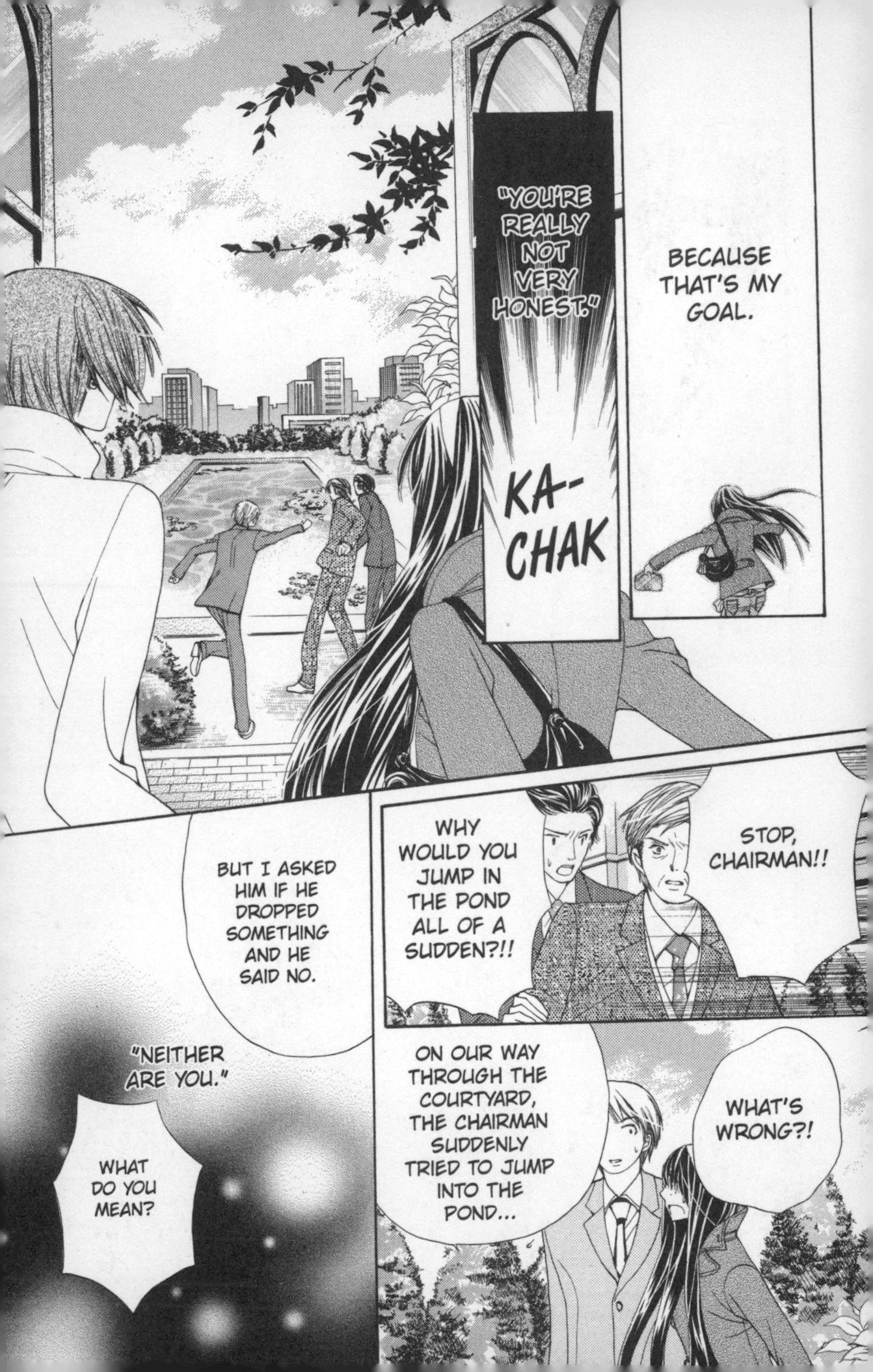
BECAUSE THAT'S MY GOAL.
"YOU'RE REALLY NOT VERY HONEST."
KA-CHAK
STOP, CHAIRMAN!!
WHY WOULD YOU JUMP IN THE POND ALL OF A SUDDEN?!!
WHAT'S WRONG?!
ON OUR WAY THROUGH THE COURTYARD, THE CHAIRMAN SUDDENLY TRIED TO JUMP INTO THE POND...
BUT I ASKED HIM IF HE DROPPED SOMETHING AND HE SAID NO.
"NEITHER ARE YOU."
WHAT DO YOU MEAN?

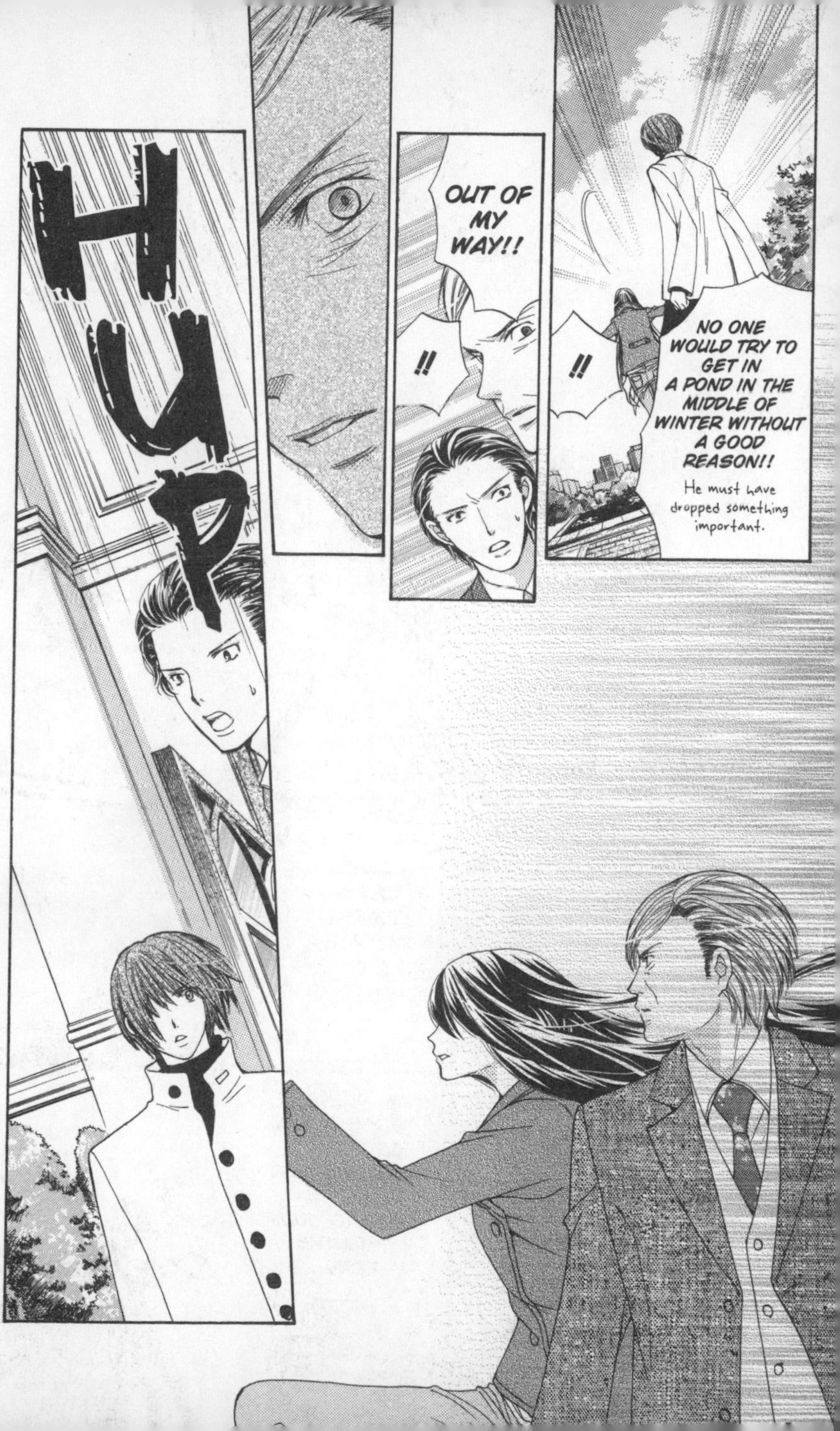
NO ONE WOULD TRY TO GET IN A POND IN THE MIDDLE OF WINTER WITHOUT A GOOD REASON!!
He must have dropped something important.
!!
OUT OF MY WAY!!
!!
HUP

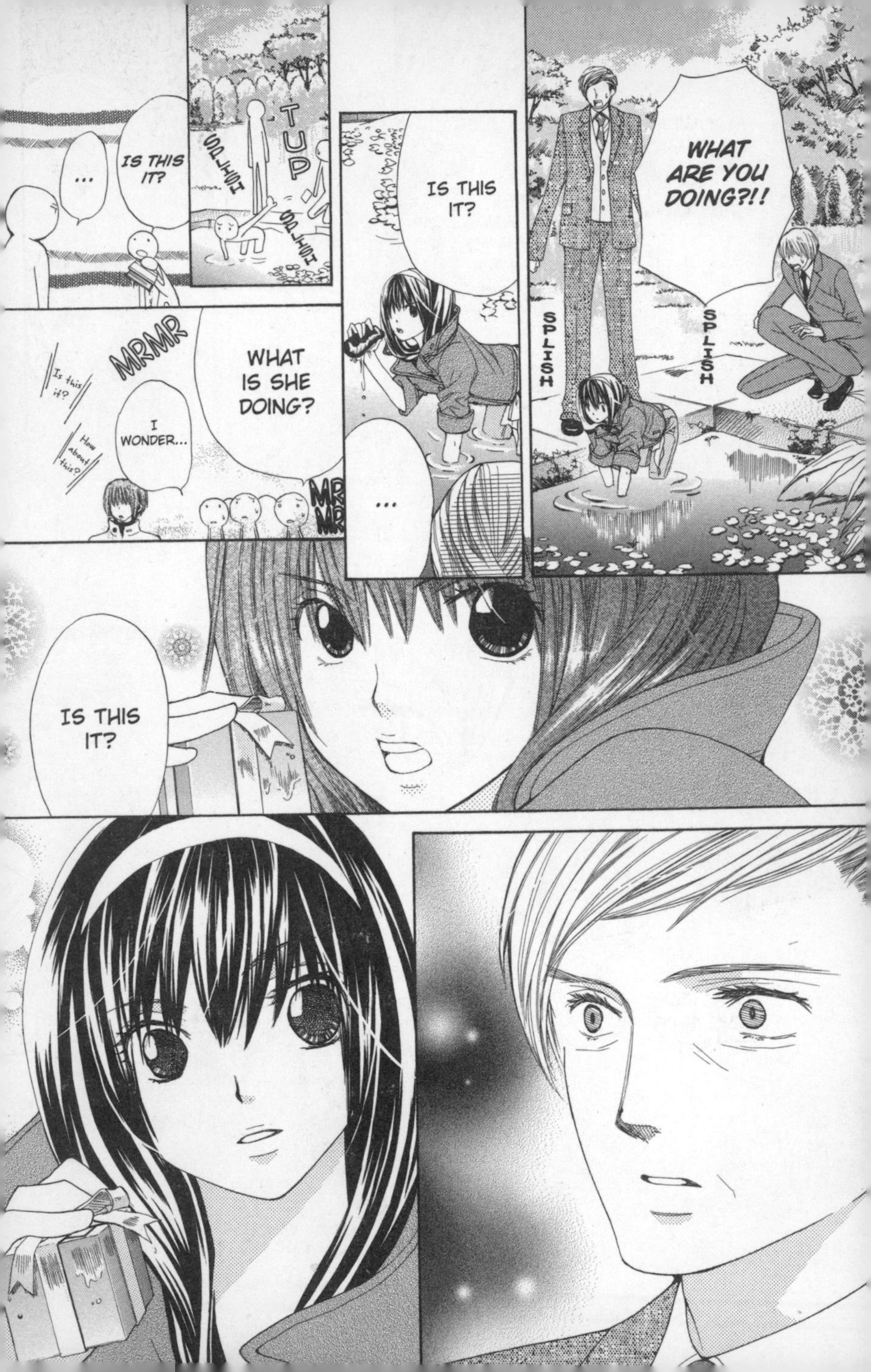
WHAT ARE YOU DOING?!!
SPLISH
SPLISH
TUP
SPLISH
SPLISH
IS THIS IT?
...
MRMR
WHAT IS SHE DOING?
I WONDER...
Is this it?
How about this?
MRMR
IS THIS IT?
...
IS THIS IT?

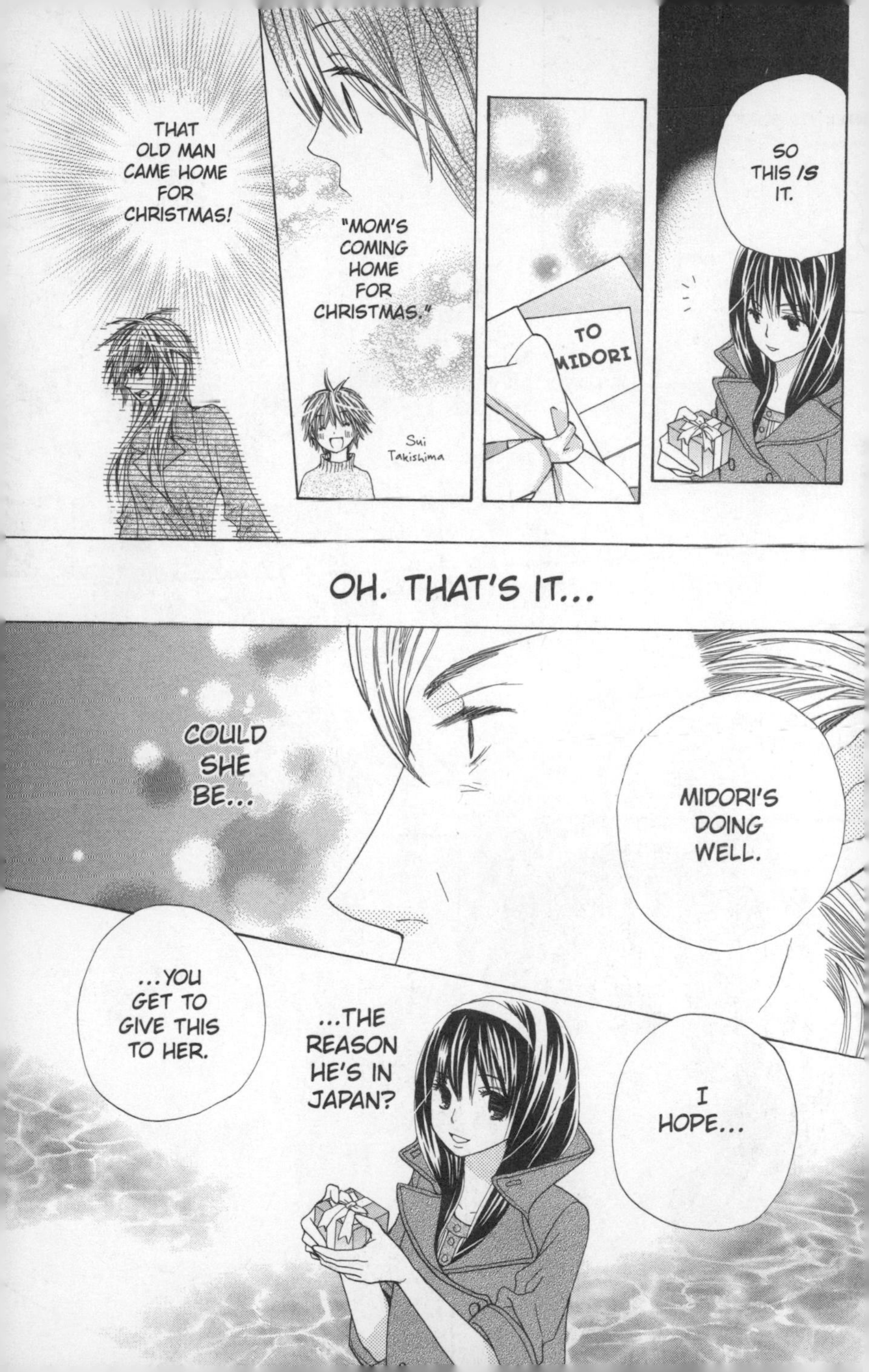
SO THIS IS IT.
TO MIDORI
"MOM'S COMING HOME FOR CHRISTMAS."
Sui Takishima
THAT OLD MAN CAME HOME FOR CHRISTMAS!
OH. THAT'S IT...
MIDORI'S DOING WELL.
COULD SHE BE...
I HOPE...
...THE REASON HE'S IN JAPAN?
...YOU GET TO GIVE THIS TO HER.

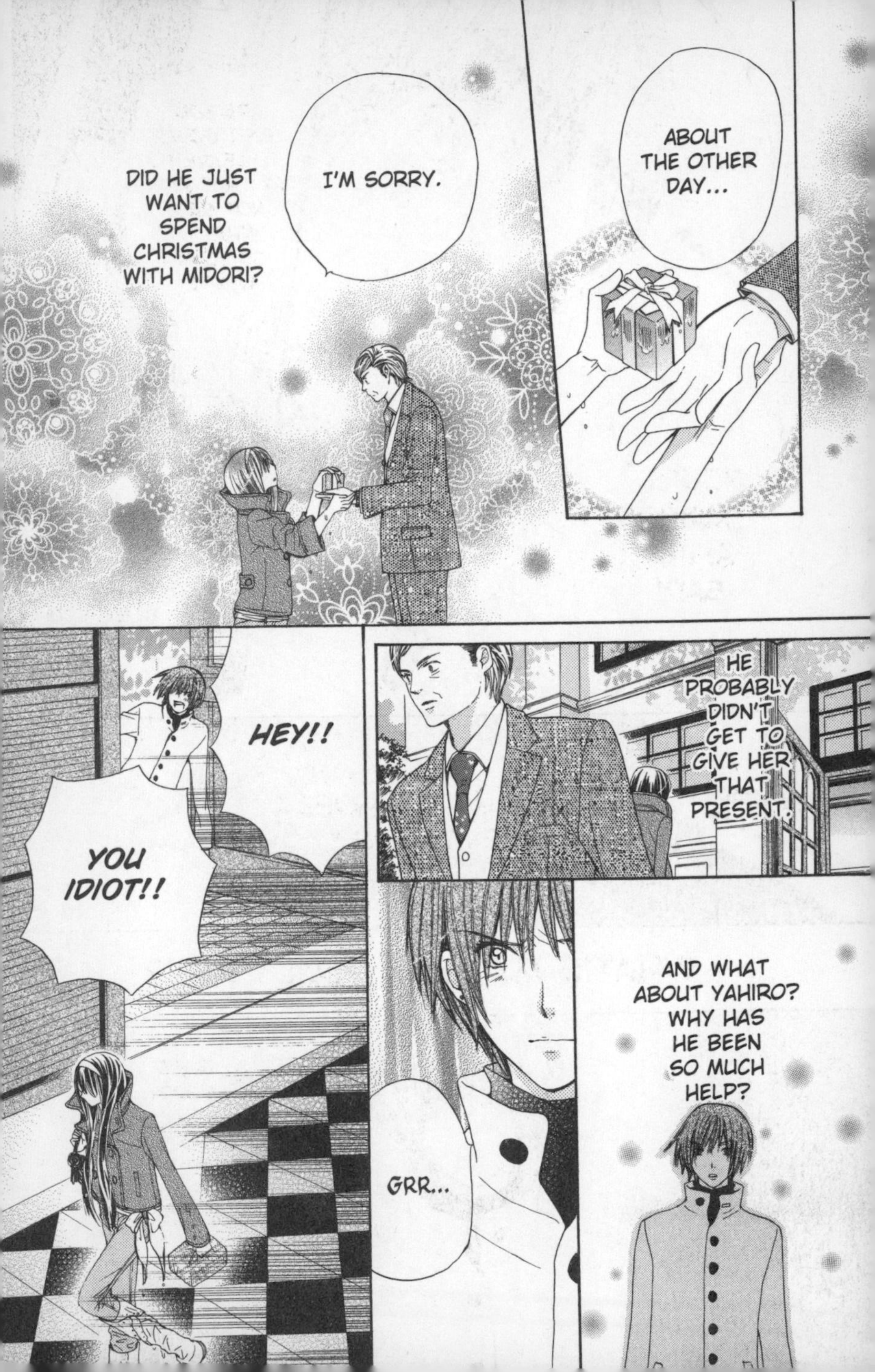
ABOUT THE OTHER DAY...
I'M SORRY.
DID HE JUST WANT TO SPEND CHRISTMAS WITH MIDORI?
HE PROBABLY DIDN'T GET TO GIVE HER THAT PRESENT.
AND WHAT ABOUT YAHIRO? WHY HAS HE BEEN SO MUCH HELP?
GRR...
HEY!!
YOU IDIOT!!

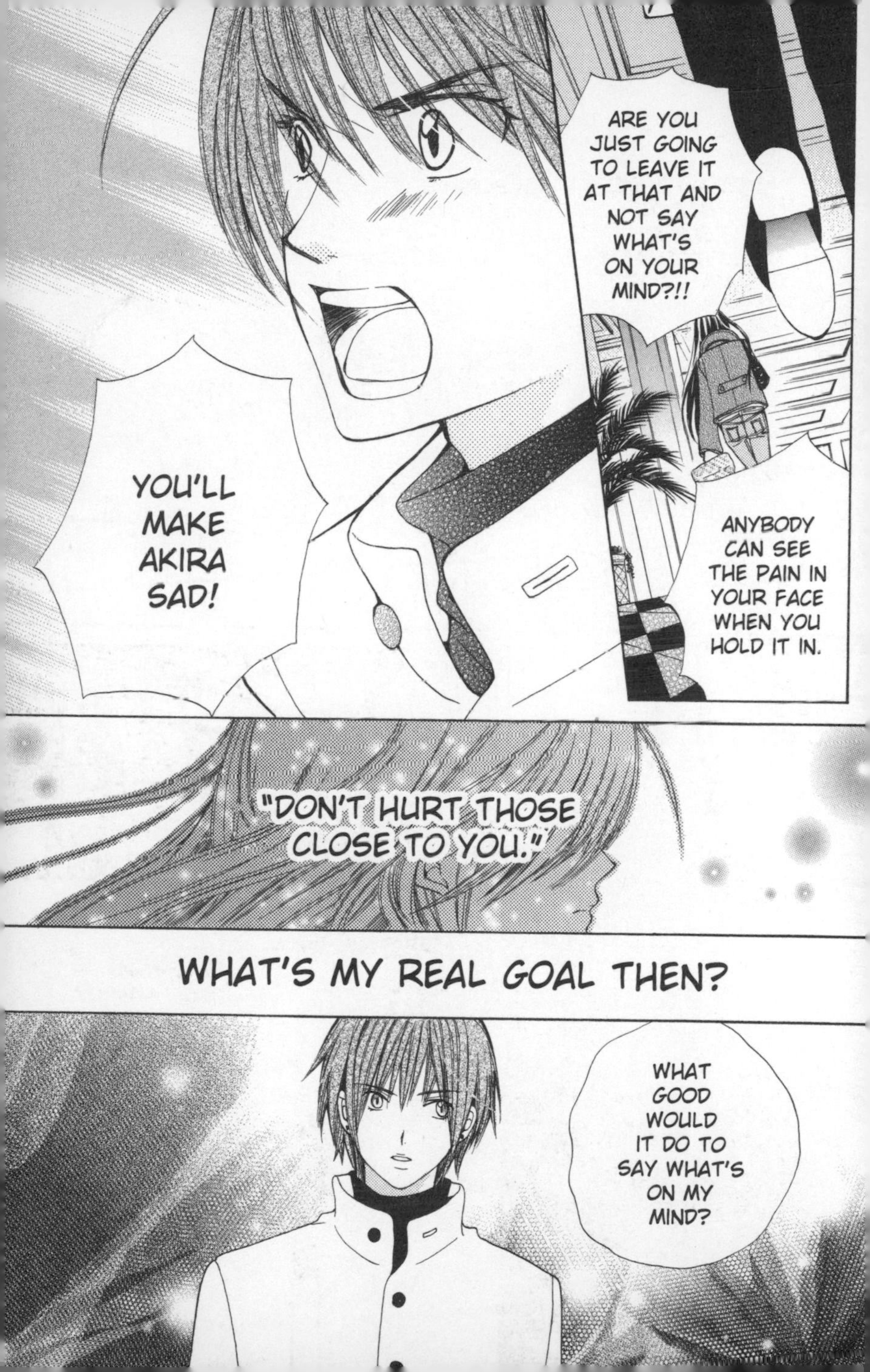
ARE YOU JUST GOING TO LEAVE IT AT THAT AND NOT SAY WHAT'S ON YOUR MIND?!!
ANYBODY CAN SEE THE PAIN IN YOUR FACE WHEN YOU HOLD IT IN.
YOU'LL MAKE AKIRA SAD!
"DON'T HURT THOSE CLOSE TO YOU."
WHAT'S MY REAL GOAL THEN?
WHAT GOOD WOULD IT DO TO SAY WHAT'S ON MY MIND?

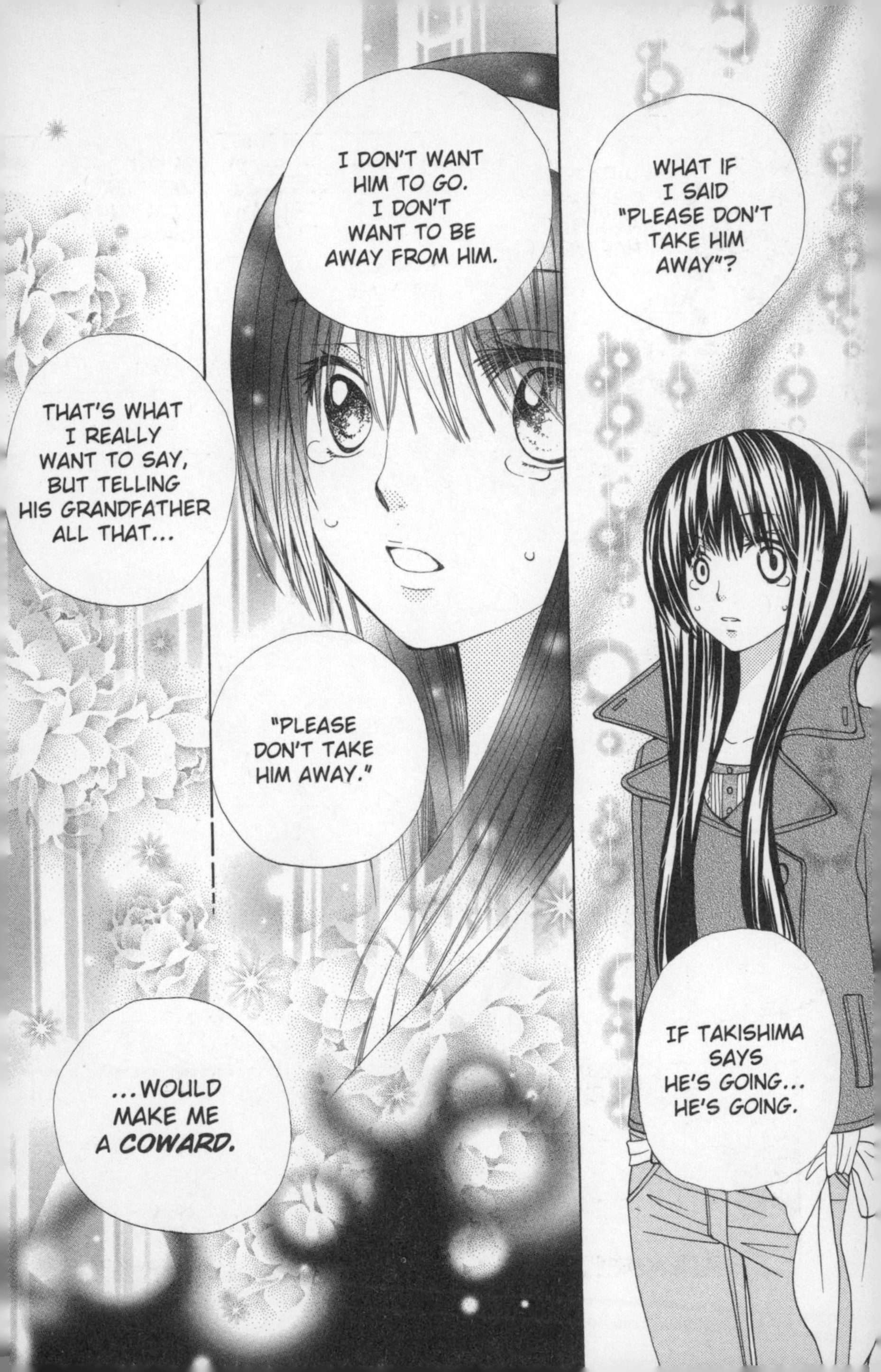
WHAT IF I SAID "PLEASE DON'T TAKE HIM AWAY"?
IF TAKISHIMA SAYS HE'S GOING... HE'S GOING.
I DON'T WANT HIM TO GO. I DON'T WANT TO BE AWAY FROM HIM.
"PLEASE DON'T TAKE HIM AWAY."
THAT'S WHAT I REALLY WANT TO SAY, BUT TELLING HIS GRANDFATHER ALL THAT...
...WOULD MAKE ME A ***COWARD.***

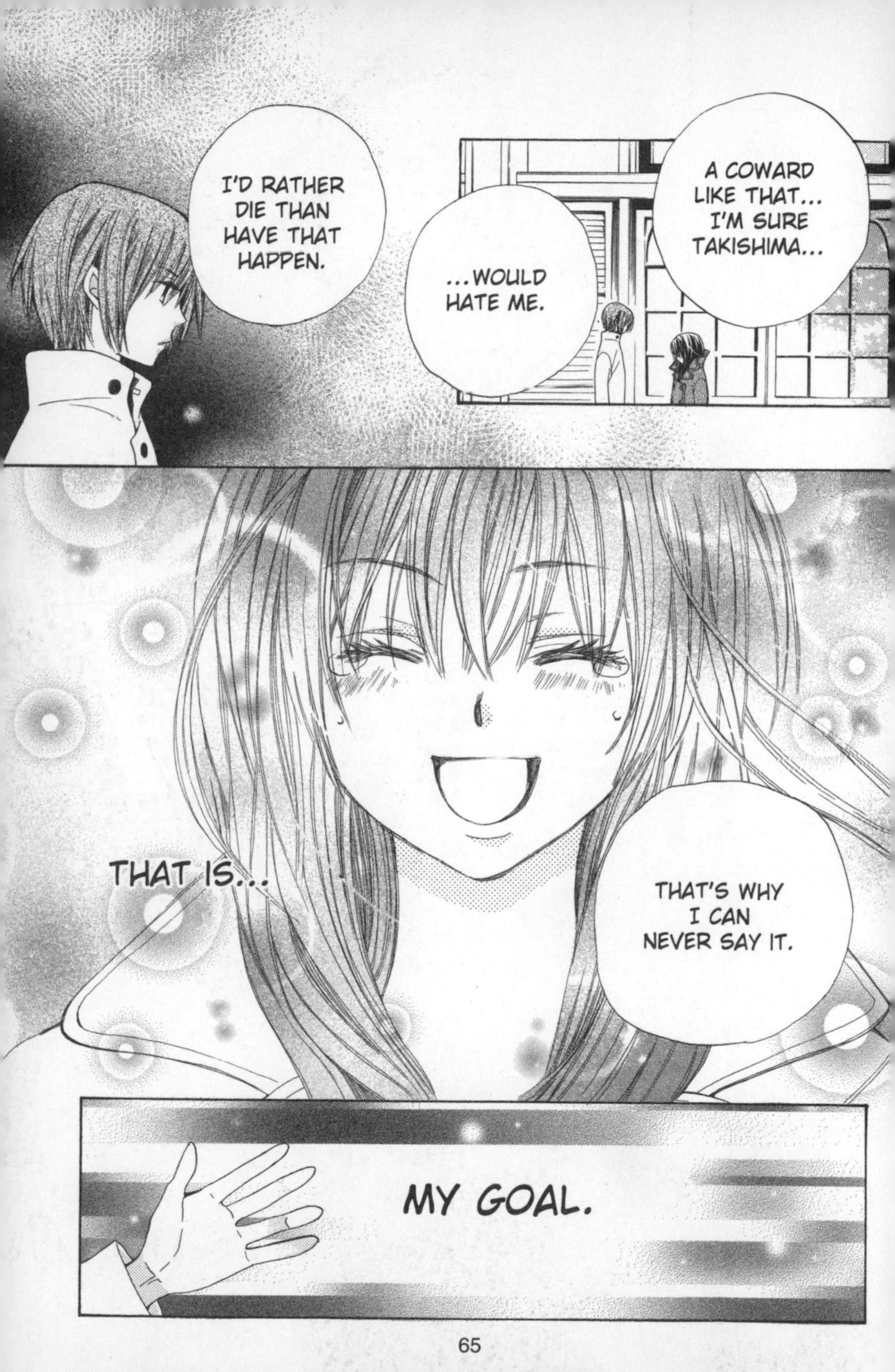
A COWARD LIKE THAT... I'M SURE TAKISHIMA...
...WOULD HATE ME.
I'D RATHER DIE THAN HAVE THAT HAPPEN.
THAT'S WHY I CAN NEVER SAY IT.
THAT IS...
MY GOAL.

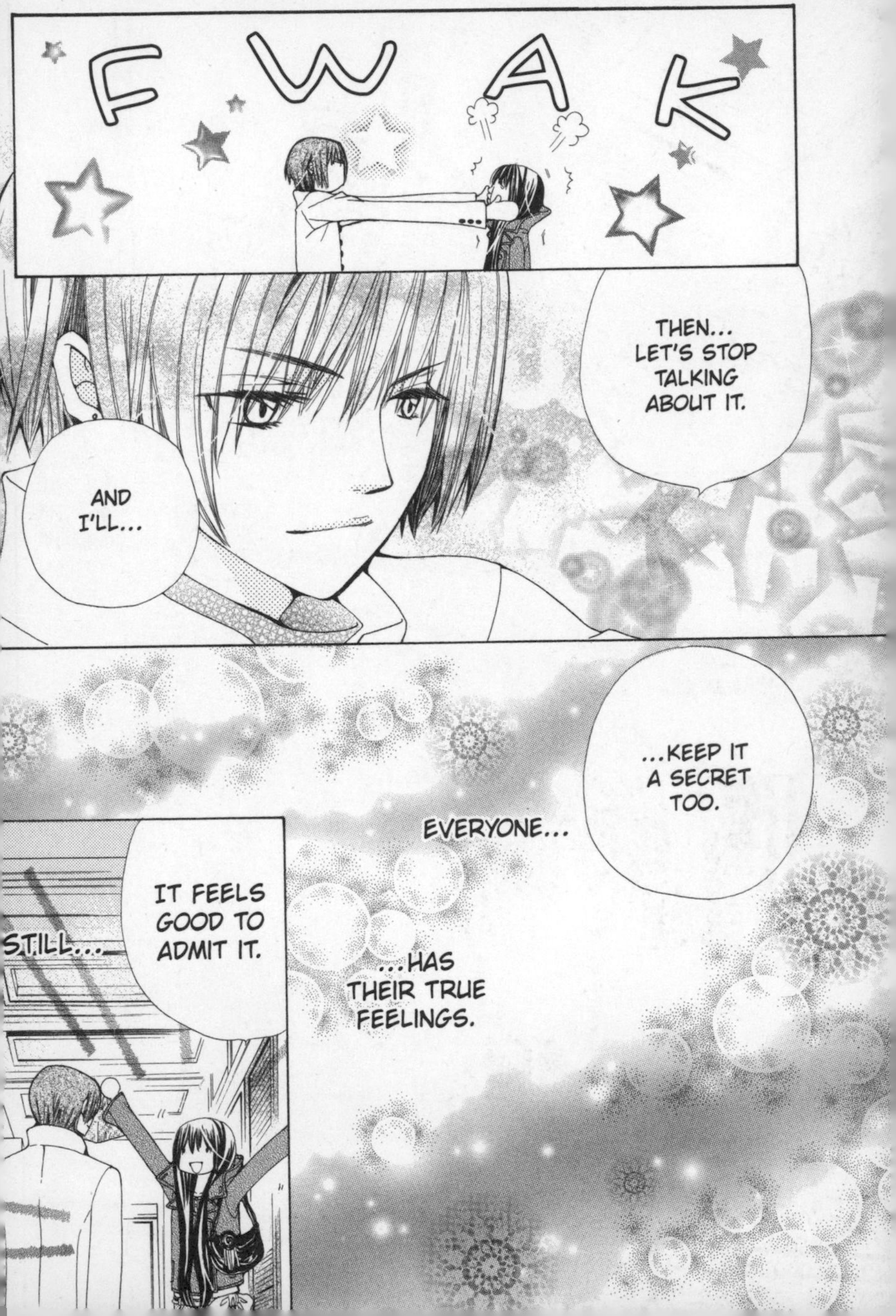
FWAK
THEN... LET'S STOP TALKING ABOUT IT.
AND I'LL...
...KEEP IT A SECRET TOO.
EVERYONE...
...HAS THEIR TRUE FEELINGS.
IT FEELS GOOD TO ADMIT IT.
STILL...

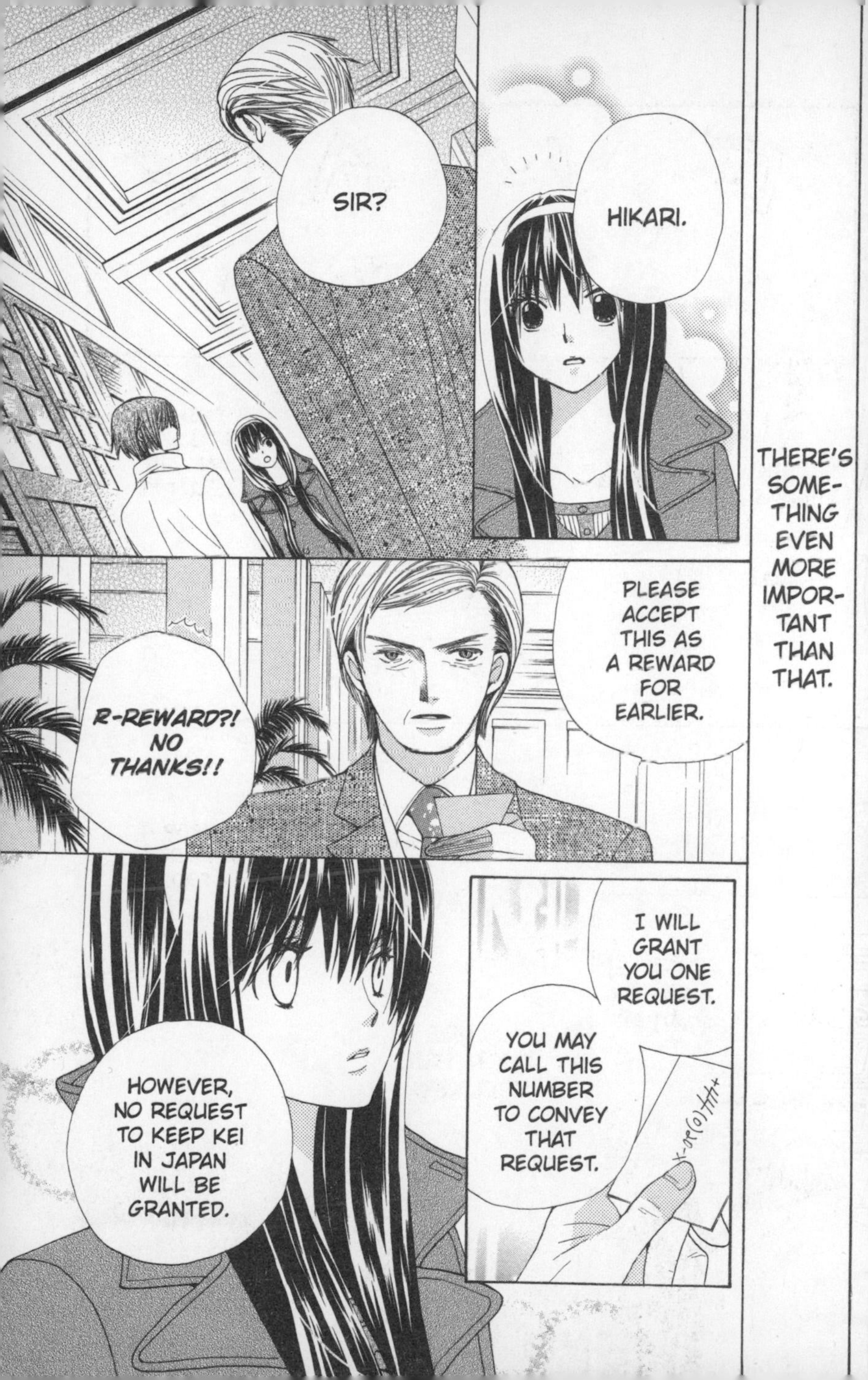
THERE'S SOME-THING EVEN MORE IMPOR-TANT THAN THAT.
HIKARI.
SIR?
PLEASE ACCEPT THIS AS A REWARD FOR EARLIER.
R-REWARD?! NO THANKS!!
I WILL GRANT YOU ONE REQUEST.
YOU MAY CALL THIS NUMBER TO CONVEY THAT REQUEST.
HOWEVER, NO REQUEST TO KEEP KEI IN JAPAN WILL BE GRANTED.

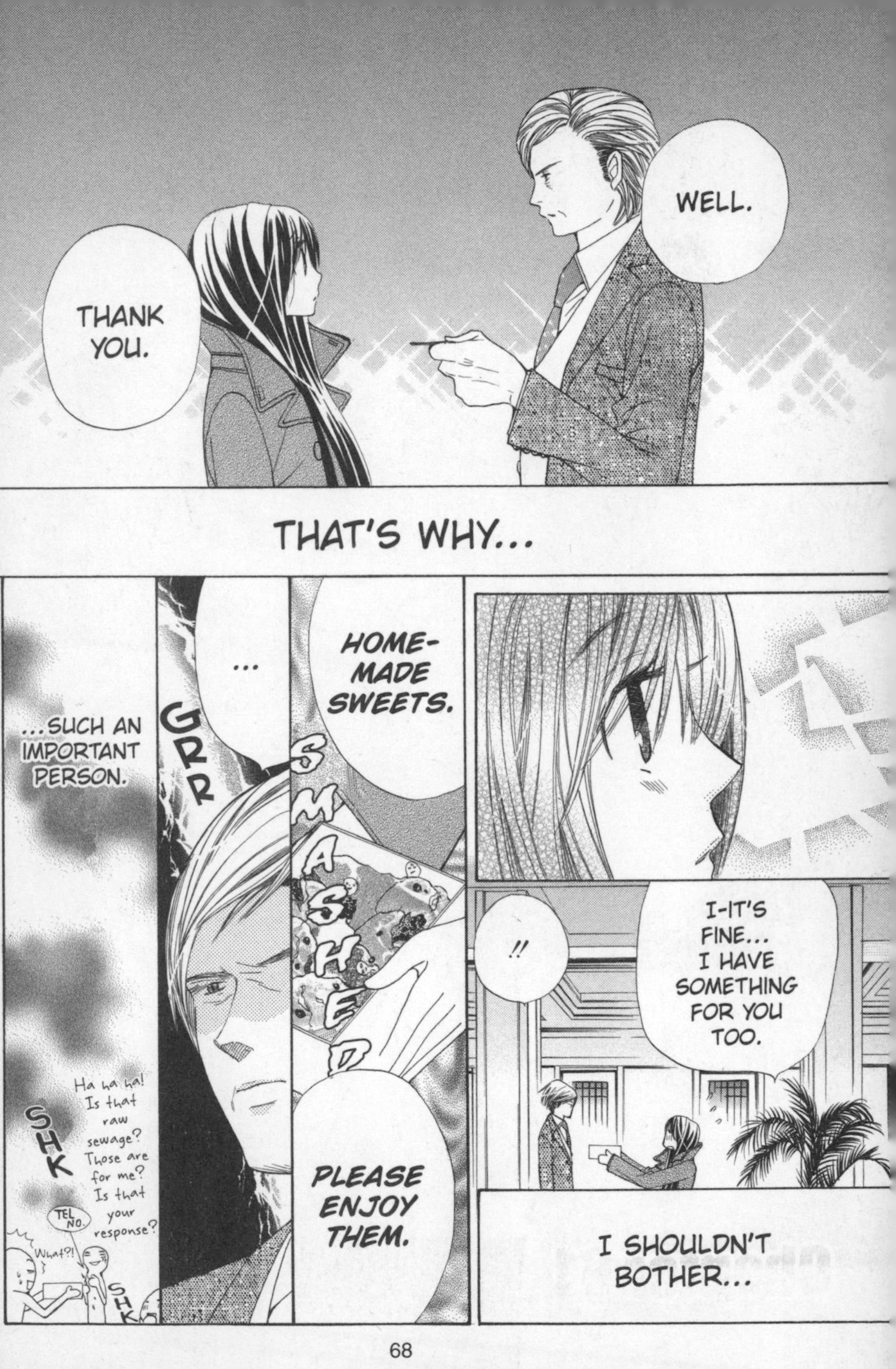
WELL.
THANK YOU.
THAT'S WHY...
I-IT'S FINE... I HAVE SOMETHING FOR YOU TOO.
!!
I SHOULDN'T BOTHER...
HOME-MADE SWEETS.
SMASHED
PLEASE ENJOY THEM.
...
GRR
...SUCH AN IMPORTANT PERSON.
SHK
Ha ha ha! Is that raw sewage? Those are for me? Is that your response?
TEL NO.
What?!
SHK

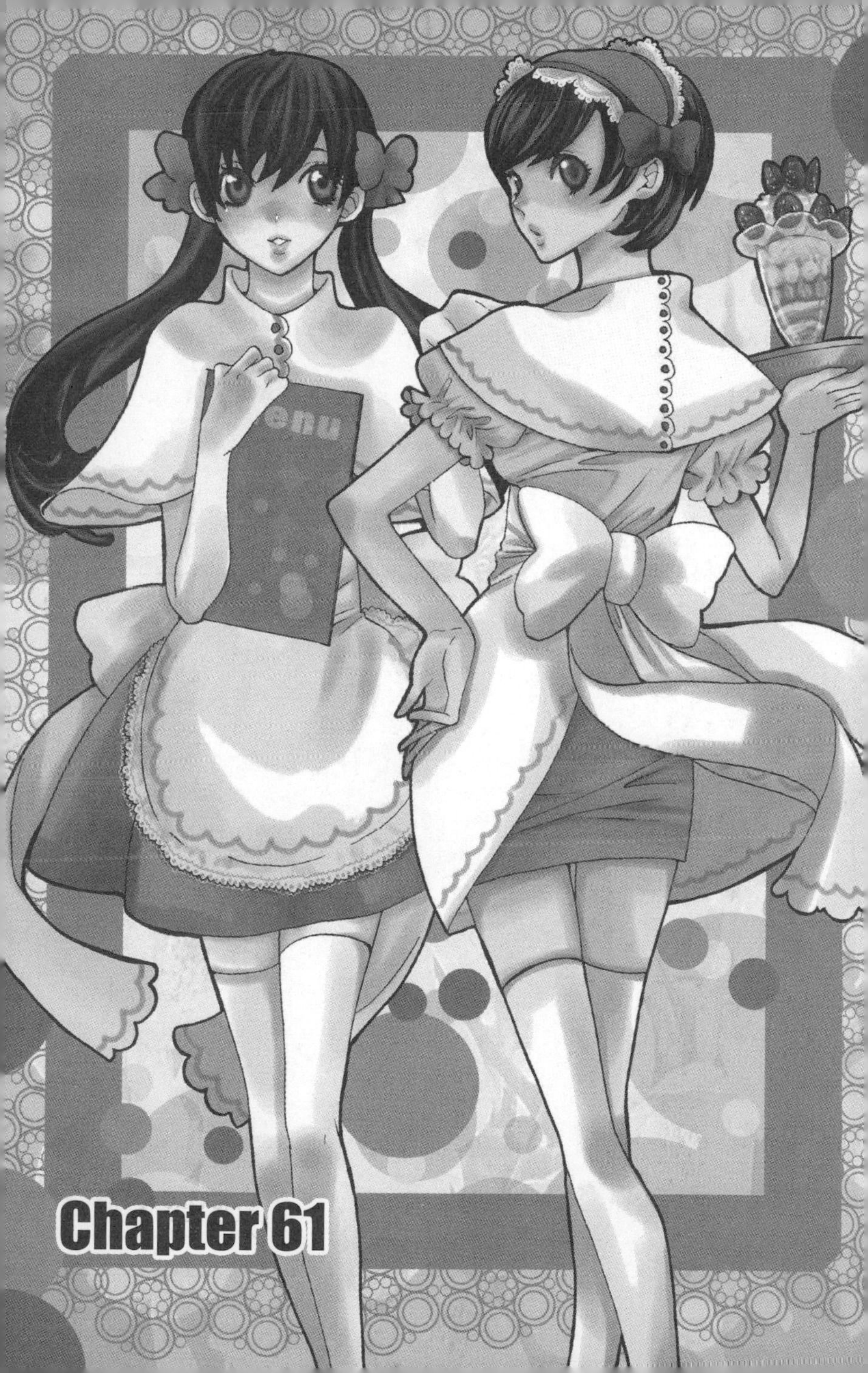

Chapter 61

SPECIAL・A

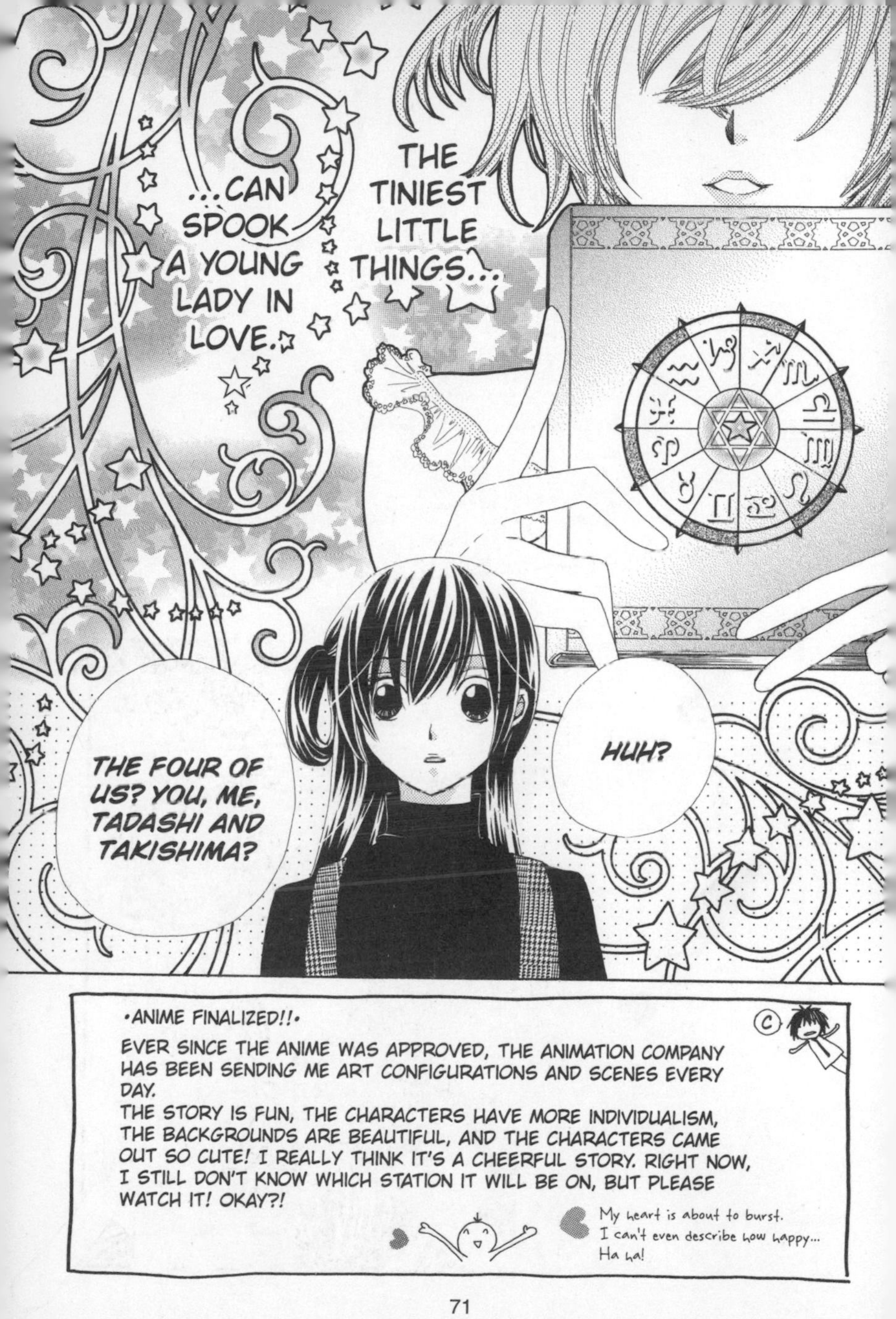
THE TINIEST LITTLE THINGS...
...CAN SPOOK A YOUNG LADY IN LOVE.
HUH?
THE FOUR OF US? YOU, ME, TADASHI AND TAKISHIMA?

•ANIME FINALIZED!!•

EVER SINCE THE ANIME WAS APPROVED, THE ANIMATION COMPANY HAS BEEN SENDING ME ART CONFIGURATIONS AND SCENES EVERY DAY.
THE STORY IS FUN, THE CHARACTERS HAVE MORE INDIVIDUALISM, THE BACKGROUNDS ARE BEAUTIFUL, AND THE CHARACTERS CAME OUT SO CUTE! I REALLY THINK IT'S A CHEERFUL STORY. RIGHT NOW, I STILL DON'T KNOW WHICH STATION IT WILL BE ON, BUT PLEASE WATCH IT! OKAY?!

My heart is about to burst. I can't even describe how happy... Ha ha!

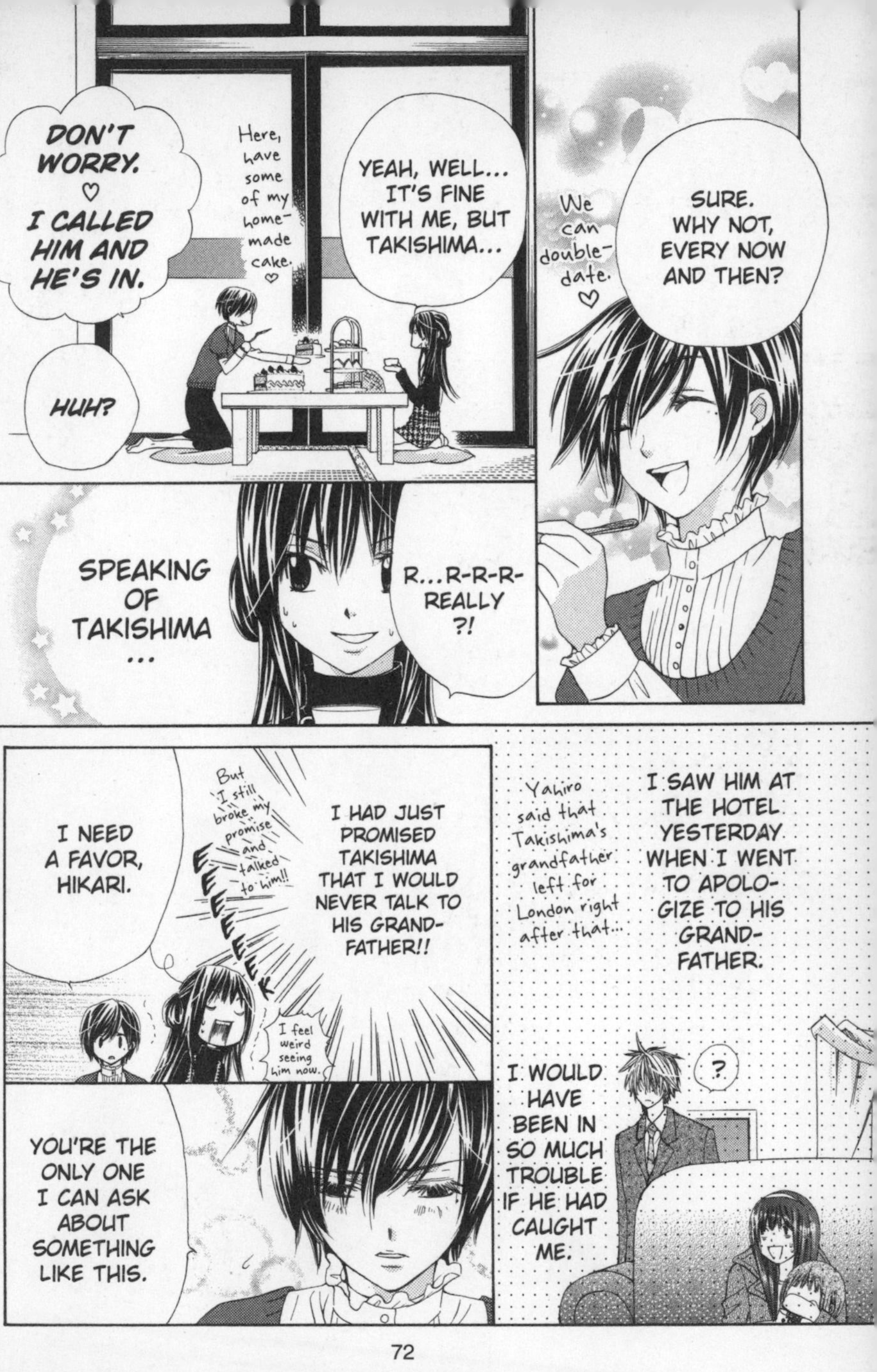
We can double-date. ♡
SURE. WHY NOT, EVERY NOW AND THEN?
YEAH, WELL... IT'S FINE WITH ME, BUT TAKISHIMA...
Here, have some of my home-made cake. ♡
DON'T WORRY. ♡ I CALLED HIM AND HE'S IN.
HUH?
R...R-R-R-REALLY ?!
SPEAKING OF TAKISHIMA ...
I SAW HIM AT THE HOTEL YESTERDAY WHEN I WENT TO APOLOGIZE TO HIS GRANDFATHER.
Yahiro said that Takishima's grandfather left for London right after that...
?
I WOULD HAVE BEEN IN SO MUCH TROUBLE IF HE HAD CAUGHT ME.
I HAD JUST PROMISED TAKISHIMA THAT I WOULD NEVER TALK TO HIS GRANDFATHER!!
But I still broke my promise and talked to him!!
EEEEEEEEK
I feel weird seeing him now.
I NEED A FAVOR, HIKARI.
YOU'RE THE ONLY ONE I CAN ASK ABOUT SOMETHING LIKE THIS.

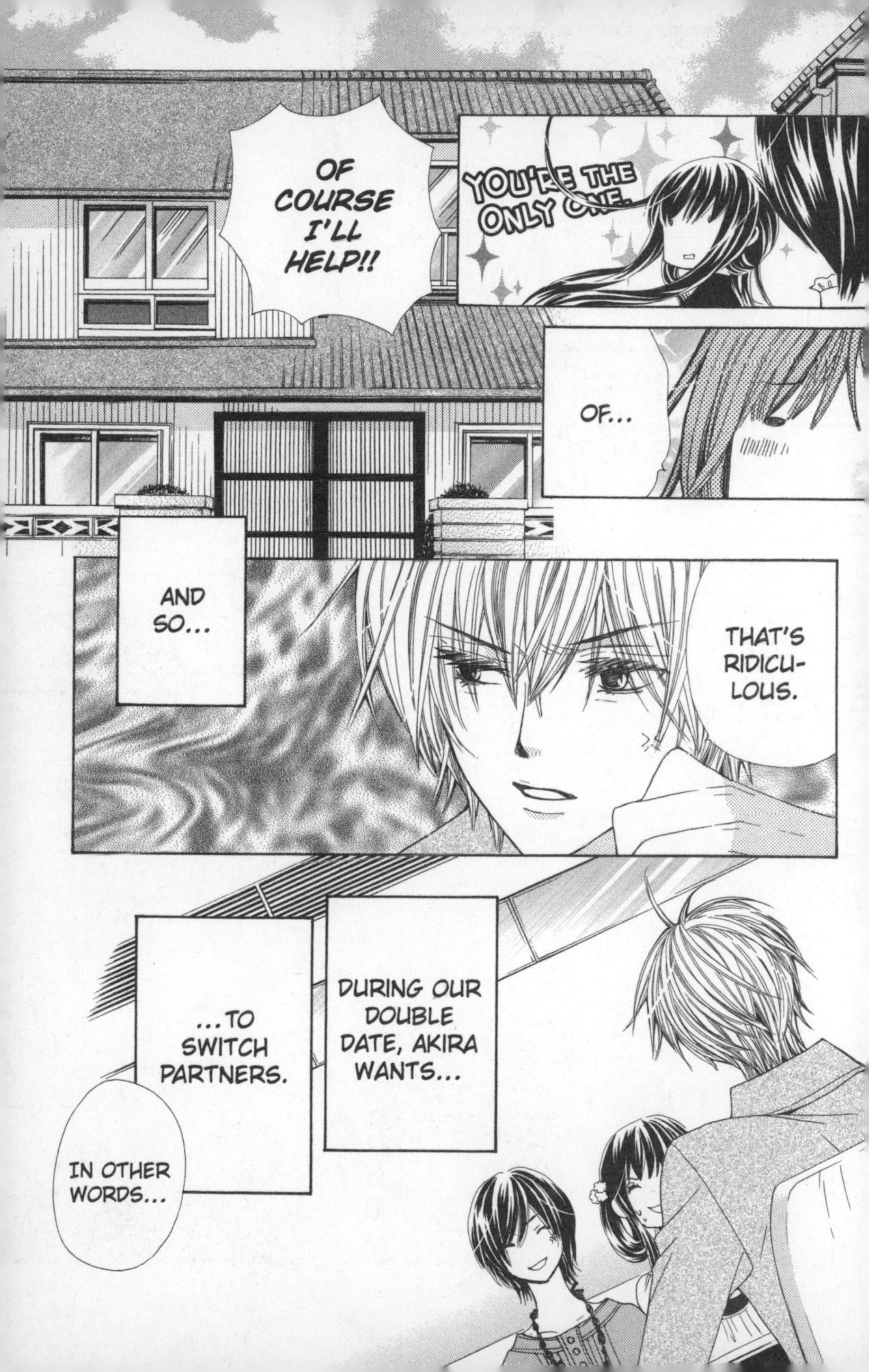
YOU'RE THE ONLY ONE.
OF...
OF COURSE I'LL HELP!!
AND SO...
THAT'S RIDICULOUS.
DURING OUR DOUBLE DATE, AKIRA WANTS...
...TO SWITCH PARTNERS.
IN OTHER WORDS...

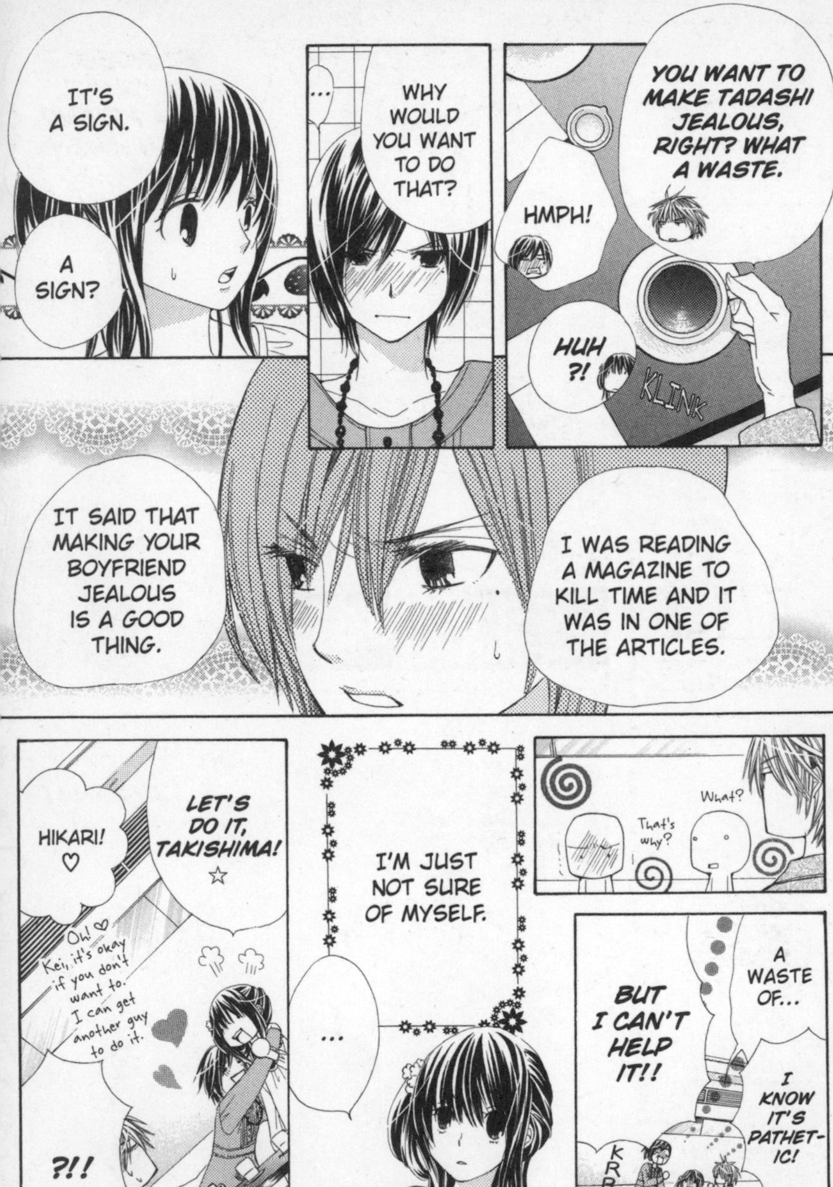

YOU WANT TO MAKE TADASHI JEALOUS, RIGHT? WHAT A WASTE.
HMPH!
HUH ?!
KLINK
...
WHY WOULD YOU WANT TO DO THAT?
IT'S A SIGN.
A SIGN?
I WAS READING A MAGAZINE TO KILL TIME AND IT WAS IN ONE OF THE ARTICLES.
IT SAID THAT MAKING YOUR BOYFRIEND JEALOUS IS A GOOD THING.
What?
That's why?
A WASTE OF...
I KNOW IT'S PATHETIC!
BUT I CAN'T HELP IT!!
KRRK
I'M JUST NOT SURE OF MYSELF.
...
LET'S DO IT, TAKISHIMA! ☆
HIKARI! ♡
Oh! ♡ Kei, it's okay if you don't want to. I can get another guy to do it.
?!!

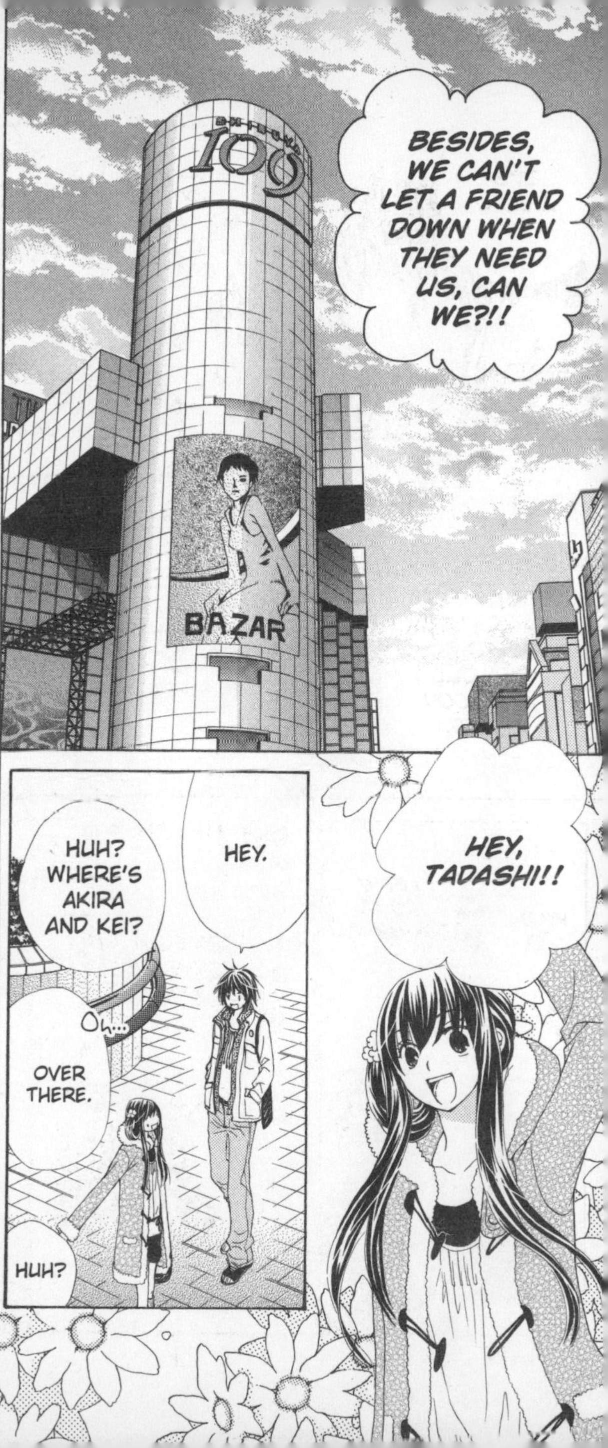
109
BESIDES, WE CAN'T LET A FRIEND DOWN WHEN THEY NEED US, CAN WE?!!
BAZAR
HEY, TADASHI!!
HEY.
HUH? WHERE'S AKIRA AND KEI?
Oh...
OVER THERE.
HUH?

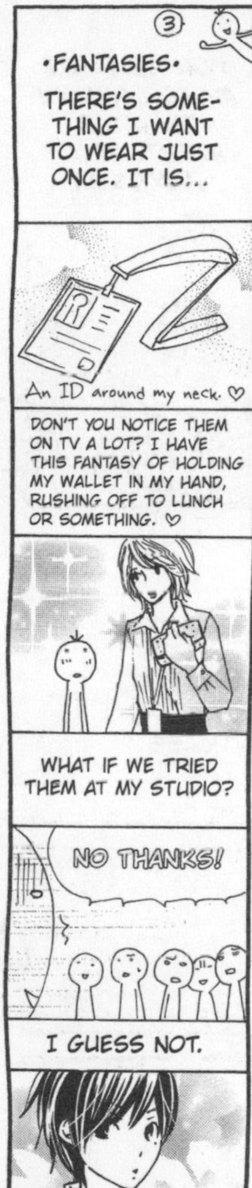
3
•FANTASIES•
THERE'S SOMETHING I WANT TO WEAR JUST ONCE. IT IS...
An ID around my neck. ♡
DON'T YOU NOTICE THEM ON TV A LOT? I HAVE THIS FANTASY OF HOLDING MY WALLET IN MY HAND, RUSHING OFF TO LUNCH OR SOMETHING. ♡
WHAT IF WE TRIED THEM AT MY STUDIO?
NO THANKS!
I GUESS NOT.

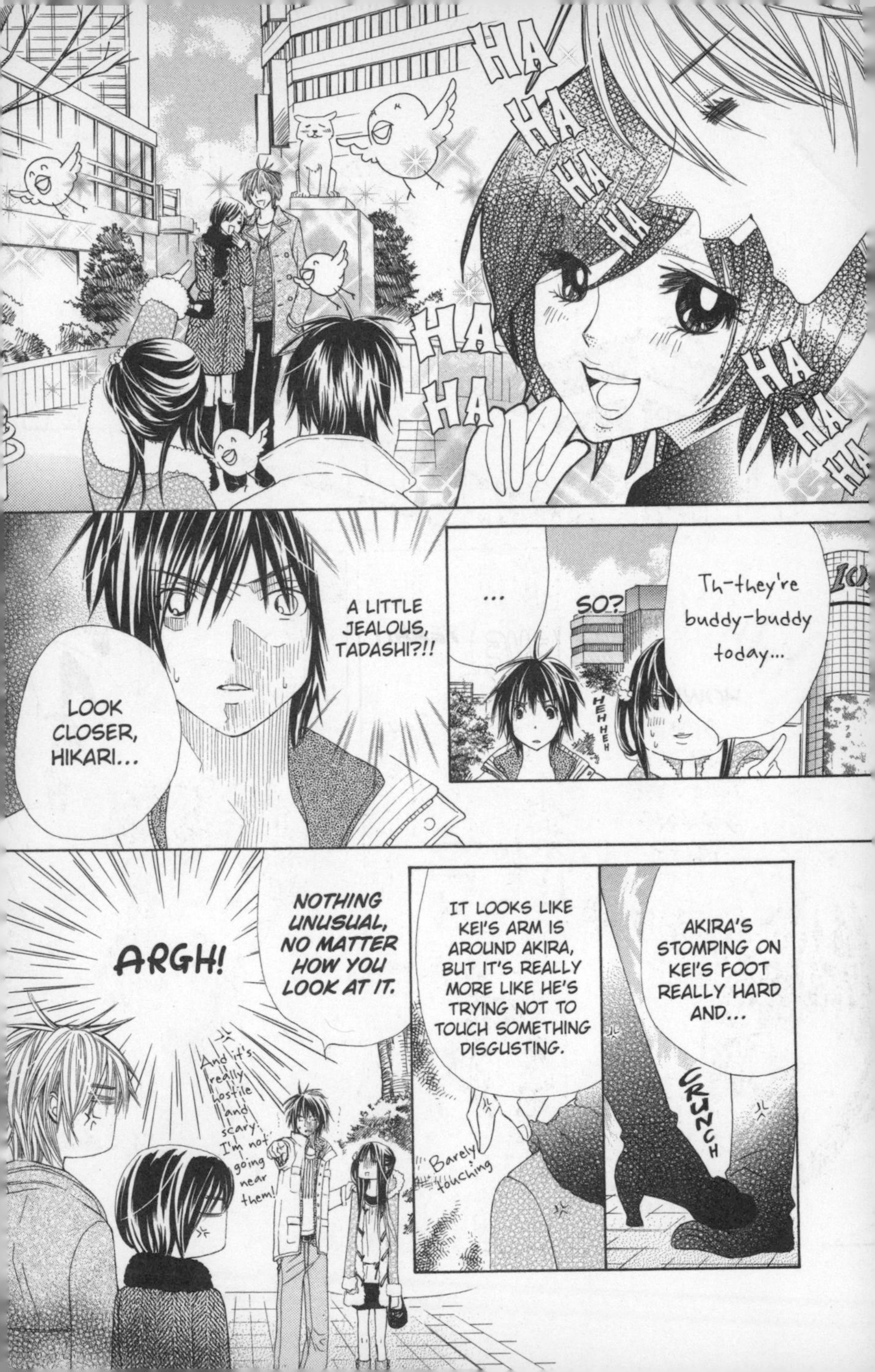
HA HA HA HA
HA HA HA
HA HA
Th-they're buddy-buddy today...
SO?
...
HEH HEH
A LITTLE JEALOUS, TADASHI?!!
LOOK CLOSER, HIKARI...
AKIRA'S STOMPING ON KEI'S FOOT REALLY HARD AND...
CRUNCH
IT LOOKS LIKE KEI'S ARM IS AROUND AKIRA, BUT IT'S REALLY MORE LIKE HE'S TRYING NOT TO TOUCH SOMETHING DISGUSTING.
Barely touching
NOTHING UNUSUAL, NO MATTER HOW YOU LOOK AT IT.
ARGH!
And it's really hostile and scary. I'm not going near them!

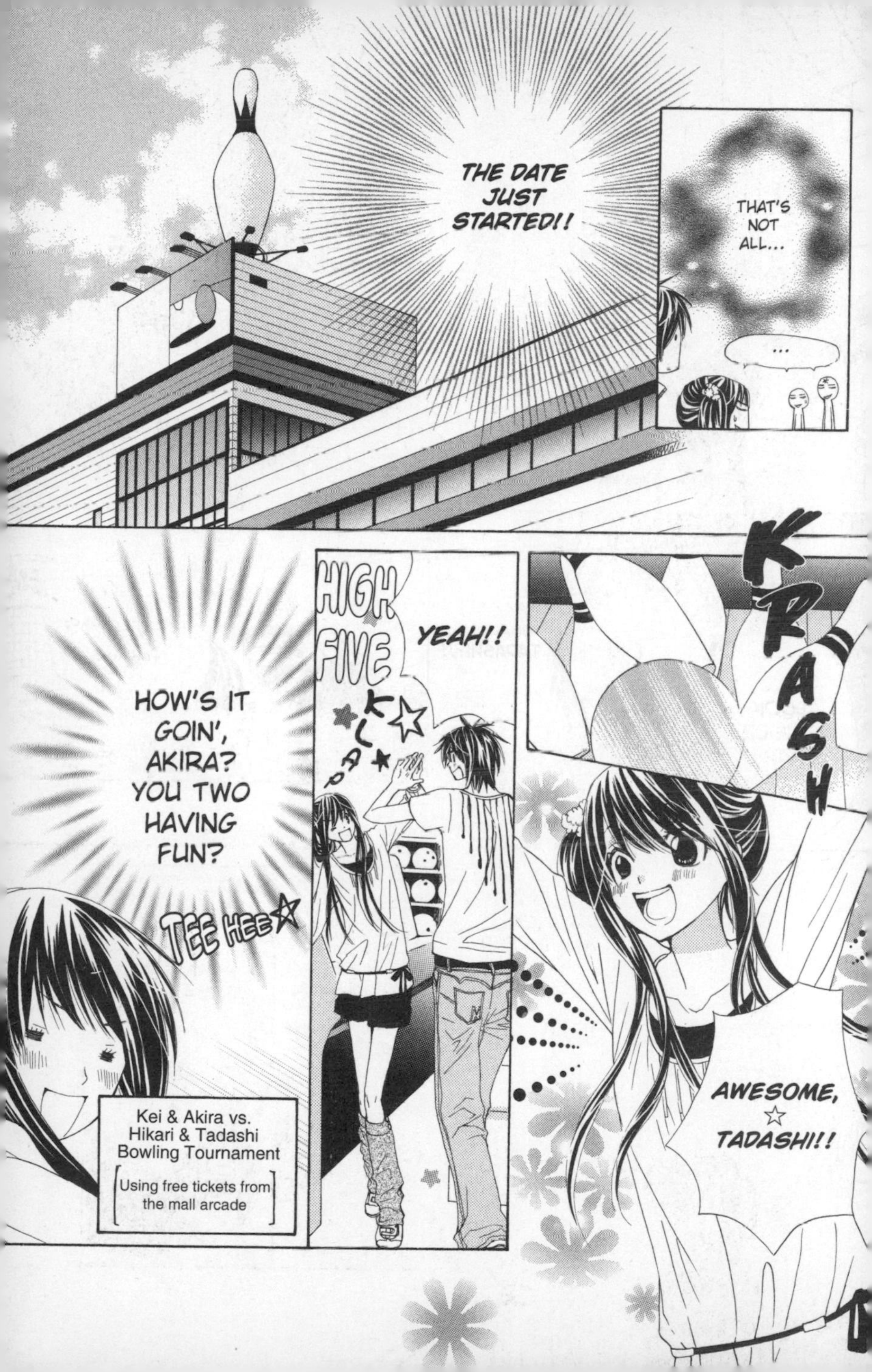
THAT'S NOT ALL...
...
THE DATE JUST STARTED!!
KRASH
AWESOME, ☆ TADASHI!!
HIGH FIVE
YEAH!!
KLAP
HOW'S IT GOIN', AKIRA? YOU TWO HAVING FUN?
TEE HEE☆
Kei & Akira vs. Hikari & Tadashi Bowling Tournament
[Using free tickets from the mall arcade]

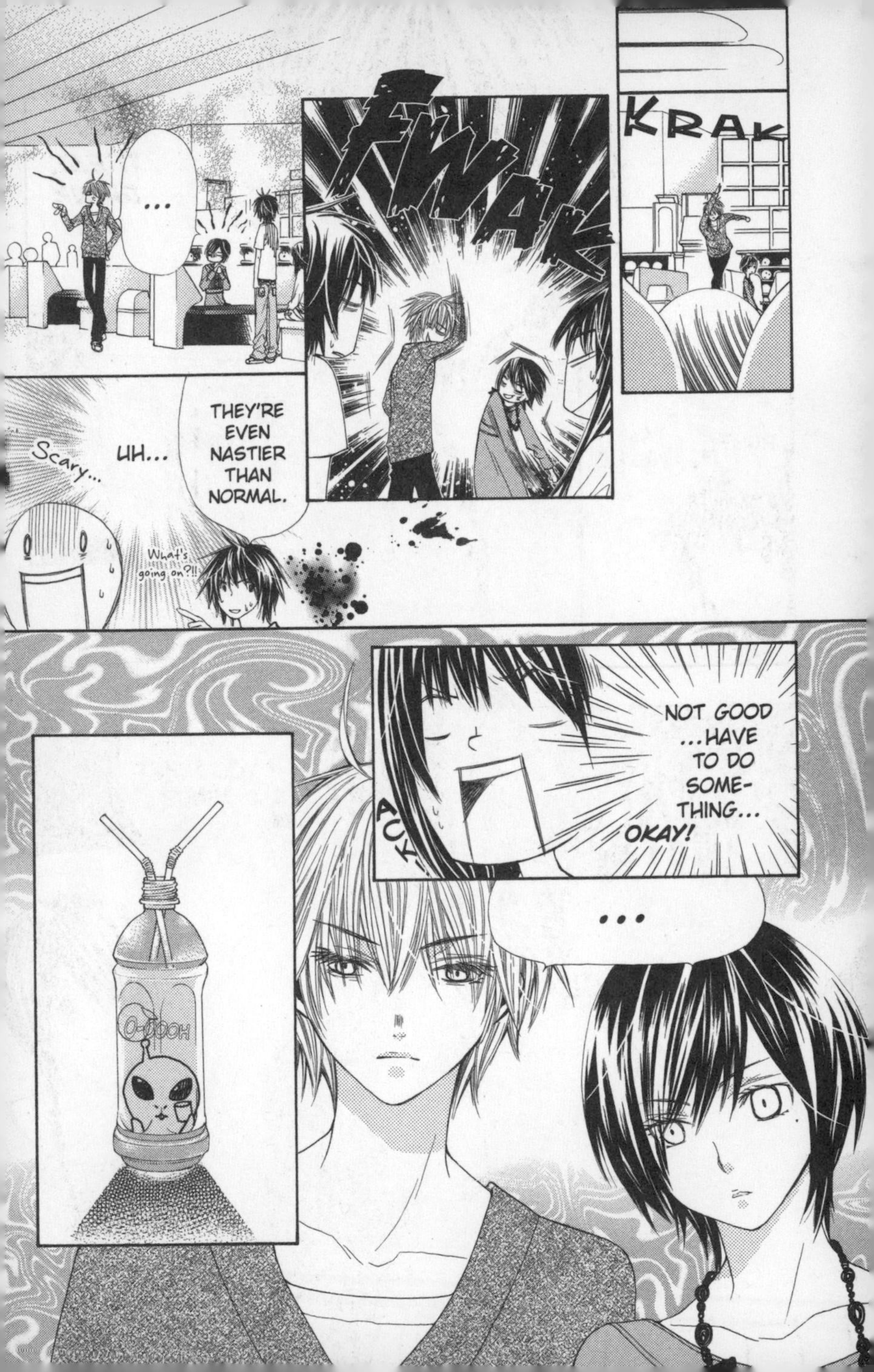
KRAK
FWAK
...
THEY'RE EVEN NASTIER THAN NORMAL.
UH...
Scary...
What's going on?!!
NOT GOOD ...HAVE TO DO SOME-THING... OKAY!
ACK
...
O-OOOH

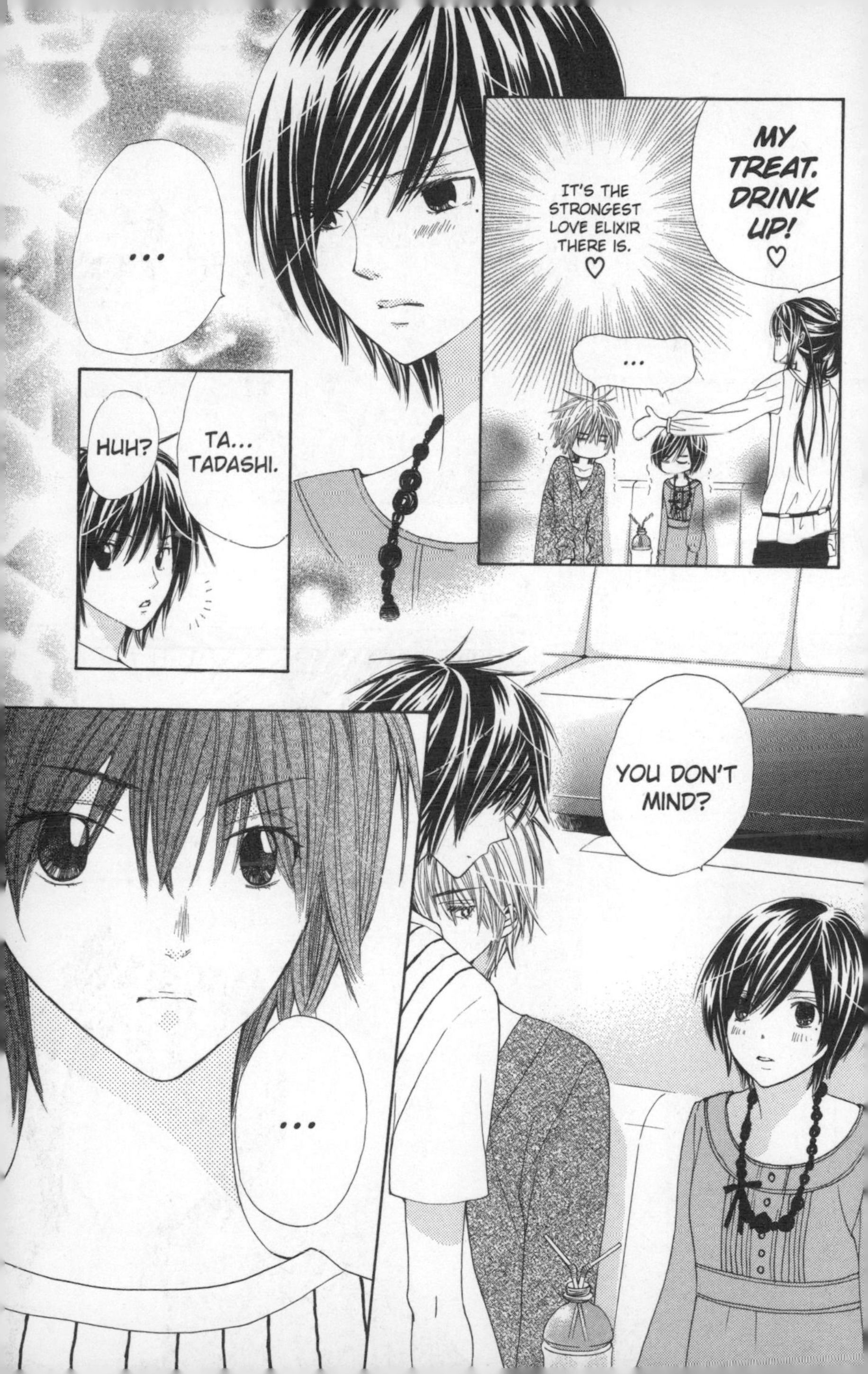
MY TREAT. DRINK UP! ♡
IT'S THE STRONGEST LOVE ELIXIR THERE IS. ♡
...
...
TA... TADASHI.
HUH?
YOU DON'T MIND?
...

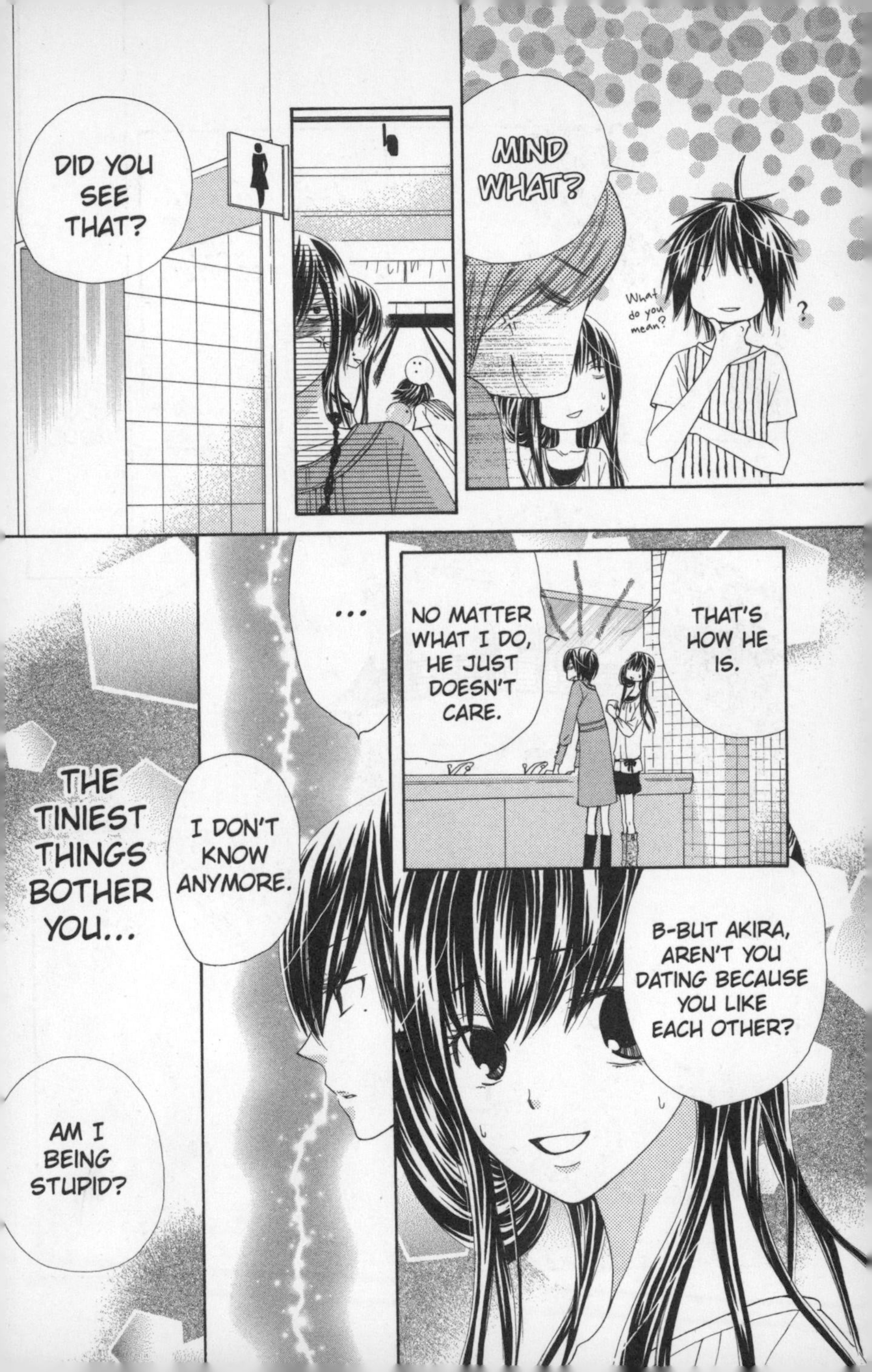
MIND WHAT?
What do you mean?
DID YOU SEE THAT?
THAT'S HOW HE IS.
NO MATTER WHAT I DO, HE JUST DOESN'T CARE.
B-BUT AKIRA, AREN'T YOU DATING BECAUSE YOU LIKE EACH OTHER?
...
I DON'T KNOW ANYMORE.
THE TINIEST THINGS BOTHER YOU...
AM I BEING STUPID?

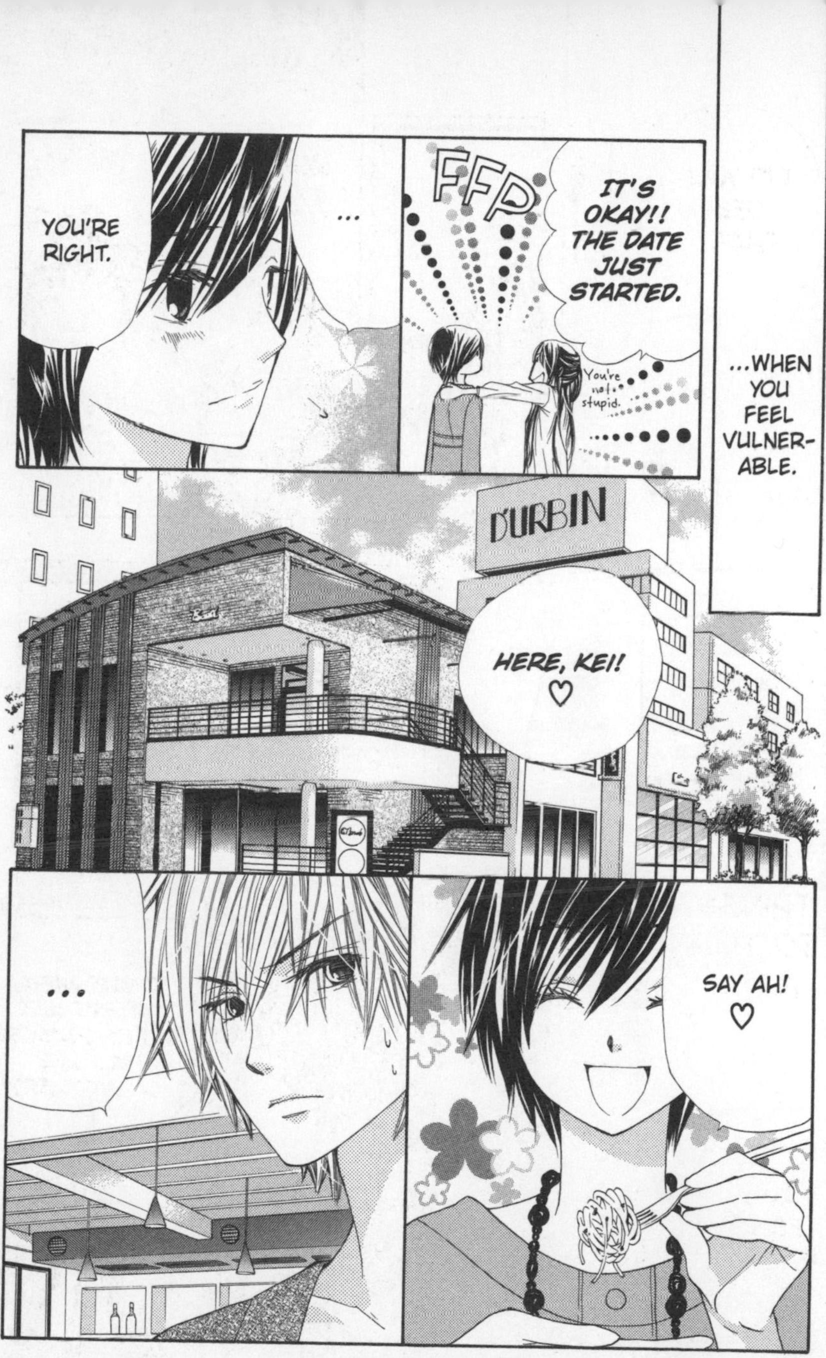
...WHEN YOU FEEL VULNER-ABLE.
FFP
IT'S OKAY!! THE DATE JUST STARTED.
You're not stupid.
...
YOU'RE RIGHT.
D'URBIN
HERE, KEI! ♡
SAY AH! ♡
...

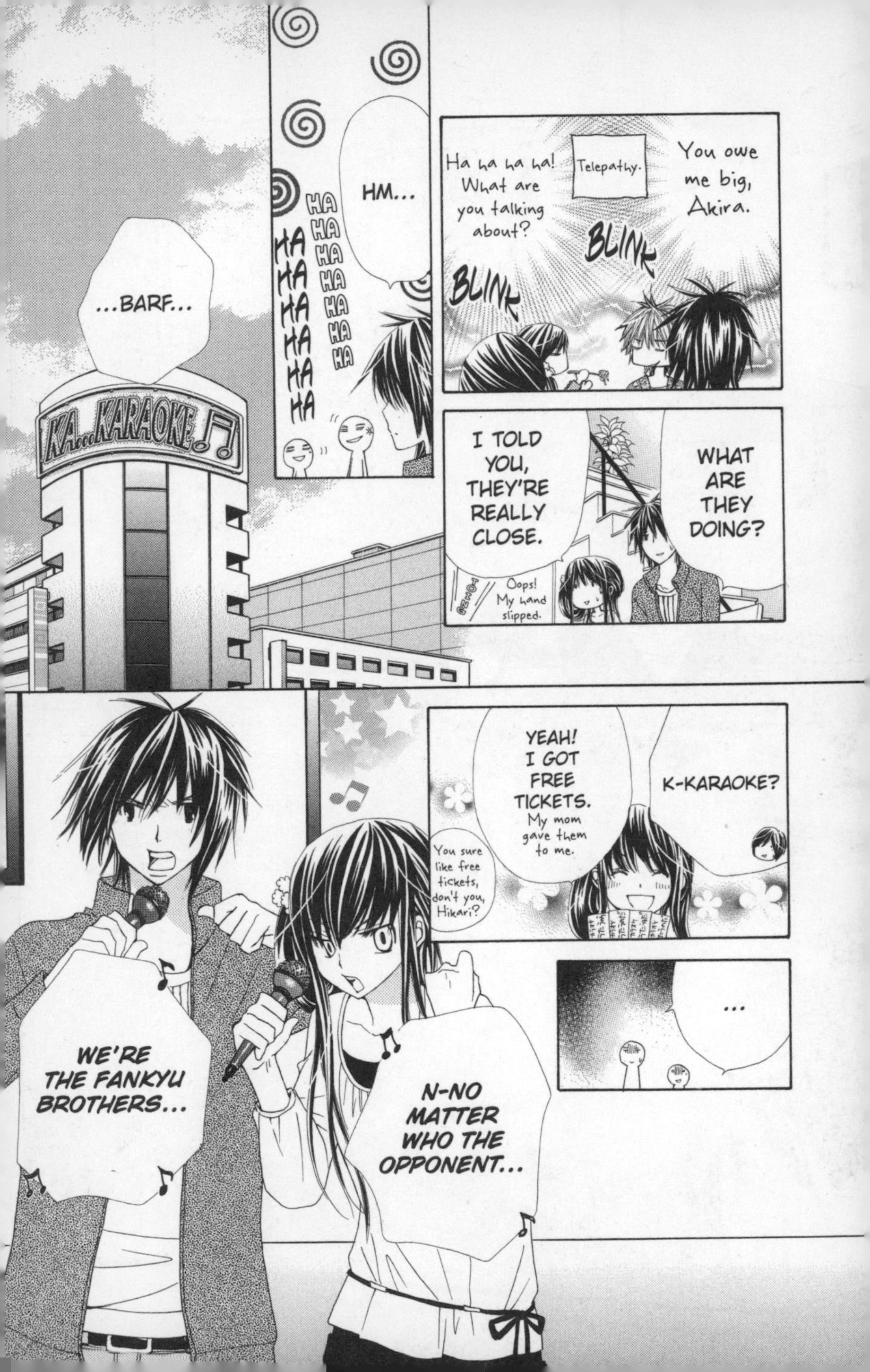
You owe me big, Akira.
Telepathy.
Ha ha ha ha! What are you talking about?
BLINK
BLINK
WHAT ARE THEY DOING?
I TOLD YOU, THEY'RE REALLY CLOSE.
Oops! My hand slipped.
HM...
HA HA HA HA HA HA HA
HA HA HA HA HA HA HA
...BARF...
KA...KARAOKE
K-KARAOKE?
YEAH! I GOT FREE TICKETS.
My mom gave them to me.
You sure like free tickets, don't you, Hikari?
...
N-NO MATTER WHO THE OPPONENT...
WE'RE THE FANKYU BROTHERS...

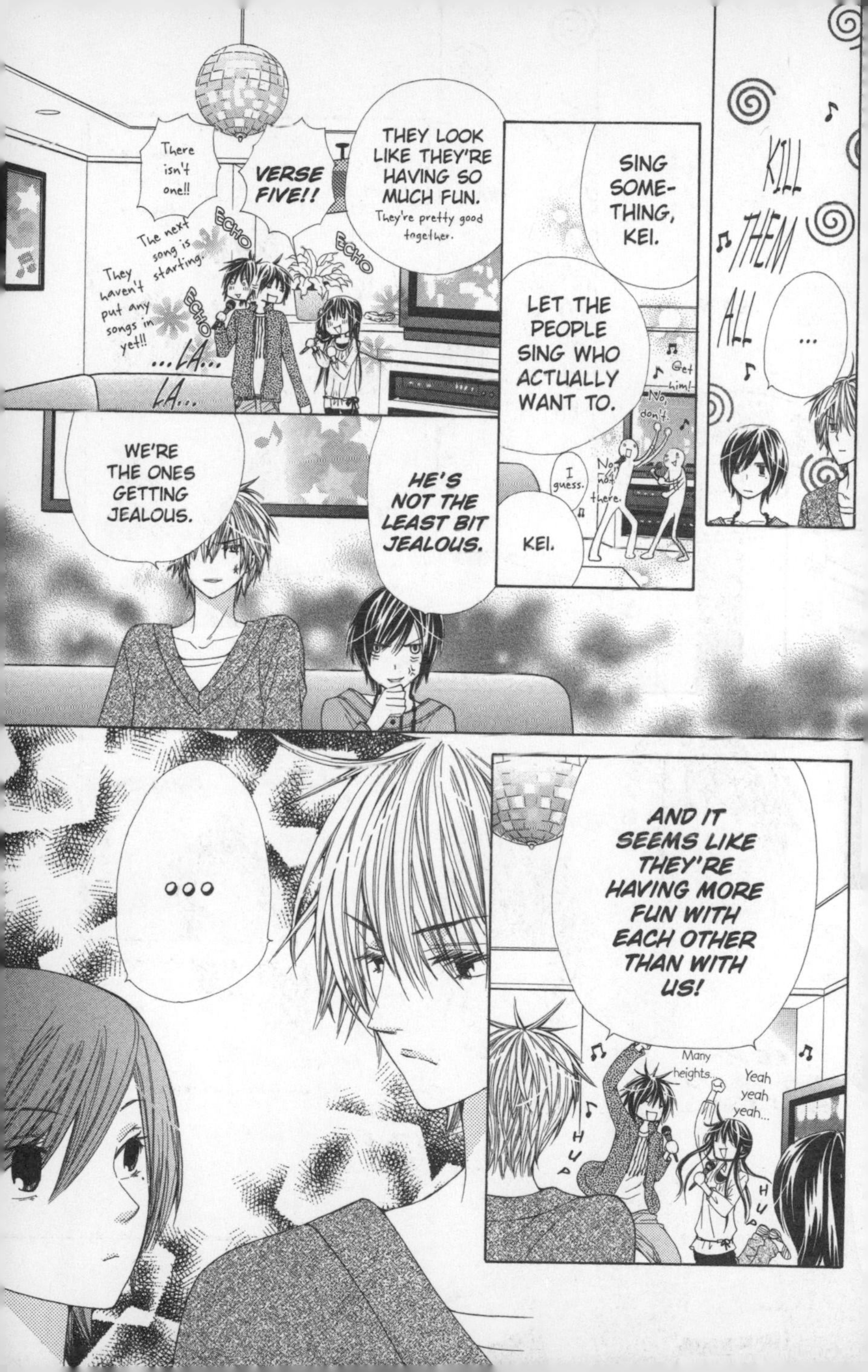
KILL THEM ALL
...
SING SOMETHING, KEI.
LET THE PEOPLE SING WHO ACTUALLY WANT TO.
KEI.
I guess.
Get him!
No, don't.
No, not there.
THEY LOOK LIKE THEY'RE HAVING SO MUCH FUN.
They're pretty good together.
VERSE FIVE!!
There isn't one!!
ECHO
ECHO
ECHO
The next song is starting.
They haven't put any songs in yet!!
...LA... LA...
HE'S NOT THE LEAST BIT JEALOUS.
WE'RE THE ONES GETTING JEALOUS.
AND IT SEEMS LIKE THEY'RE HAVING MORE FUN WITH EACH OTHER THAN WITH US!
Many heights...
Yeah yeah yeah...
HUP
HUP
ooo

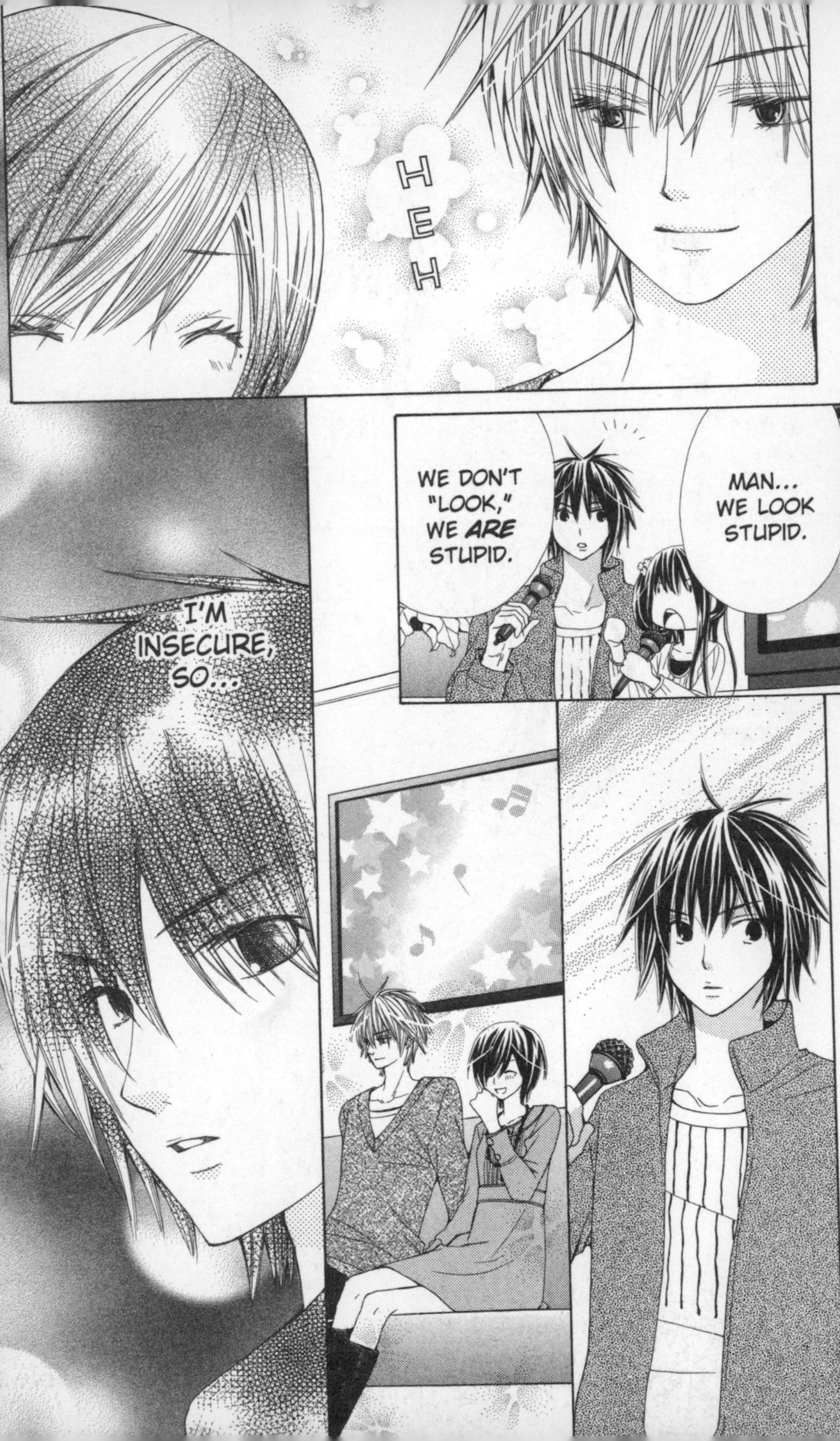
HEH
MAN... WE LOOK STUPID.
WE DON'T "LOOK," WE *ARE* STUPID.
I'M INSECURE, SO...

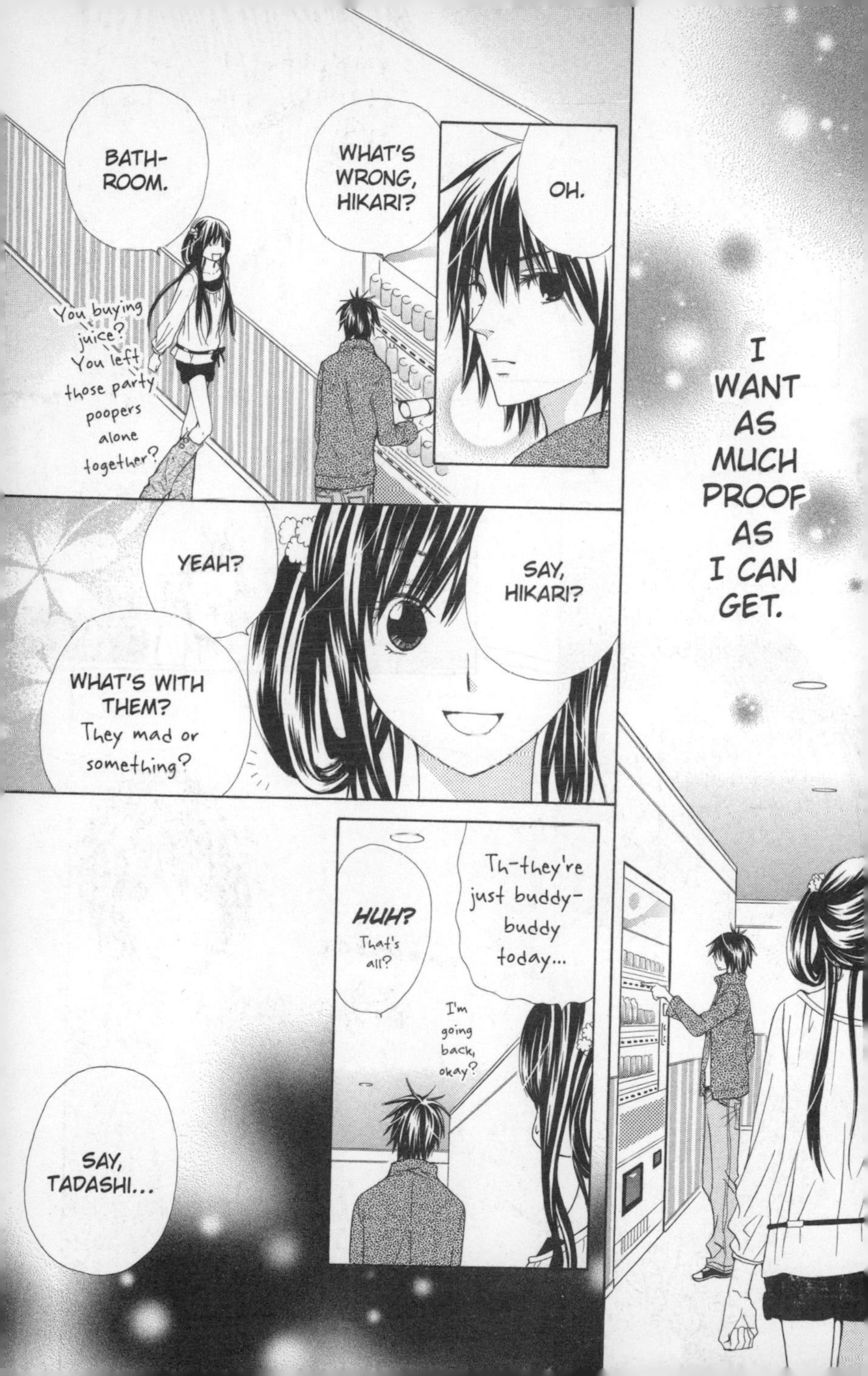
I WANT AS MUCH PROOF AS I CAN GET.
WHAT'S WRONG, HIKARI?
BATH-ROOM.
OH.
You buying juice? You left those party poopers alone together?
SAY, HIKARI?
YEAH?
WHAT'S WITH THEM? They mad or something?
Th-they're just buddy-buddy today...
HUH? That's all?
I'm going back, okay?
SAY, TADASHI...

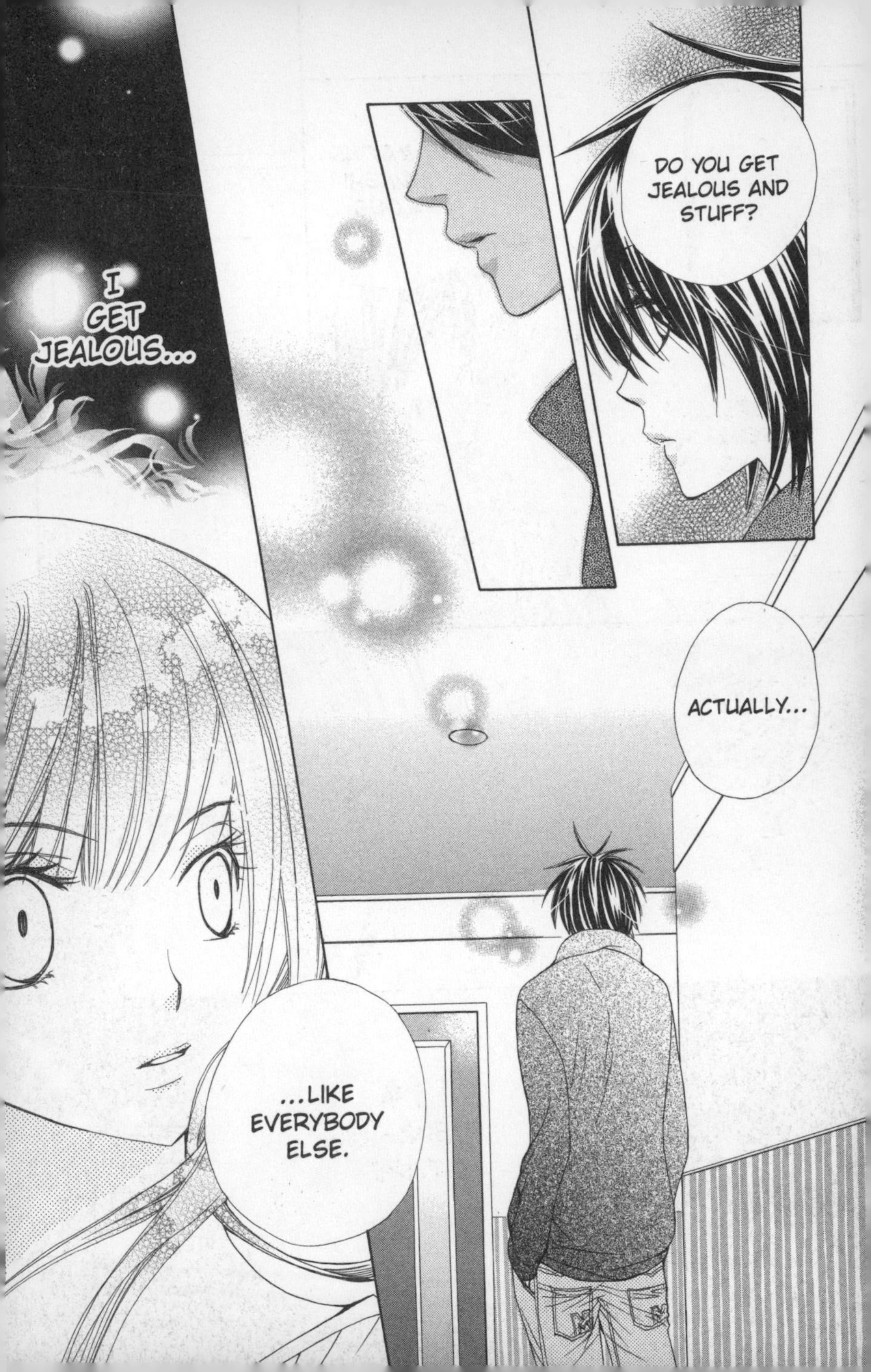
DO YOU GET JEALOUS AND STUFF?
I GET JEALOUS...
ACTUALLY...
...LIKE EVERYBODY ELSE.

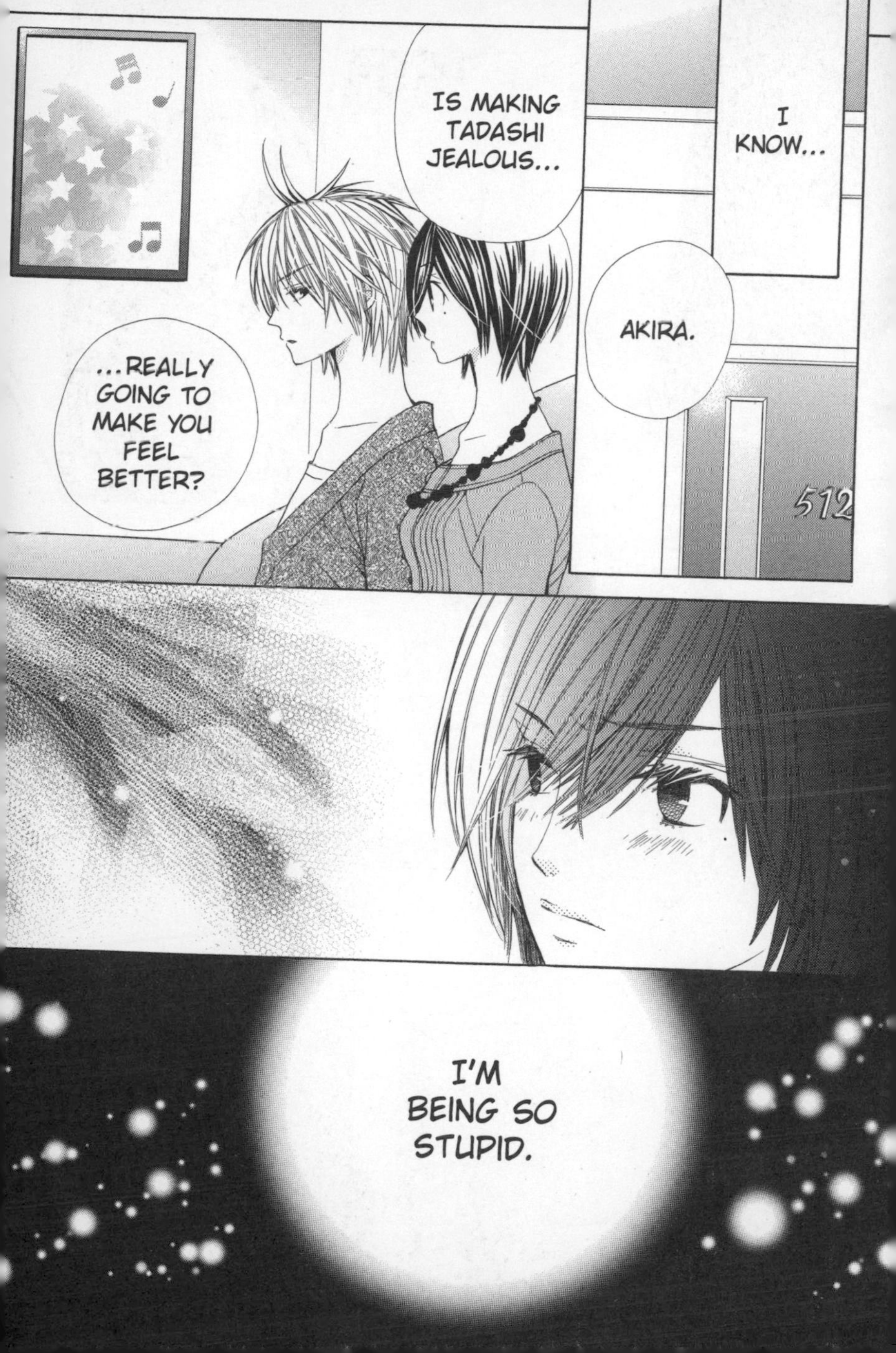
I KNOW...
AKIRA.
IS MAKING TADASHI JEALOUS...
...REALLY GOING TO MAKE YOU FEEL BETTER?
512
I'M BEING SO STUPID.

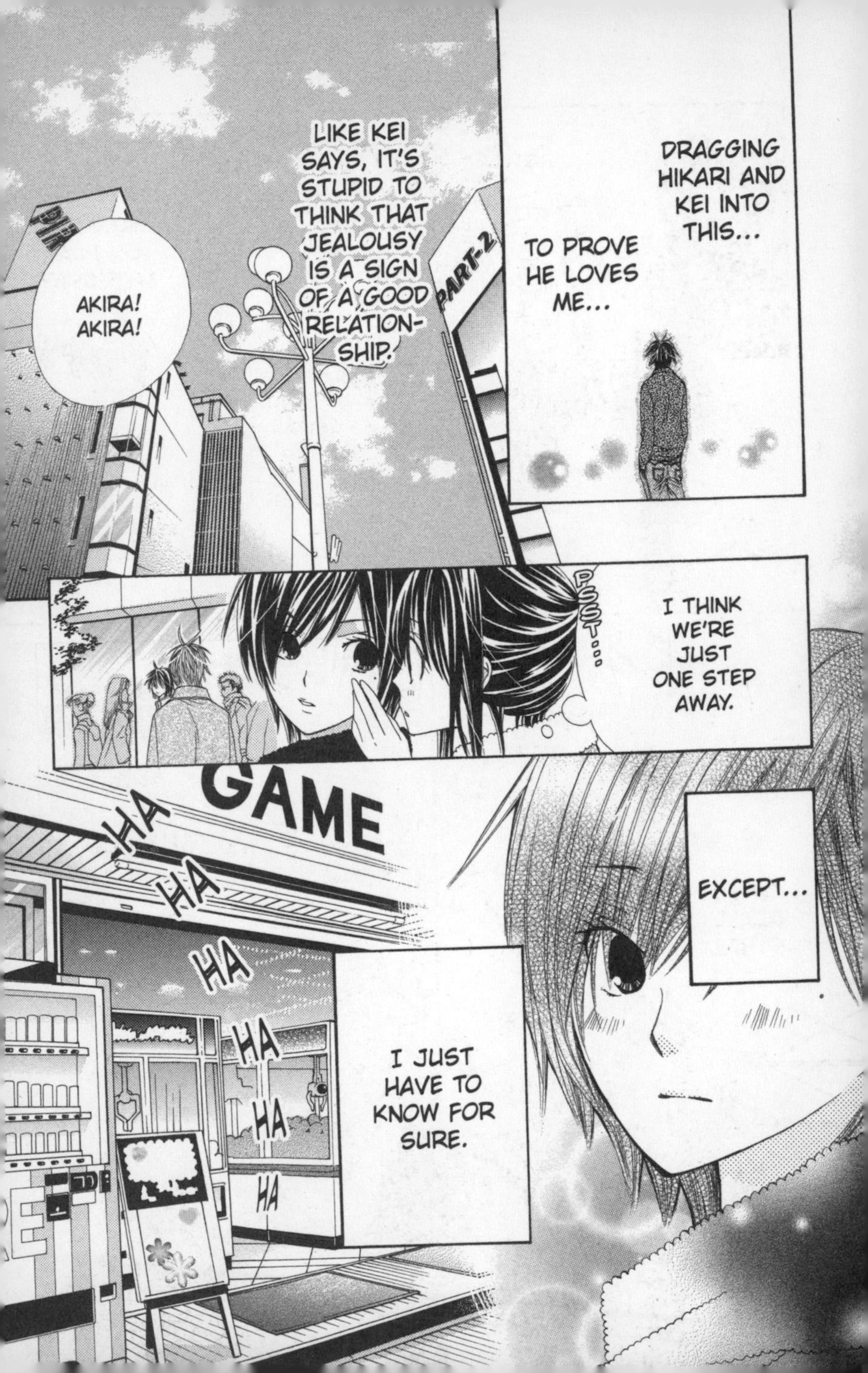

DRAGGING HIKARI AND KEI INTO THIS...
TO PROVE HE LOVES ME...
PART-2
LIKE KEI SAYS, IT'S STUPID TO THINK THAT JEALOUSY IS A SIGN OF A GOOD RELATION-SHIP.
AKIRA! AKIRA!
I THINK WE'RE JUST ONE STEP AWAY.
PSST...
EXCEPT...
GAME
HA HA HA HA HA HA
I JUST HAVE TO KNOW FOR SURE.

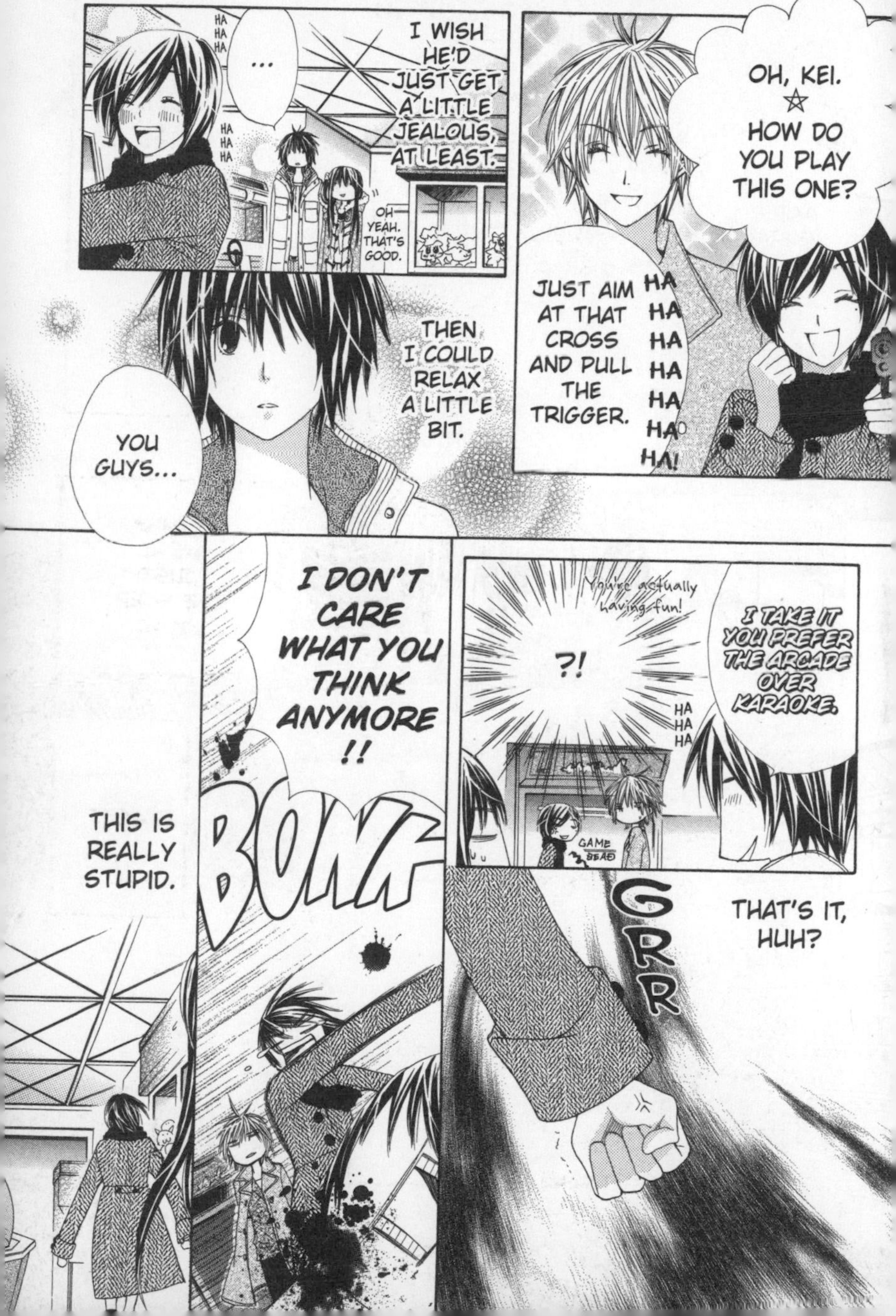
OH, KEI. ☆ HOW DO YOU PLAY THIS ONE?
JUST AIM AT THAT CROSS AND PULL THE TRIGGER.
HA HA HA HA HA HA HA!
I WISH HE'D JUST GET A LITTLE JEALOUS, AT LEAST.
...
HA HA HA
HA HA HA
OH YEAH. THAT'S GOOD.
THEN I COULD RELAX A LITTLE BIT.
YOU GUYS...
I TAKE IT YOU PREFER THE ARCADE OVER KARAOKE.
You're actually having fun!
?!
HA HA HA
GAME DEAD
THAT'S IT, HUH?
GRR
I DON'T CARE WHAT YOU THINK ANYMORE!!
BONK
THIS IS REALLY STUPID.

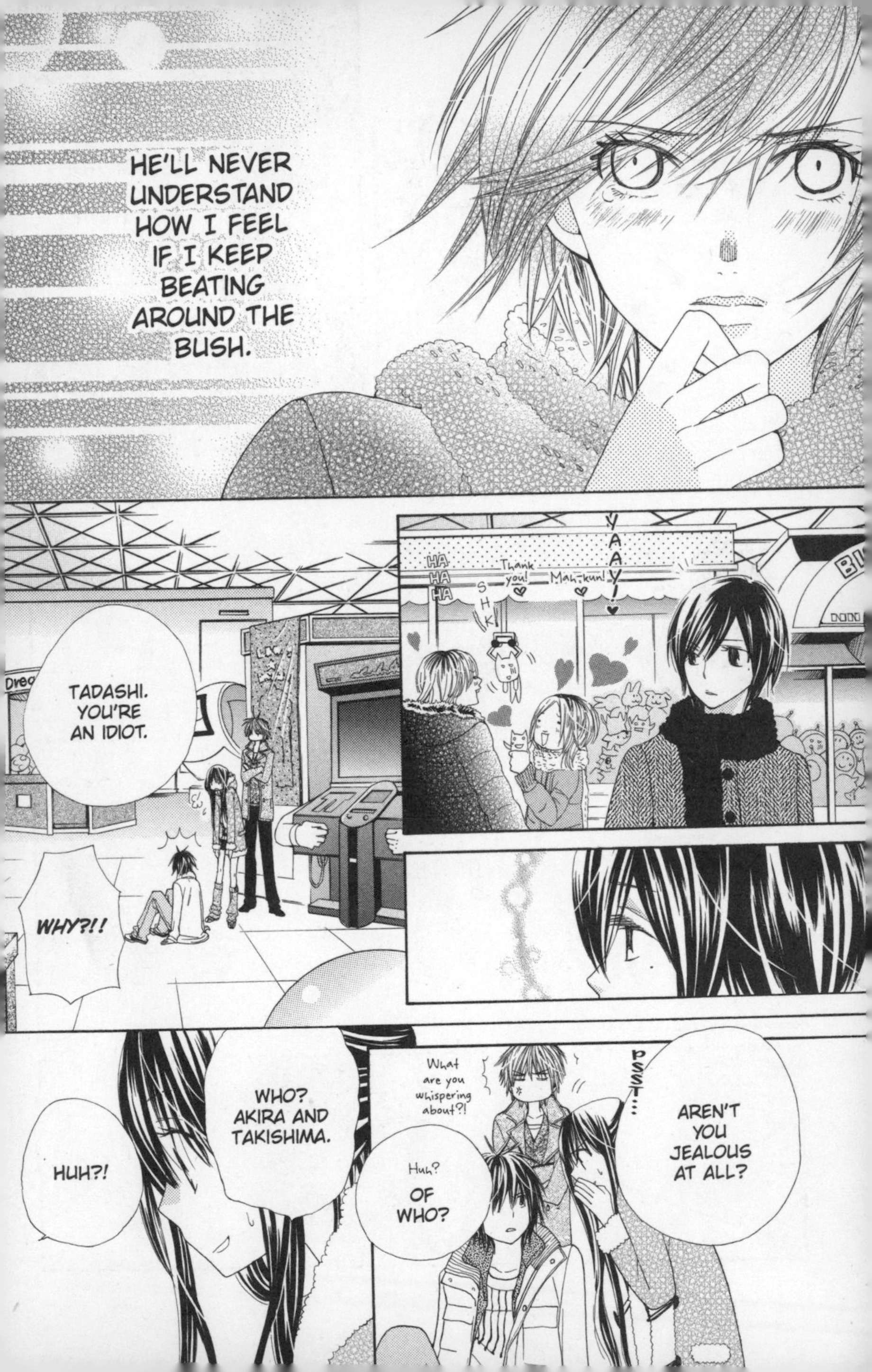
HE'LL NEVER UNDERSTAND HOW I FEEL IF I KEEP BEATING AROUND THE BUSH.
YAAAY!
Mah-kun!
Thank you!
HA HA HA
SHK
TADASHI. YOU'RE AN IDIOT.
WHY?!!
PSSST...
AREN'T YOU JEALOUS AT ALL?
What are you whispering about?!
Huh? OF WHO?
WHO? AKIRA AND TAKISHIMA.
HUH?!

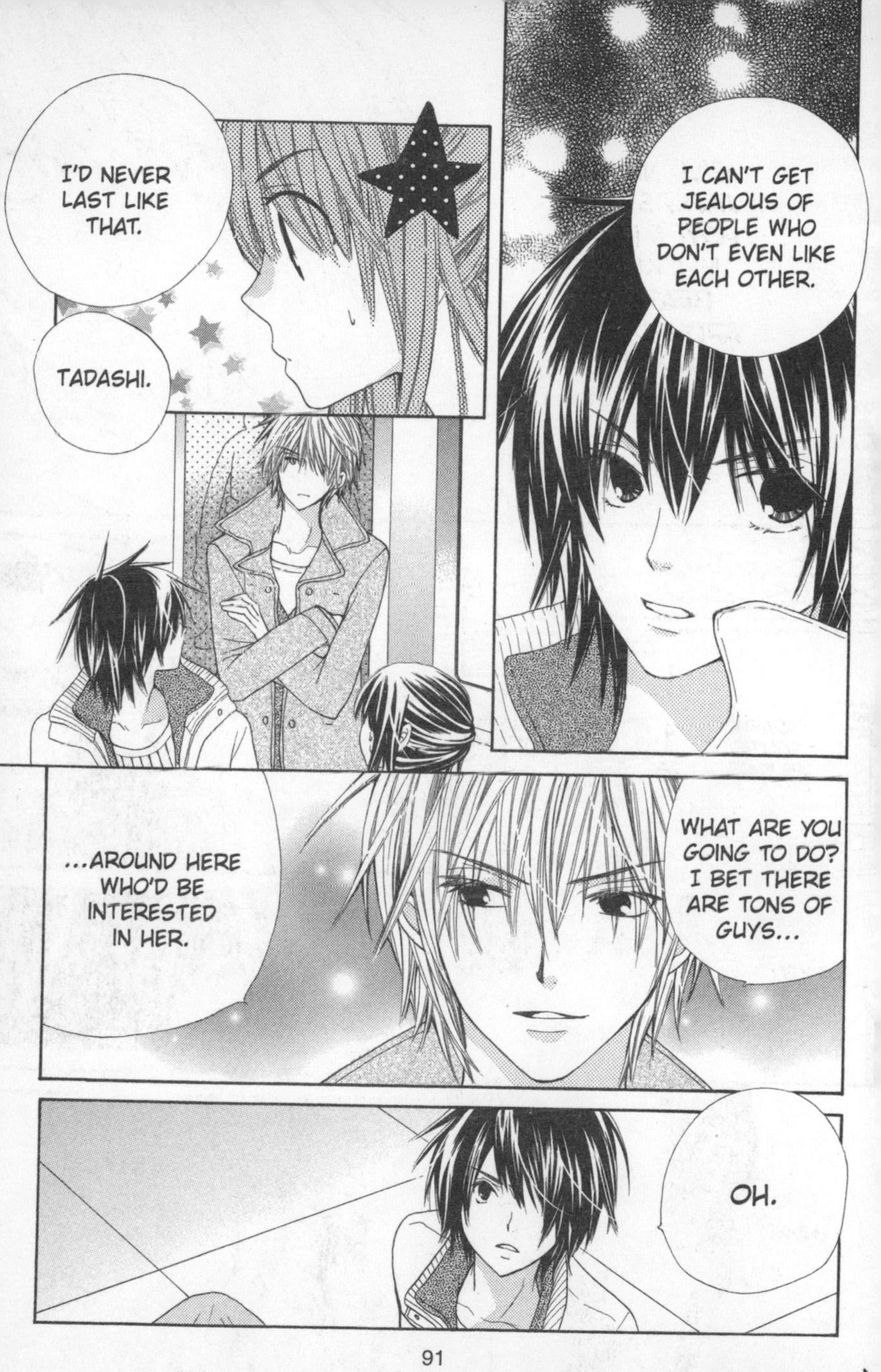
I CAN'T GET JEALOUS OF PEOPLE WHO DON'T EVEN LIKE EACH OTHER.
I'D NEVER LAST LIKE THAT.
TADASHI.
WHAT ARE YOU GOING TO DO? I BET THERE ARE TONS OF GUYS...
...AROUND HERE WHO'D BE INTERESTED IN HER.
OH.

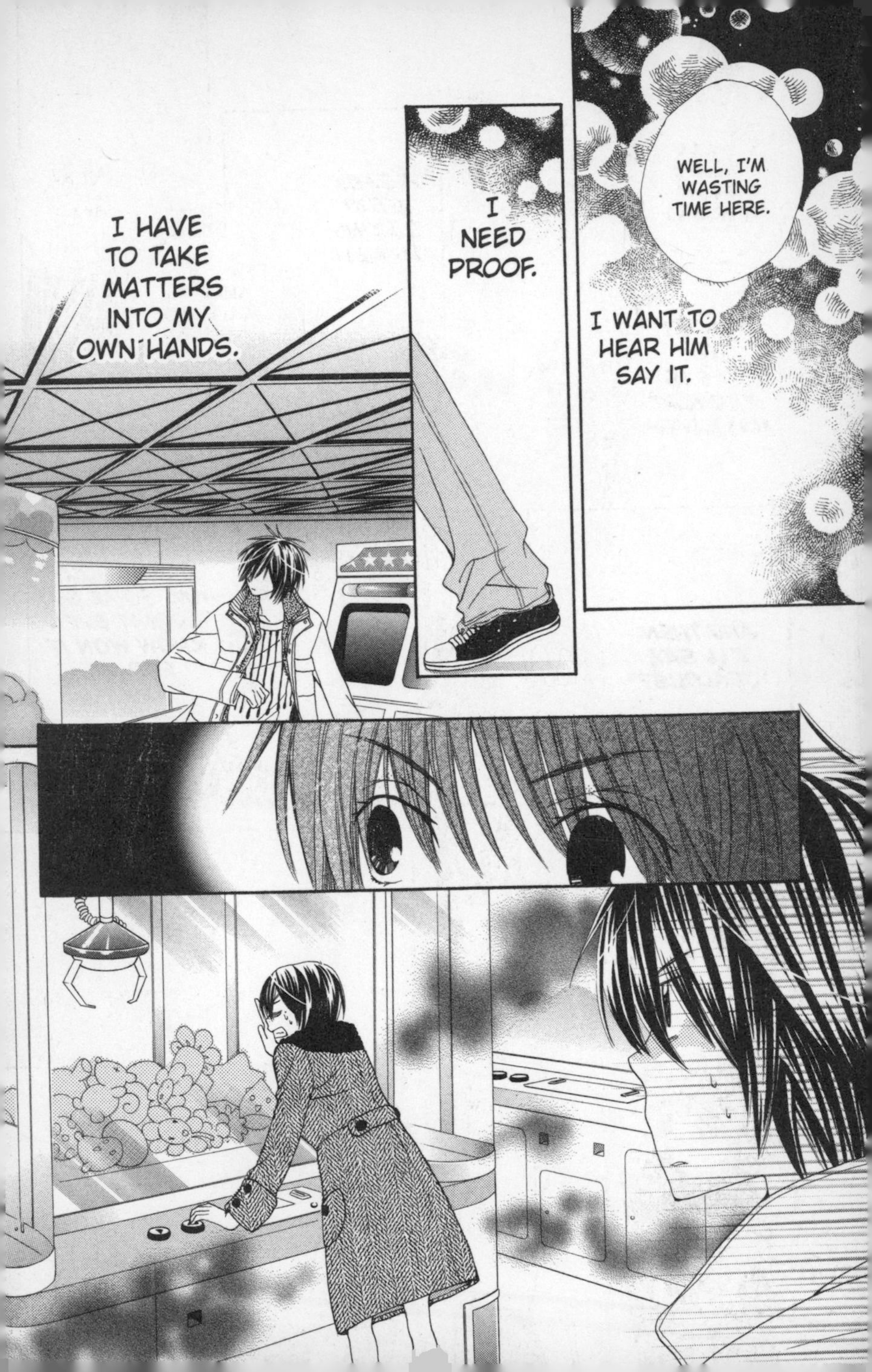
WELL, I'M WASTING TIME HERE.
I WANT TO HEAR HIM SAY IT.
I NEED PROOF.
I HAVE TO TAKE MATTERS INTO MY OWN HANDS.

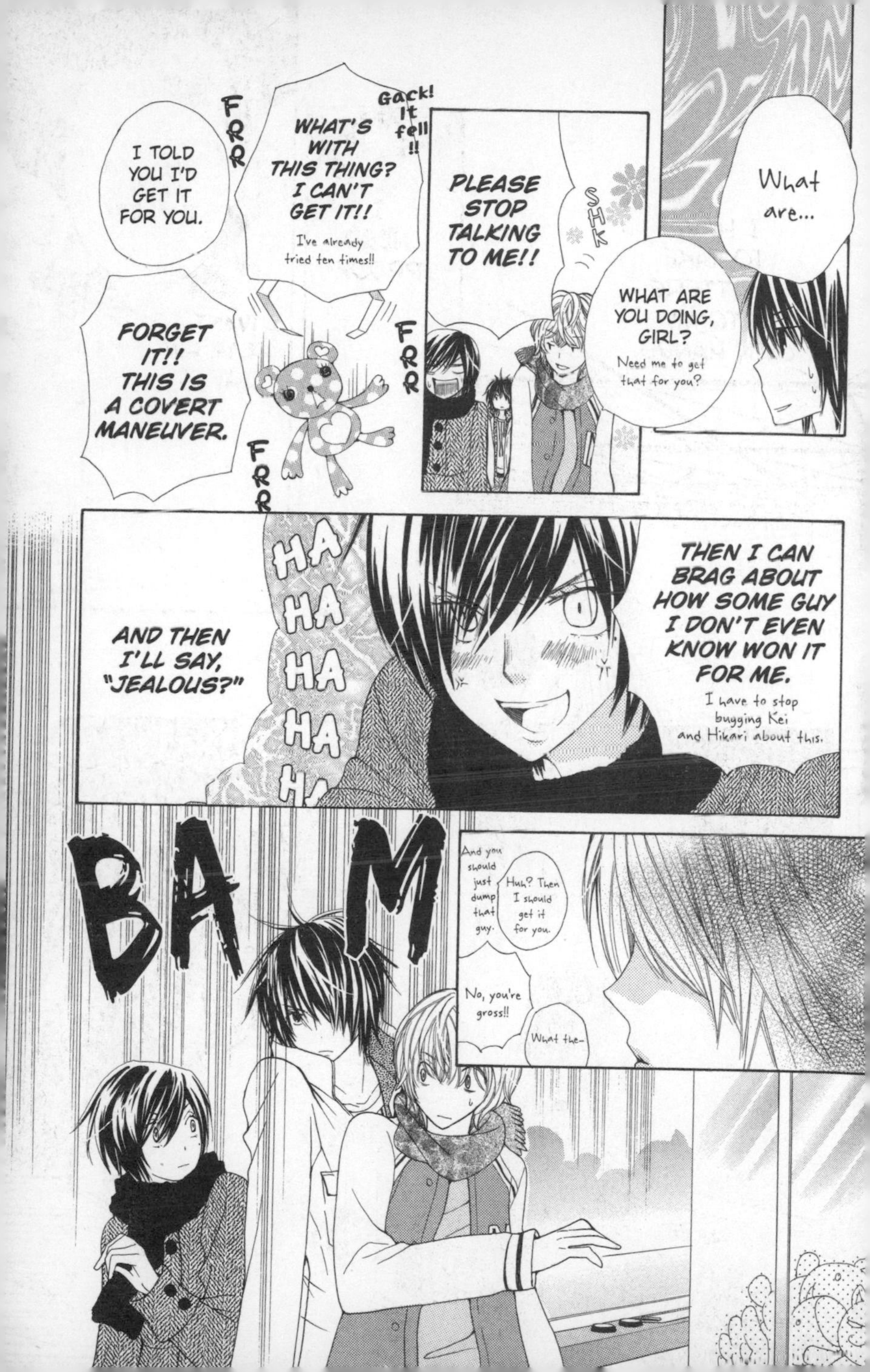
What are...
WHAT ARE YOU DOING, GIRL?
Need me to get that for you?
SHK
PLEASE STOP TALKING TO ME!!
Gack! It fell!!
WHAT'S WITH THIS THING? I CAN'T GET IT!!
I've already tried ten times!!
FRR
I TOLD YOU I'D GET IT FOR YOU.
FRR
FORGET IT!! THIS IS A COVERT MANEUVER.
FRR
THEN I CAN BRAG ABOUT HOW SOME GUY I DON'T EVEN KNOW WON IT FOR ME.
I have to stop bugging Kei and Hikari about this.
HA HA HA HA
AND THEN I'LL SAY, "JEALOUS?"
Huh? Then I should get it for you.
And you should just dump that guy.
No, you're gross!!
What the-
BAM

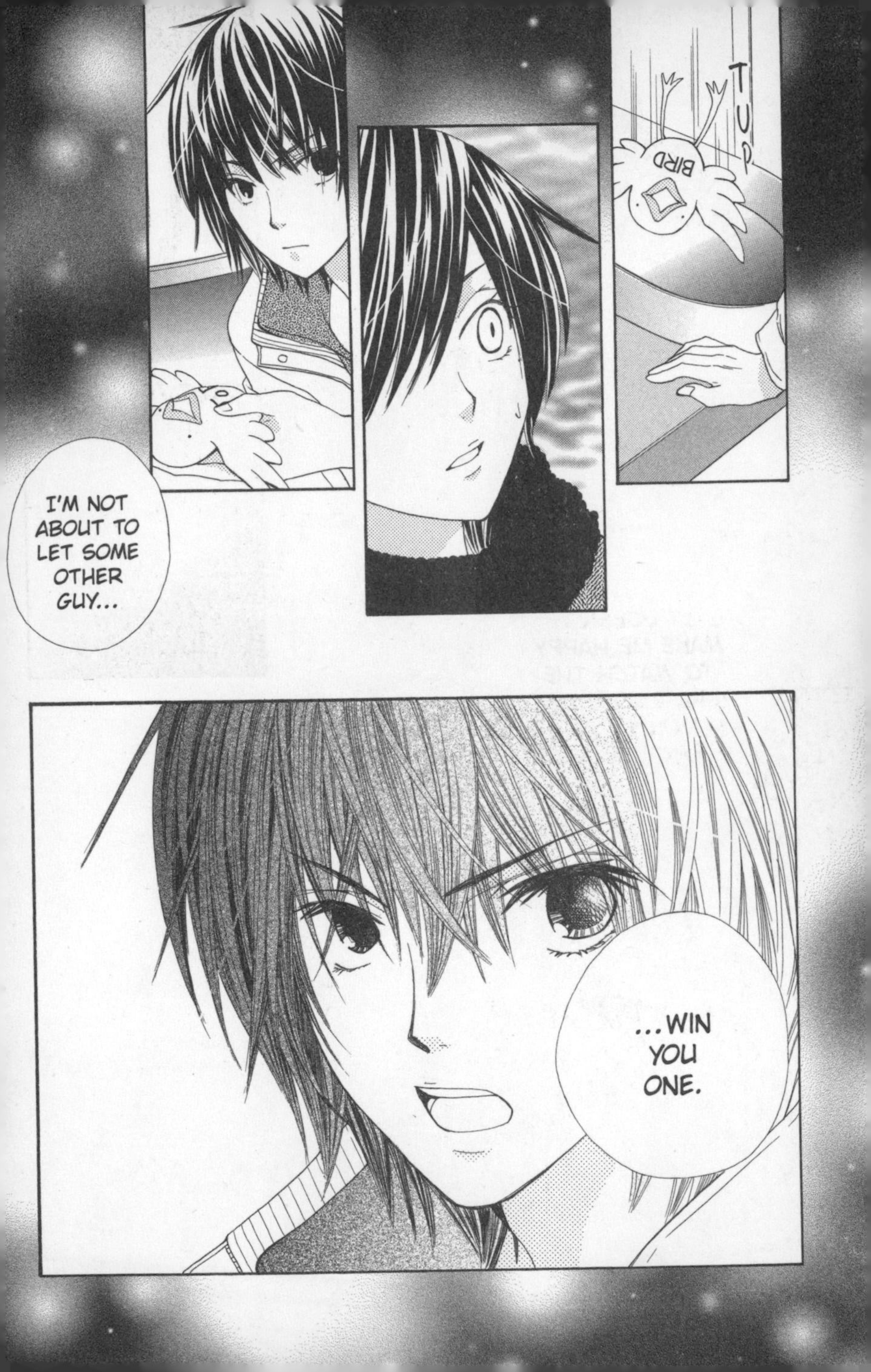
TUP
BIRD
I'M NOT ABOUT TO LET SOME OTHER GUY...
...WIN YOU ONE.

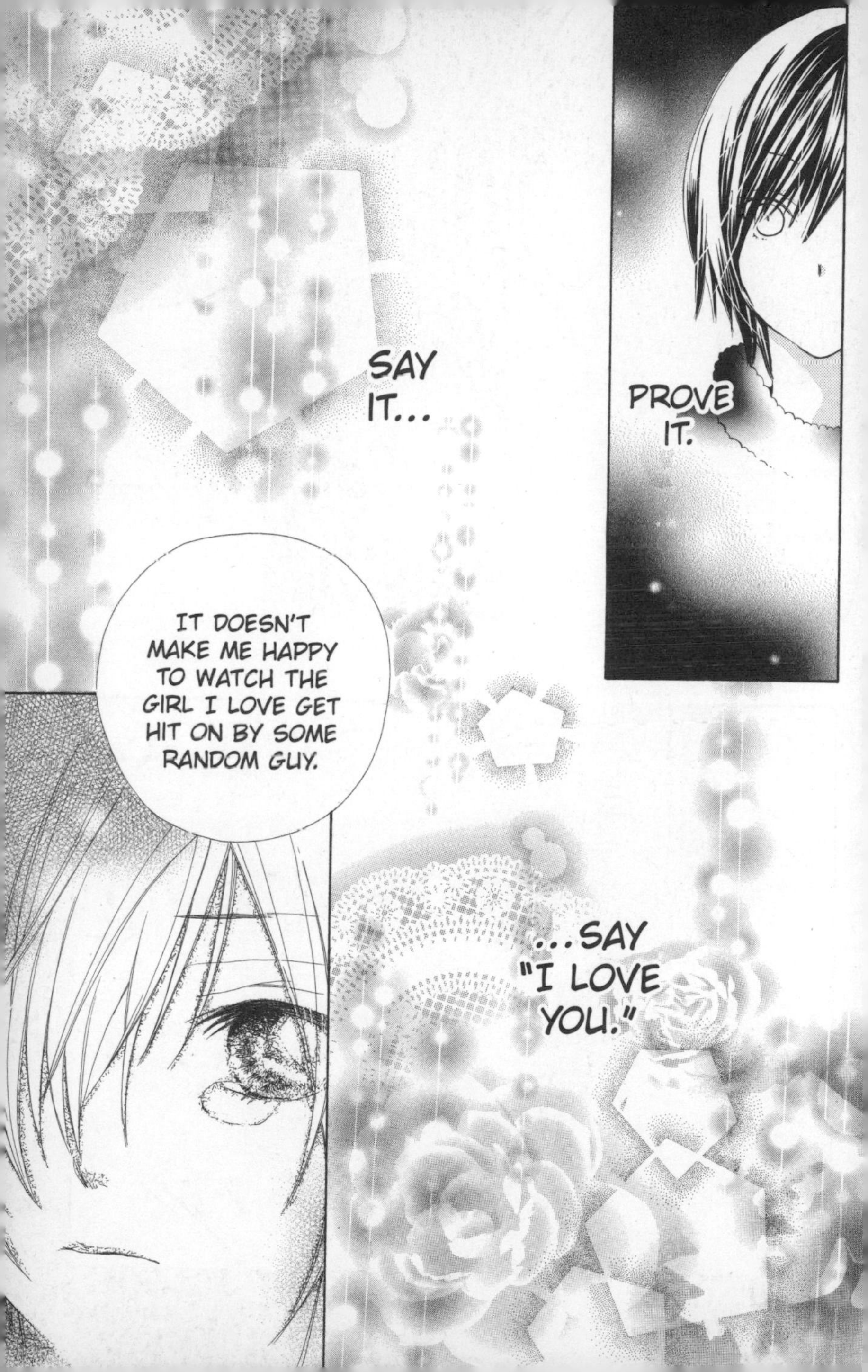
PROVE IT.
SAY IT...
IT DOESN'T MAKE ME HAPPY TO WATCH THE GIRL I LOVE GET HIT ON BY SOME RANDOM GUY.
...SAY "I LOVE YOU."

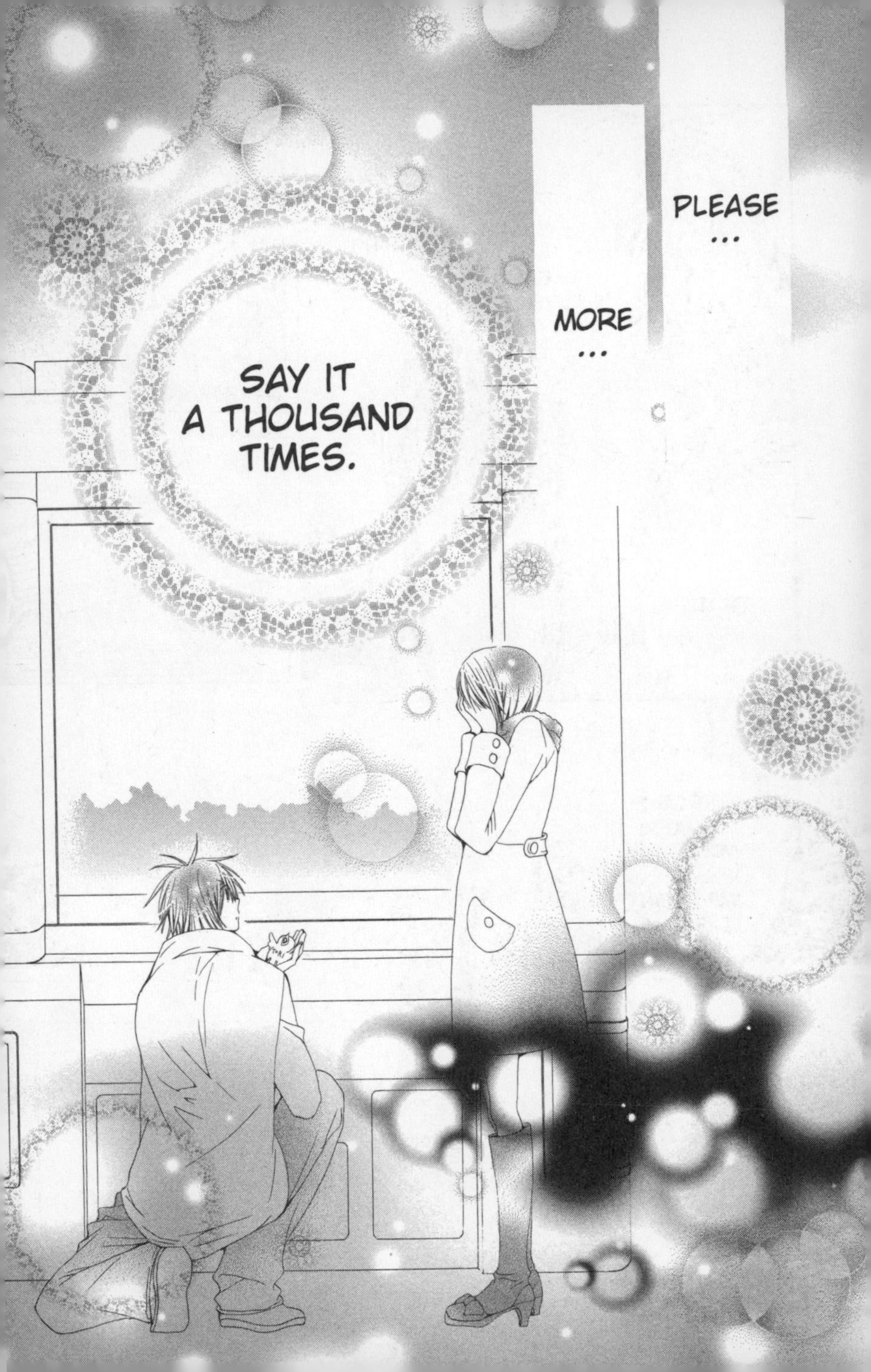
PLEASE ...
MORE ...
SAY IT A THOUSAND TIMES.

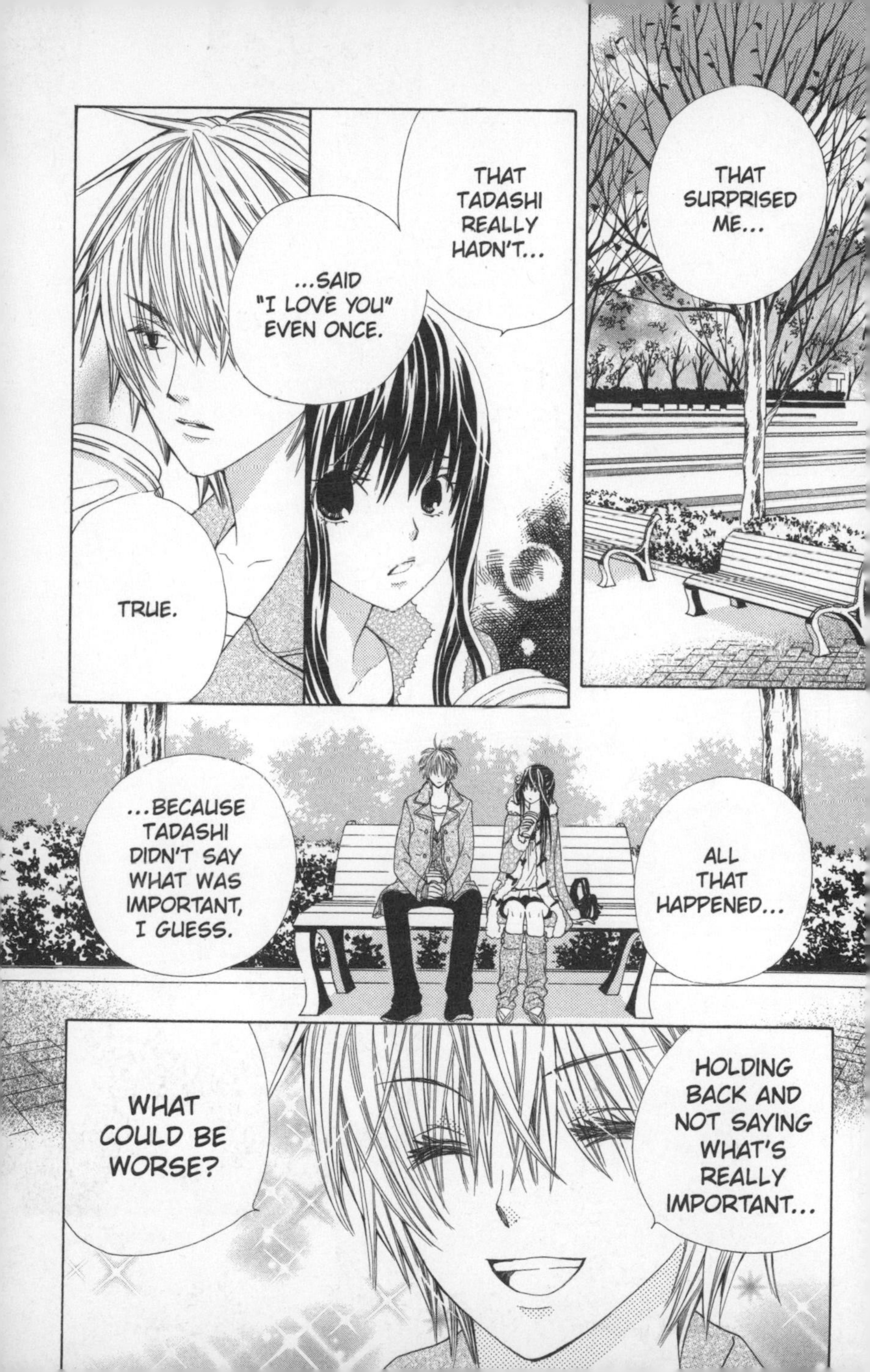
THAT SURPRISED ME...
THAT TADASHI REALLY HADN'T...
...SAID "I LOVE YOU" EVEN ONCE.
TRUE.
ALL THAT HAPPENED...
...BECAUSE TADASHI DIDN'T SAY WHAT WAS IMPORTANT, I GUESS.
HOLDING BACK AND NOT SAYING WHAT'S REALLY IMPORTANT...
WHAT COULD BE WORSE?

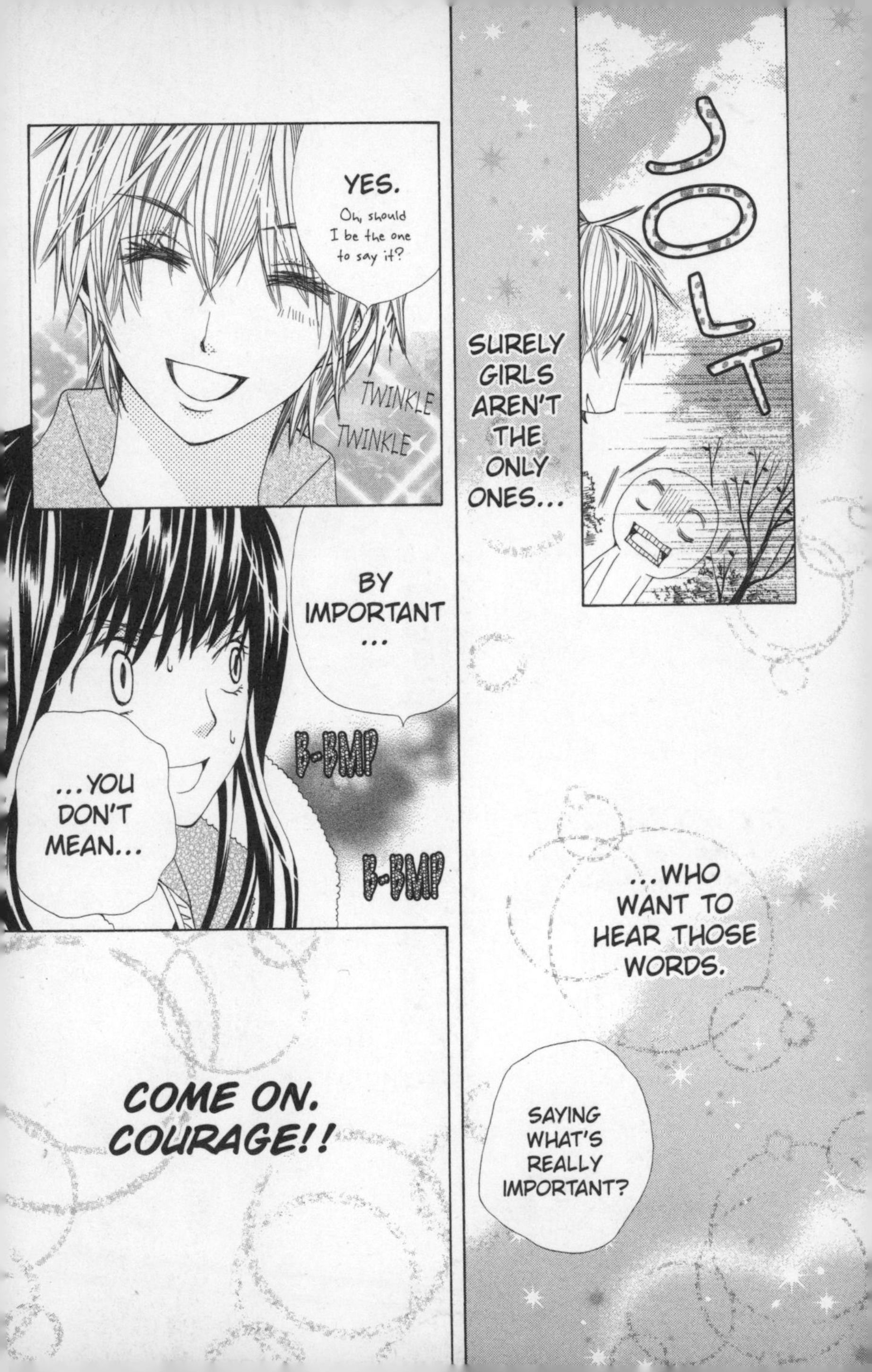
JOLT
SURELY GIRLS AREN'T THE ONLY ONES...
...WHO WANT TO HEAR THOSE WORDS.
SAYING WHAT'S REALLY IMPORTANT?
YES.
Oh, should I be the one to say it?
TWINKLE
TWINKLE
BY IMPORTANT...
...YOU DON'T MEAN...
B-BMP
B-BMP
COME ON. COURAGE!!

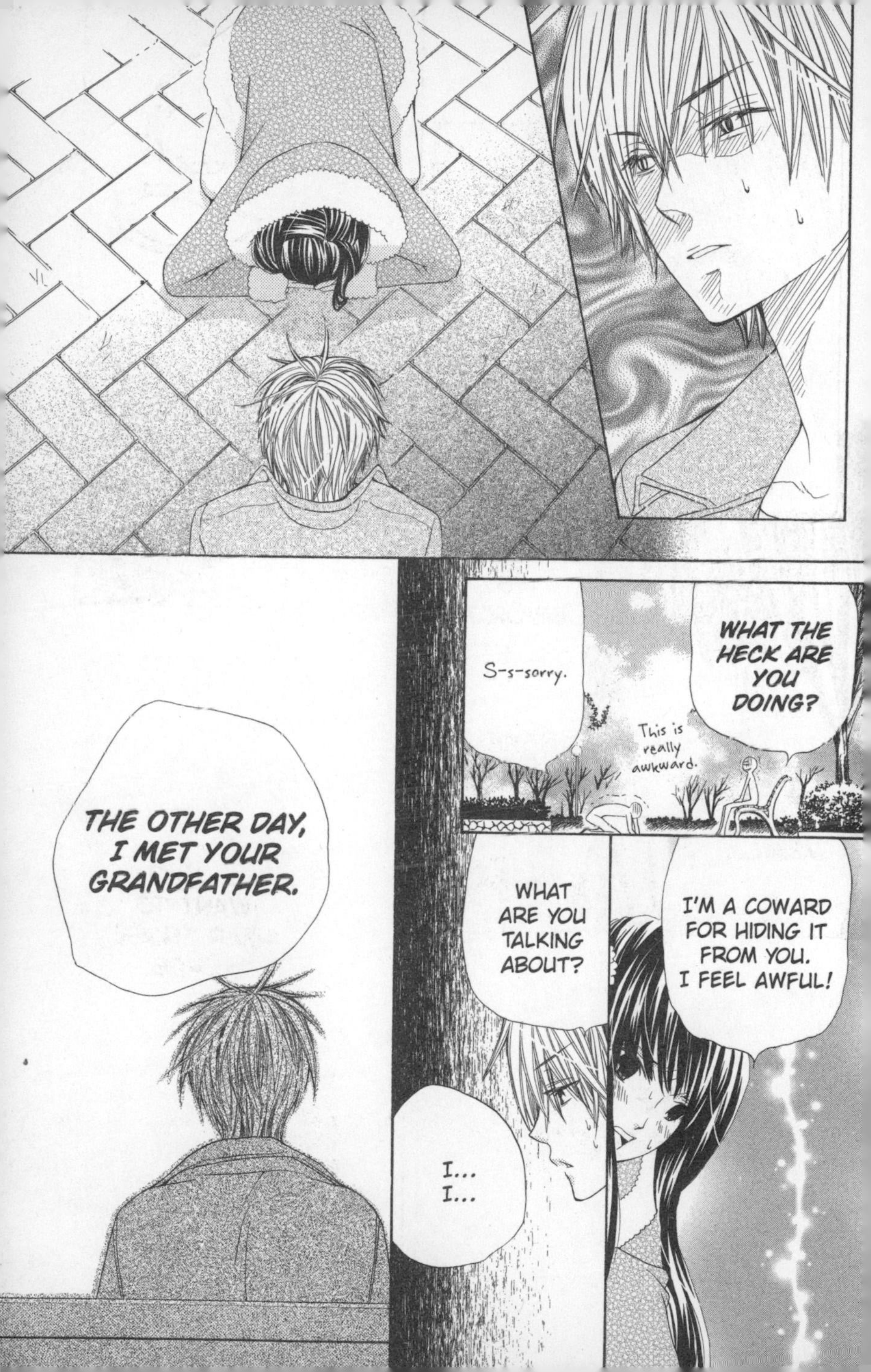
WHAT THE HECK ARE YOU DOING?
S-s-sorry.
This is really awkward.
I'M A COWARD FOR HIDING IT FROM YOU. I FEEL AWFUL!
WHAT ARE YOU TALKING ABOUT?
I... I...
THE OTHER DAY, I MET YOUR GRANDFATHER.

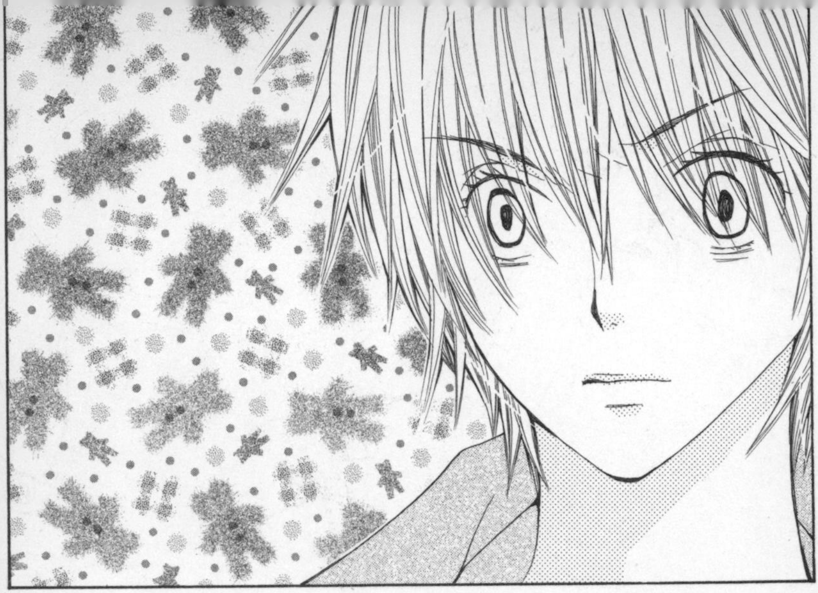

EMOTIONS TAKE MANY SHAPES.

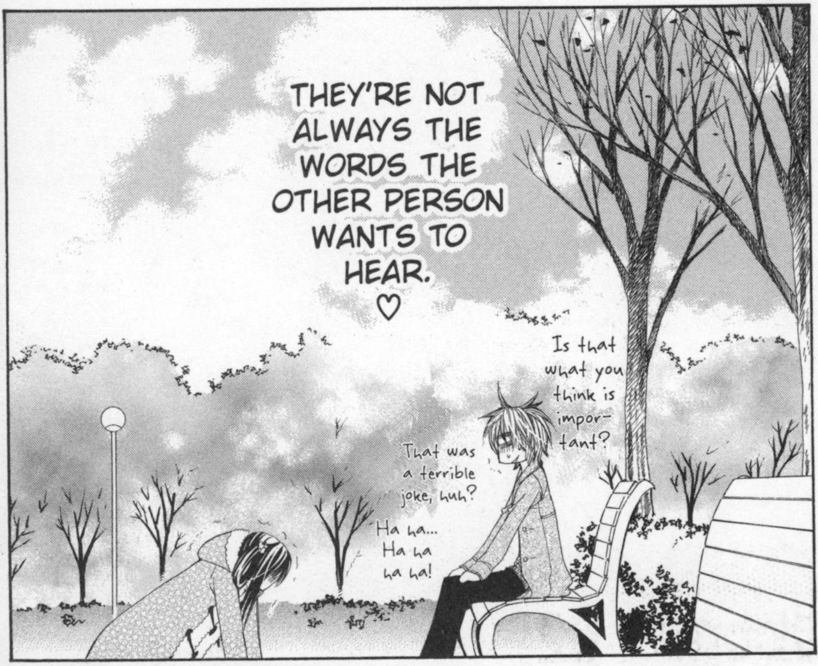
THEY'RE NOT ALWAYS THE WORDS THE OTHER PERSON WANTS TO HEAR. ♡
Is that what you think is impor-tant?
That was a terrible joke, huh?
Ha ha... Ha ha ha ha!

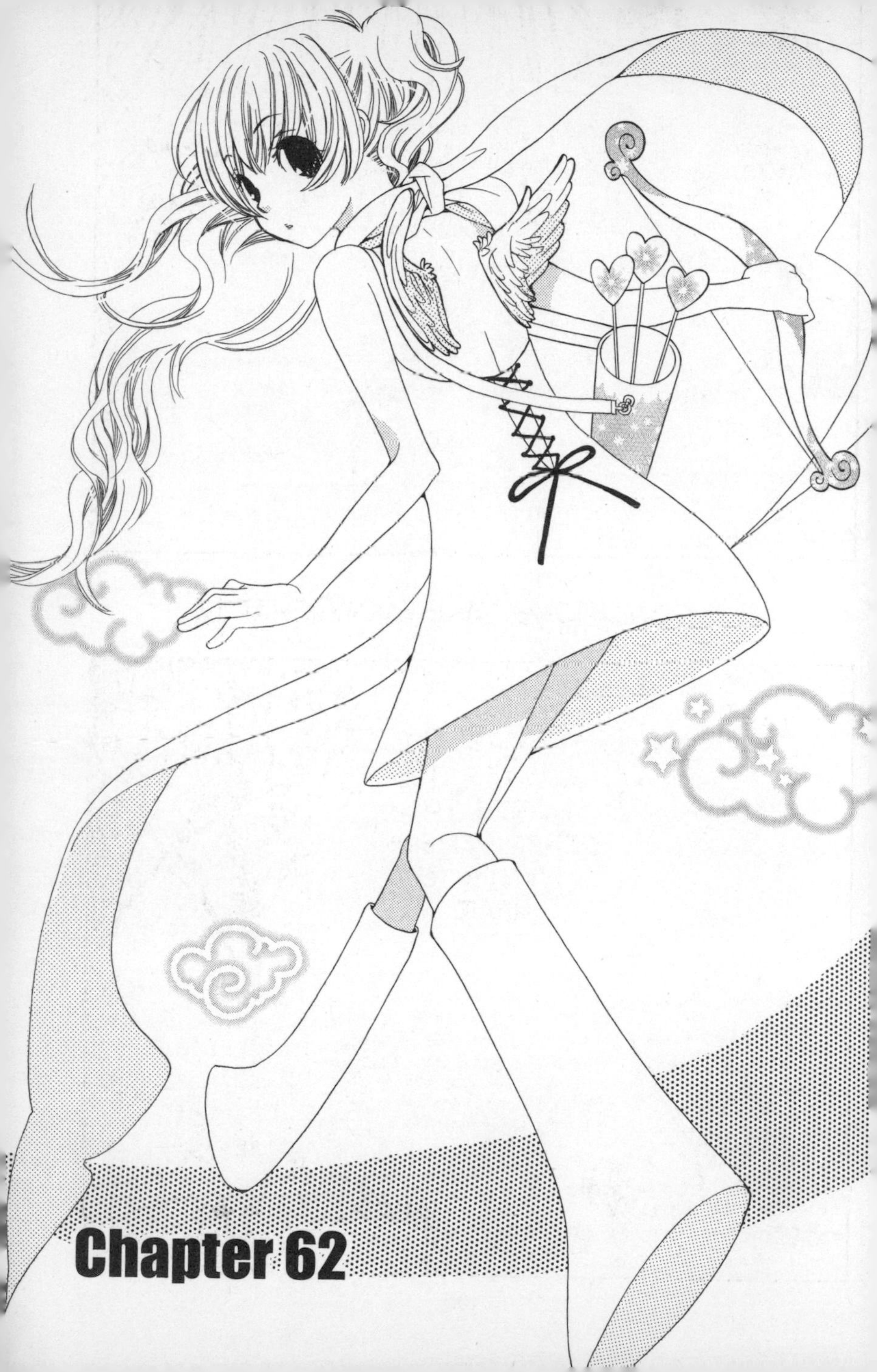

Chapter 62

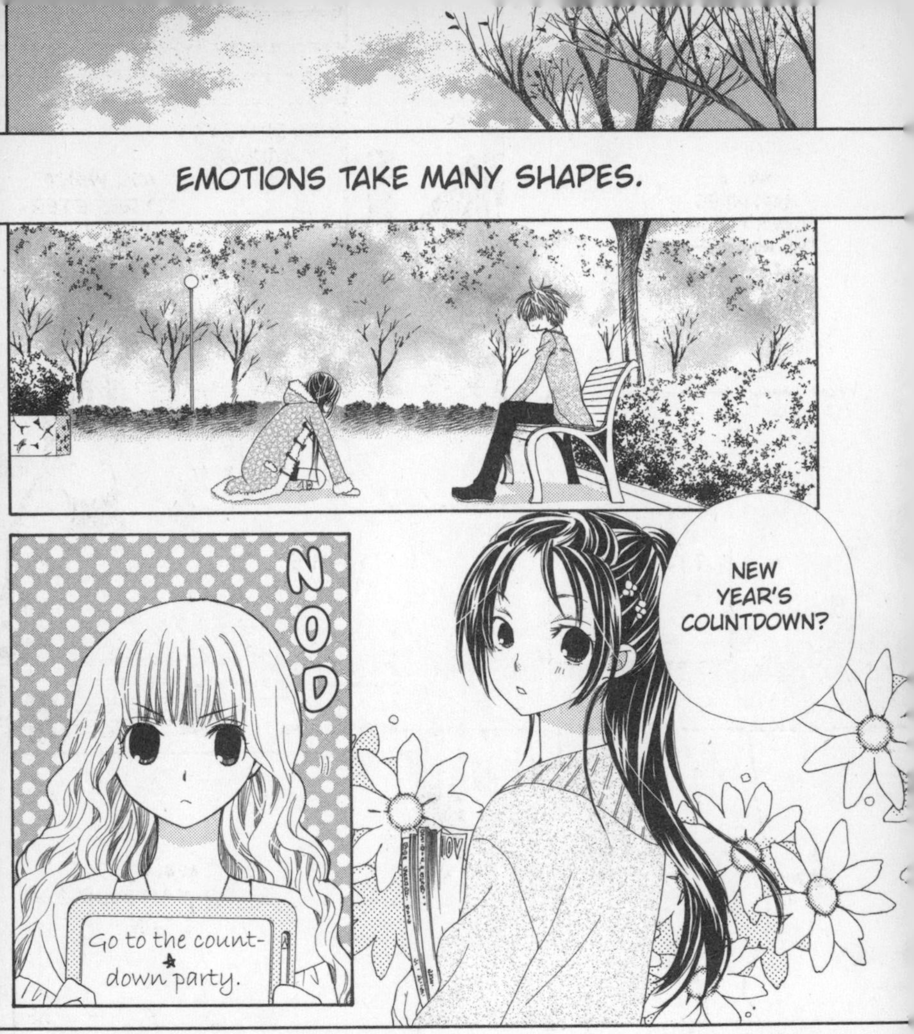
EMOTIONS TAKE MANY SHAPES.
NEW YEAR'S COUNTDOWN?
NOD
Go to the count-down party.

·COLORS·

LATELY I'VE BEEN DRAWING WITH CG AND ANALOG METHODS.
THEY'RE BOTH VERY COMPLICATED AND A LOT OF FUN.
WHICH CG SOFTWARE DO I USE? I'M ASKED THAT A LOT, SO I'LL ANSWER HERE.

I USE FONT SHOP 6 AND PAINTER 9. AND FOR A STYLUS TABLET,
I USE SOMETHING CALLED INTUOS. AFTER ALL IS SAID AND DONE,
ANALOG IS SO MUCH EASIER TO USE...
BUT I THINK I'LL KEEP USING BOTH!

I like the colored ink bottles.

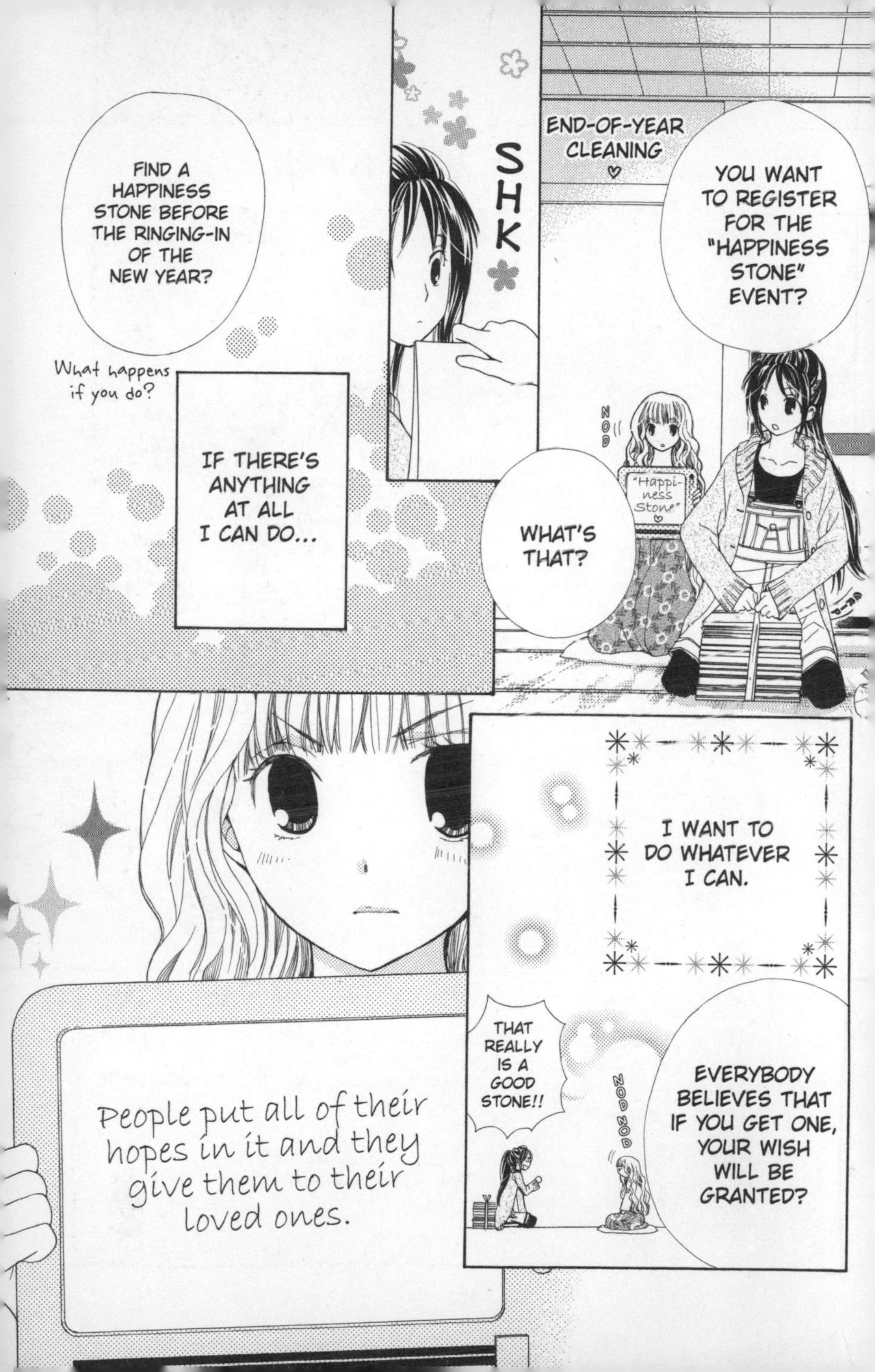
END-OF-YEAR CLEANING ♡
YOU WANT TO REGISTER FOR THE "HAPPINESS STONE" EVENT?
NOD
"Happi-ness Stone" ♡
WHAT'S THAT?
SHK
FIND A HAPPINESS STONE BEFORE THE RINGING-IN OF THE NEW YEAR?
What happens if you do?
IF THERE'S ANYTHING AT ALL I CAN DO...
I WANT TO DO WHATEVER I CAN.
EVERYBODY BELIEVES THAT IF YOU GET ONE, YOUR WISH WILL BE GRANTED?
NOD NOD
THAT REALLY IS A GOOD STONE!!
People put all of their hopes in it and they give them to their loved ones.

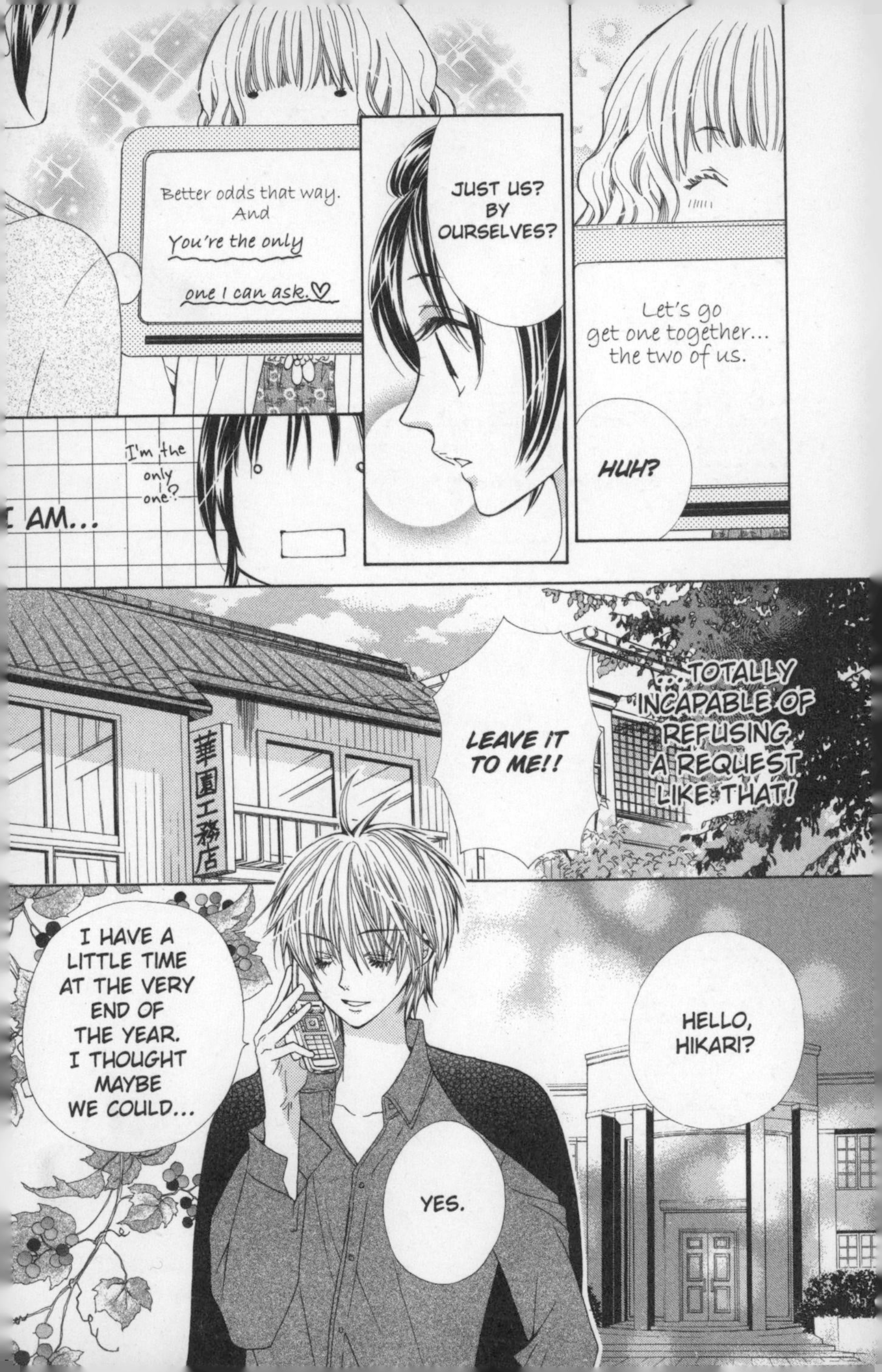
Let's go get one together... the two of us.
HUH?
JUST US? BY OURSELVES?
Better odds that way. And You're the only one I can ask.♡
I'm the only one?
I AM...
...TOTALLY INCAPABLE OF REFUSING A REQUEST LIKE THAT!
LEAVE IT TO ME!!
HELLO, HIKARI?
YES.
I HAVE A LITTLE TIME AT THE VERY END OF THE YEAR. I THOUGHT MAYBE WE COULD...

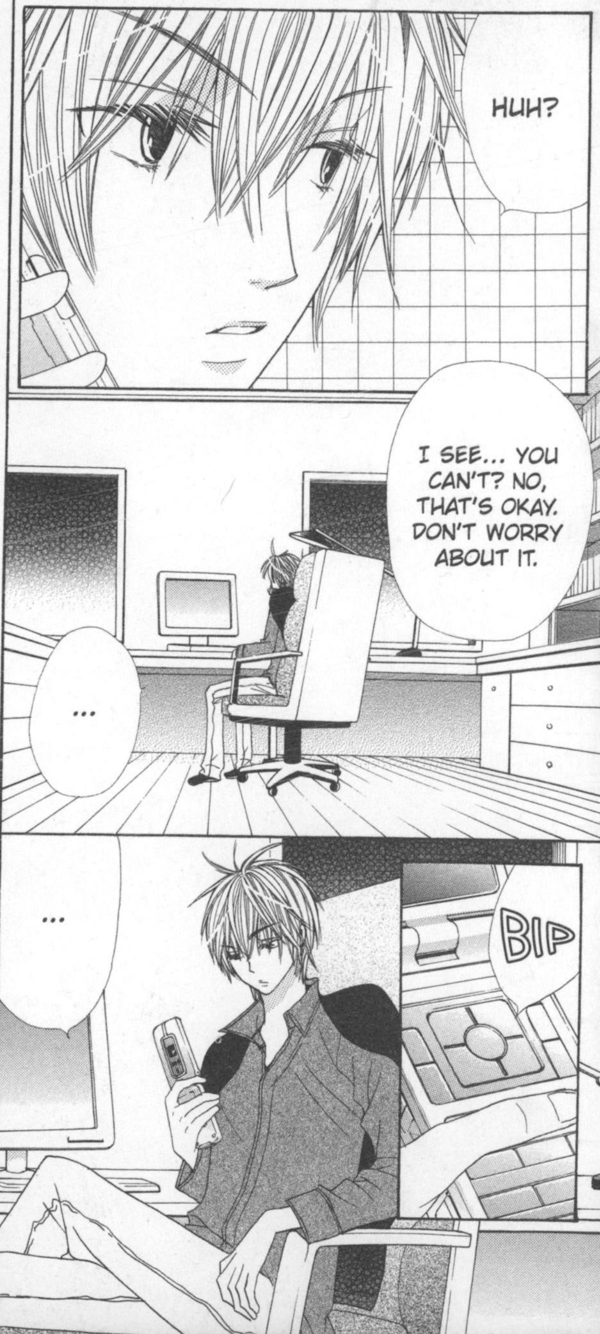
HUH?
I SEE... YOU CAN'T? NO, THAT'S OKAY. DON'T WORRY ABOUT IT.
...
BIP
...

④

•A WEIRD EXPERIENCE•

THE OTHER DAY, MY MOTHER SAID SHE HAD A WEIRD EXPERIENCE.

SHE HAS LIVED HERE FOR DECADES AND SHE KNOWS THE AREA LIKE THE BACK OF HER HAND. BUT THE OTHER DAY, SHE WAS WALKING OUR DOG IN THE NEIGHBORHOOD AND SHE ENDED UP IN A RIVERBED SHE DIDN'T RECOGNIZE.

SHE HAS LIVED HERE FOR DECADES, BUT THERE WAS A RIVERBED SHE HAD NEVER EVEN SEEN.

SHE WALKED A LITTLE FURTHER AND SAW A MAN WALKING SLOWLY BY HIMSELF.

WHEN SHE GOT CLOSE TO HIM, HE SUDDENLY STOPPED AND TURNED HIS HEAD.

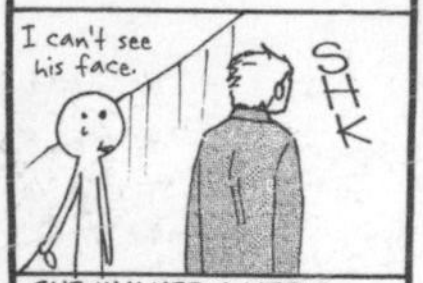
I can't see his face.
SHK

SHE WALKED A LITTLE MORE AND TURNED BACK TO LOOK. HE DIDN'T MOVE AN INCH AFTER SHE PASSED HIM.

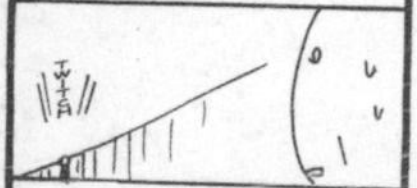

LATER, THERE WAS A WOMAN DRESSED ALL IN BLACK, WALKING WITH HER HEAD DOWN, FOLLOWING MY MOM. AND THEN SHE SAW A BIG BLACK PIG. WHEN SHE FINALLY GOT BACK HOME, IT WAS COMPLETELY DARK, EVEN THOUGH SHE HAD LEFT AT NOON. SHE SAID IT WAS AN INCREDIBLE EXPERIENCE.

HOWEVER...IF THEY WERE ALL NEIGHBORS, THEN WHAT... DOESN'T THAT MAKE THIS STORY KIND OF RUDE? HA HA! SORRY.

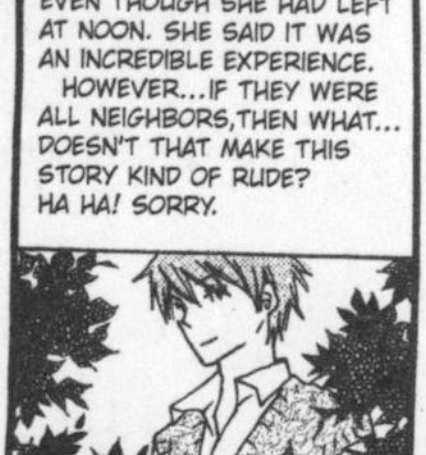

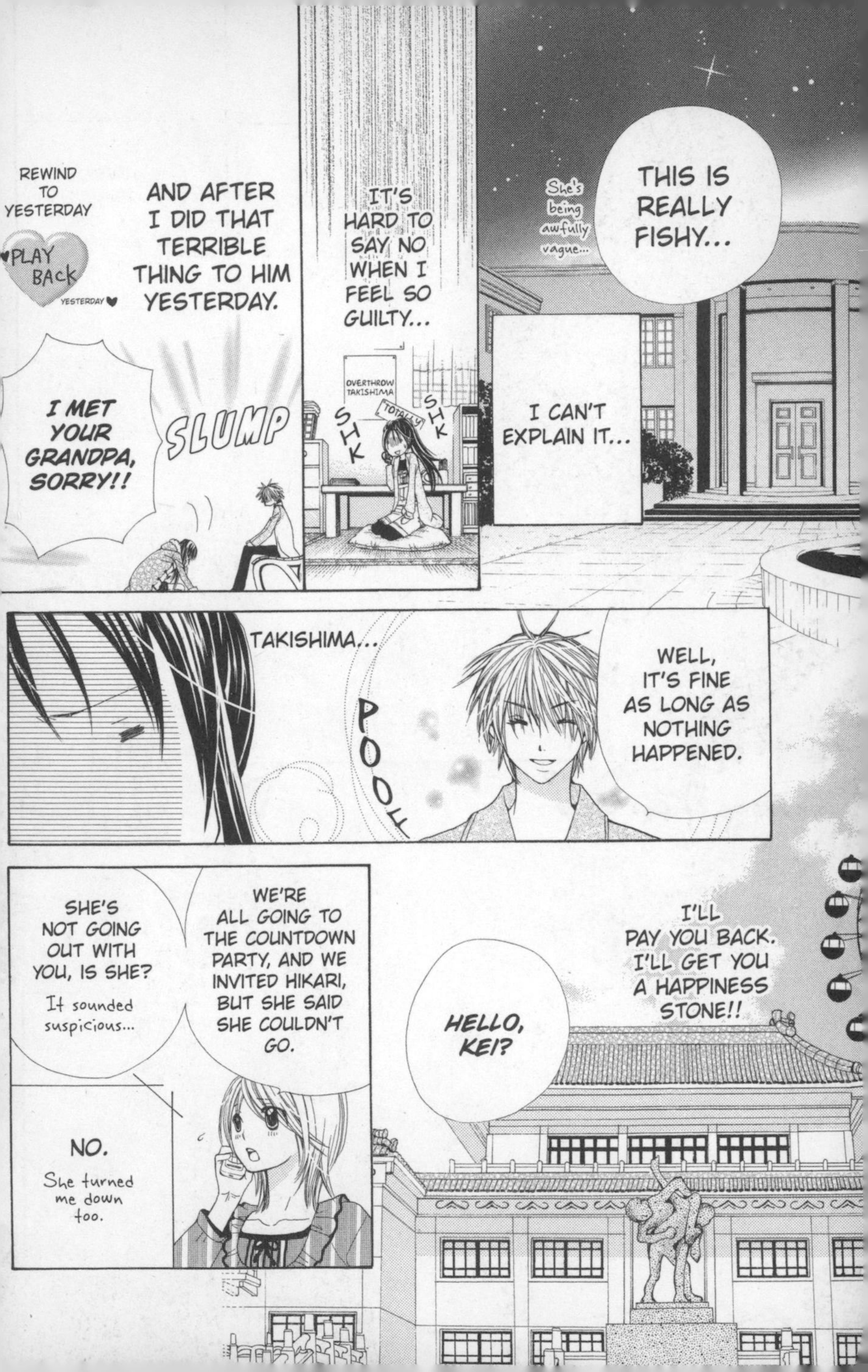
THIS IS REALLY FISHY...
She's being awfully vague...
I CAN'T EXPLAIN IT...
IT'S HARD TO SAY NO WHEN I FEEL SO GUILTY...
OVERTHROW TAKISHIMA
TOTALLY
SHK
SHK
AND AFTER I DID THAT TERRIBLE THING TO HIM YESTERDAY.
REWIND TO YESTERDAY
PLAY BACK
YESTERDAY
SLUMP
I MET YOUR GRANDPA, SORRY!!
WELL, IT'S FINE AS LONG AS NOTHING HAPPENED.
POOF
TAKISHIMA...
I'LL PAY YOU BACK. I'LL GET YOU A HAPPINESS STONE!!
HELLO, KEI?
WE'RE ALL GOING TO THE COUNTDOWN PARTY, AND WE INVITED HIKARI, BUT SHE SAID SHE COULDN'T GO.
SHE'S NOT GOING OUT WITH YOU, IS SHE?
It sounded suspicious...
NO.
She turned me down too.

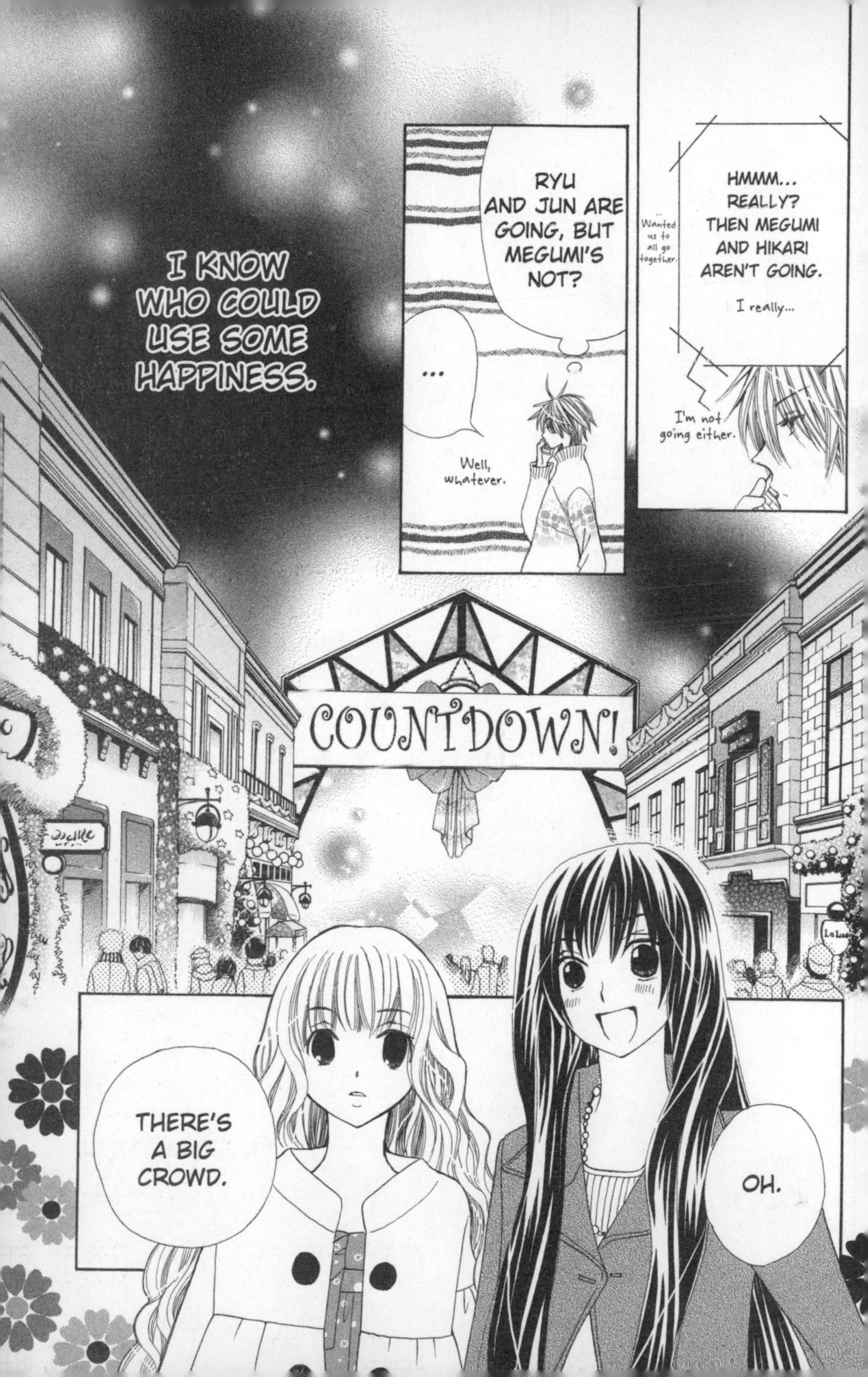
HMMM... REALLY? THEN MEGUMI AND HIKARI AREN'T GOING.
I really...
...Wanted us to all go together.
I'm not going either.
RYU AND JUN ARE GOING, BUT MEGUMI'S NOT?
...
Well, whatever.
I KNOW WHO COULD USE SOME HAPPINESS.
COUNTDOWN!
THERE'S A BIG CROWD.
OH.

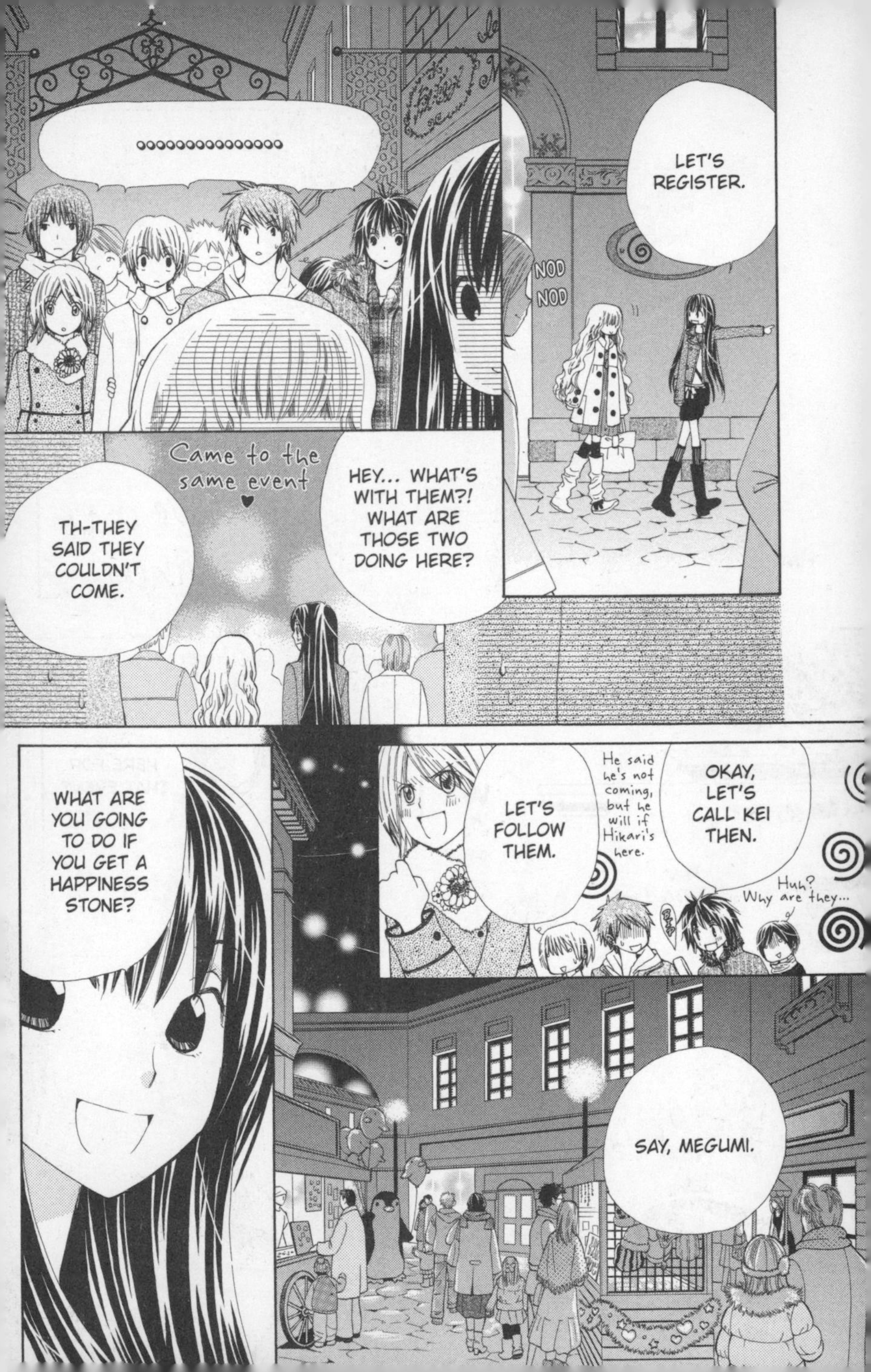
LET'S REGISTER.
NOD NOD
oooooooooooooooo
HEY... WHAT'S WITH THEM?! WHAT ARE THOSE TWO DOING HERE?
Came to the same event
TH-THEY SAID THEY COULDN'T COME.
OKAY, LET'S CALL KEI THEN.
Huh? Why are they...
He said he's not coming, but he will if Hikari's here.
LET'S FOLLOW THEM.
SAY, MEGUMI.
WHAT ARE YOU GOING TO DO IF YOU GET A HAPPINESS STONE?

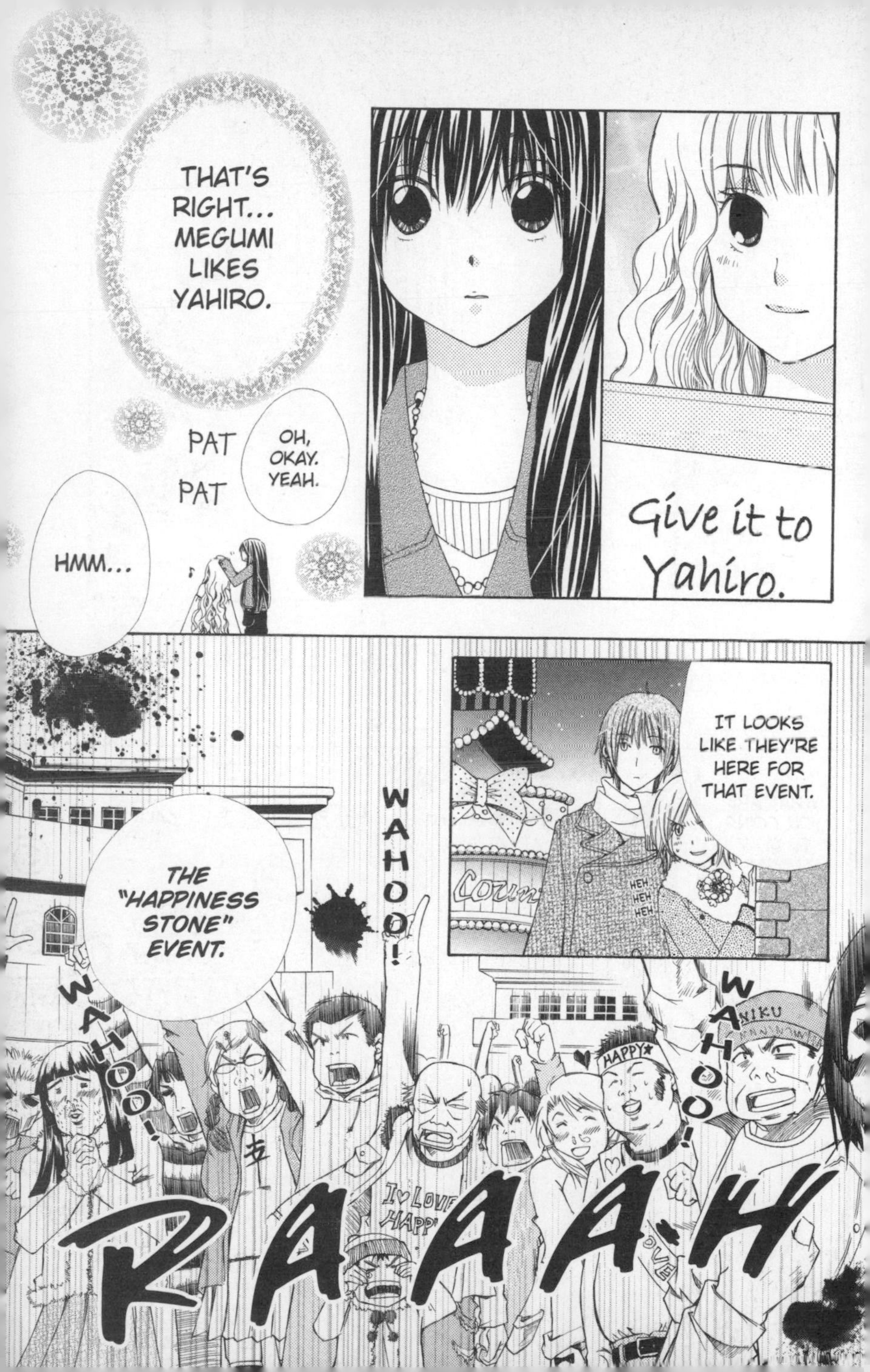
Give it to Yahiro.
THAT'S RIGHT... MEGUMI LIKES YAHIRO.
OH, OKAY. YEAH.
PAT PAT
HMM...
IT LOOKS LIKE THEY'RE HERE FOR THAT EVENT.
HEH HEH HEH
WAHOO!
WAHOO!
THE "HAPPINESS STONE" EVENT.
WAHOO!
RAAAH

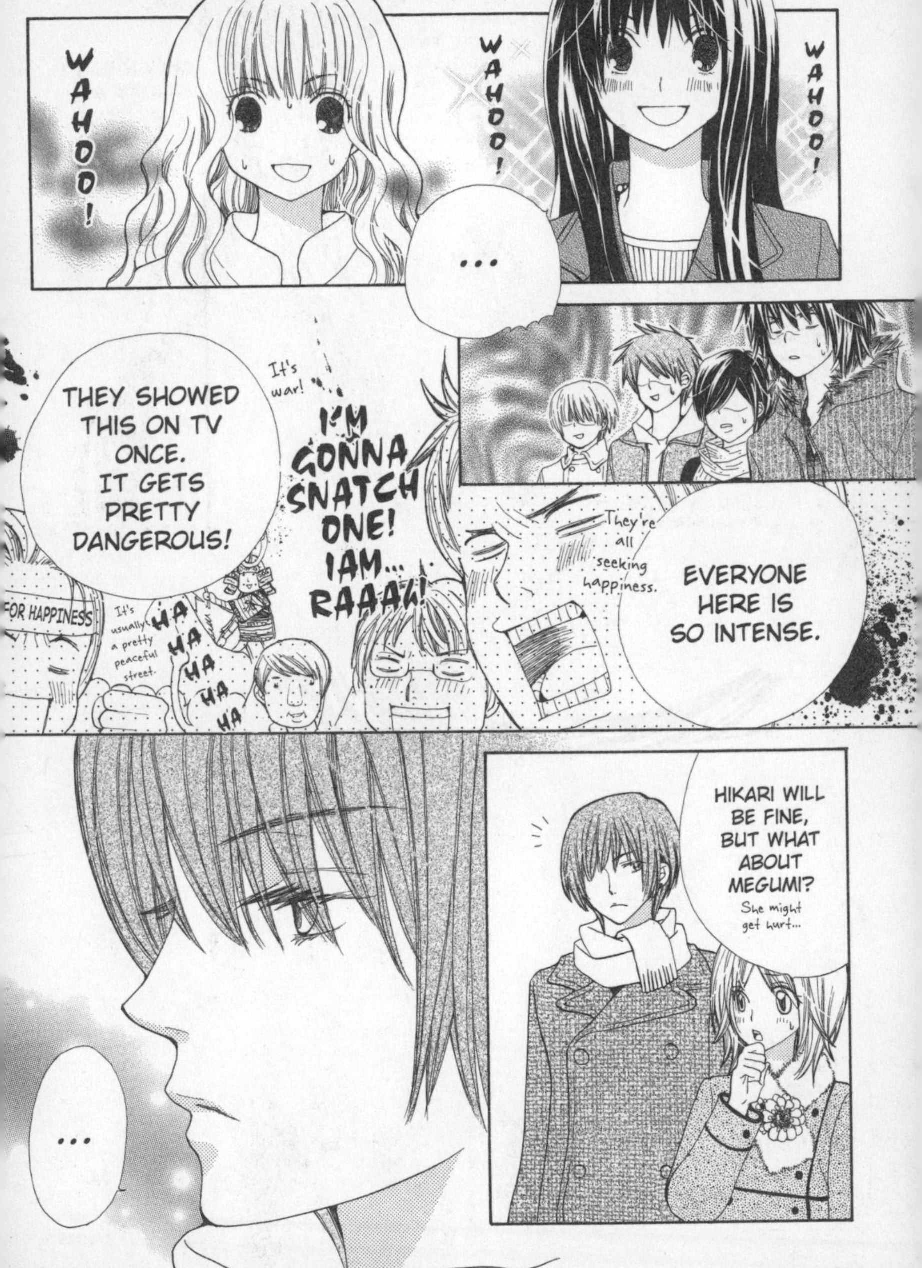

WAHOO!
WAHOO!
WAHOO!
...
EVERYONE HERE IS SO INTENSE.
They're all seeking happiness.
I'M GONNA SNATCH ONE! IAM... RAAAH!
It's war!
THEY SHOWED THIS ON TV ONCE. IT GETS PRETTY DANGEROUS!
FOR HAPPINESS
HA HA HA HA HA
It's usually a pretty peaceful street.
HIKARI WILL BE FINE, BUT WHAT ABOUT MEGUMI?
She might get hurt...
...

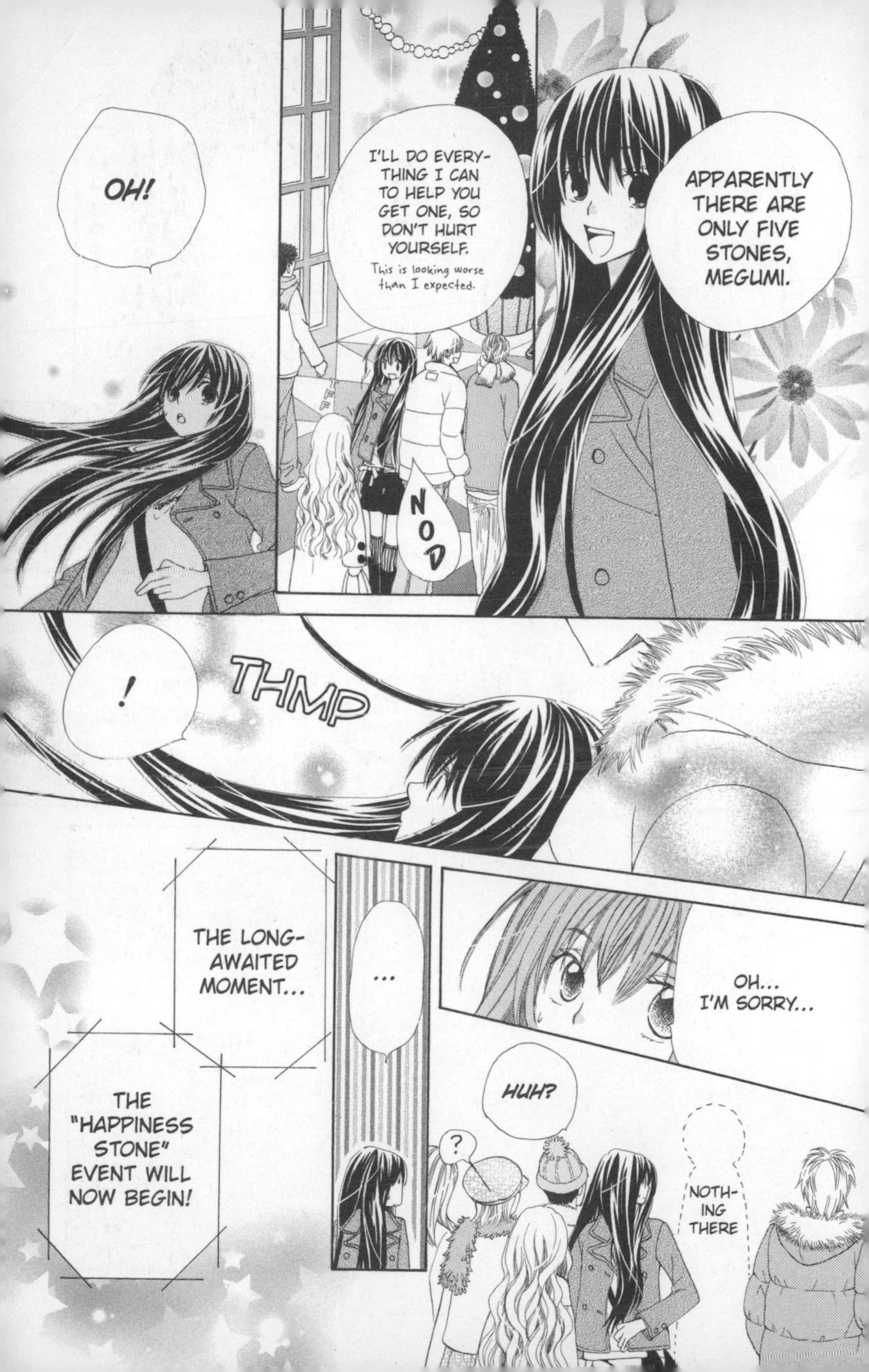
APPARENTLY THERE ARE ONLY FIVE STONES, MEGUMI.
I'LL DO EVERYTHING I CAN TO HELP YOU GET ONE, SO DON'T HURT YOURSELF.
This is looking worse than I expected.
NOD
TFF
OH!
THMP
!
OH... I'M SORRY...
HUH?
?
NOTHING THERE
...
THE LONG-AWAITED MOMENT...
THE "HAPPINESS STONE" EVENT WILL NOW BEGIN!

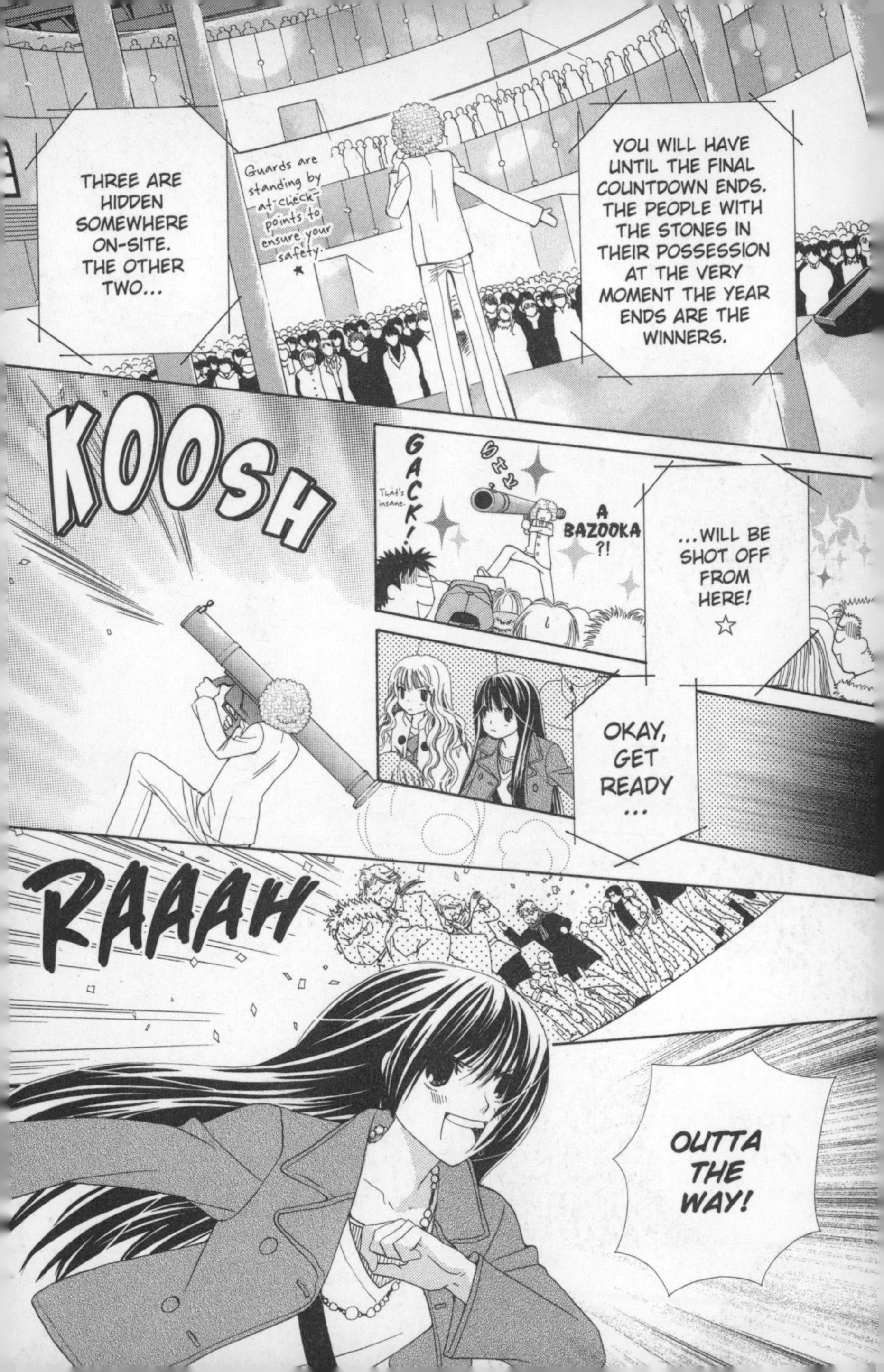
YOU WILL HAVE UNTIL THE FINAL COUNTDOWN ENDS. THE PEOPLE WITH THE STONES IN THEIR POSSESSION AT THE VERY MOMENT THE YEAR ENDS ARE THE WINNERS.
Guards are standing by at check-points to ensure your safety. ★
THREE ARE HIDDEN SOMEWHERE ON-SITE. THE OTHER TWO...
...WILL BE SHOT OFF FROM HERE! ☆
A BAZOOKA ?!
GACK!
That's insane.
KOOSH
OKAY, GET READY ...
RAAAH
OUTTA THE WAY!

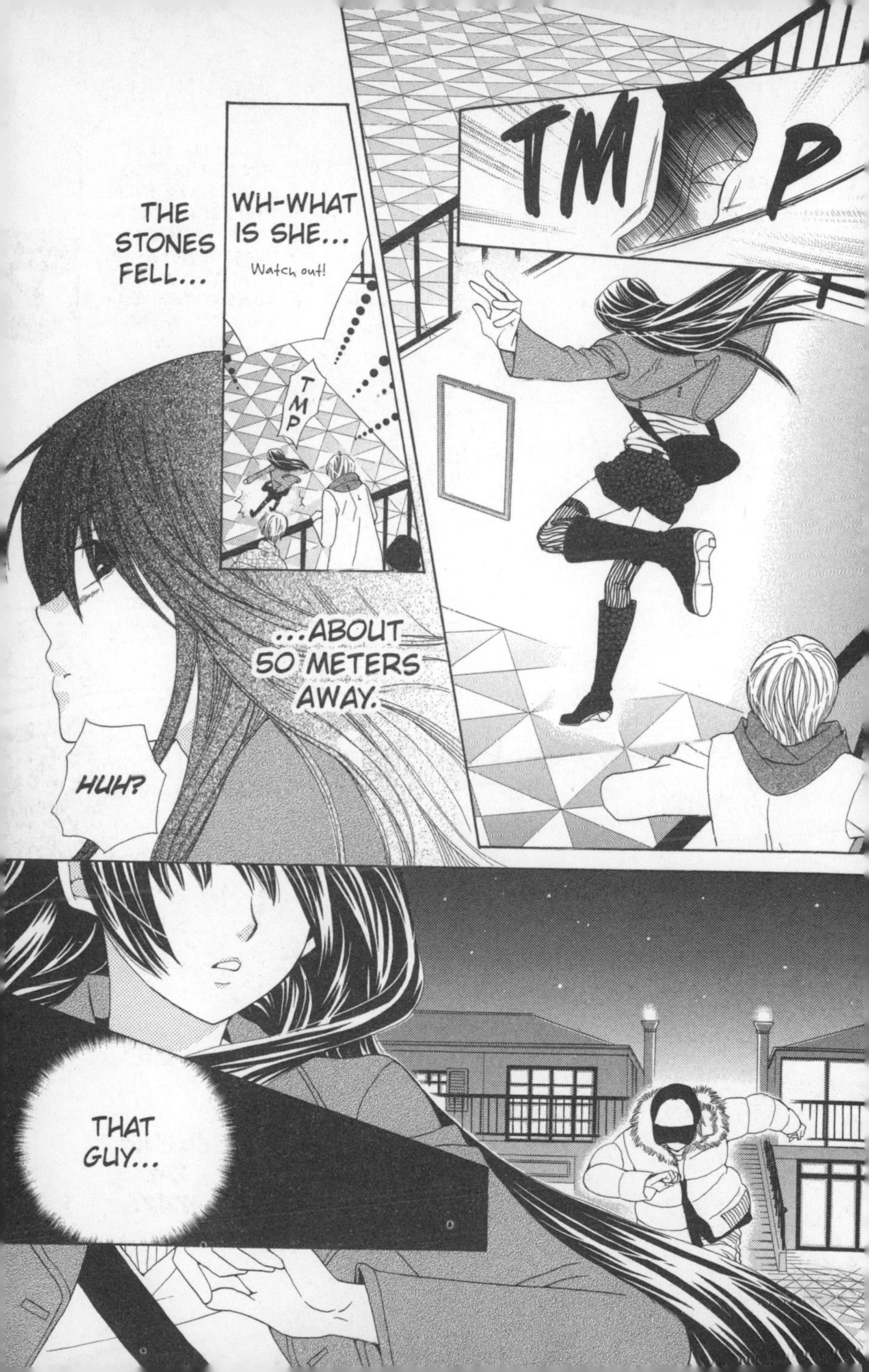
TMP
WH-WHAT IS SHE...
Watch out!
TMP
THE STONES FELL...
...ABOUT 50 METERS AWAY.
HUH?
THAT GUY...

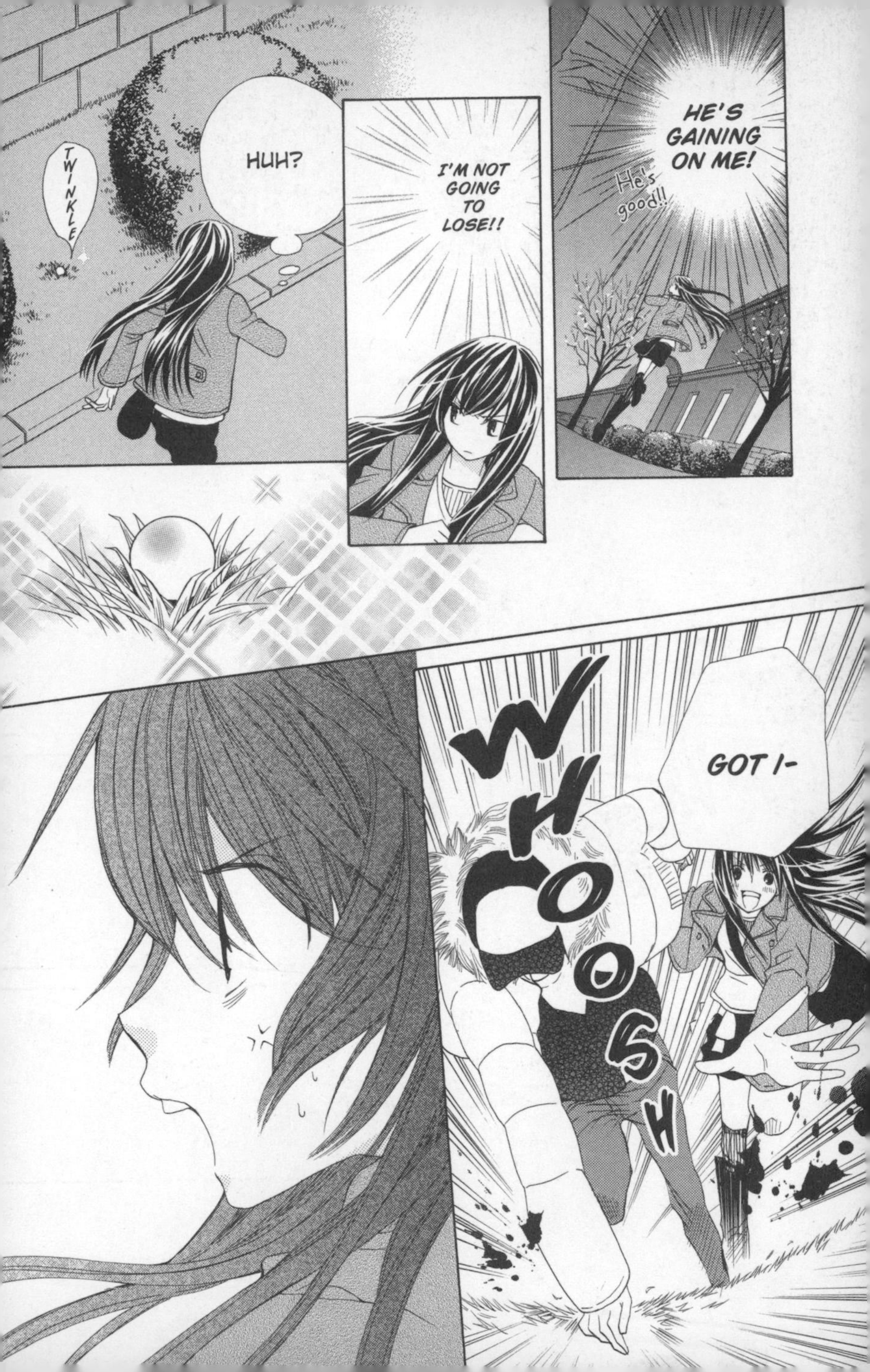
HE'S GAINING ON ME!
He's good!!
I'M NOT GOING TO LOSE!!
HUH?
TWINKLE
GOT I-
WHOOSH

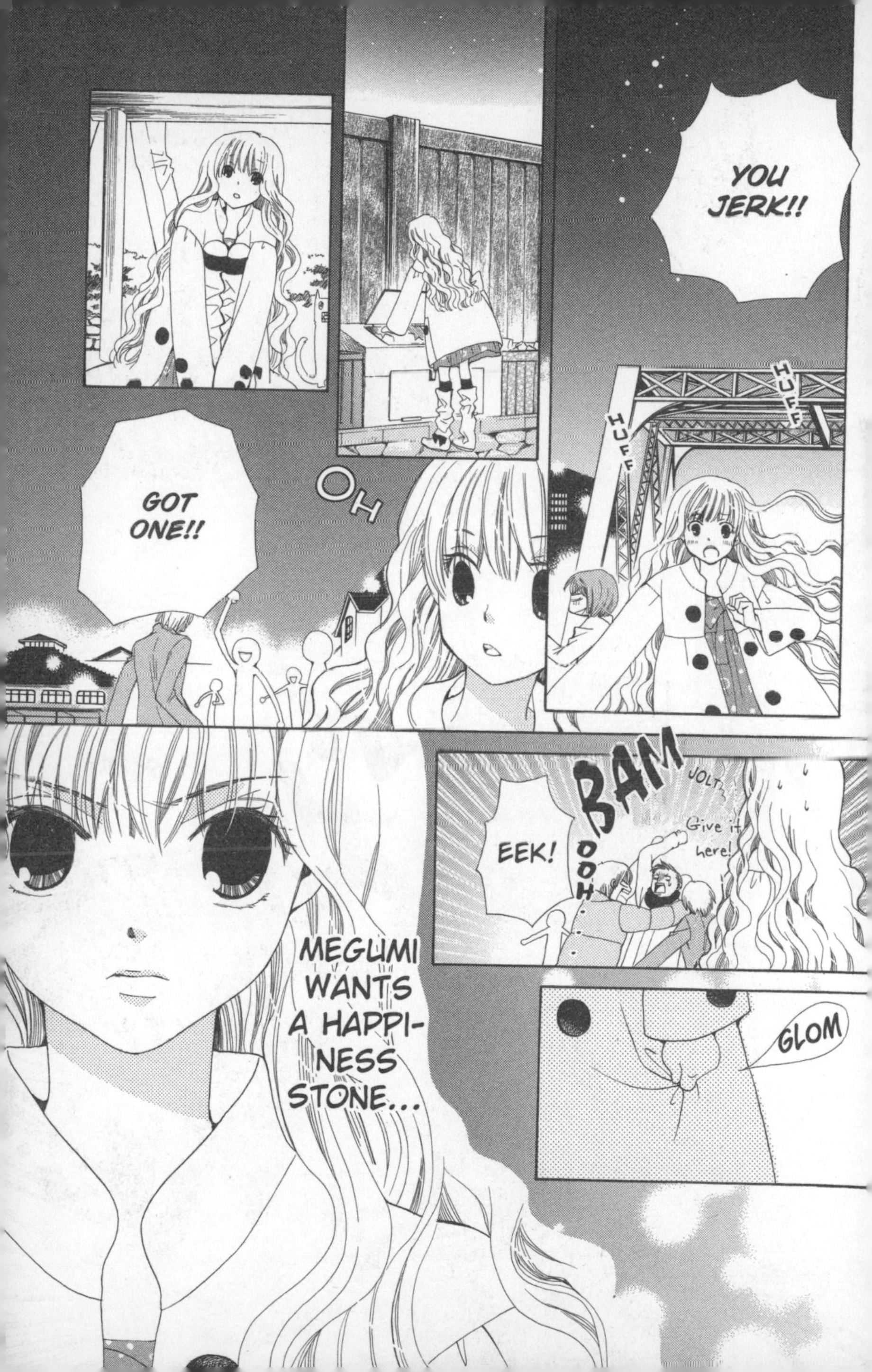
YOU JERK!!
HUFF HUFF
GOT ONE!!
OH
BAM
JOLT
Give it here!
EEK!
OOH
GLOM
MEGUMI WANTS A HAPPINESS STONE...

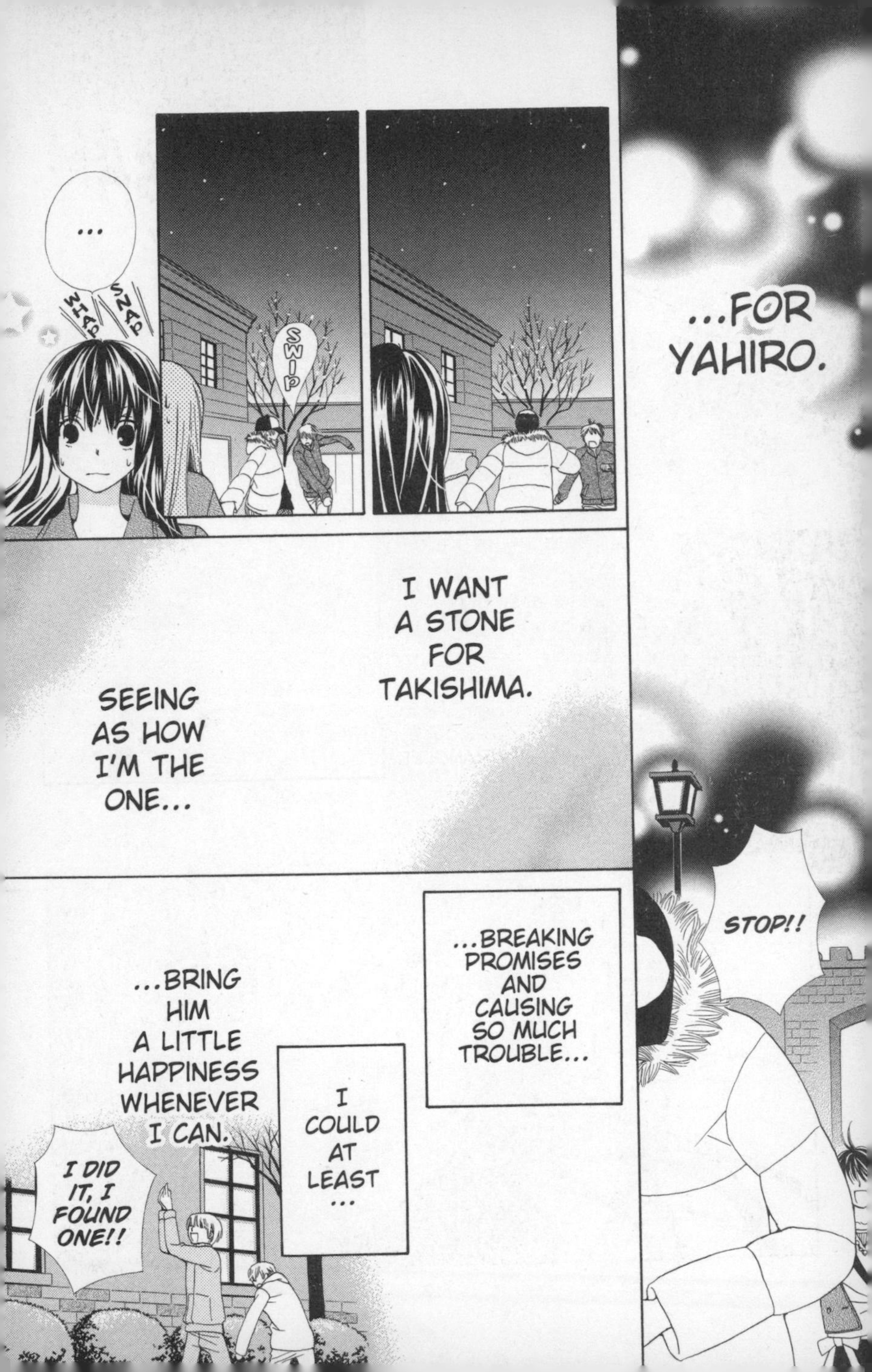
...FOR YAHIRO.
STOP!!
SWIP
...
WHAP
SNAP
I WANT A STONE FOR TAKISHIMA.
SEEING AS HOW I'M THE ONE...
...BREAKING PROMISES AND CAUSING SO MUCH TROUBLE...
I COULD AT LEAST...
...BRING HIM A LITTLE HAPPINESS WHENEVER I CAN.
I DID IT, I FOUND ONE!!

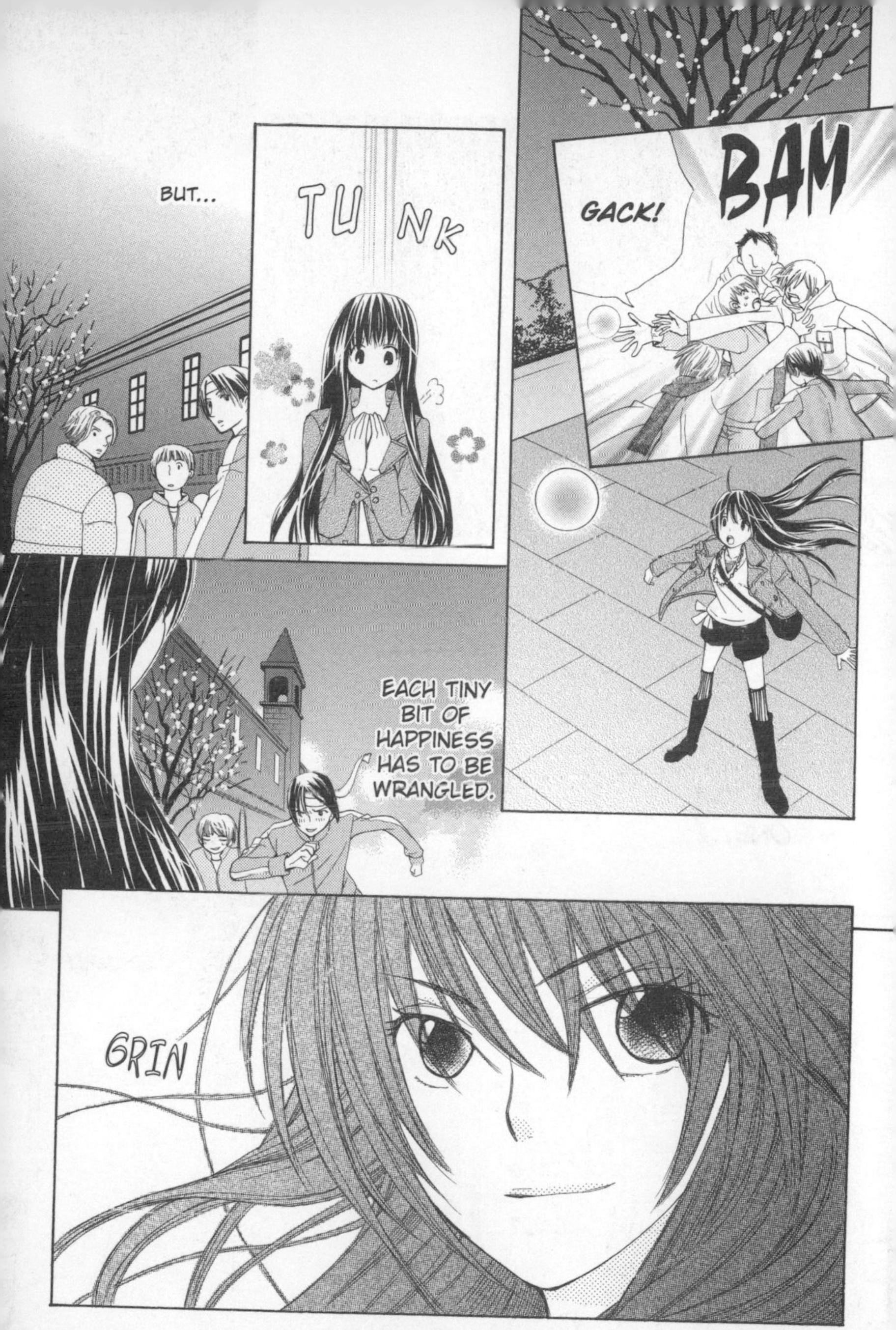
BAM
GACK!
TUNK
BUT...
EACH TINY BIT OF HAPPINESS HAS TO BE WRANGLED.
GRIN

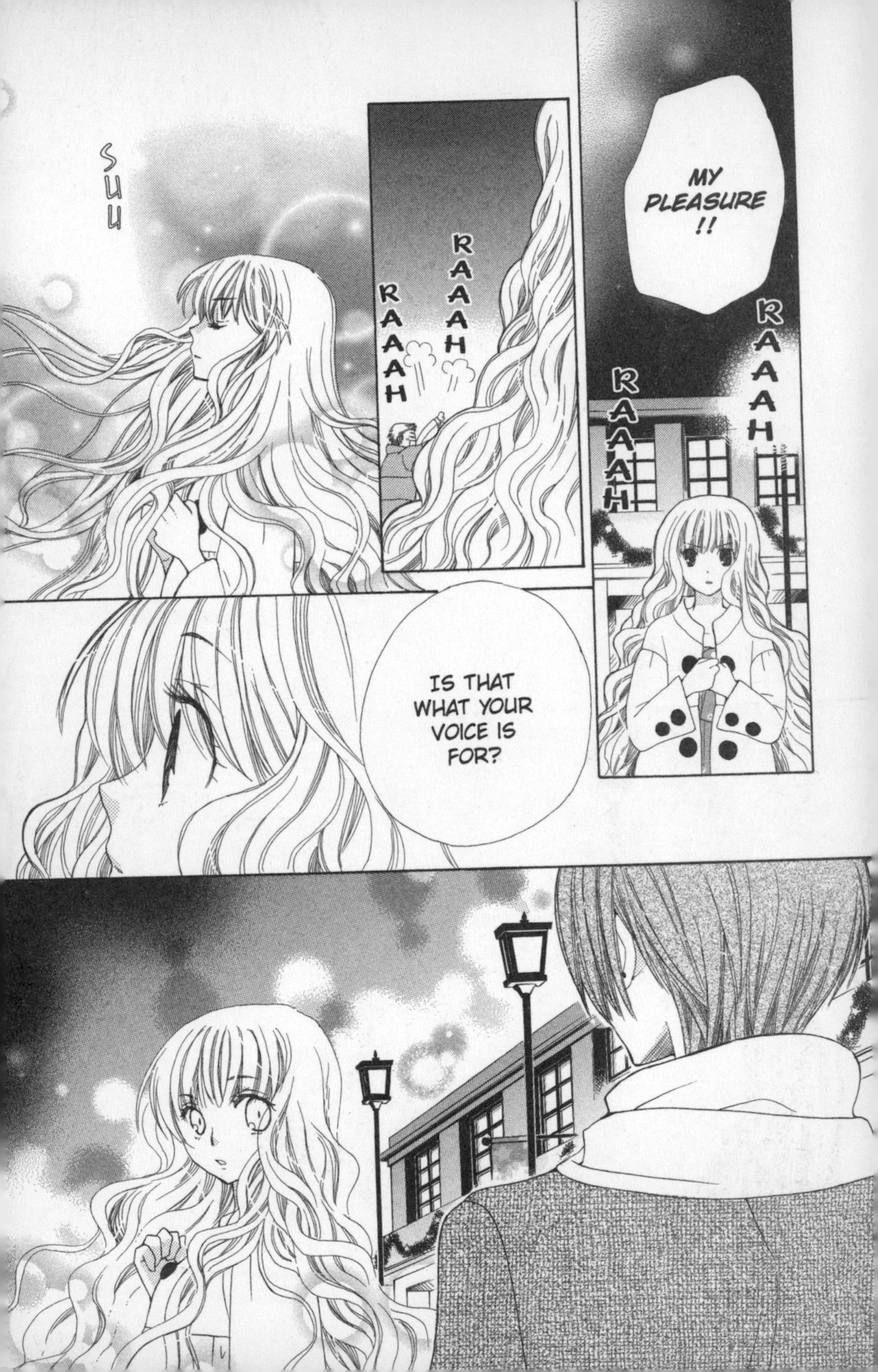
MY PLEASURE!!
RAAAH
RAAAH
RAAAH
RAAAH
SUU
IS THAT WHAT YOUR VOICE IS FOR?

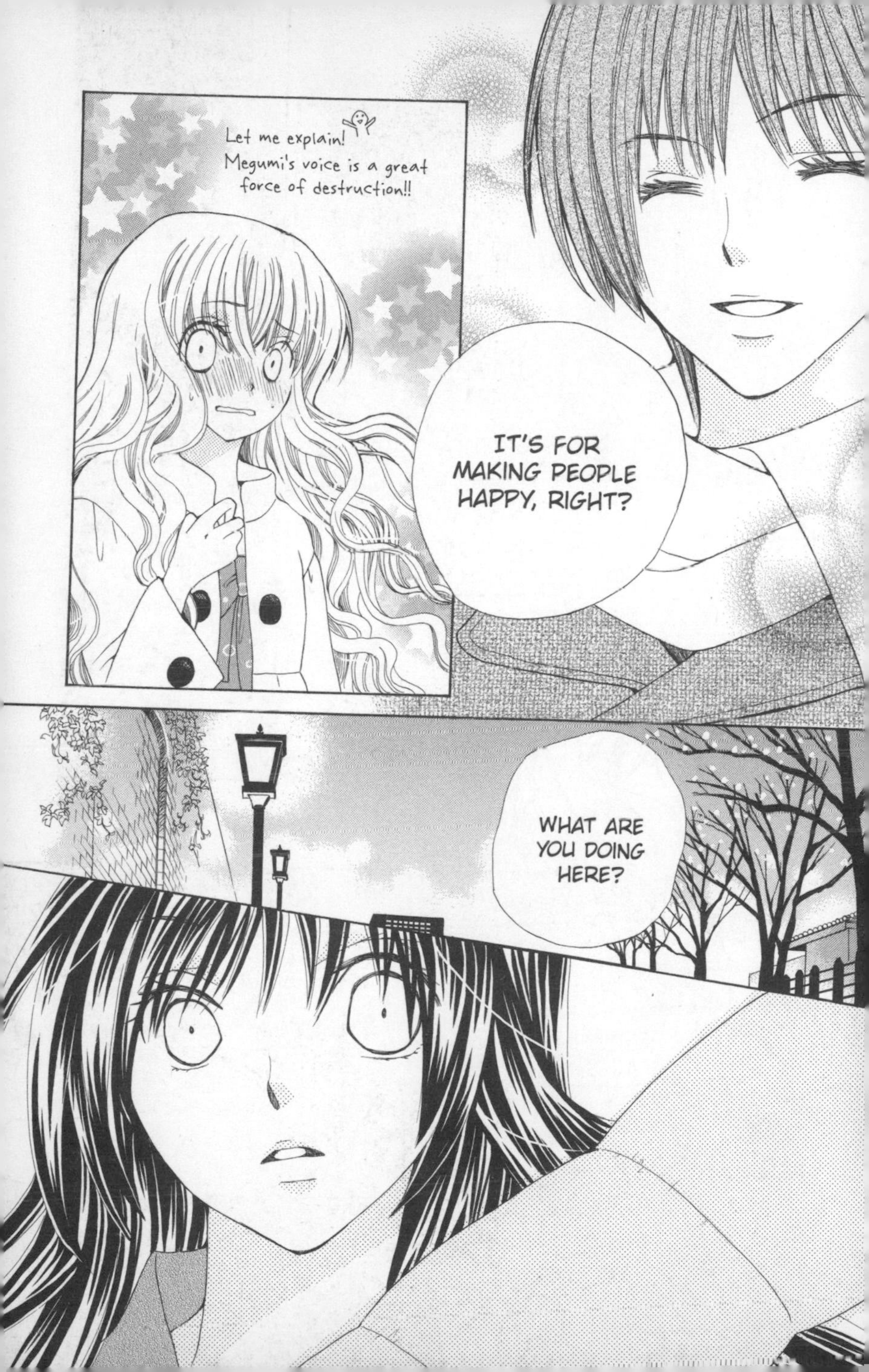
IT'S FOR MAKING PEOPLE HAPPY, RIGHT?
Let me explain! Megumi's voice is a great force of destruction!!
WHAT ARE YOU DOING HERE?

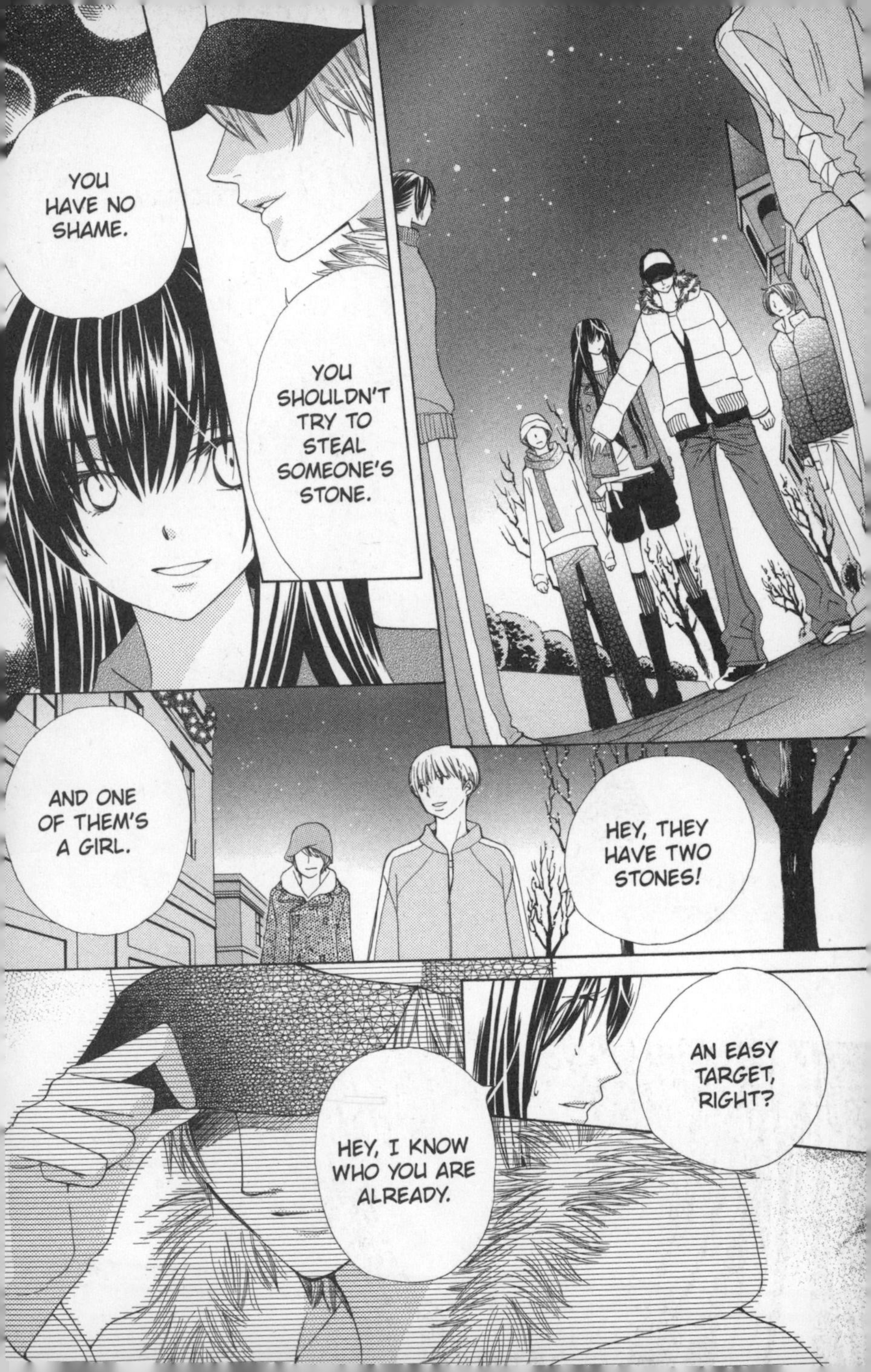
YOU SHOULDN'T TRY TO STEAL SOMEONE'S STONE.
YOU HAVE NO SHAME.
HEY, THEY HAVE TWO STONES!
AND ONE OF THEM'S A GIRL.
AN EASY TARGET, RIGHT?
HEY, I KNOW WHO YOU ARE ALREADY.

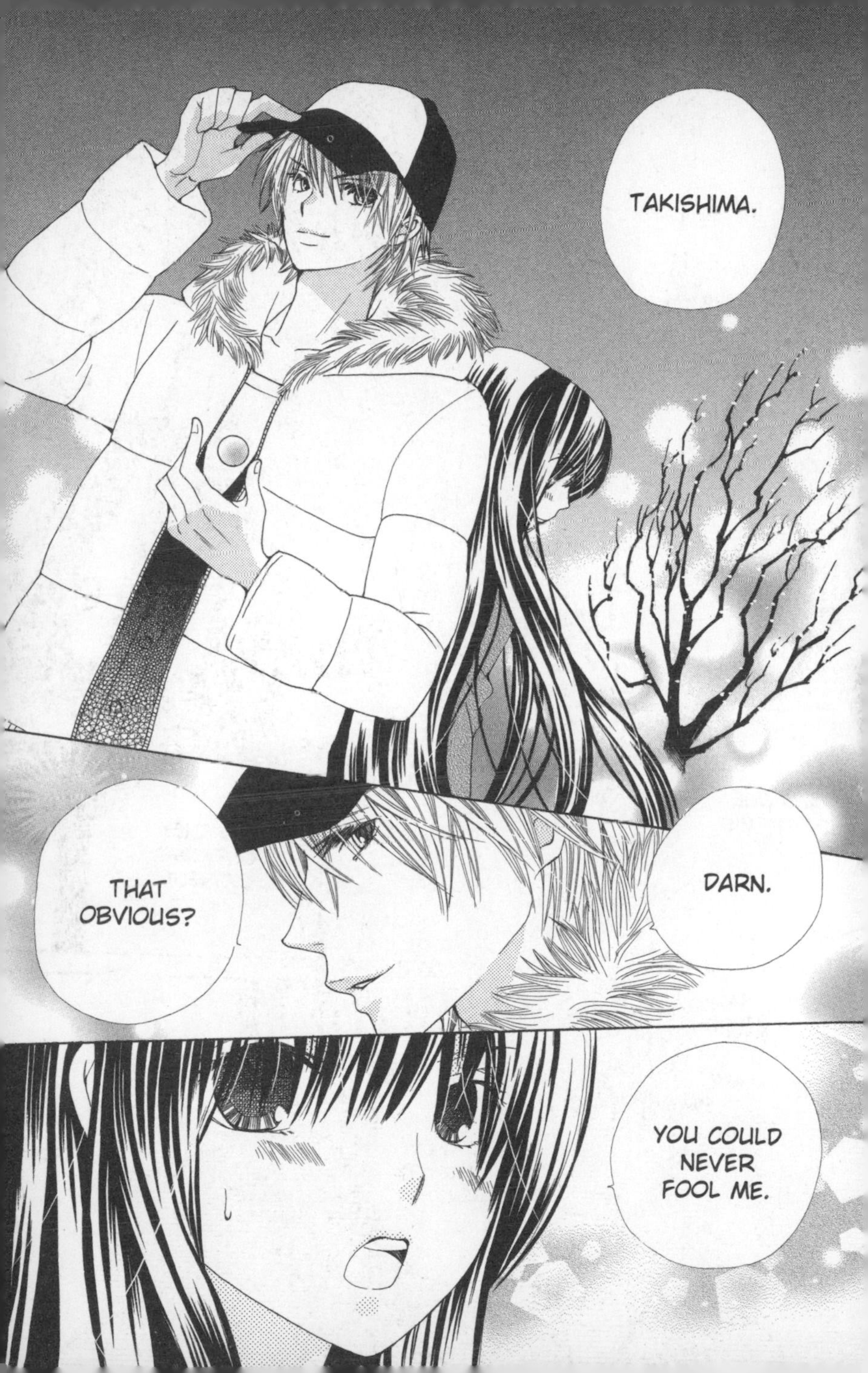
TAKISHIMA.
DARN.
THAT OBVIOUS?
YOU COULD NEVER FOOL ME.

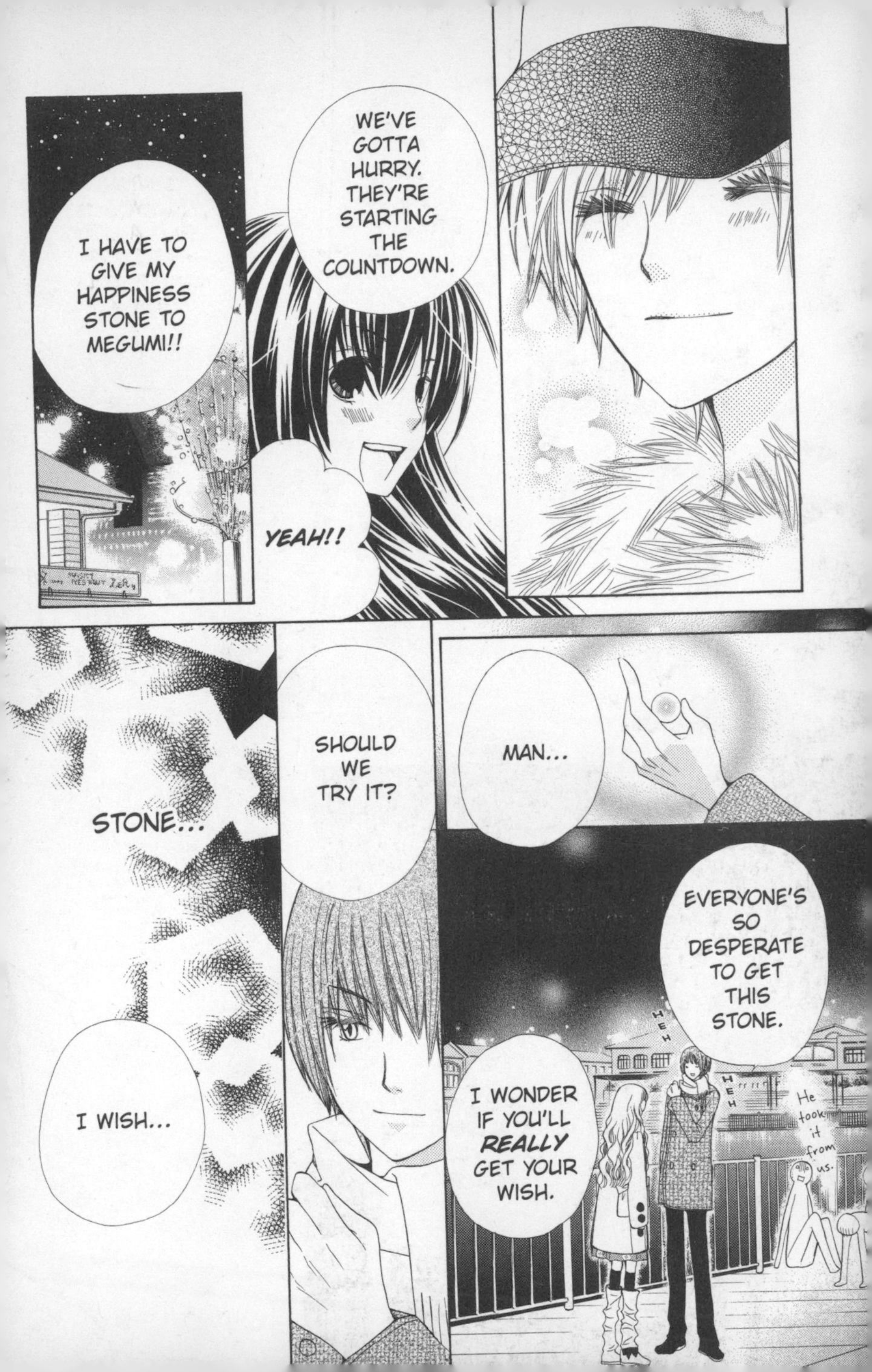
WE'VE GOTTA HURRY. THEY'RE STARTING THE COUNTDOWN.
YEAH!!
I HAVE TO GIVE MY HAPPINESS STONE TO MEGUMI!!
MAN...
EVERYONE'S SO DESPERATE TO GET THIS STONE.
HEH
HEH
He took it from us.
I WONDER IF YOU'LL *REALLY* GET YOUR WISH.
SHOULD WE TRY IT?
STONE...
I WISH...

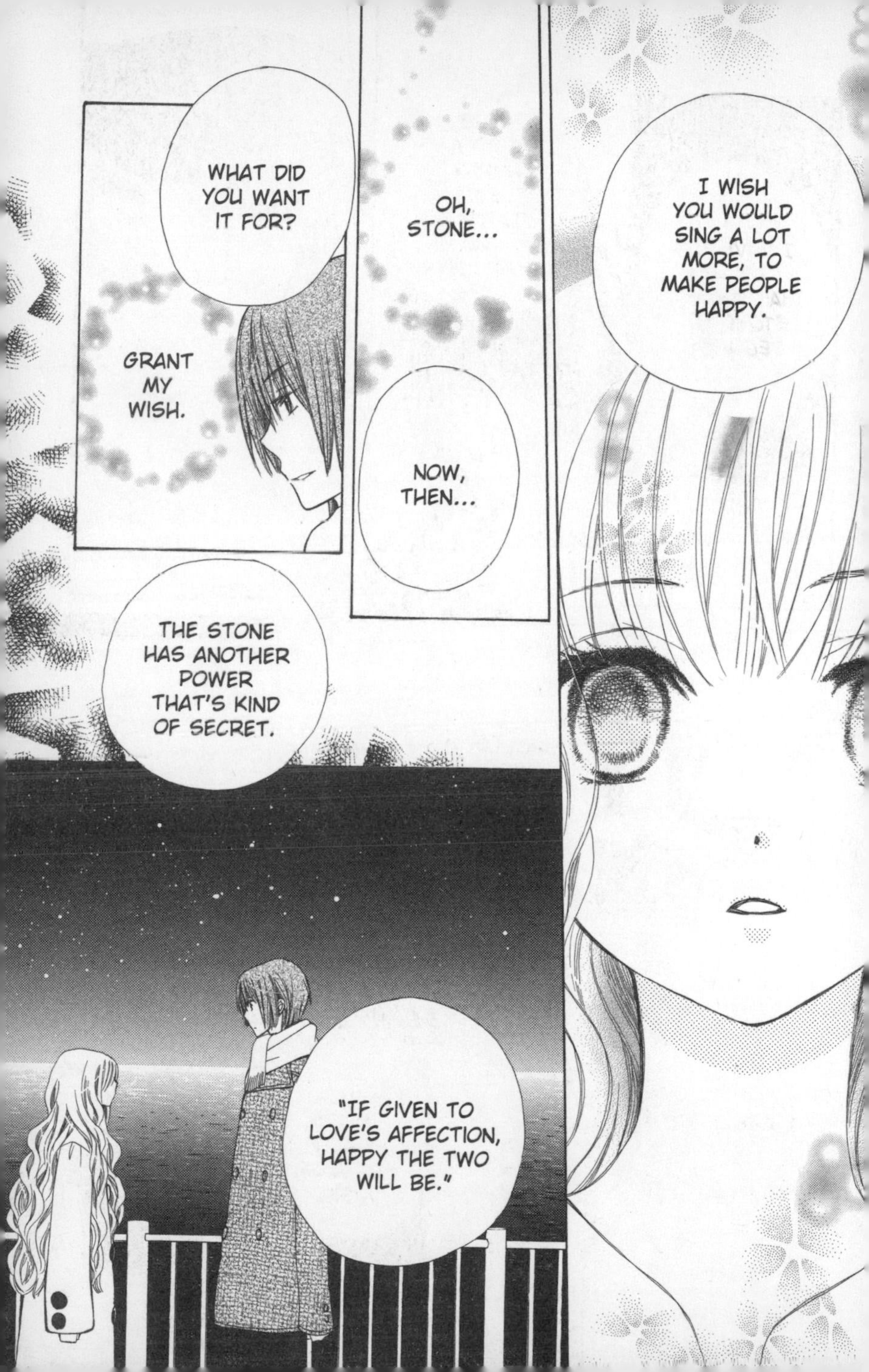

I WISH YOU WOULD SING A LOT MORE, TO MAKE PEOPLE HAPPY.
OH, STONE...
NOW, THEN...
WHAT DID YOU WANT IT FOR?
GRANT MY WISH.
THE STONE HAS ANOTHER POWER THAT'S KIND OF SECRET.
"IF GIVEN TO LOVE'S AFFECTION, HAPPY THE TWO WILL BE."

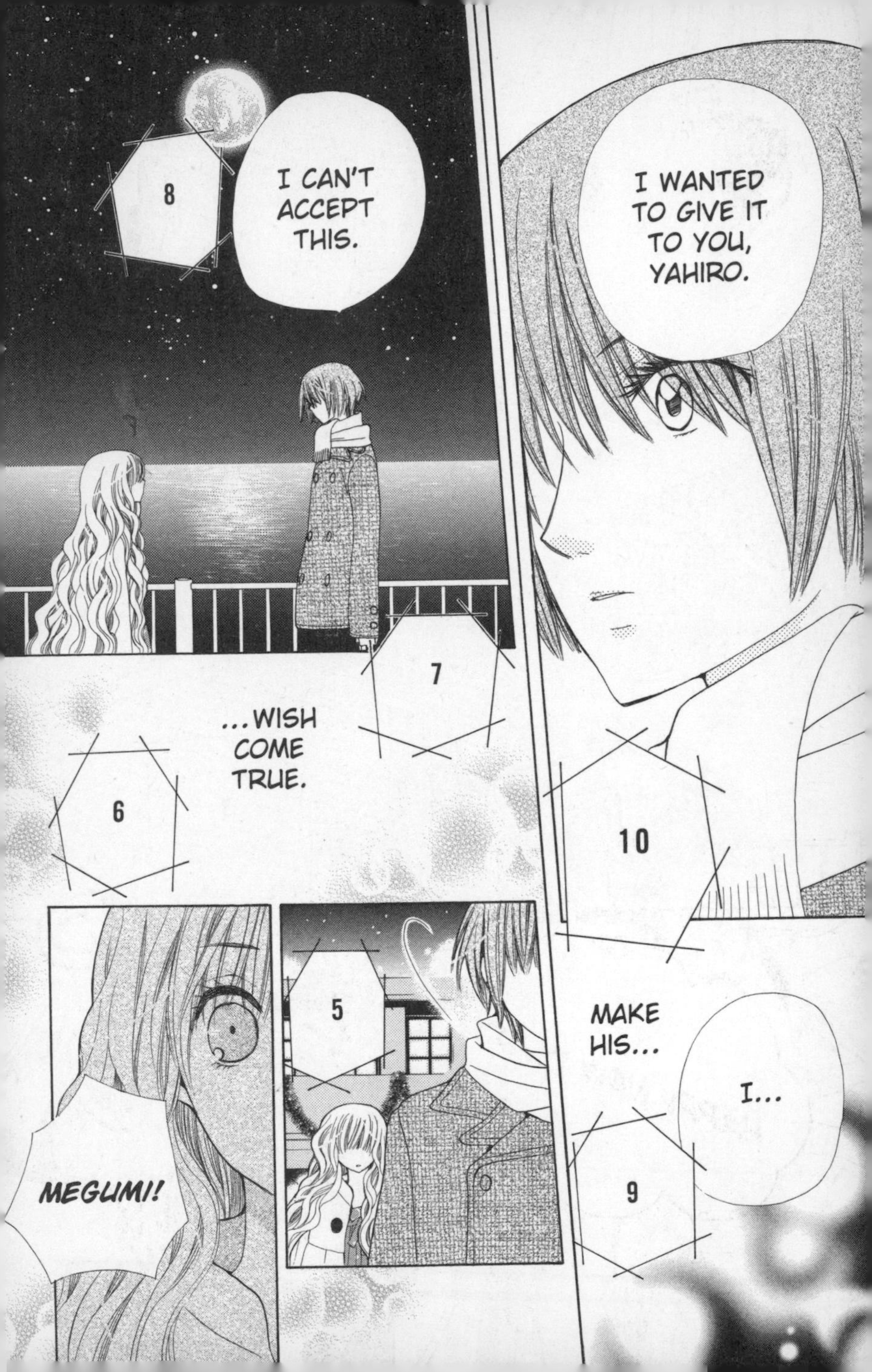
I WANTED TO GIVE IT TO YOU, YAHIRO.
I CAN'T ACCEPT THIS.
8
7
10
MAKE HIS...
...WISH COME TRUE.
6
I...
9
5
MEGUMI!

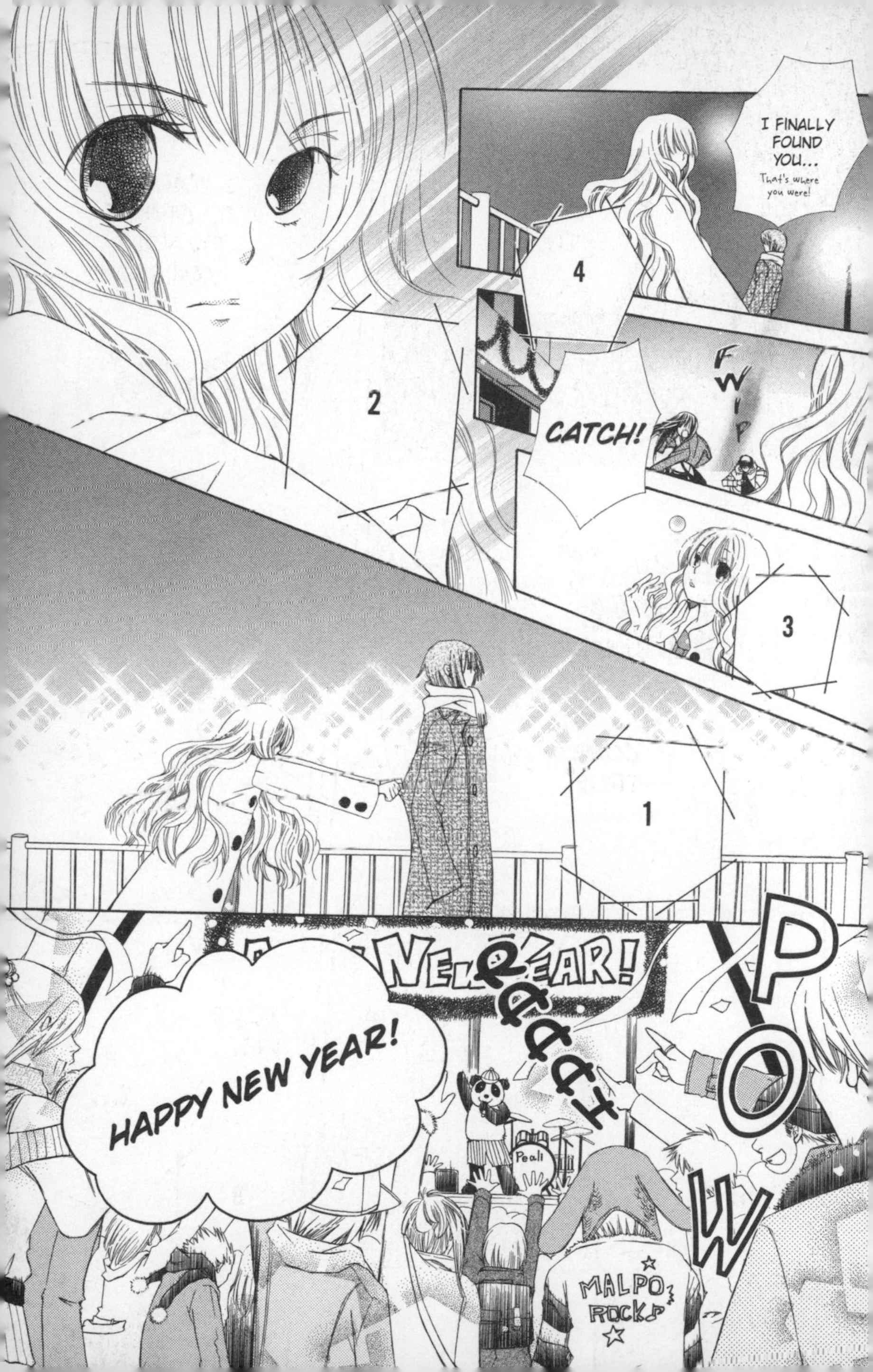
I FINALLY FOUND YOU...
That's where you were!
4
FWIP
CATCH!
3
2
1
POW
REAAAH
HAPPY NEW YEAR!
Peali
MALPO ROCK

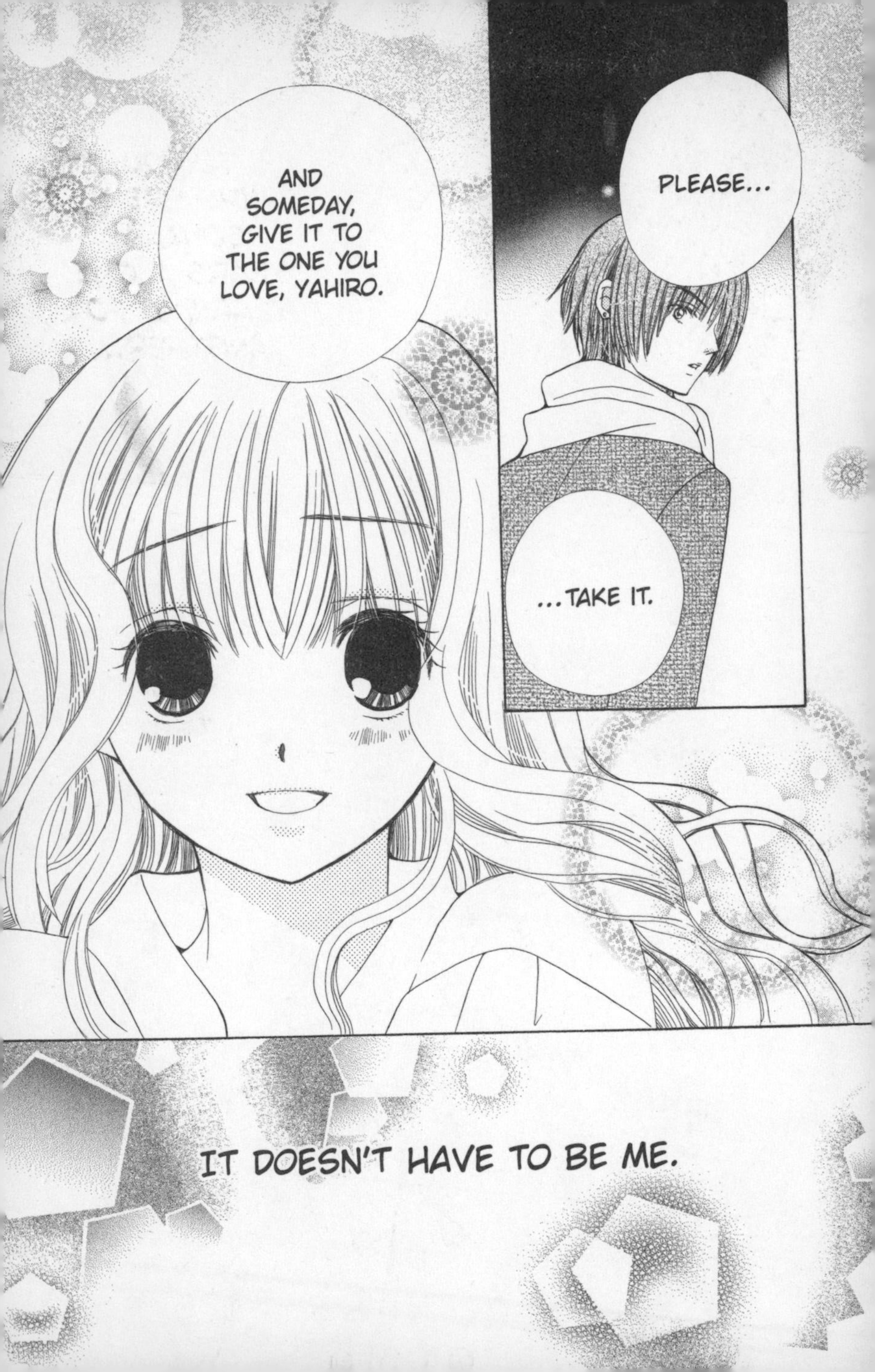
PLEASE...
...TAKE IT.
AND SOMEDAY, GIVE IT TO THE ONE YOU LOVE, YAHIRO.
IT DOESN'T HAVE TO BE ME.

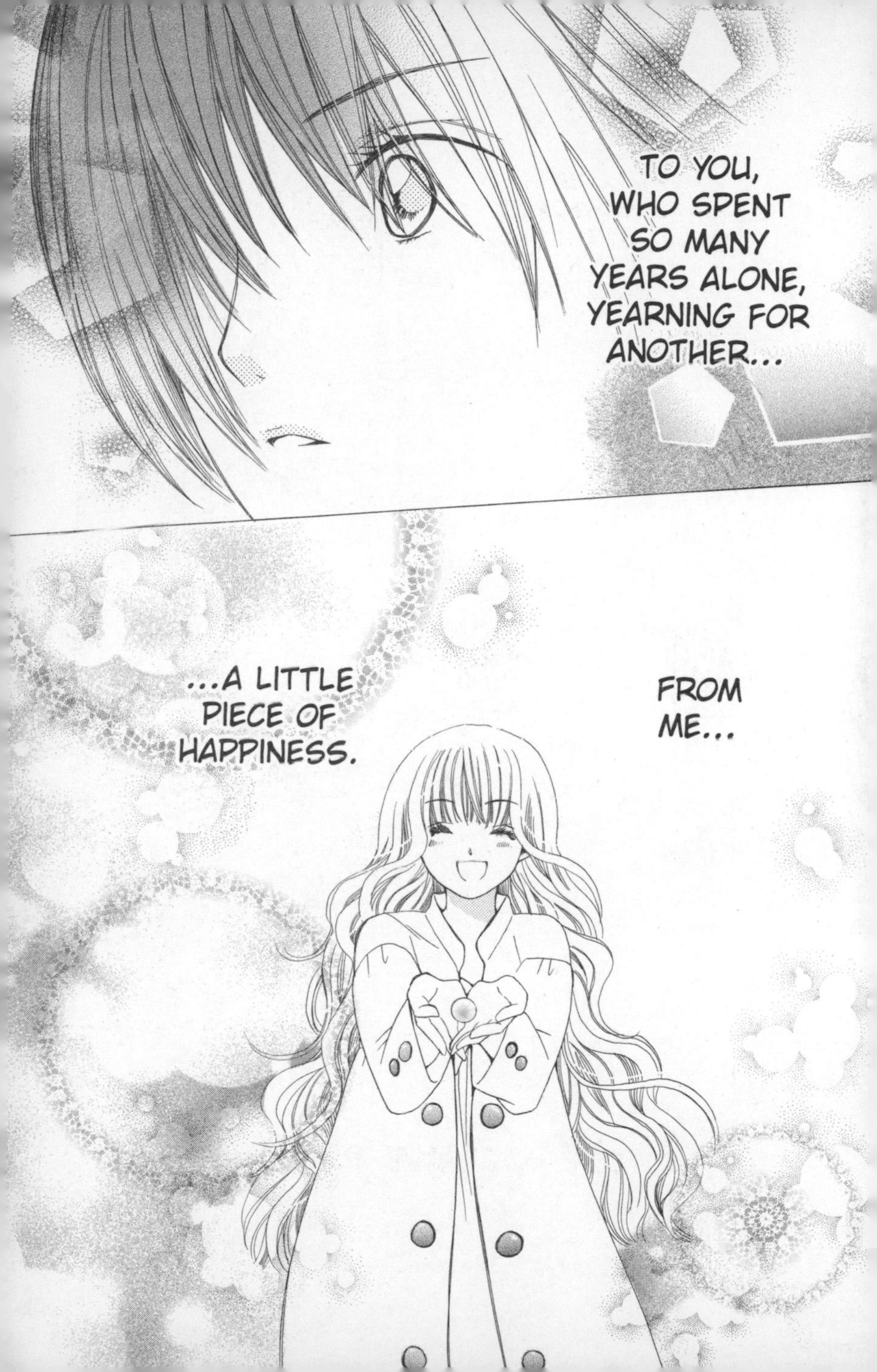
TO YOU, WHO SPENT SO MANY YEARS ALONE, YEARNING FOR ANOTHER...
FROM ME...
...A LITTLE PIECE OF HAPPINESS.

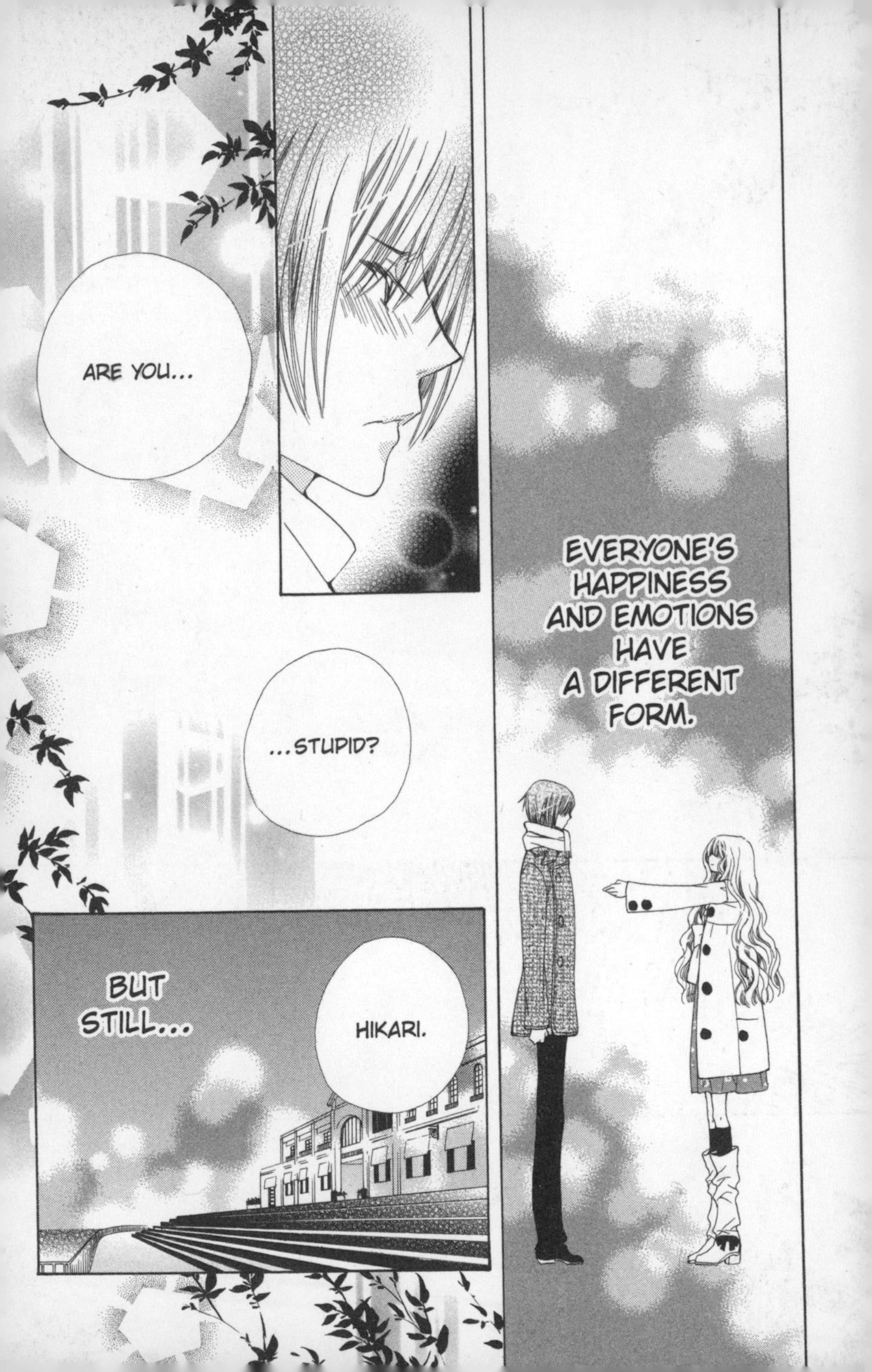
EVERYONE'S HAPPINESS AND EMOTIONS HAVE A DIFFERENT FORM.
ARE YOU...
...STUPID?
HIKARI.
BUT STILL...

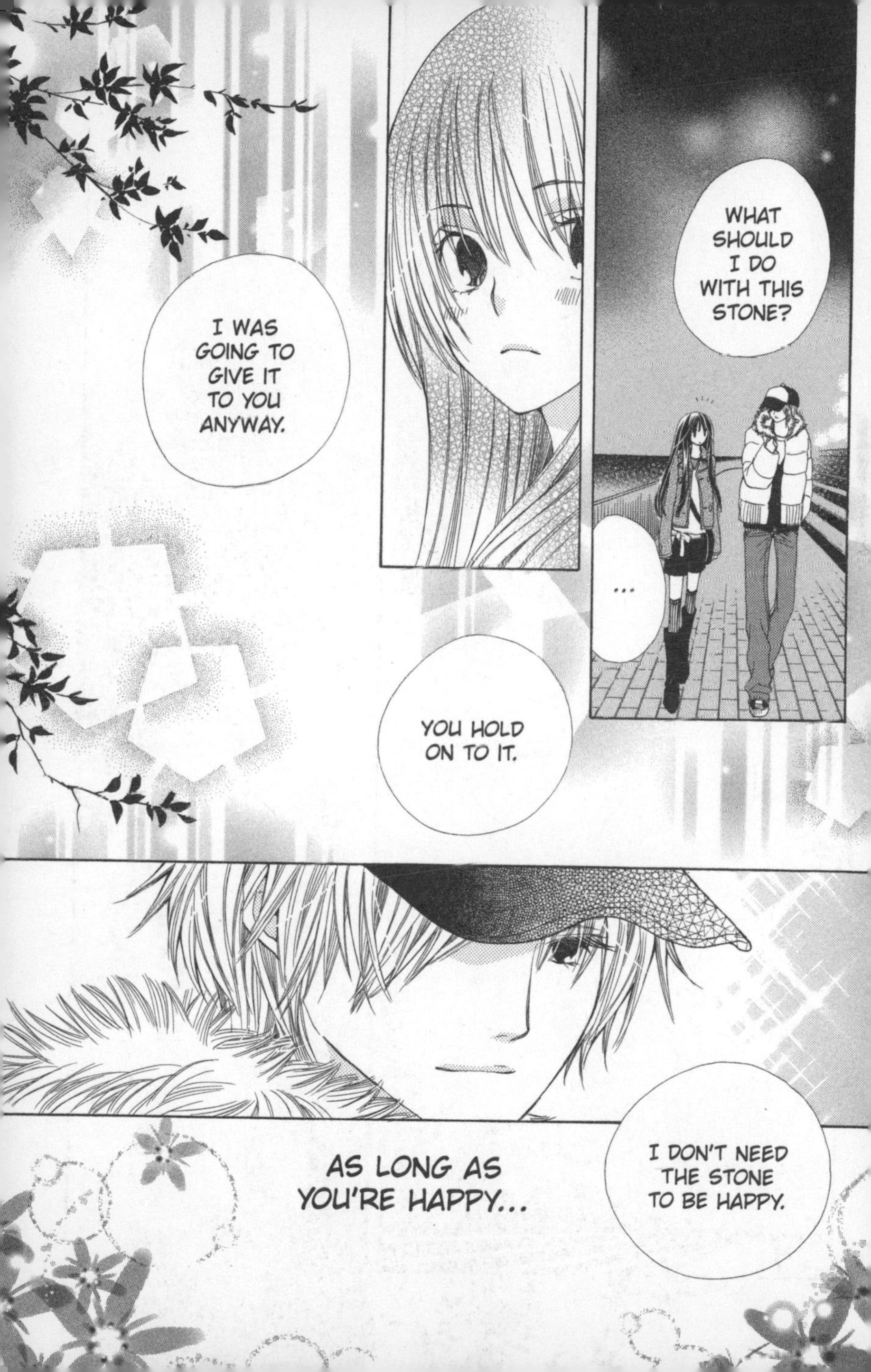
WHAT SHOULD I DO WITH THIS STONE?
...
I WAS GOING TO GIVE IT TO YOU ANYWAY.
YOU HOLD ON TO IT.
I DON'T NEED THE STONE TO BE HAPPY.
AS LONG AS YOU'RE HAPPY...

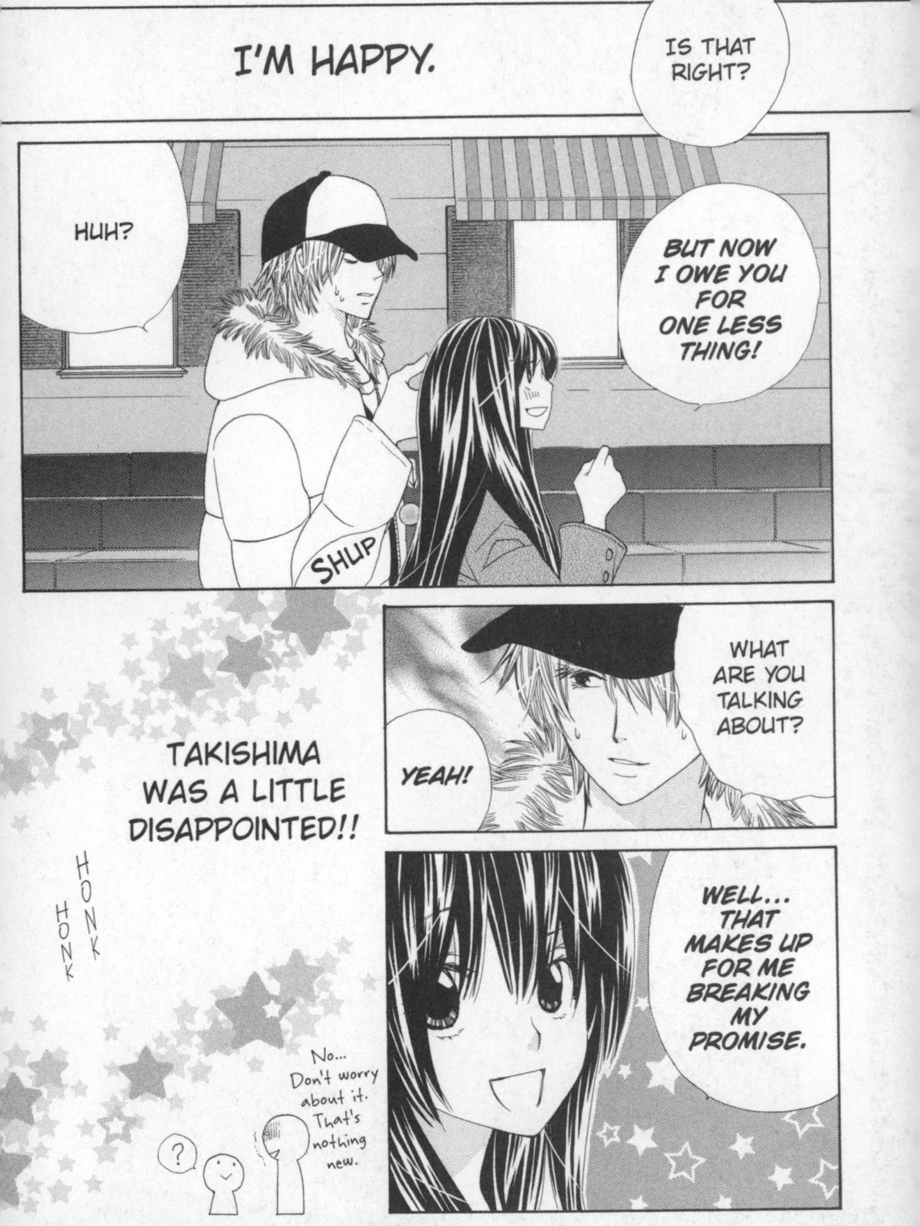
IS THAT RIGHT?
I'M HAPPY.
BUT NOW I OWE YOU FOR ONE LESS THING!
SHUP
HUH?
WHAT ARE YOU TALKING ABOUT?
YEAH!
WELL... THAT MAKES UP FOR ME BREAKING MY PROMISE.
TAKISHIMA WAS A LITTLE DISAPPOINTED!!
HONK HONK
No... Don't worry about it. That's nothing new.
?

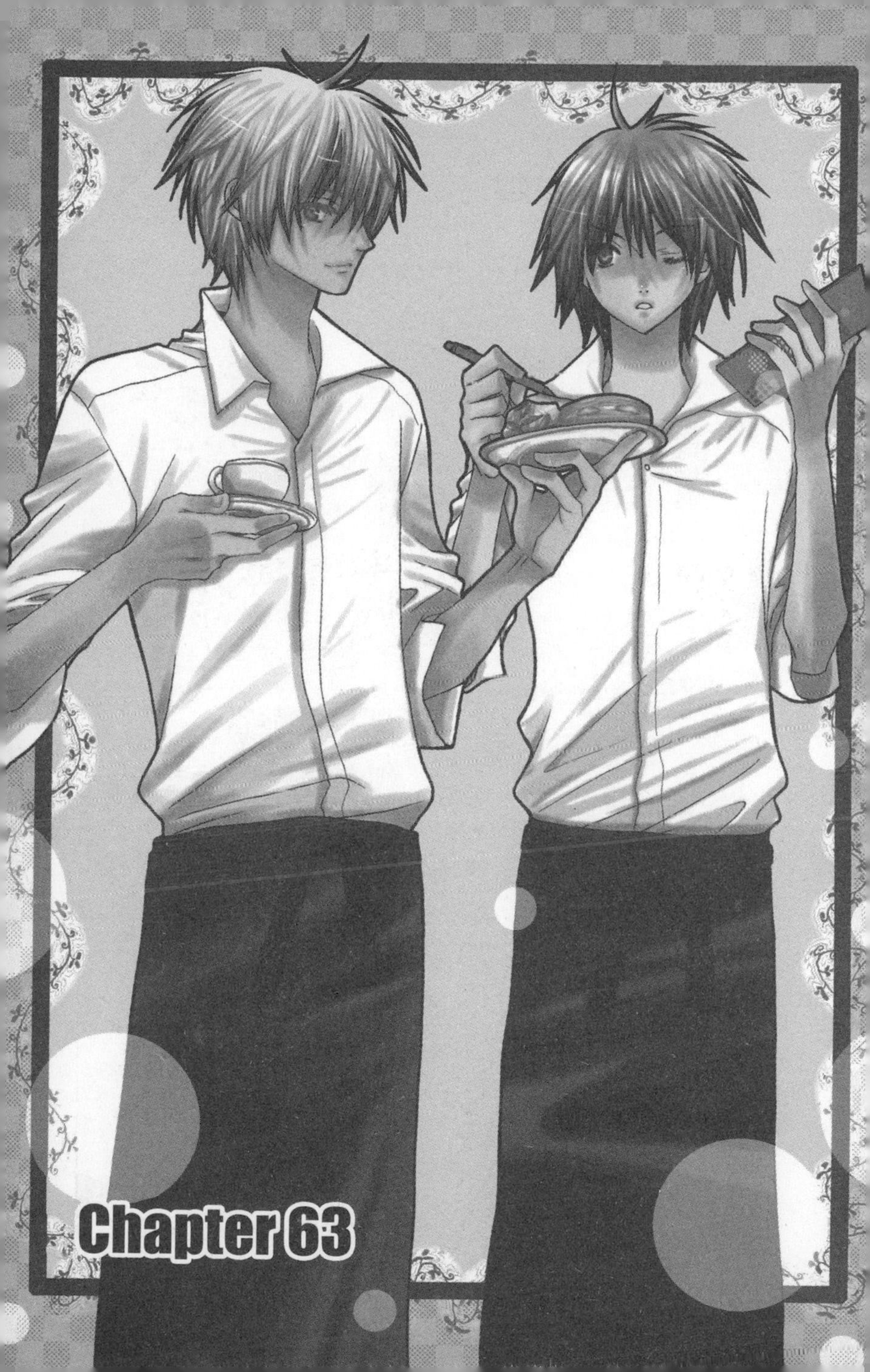
Chapter 63

FOOD PARADISE

THIS IS THE TITLE OF THE BONUS STORY AT THE END OF THE BOOK.

I WROTE IT ABOUT FOUR YEARS AGO.

BACK THEN I DREW EVERYTHING MYSELF. NOW I HAVE ASSISTANTS WHO DRAW THE BEAUTIFUL BACKGROUNDS. IT'S SO ENCOURAGING!

THIS IS A STORY ABOUT A GIRL WHO LOVES TO EAT AND A CHEF WHO IS SOCIALLY AWKWARD.

DRAWING THE CHEF WAS FUN. AND DRAWING THE GIRL WITH BOBBED HAIR WAS FUN. I LOVE PEOPLE WHO LIKE GIRLS WITH BOBBED HAIR. ♡ ♡

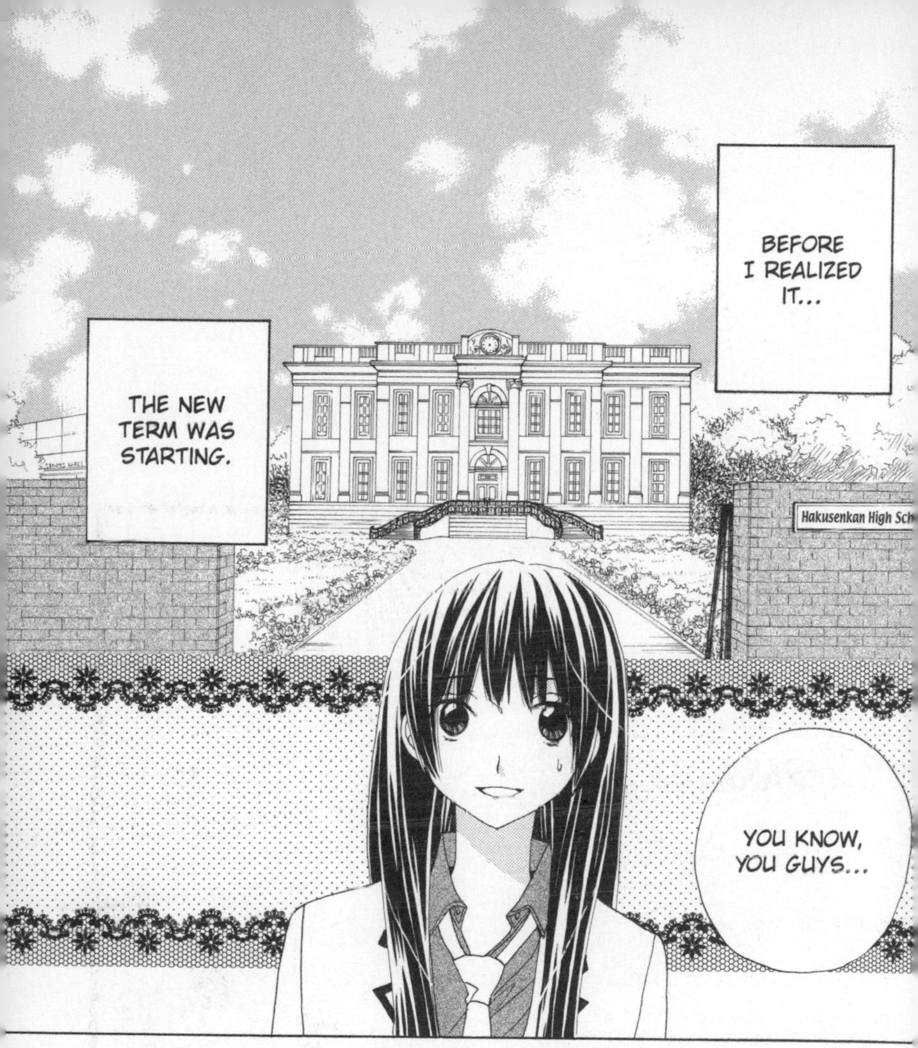
BEFORE I REALIZED IT...
THE NEW TERM WAS STARTING.
Hakusenkan High Sch
YOU KNOW, YOU GUYS...

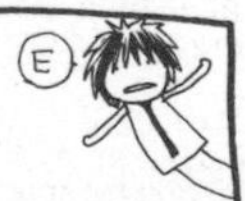
E

· THIS AND THAT ·

· THANK YOU FOR ALL THE LETTERS! THEY REALLY DO MAKE ME WANT TO WORK HARDER!! I'M ABOUT TO START WRITING MY RESPONSES TO MY NEW YEAR'S CARDS!! KEEP AN EYE OUT FOR THEM!

· THIS TIME WE INCLUDED A SEPARATE STORY I WROTE A LONG TIME AGO!! IT'S VERY NOSTALGIC FOR ME. IF YOU DON'T MIND, PLEASE READ TO THE END!!

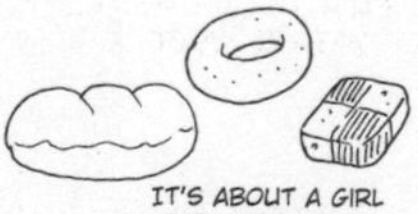

IT'S ABOUT A GIRL WHO LIKES FOOD.

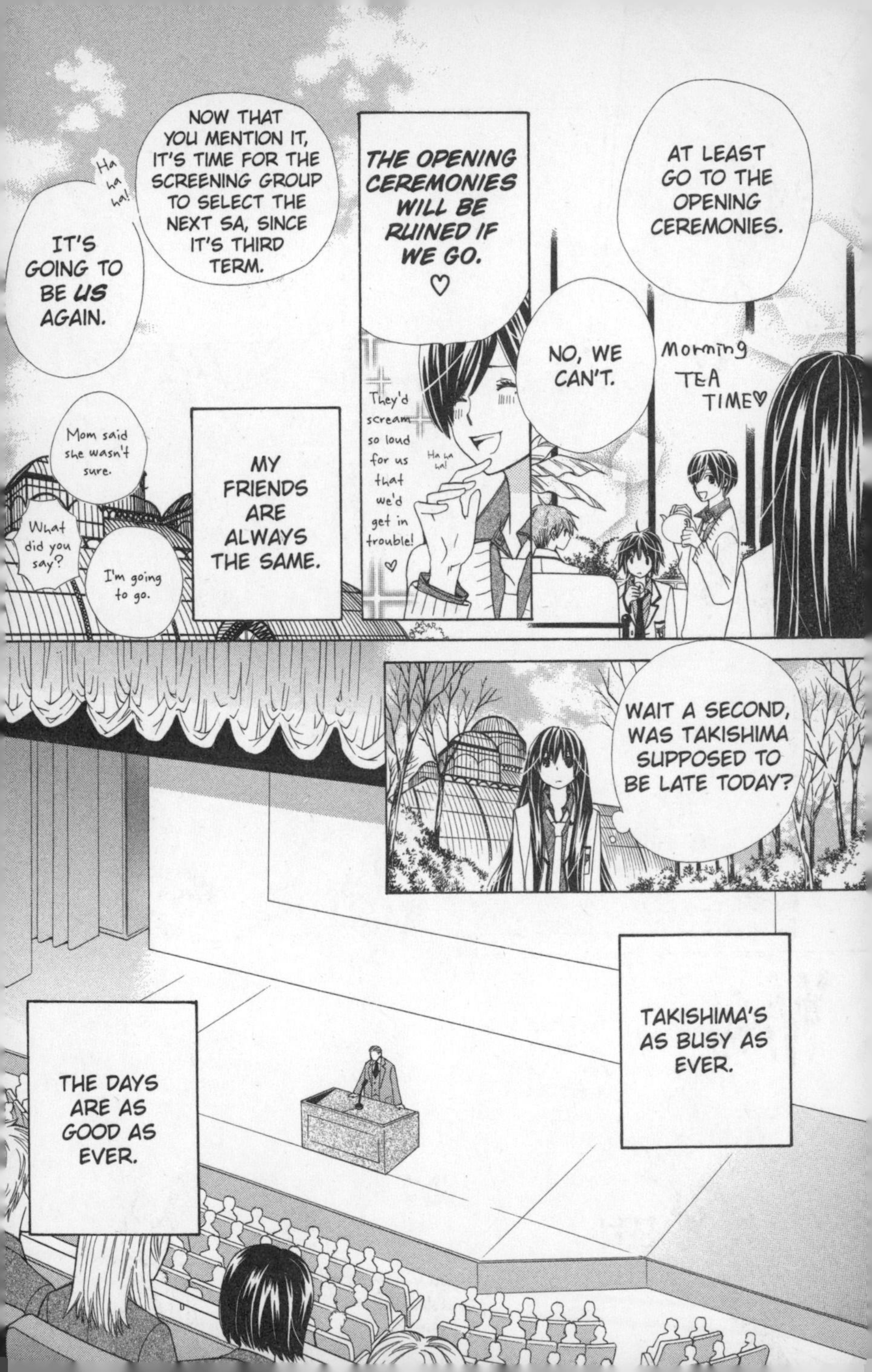
AT LEAST GO TO THE OPENING CEREMONIES.
Morning TEA TIME♡
NO, WE CAN'T.
THE OPENING CEREMONIES WILL BE RUINED IF WE GO. ♡
They'd scream so loud for us that we'd get in trouble! ♡
Ha ha ha!
NOW THAT YOU MENTION IT, IT'S TIME FOR THE SCREENING GROUP TO SELECT THE NEXT SA, SINCE IT'S THIRD TERM.
Ha ha ha!
IT'S GOING TO BE *US* AGAIN.
MY FRIENDS ARE ALWAYS THE SAME.
Mom said she wasn't sure.
What did you say?
I'm going to go.
WAIT A SECOND, WAS TAKISHIMA SUPPOSED TO BE LATE TODAY?
TAKISHIMA'S AS BUSY AS EVER.
THE DAYS ARE AS GOOD AS EVER.

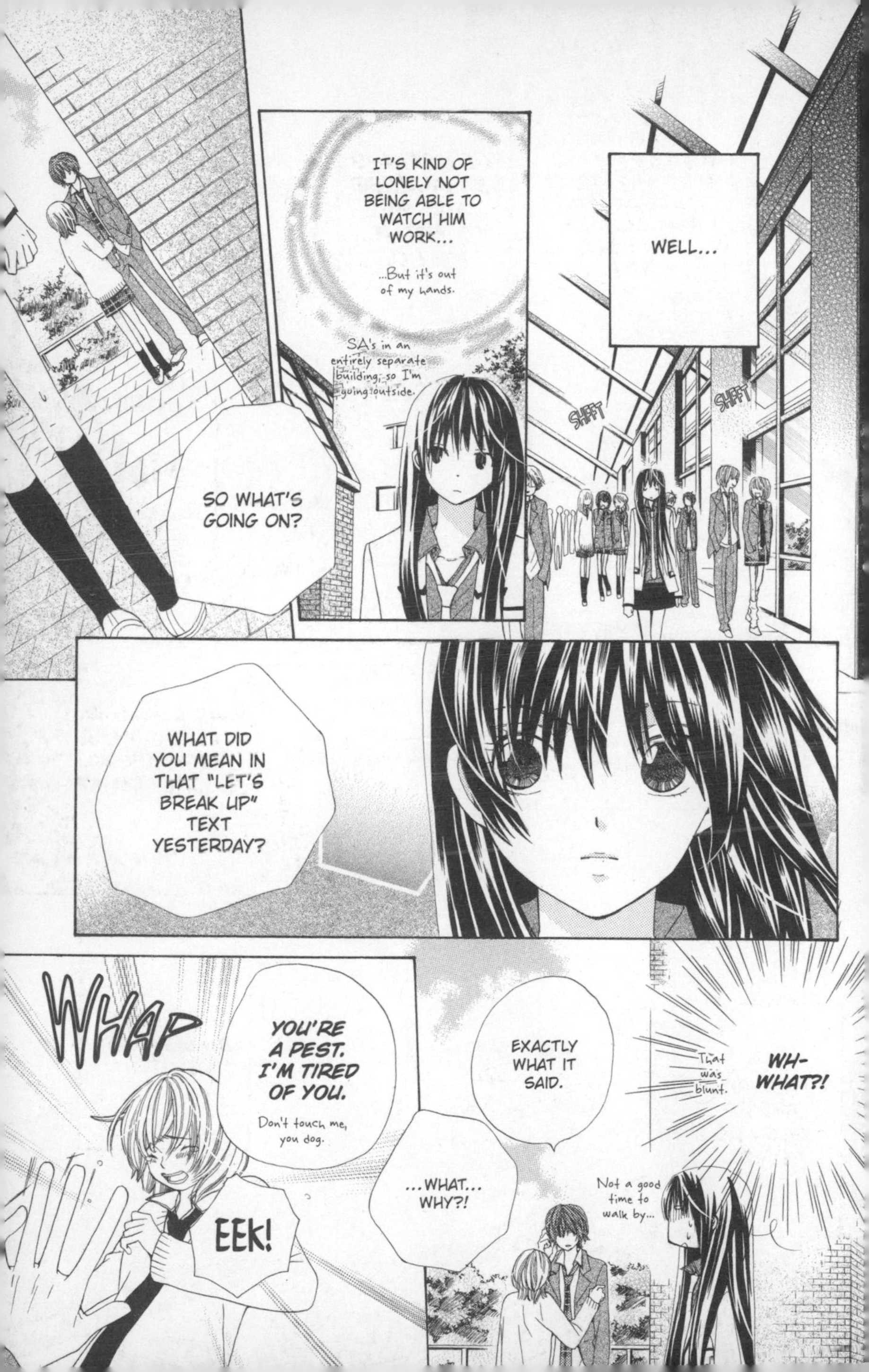
WELL...
SHFFT
SHFFT
IT'S KIND OF LONELY NOT BEING ABLE TO WATCH HIM WORK...
...But it's out of my hands.
SA's in an entirely separate building, so I'm going outside.
SO WHAT'S GOING ON?
WHAT DID YOU MEAN IN THAT "LET'S BREAK UP" TEXT YESTERDAY?
WH-WHAT?!
That was blunt.
EXACTLY WHAT IT SAID.
Not a good time to walk by...
...WHAT... WHY?!
YOU'RE A PEST. I'M TIRED OF YOU.
Don't touch me, you dog.
WHAP
EEK!

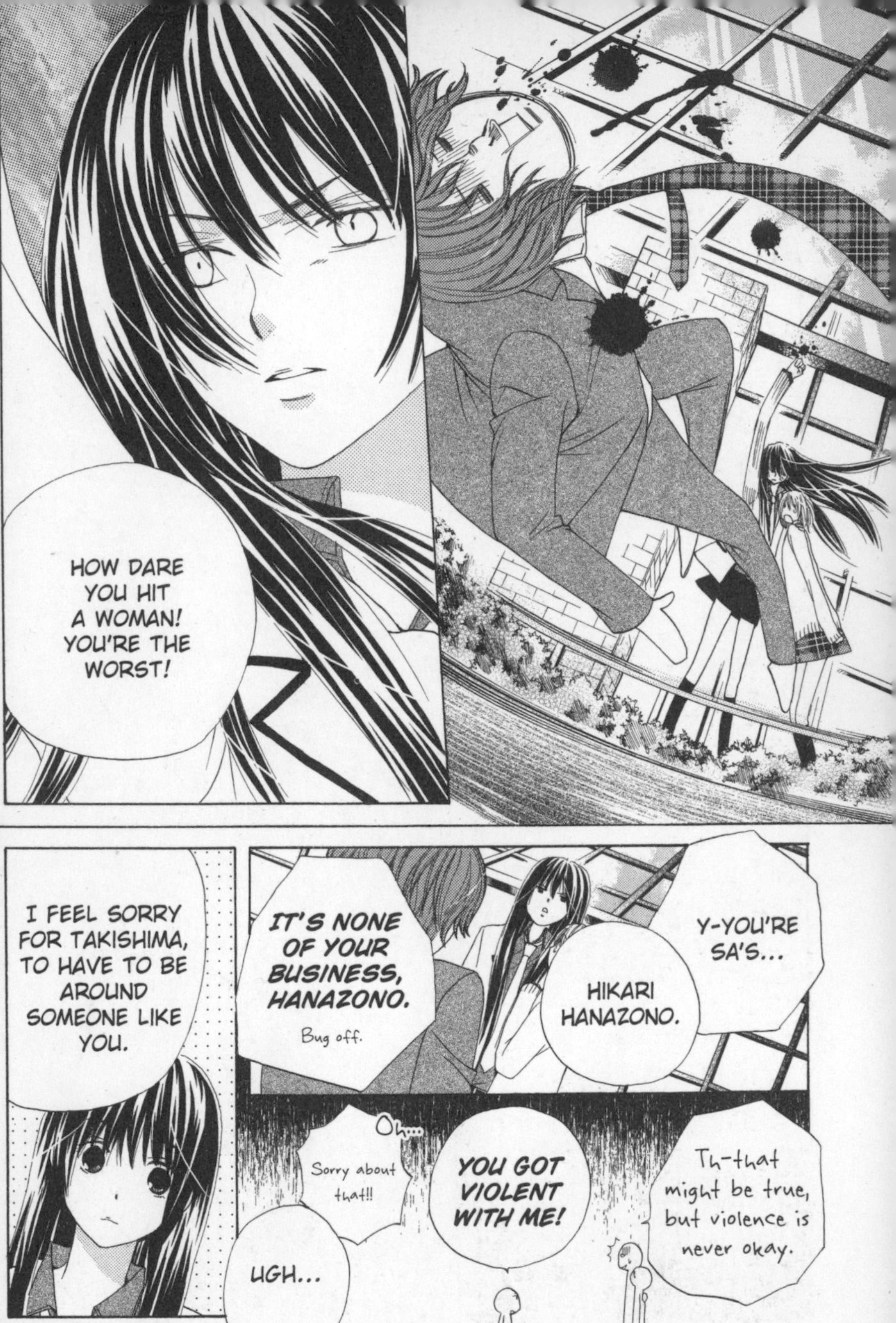
HOW DARE YOU HIT A WOMAN! YOU'RE THE WORST!
Y-YOU'RE SA'S...
HIKARI HANAZONO.
IT'S NONE OF YOUR BUSINESS, HANAZONO.
Bug off.
Th-that might be true, but violence is never okay.
YOU GOT VIOLENT WITH ME!
Oh...
Sorry about that!!
UGH...
I FEEL SORRY FOR TAKISHIMA, TO HAVE TO BE AROUND SOMEONE LIKE YOU.

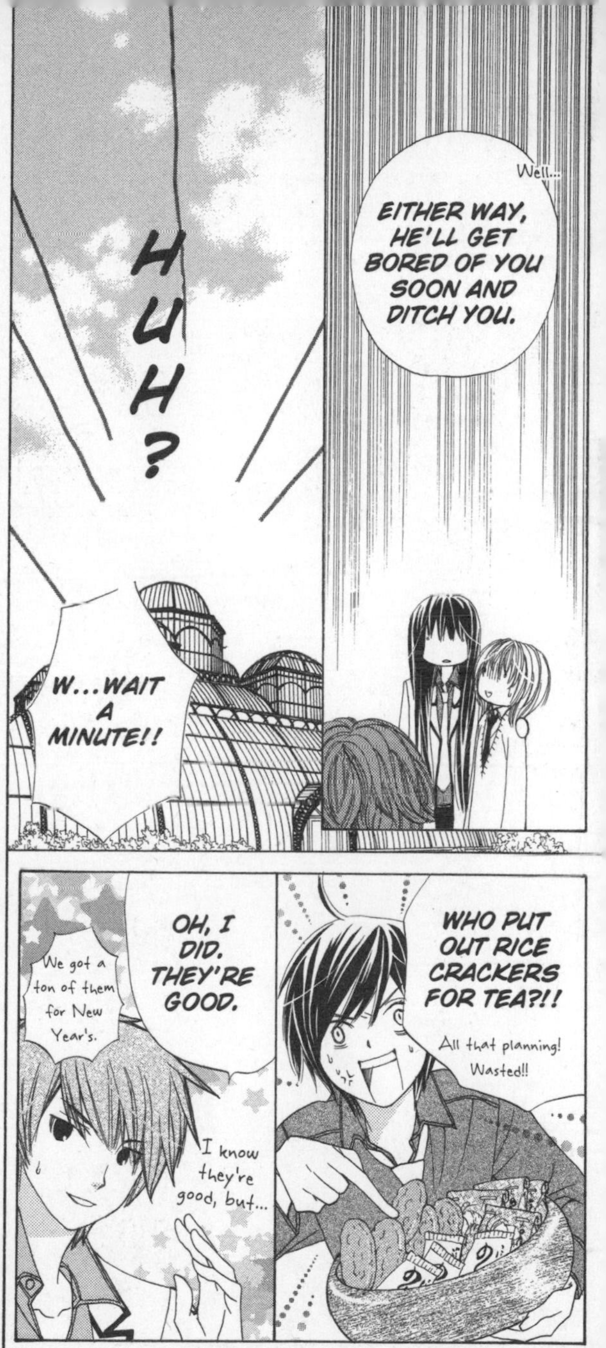

Well...
EITHER WAY, HE'LL GET BORED OF YOU SOON AND DITCH YOU.
HUH?
W...WAIT A MINUTE!!
WHO PUT OUT RICE CRACKERS FOR TEA?!!
All that planning! Wasted!!
OH, I DID. THEY'RE GOOD.
We got a ton of them for New Year's.
I know they're good, but...

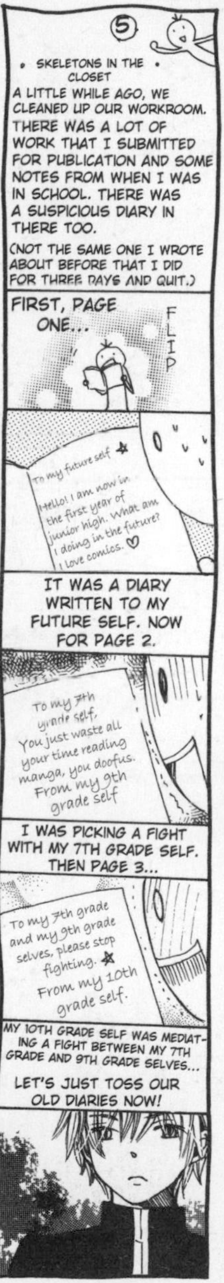

5
SKELETONS IN THE CLOSET
A LITTLE WHILE AGO, WE CLEANED UP OUR WORKROOM. THERE WAS A LOT OF WORK THAT I SUBMITTED FOR PUBLICATION AND SOME NOTES FROM WHEN I WAS IN SCHOOL. THERE WAS A SUSPICIOUS DIARY IN THERE TOO.
(NOT THE SAME ONE I WROTE ABOUT BEFORE THAT I DID FOR THREE DAYS AND QUIT.)
FIRST, PAGE ONE...
FLIP
To my future self ☆
Hello! I am now in the first year of junior high. What am I doing in the future? I love comics. ♡
IT WAS A DIARY WRITTEN TO MY FUTURE SELF. NOW FOR PAGE 2.
To my 7th grade self, You just waste all your time reading manga, you doofus. From my 9th grade self
I WAS PICKING A FIGHT WITH MY 7TH GRADE SELF. THEN PAGE 3...
To my 7th grade and my 9th grade selves, please stop fighting. ☆ From my 10th grade self.
MY 10TH GRADE SELF WAS MEDIATING A FIGHT BETWEEN MY 7TH GRADE AND 9TH GRADE SELVES...
LET'S JUST TOSS OUR OLD DIARIES NOW!

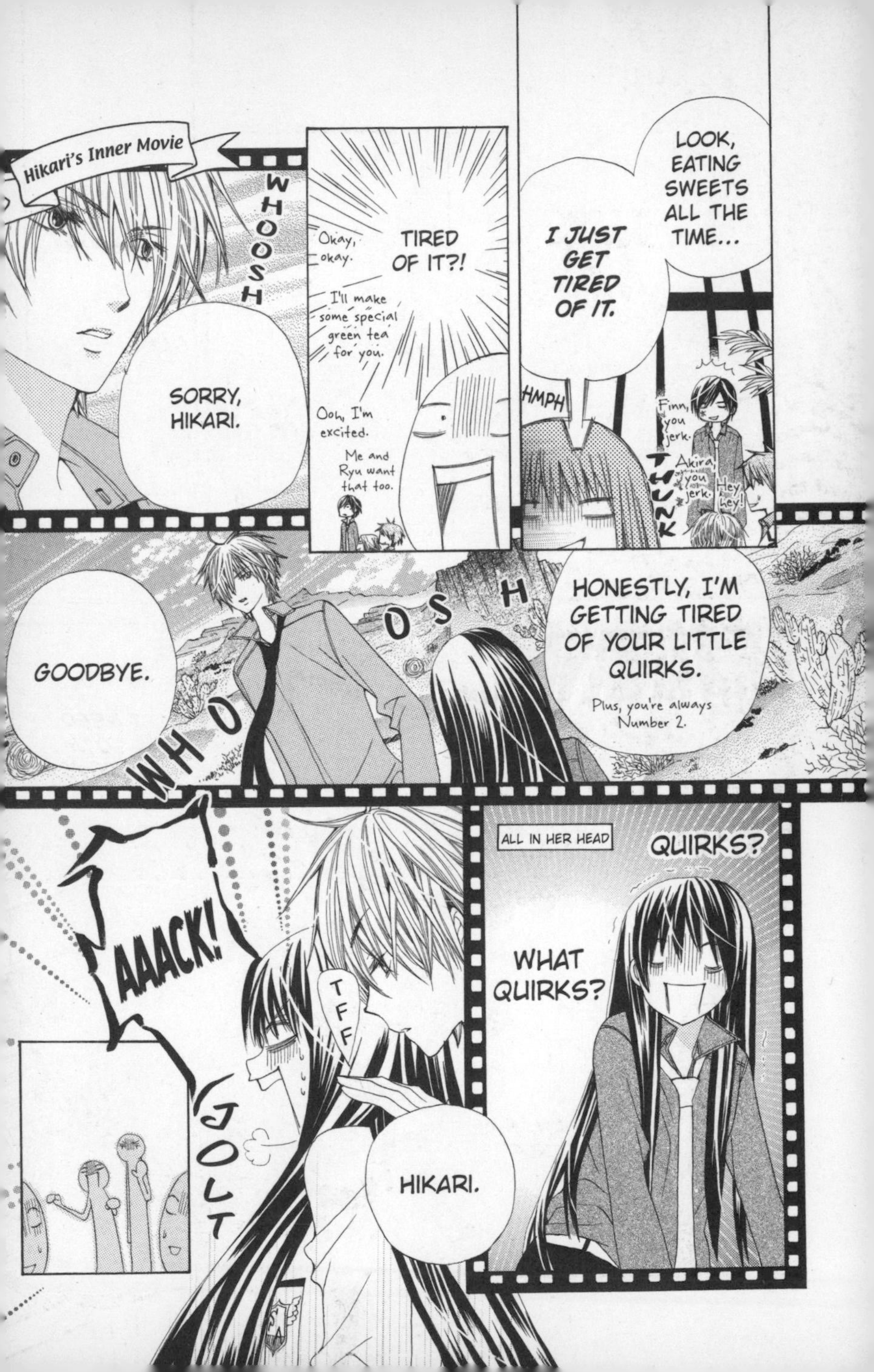
LOOK, EATING SWEETS ALL THE TIME...
I JUST GET TIRED OF IT.
HMPH
Finn, you jerk.
THUNK
Akira, you jerk.
Hey hey!
TIRED OF IT?!
Okay, okay.
I'll make some special green tea for you.
Ooh, I'm excited.
Me and Ryu want that too.
Hikari's Inner Movie
WHOOSH
SORRY, HIKARI.
HONESTLY, I'M GETTING TIRED OF YOUR LITTLE QUIRKS.
Plus, you're always Number 2.
WHOOSH
GOODBYE.
ALL IN HER HEAD
QUIRKS?
WHAT QUIRKS?
HIKARI.
TFF
JOLT
AAACK!

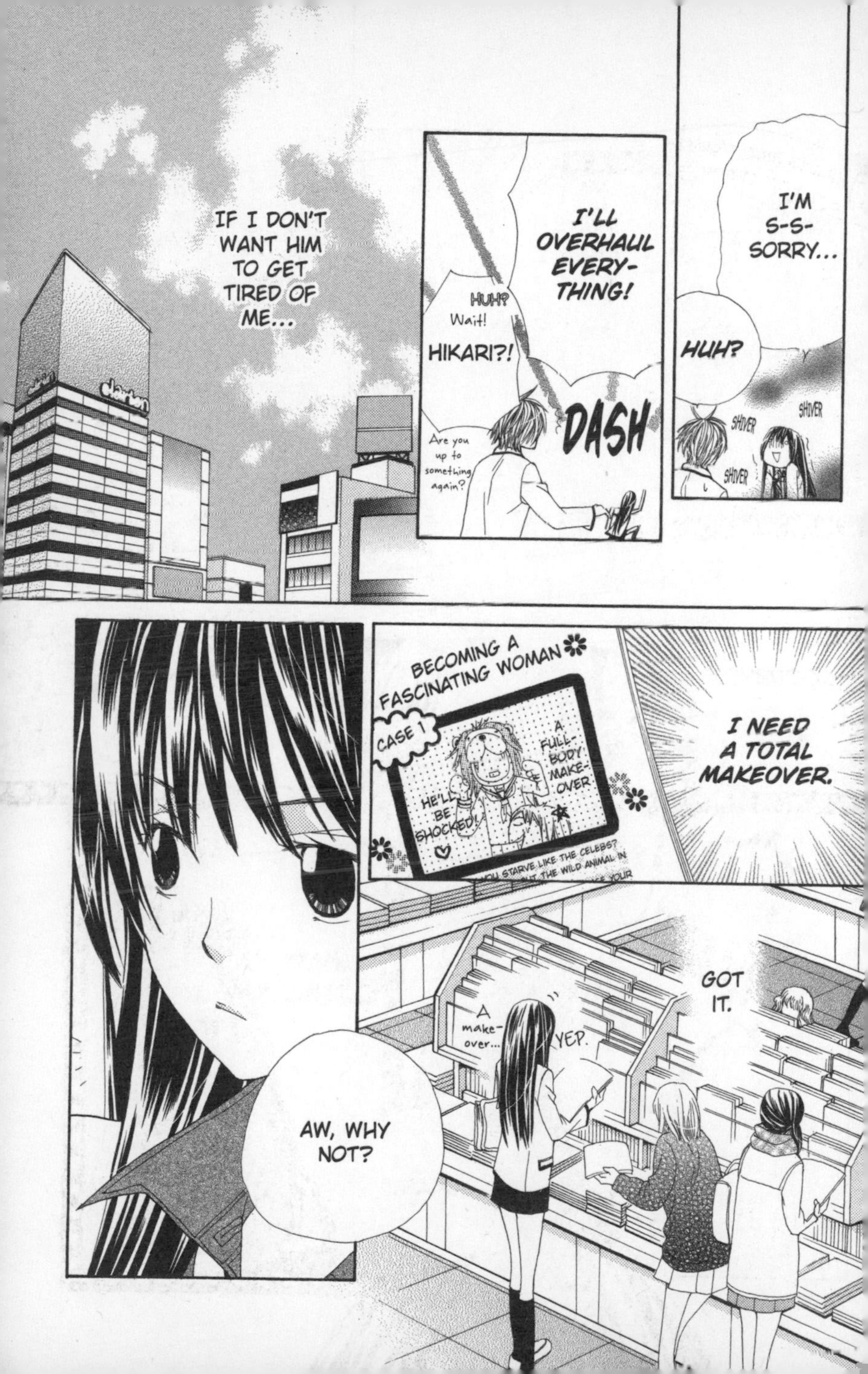
I'M S-S-SORRY...
HUH?
SHIVER
SHIVER
SHIVER
I'LL OVERHAUL EVERY-THING!
HUH? Wait!
HIKARI?!
DASH
Are you up to something again?
IF I DON'T WANT HIM TO GET TIRED OF ME...
I NEED A TOTAL MAKEOVER.
BECOMING A FASCINATING WOMAN
CASE 1
A FULL-BODY MAKE-OVER
HE'LL BE SHOCKED!
GOT IT.
YEP.
A make-over...
AW, WHY NOT?

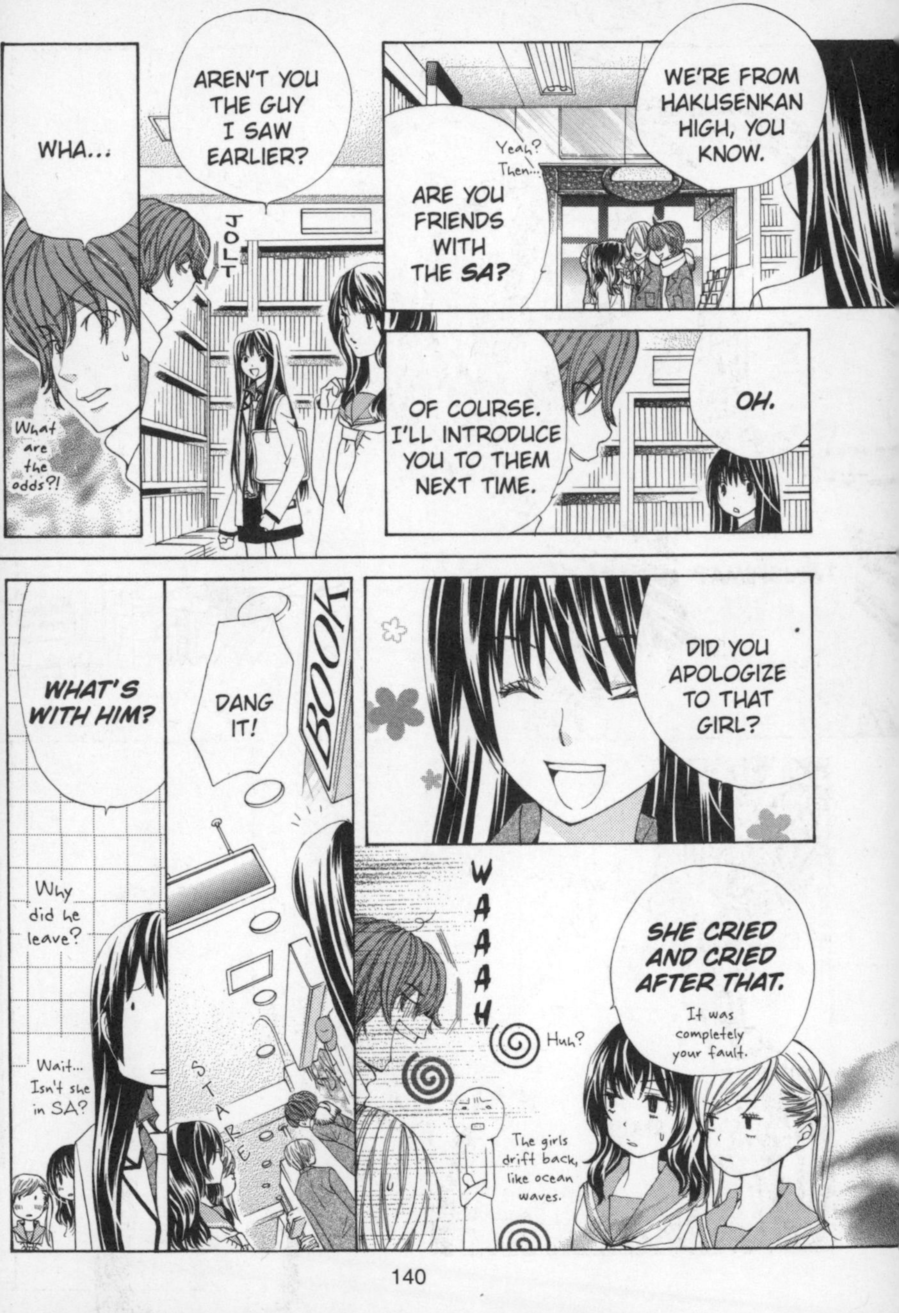
WE'RE FROM HAKUSENKAN HIGH, YOU KNOW.
Yeah? Then...
ARE YOU FRIENDS WITH THE SA?
OH.
OF COURSE. I'LL INTRODUCE YOU TO THEM NEXT TIME.
AREN'T YOU THE GUY I SAW EARLIER?
JOLT
WHA...
What are the odds?!
DID YOU APOLOGIZE TO THAT GIRL?
SHE CRIED AND CRIED AFTER THAT.
It was completely your fault.
WAAAAH
Huh?
The girls drift back, like ocean waves.
BOOK
DANG IT!
STARE
WHAT'S WITH HIM?
Why did he leave?
Wait... Isn't she in SA?

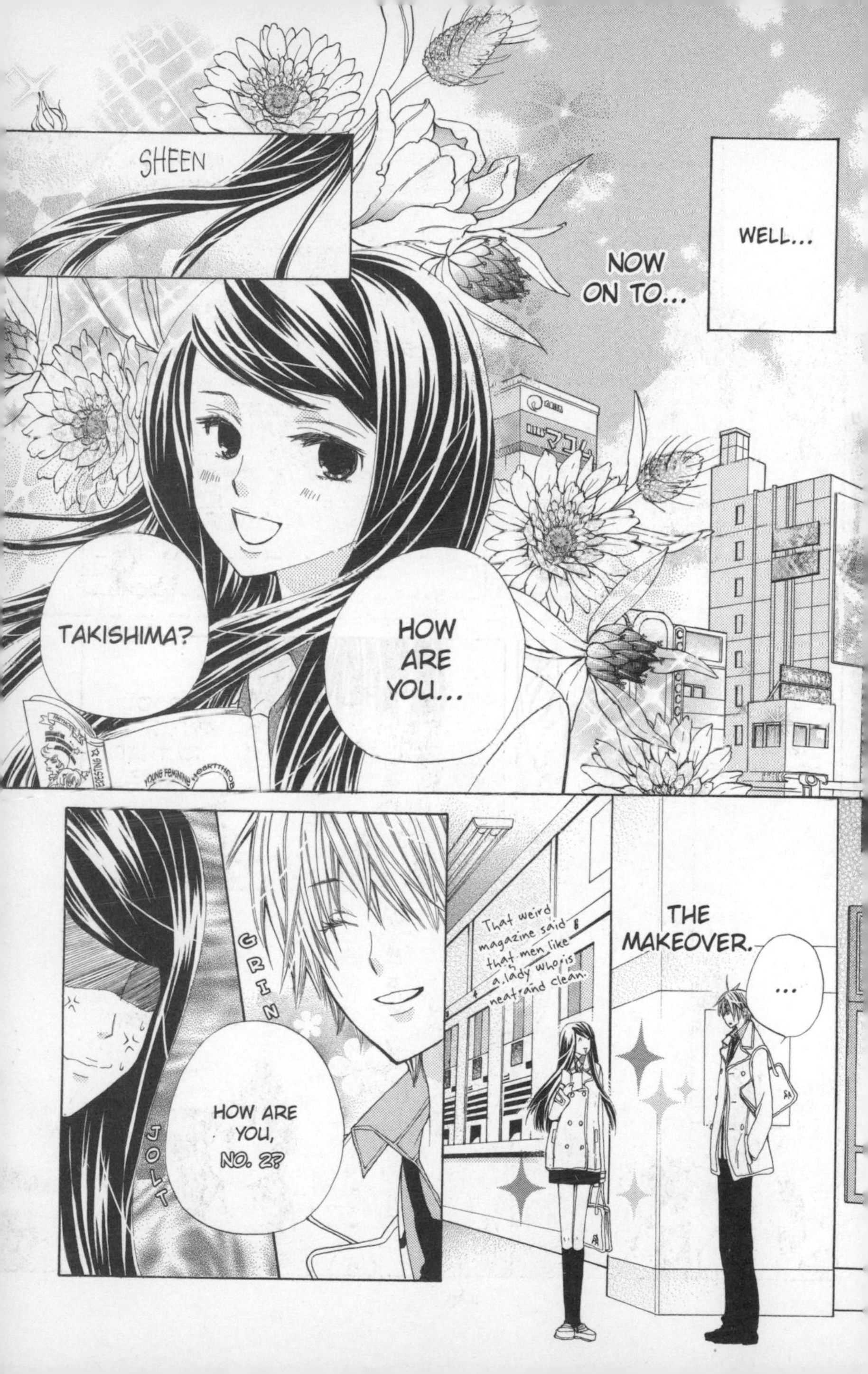
WELL...
NOW ON TO...
SHEEN
HOW ARE YOU...
TAKISHIMA?
...
THE MAKEOVER.
That weird magazine said that men like a lady who is neat and clean.
GRIN
HOW ARE YOU, NO. 2?
JOLT

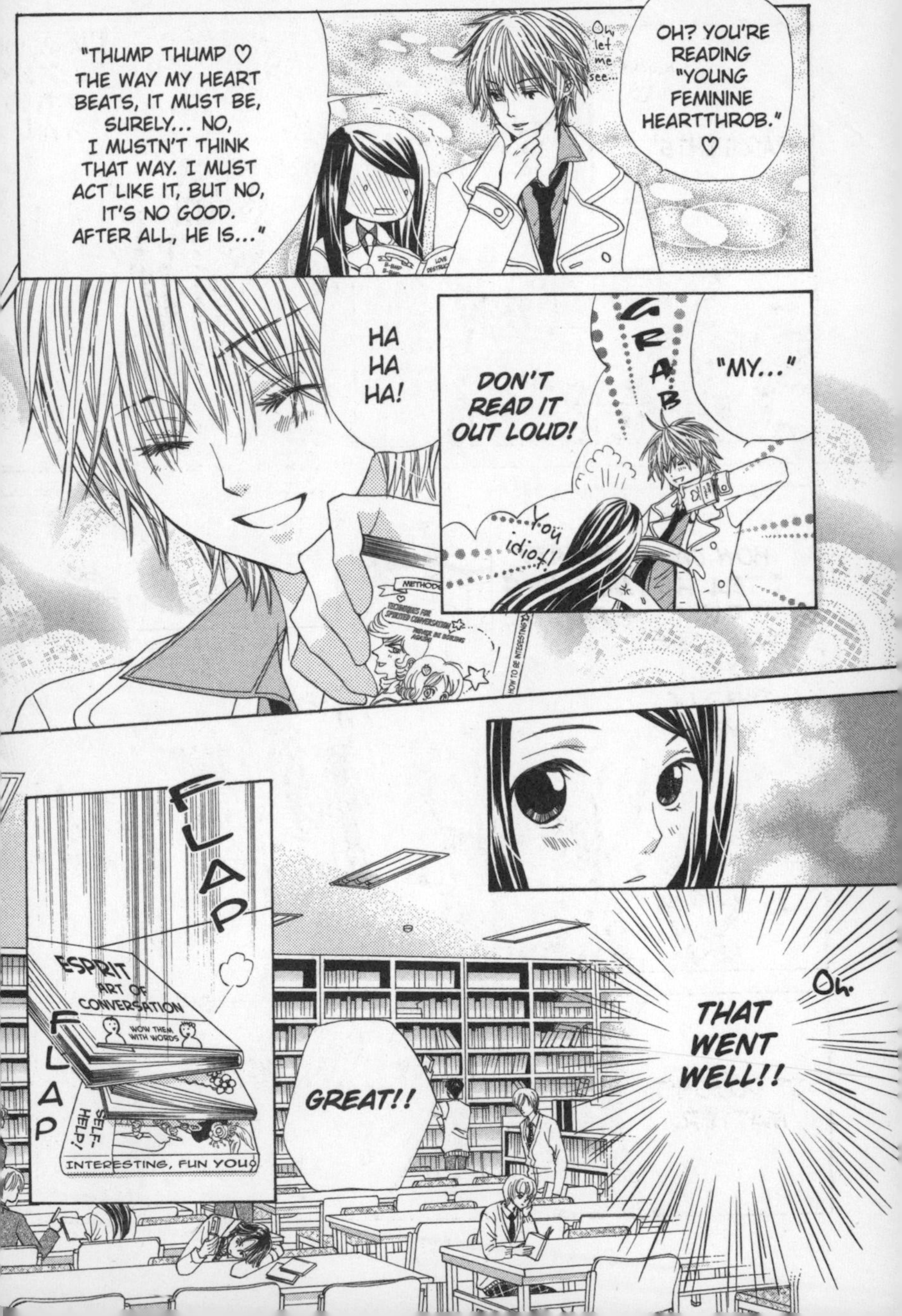
OH? YOU'RE READING "YOUNG FEMININE HEARTTHROB." ♡
Oh, let me see...
"THUMP THUMP ♡ THE WAY MY HEART BEATS, IT MUST BE, SURELY... NO, I MUSTN'T THINK THAT WAY. I MUST ACT LIKE IT, BUT NO, IT'S NO GOOD. AFTER ALL, HE IS..."
"MY..."
GRAB
DON'T READ IT OUT LOUD!
You idiot!
HA HA HA!
METHODS
TECHNIQUES FOR SPIRITED CONVERSATION
HOW TO BE INTERESTING
Oh.
THAT WENT WELL!!
GREAT!!
FLAP
FLAP
ESPRIT
ART OF CONVERSATION
WOW THEM WITH WORDS
SELF-HELP!
INTERESTING, FUN YOU

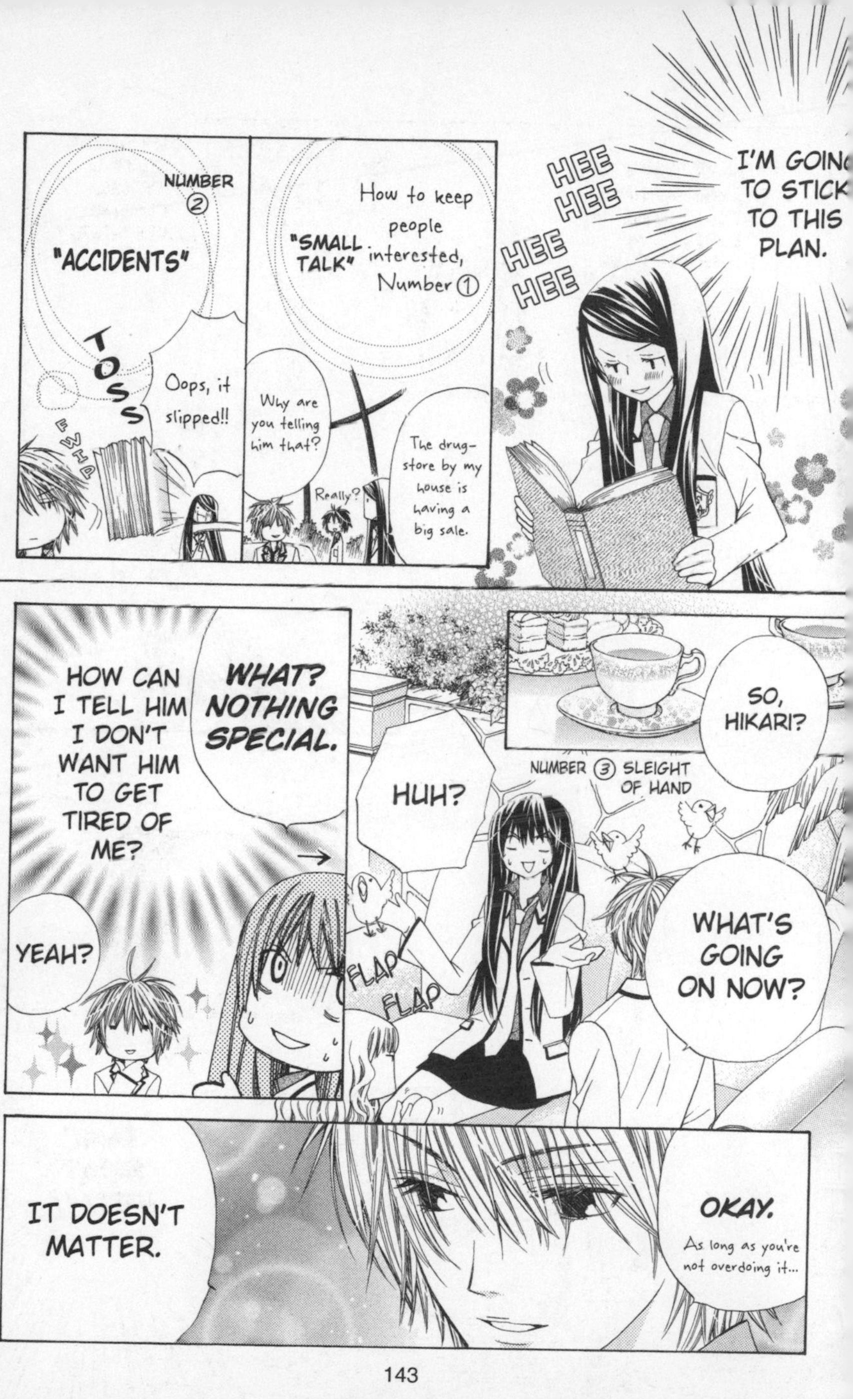
I'M GOING TO STICK TO THIS PLAN.
HEE HEE
HEE HEE
How to keep people interested, Number ①
"SMALL TALK"
The drug-store by my house is having a big sale.
Really?
Why are you telling him that?
NUMBER ②
"ACCIDENTS"
TOSS
Oops, it slipped!!
FWIP
SO, HIKARI?
WHAT'S GOING ON NOW?
NUMBER ③ SLEIGHT OF HAND
HUH?
FLAP
FLAP
WHAT? NOTHING SPECIAL.
HOW CAN I TELL HIM I DON'T WANT HIM TO GET TIRED OF ME?
YEAH?
OKAY.
As long as you're not overdoing it...
IT DOESN'T MATTER.

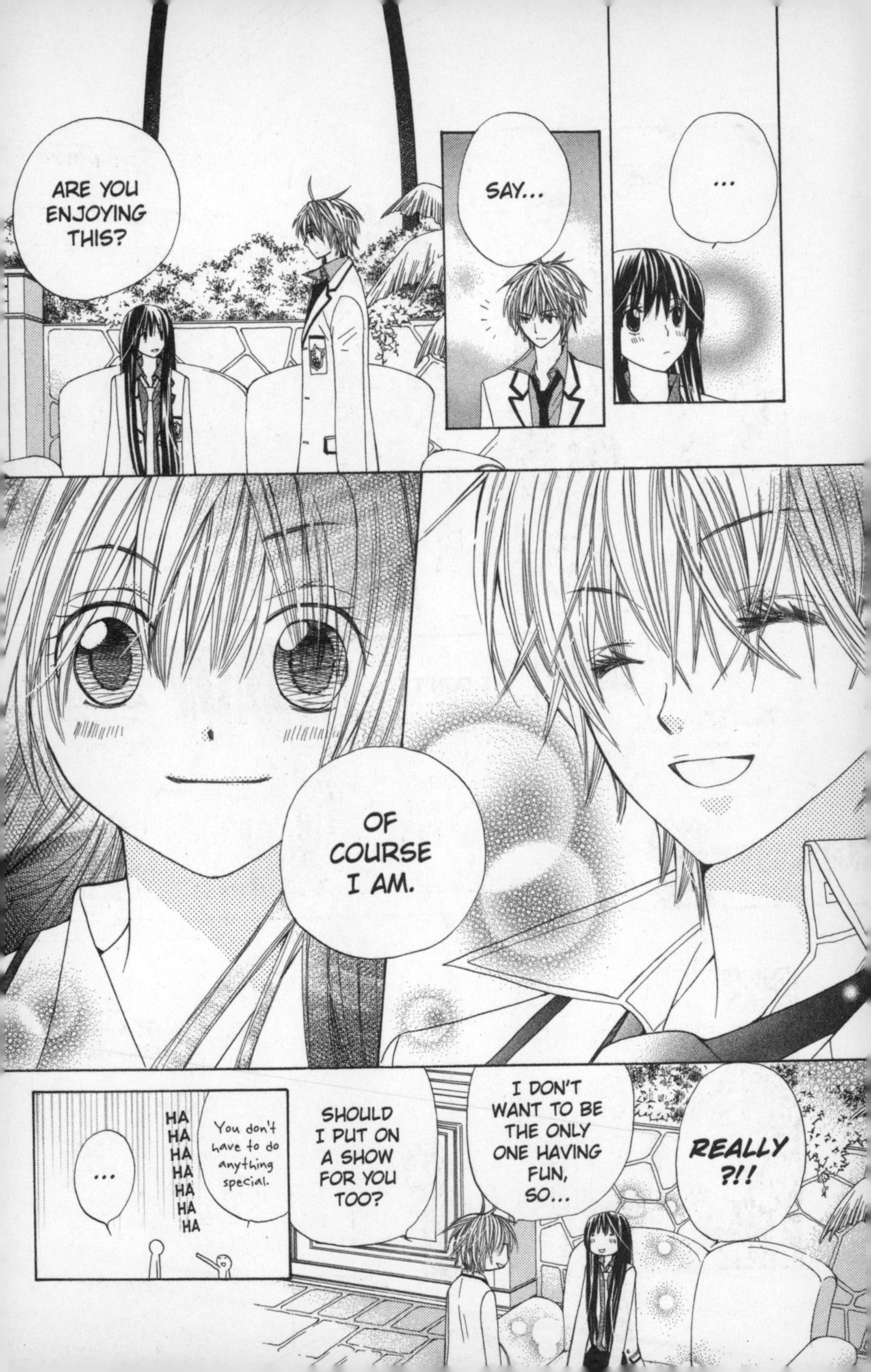
...
SAY...
ARE YOU ENJOYING THIS?
OF COURSE I AM.
REALLY ?!!
I DON'T WANT TO BE THE ONLY ONE HAVING FUN, SO...
SHOULD I PUT ON A SHOW FOR YOU TOO?
You don't have to do anything special.
HA HA HA HA HA HA HA
...

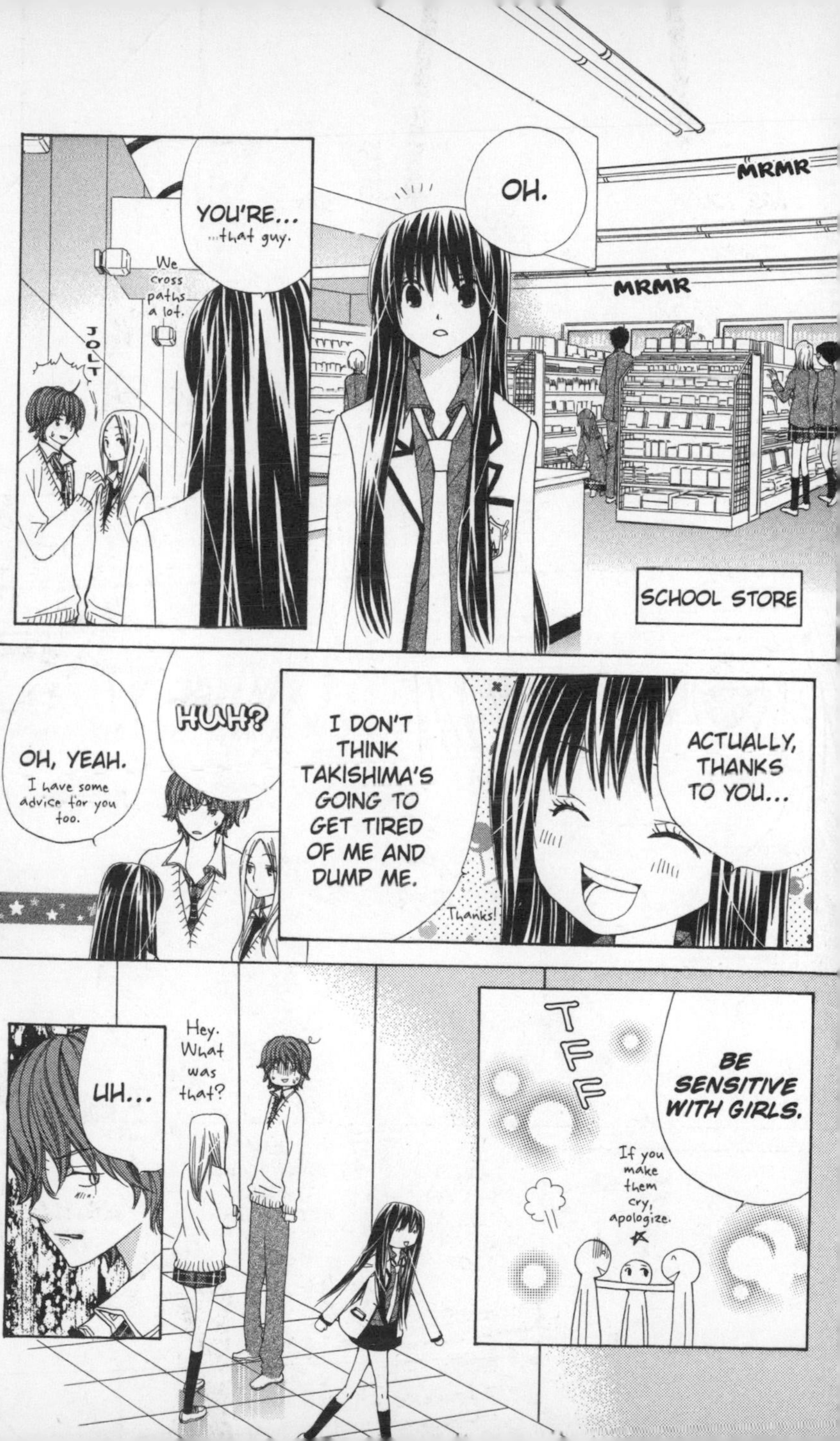
MRMR
OH.
MRMR
SCHOOL STORE
YOU'RE... ...that guy.
We cross paths a lot.
JOLT
ACTUALLY, THANKS TO YOU...
I DON'T THINK TAKISHIMA'S GOING TO GET TIRED OF ME AND DUMP ME.
Thanks!
HUH?
OH, YEAH. I have some advice for you too.
TFF
BE SENSITIVE WITH GIRLS.
If you make them cry, apologize.
Hey. What was that?
UH...

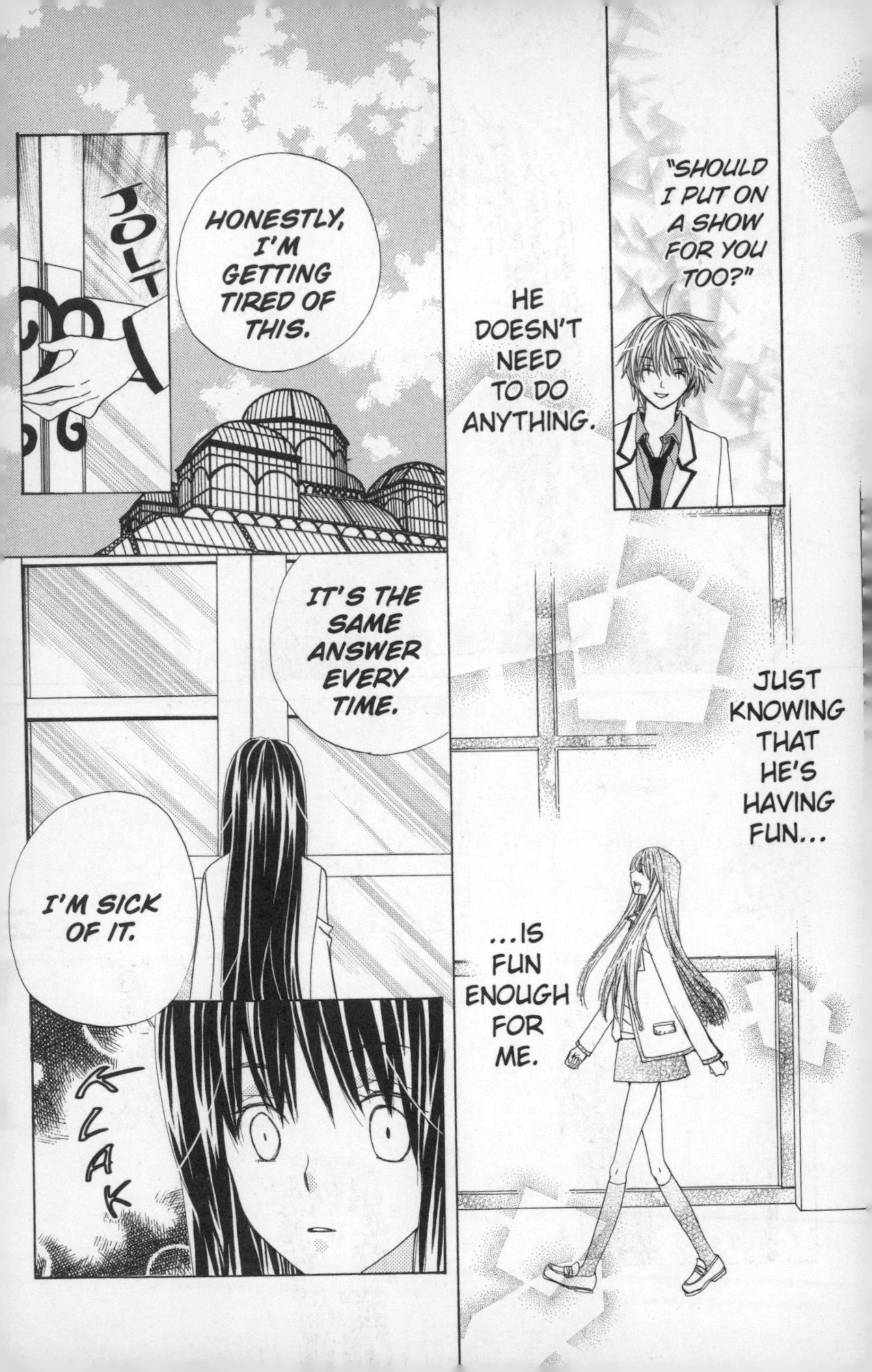
"SHOULD I PUT ON A SHOW FOR YOU TOO?"
HE DOESN'T NEED TO DO ANYTHING.
JUST KNOWING THAT HE'S HAVING FUN...
...IS FUN ENOUGH FOR ME.
JOLT
HONESTLY, I'M GETTING TIRED OF THIS.
IT'S THE SAME ANSWER EVERY TIME.
I'M SICK OF IT.
KLAK

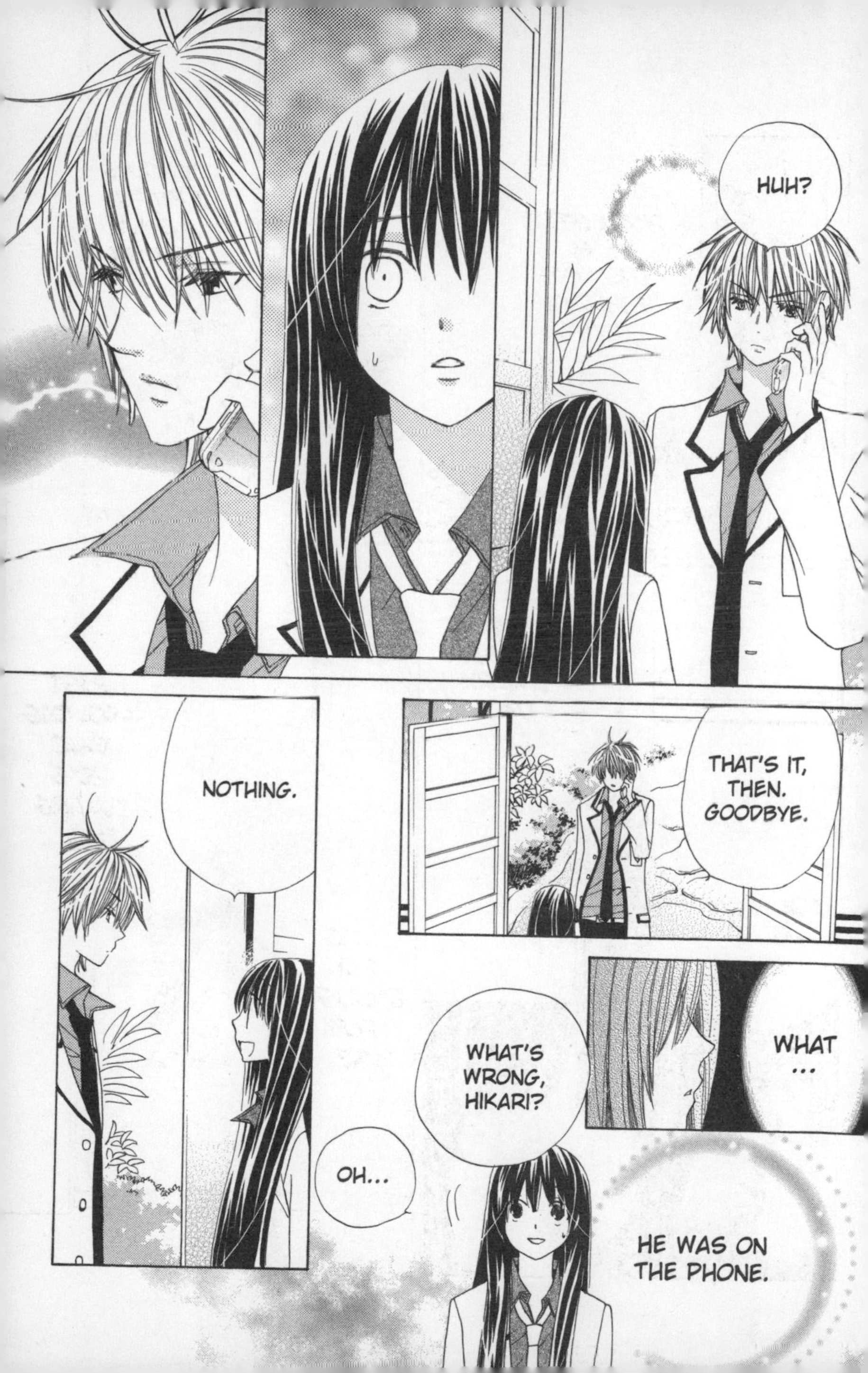
HUH?
THAT'S IT, THEN. GOODBYE.
WHAT ...
WHAT'S WRONG, HIKARI?
OH...
HE WAS ON THE PHONE.
NOTHING.

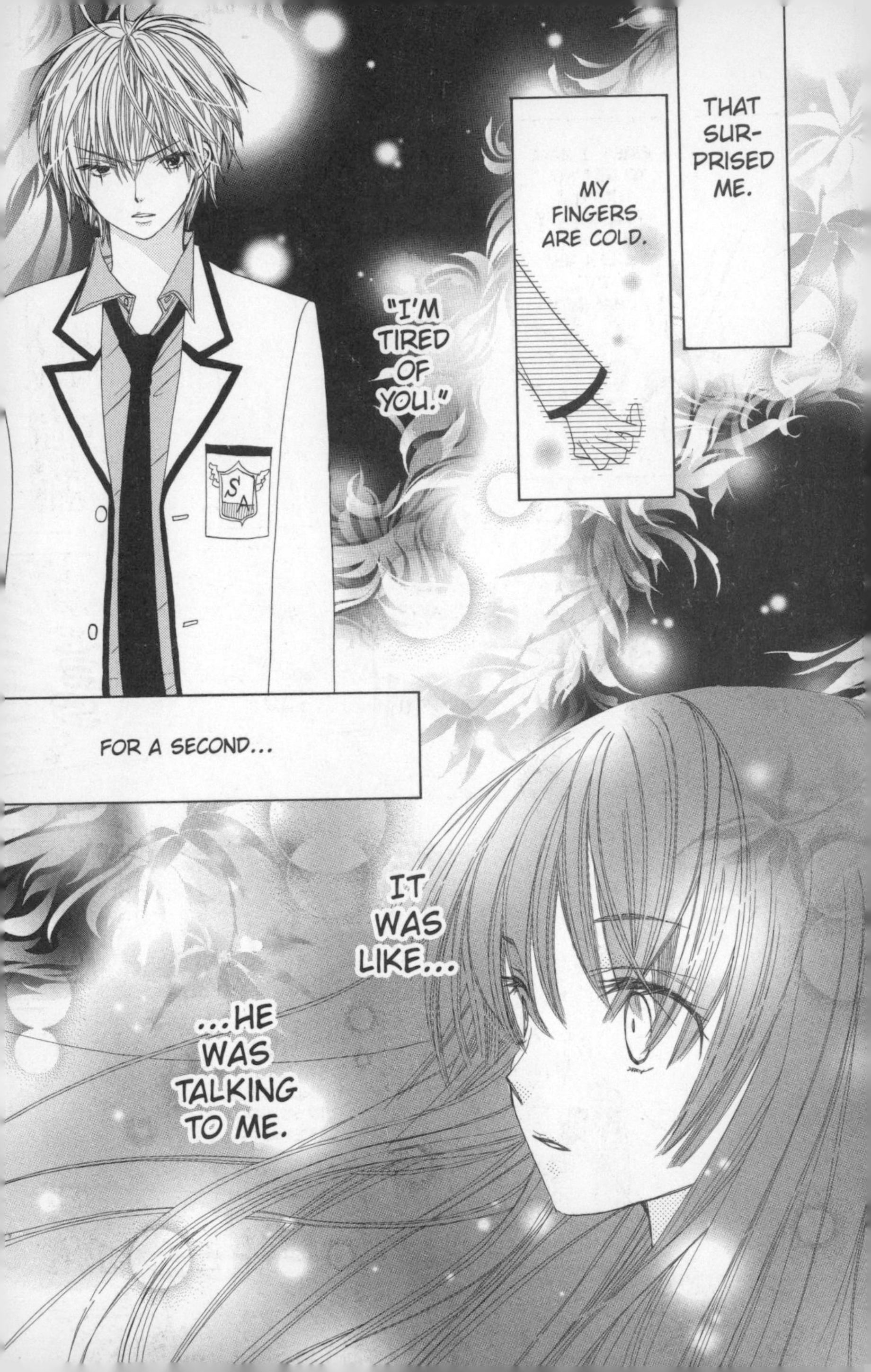
THAT SUR-PRISED ME.
MY FINGERS ARE COLD.
"I'M TIRED OF YOU."
FOR A SECOND...
IT WAS LIKE...
...HE WAS TALKING TO ME.

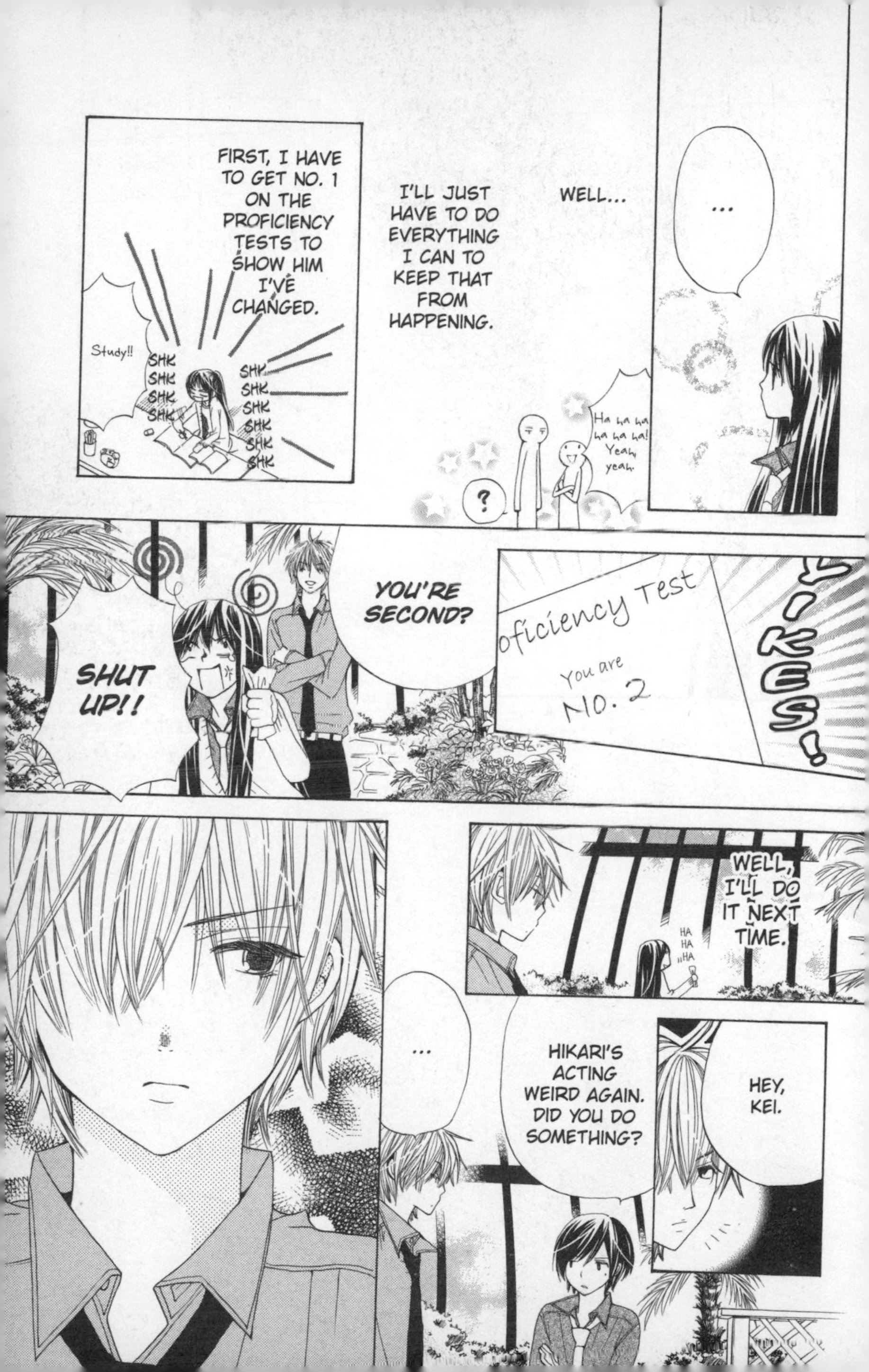
...
WELL...
I'LL JUST HAVE TO DO EVERYTHING I CAN TO KEEP THAT FROM HAPPENING.
Ha ha ha ha ha ha! Yeah yeah.
?
FIRST, I HAVE TO GET NO. 1 ON THE PROFICIENCY TESTS TO SHOW HIM I'VE CHANGED.
SHK SHK SHK SHK SHK SHK
SHK SHK SHK SHK
Study!!
YIKES!
oficiency Test
You are
NO. 2
YOU'RE SECOND?
SHUT UP!!
WELL, I'LL DO IT NEXT TIME.
HA HA HA
HEY, KEI.
HIKARI'S ACTING WEIRD AGAIN. DID YOU DO SOMETHING?
...

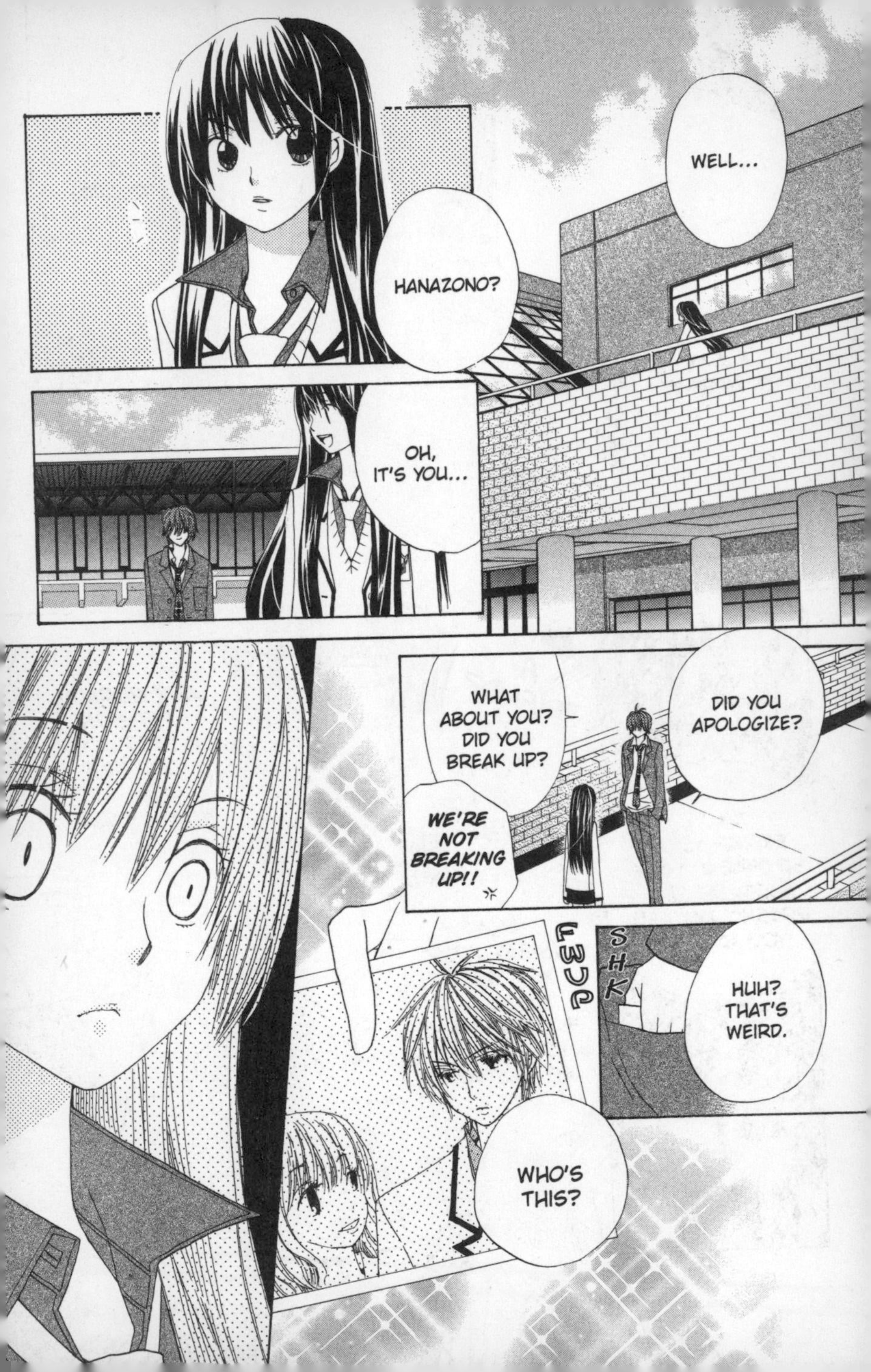
WELL...
HANAZONO?
OH, IT'S YOU...
DID YOU APOLOGIZE?
WHAT ABOUT YOU? DID YOU BREAK UP?
WE'RE NOT BREAKING UP!!
SHK
HUH? THAT'S WEIRD.
FWUP
WHO'S THIS?

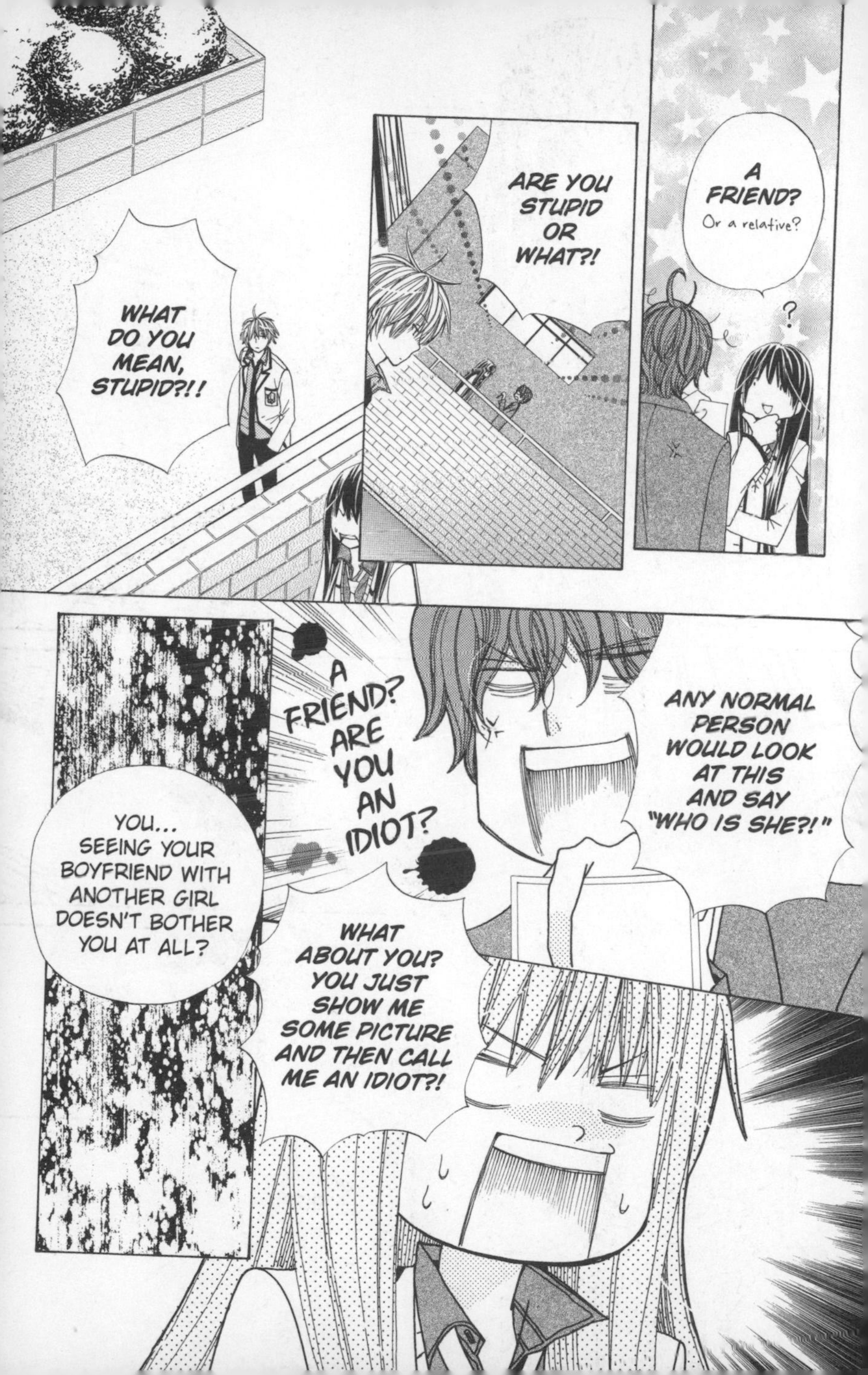
A FRIEND?
Or a relative?
ARE YOU STUPID OR WHAT?!
WHAT DO YOU MEAN, STUPID?!!
A FRIEND? ARE YOU AN IDIOT?
ANY NORMAL PERSON WOULD LOOK AT THIS AND SAY "WHO IS SHE?!"
WHAT ABOUT YOU? YOU JUST SHOW ME SOME PICTURE AND THEN CALL ME AN IDIOT?!
YOU... SEEING YOUR BOYFRIEND WITH ANOTHER GIRL DOESN'T BOTHER YOU AT ALL?

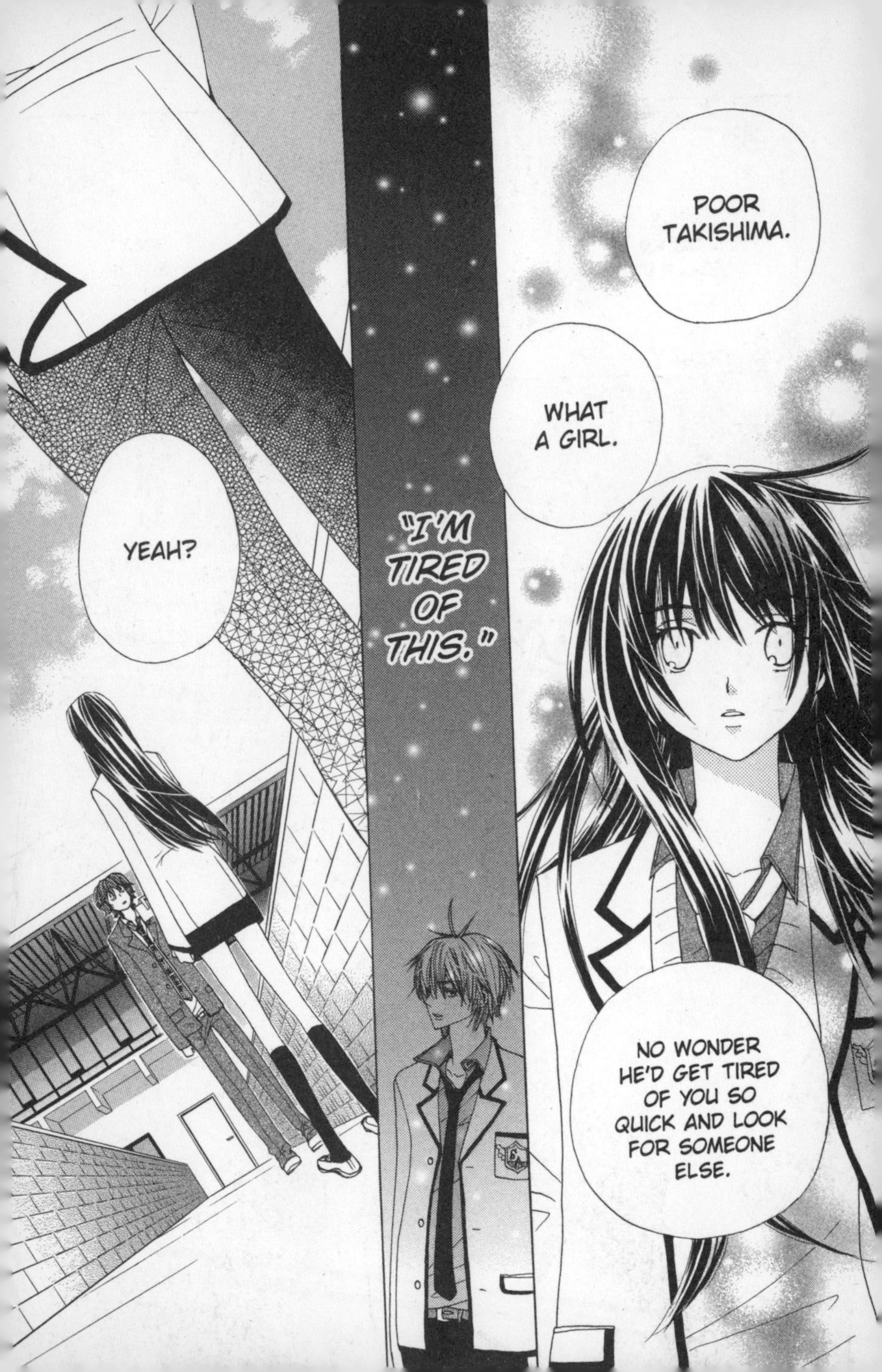
POOR TAKISHIMA.
WHAT A GIRL.
NO WONDER HE'D GET TIRED OF YOU SO QUICK AND LOOK FOR SOMEONE ELSE.
"I'M TIRED OF THIS."
YEAH?

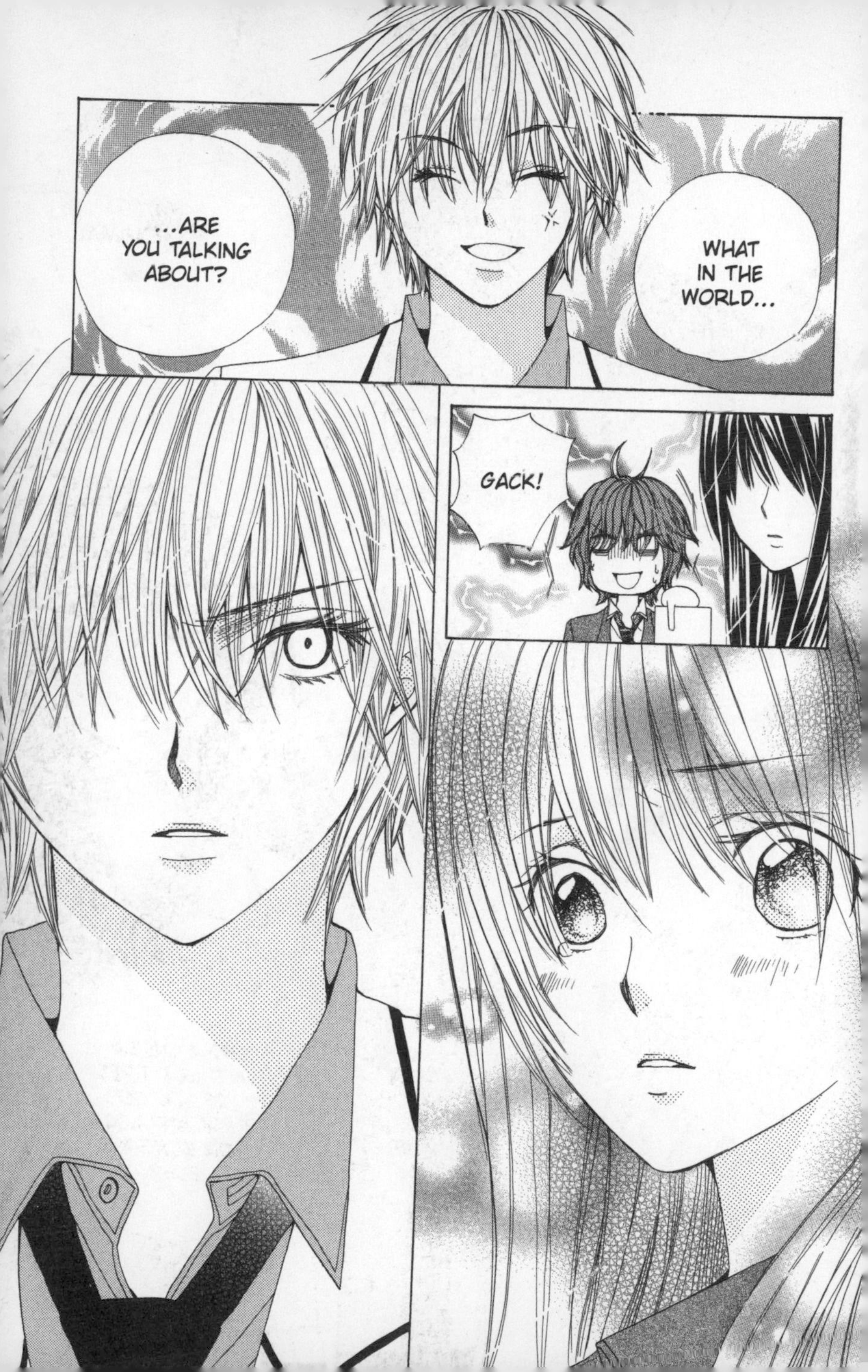
WHAT IN THE WORLD...
...ARE YOU TALKING ABOUT?
GACK!

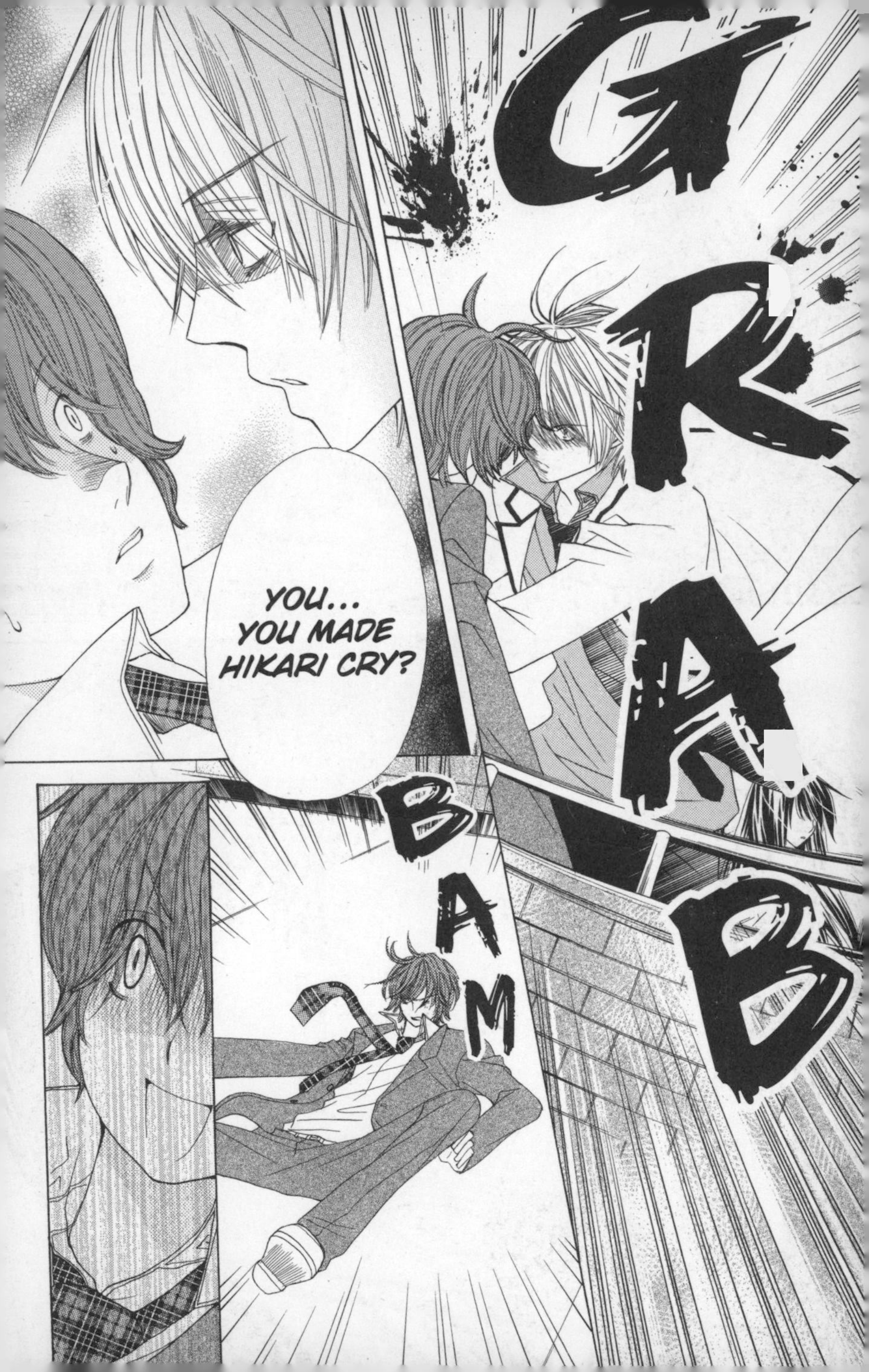
GRAB
YOU... YOU MADE HIKARI CRY?
BAM

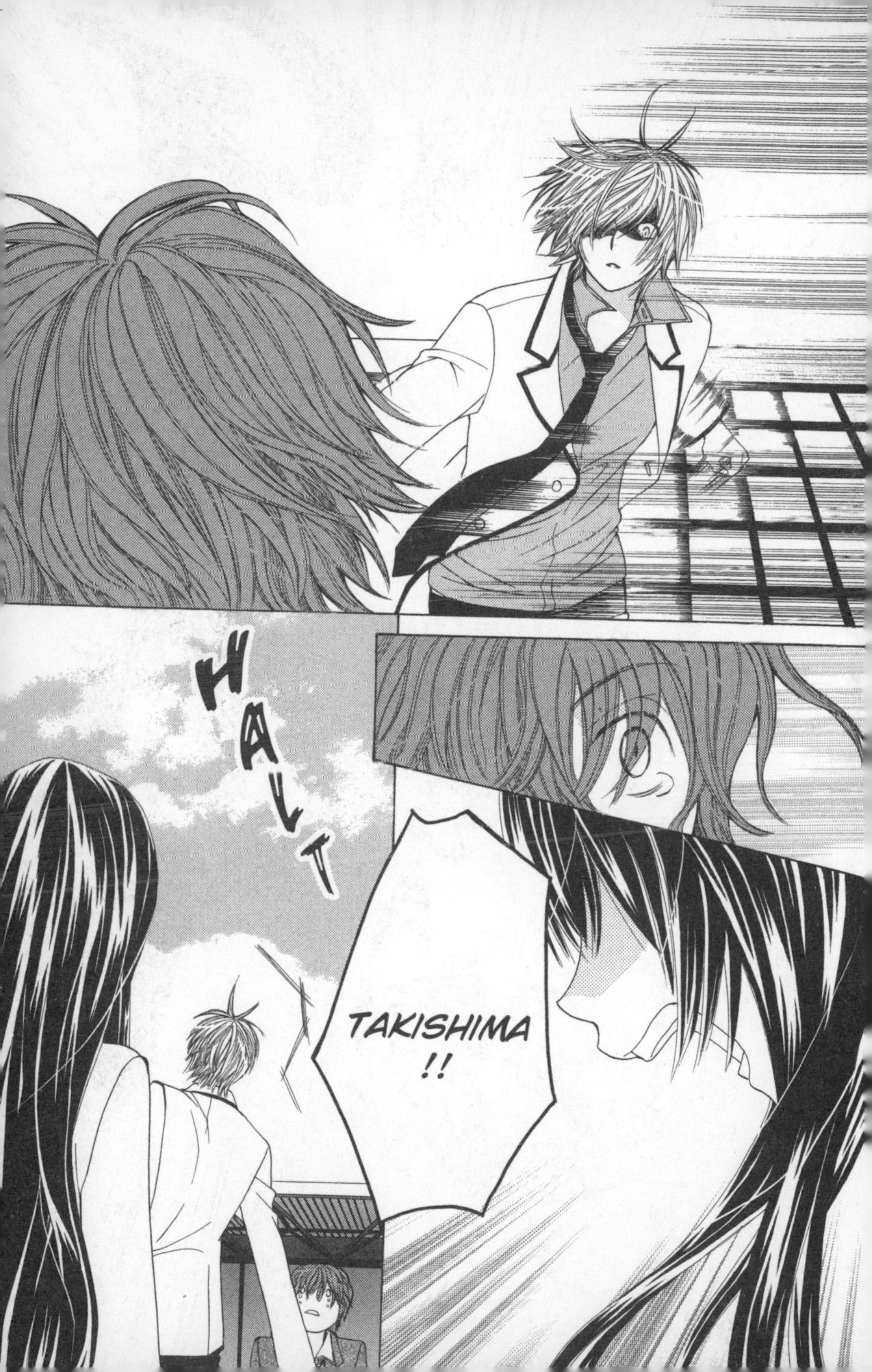
HALT
TAKISHIMA !!

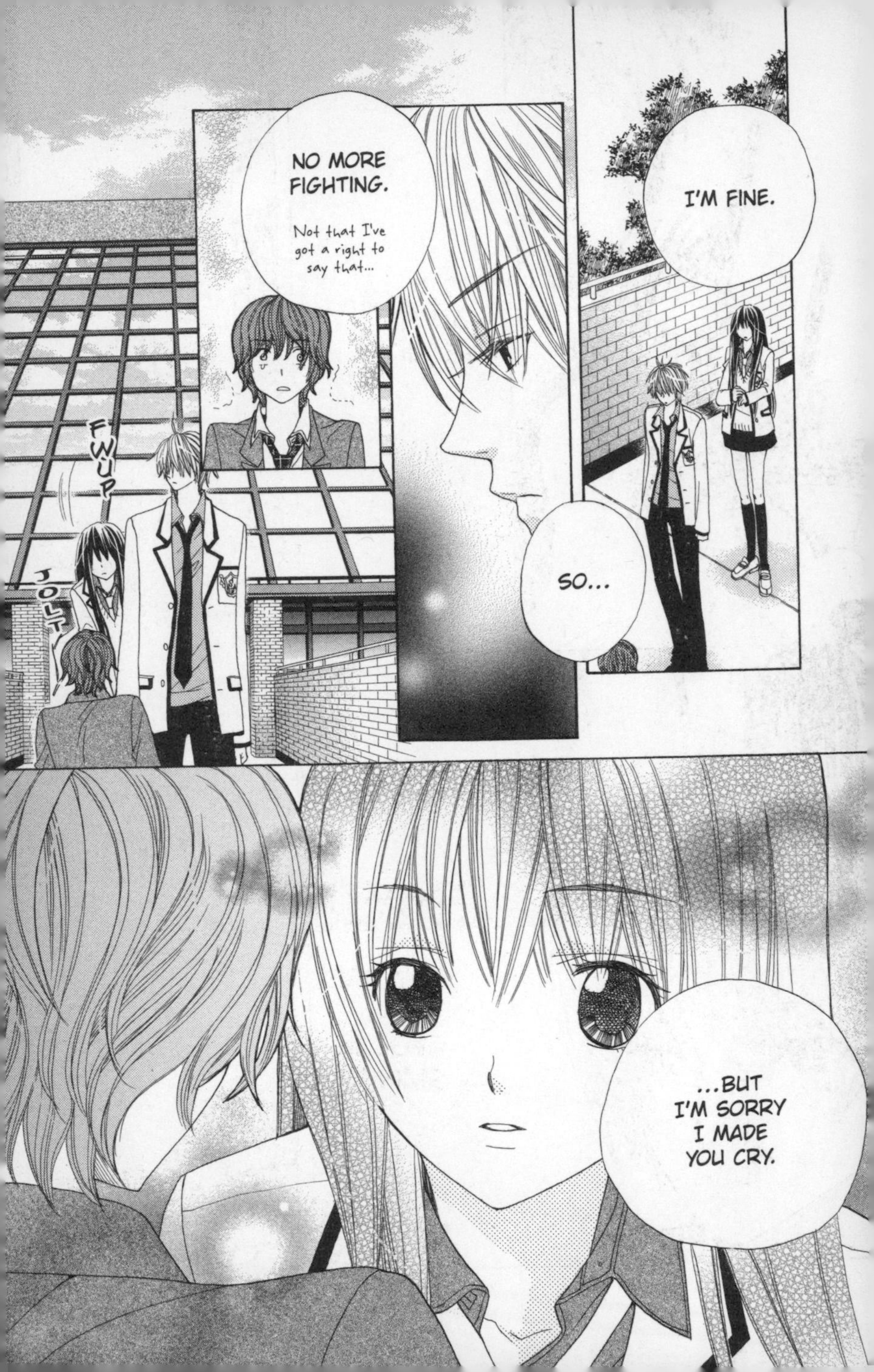
I'M FINE.
SO...
NO MORE FIGHTING.
Not that I've got a right to say that...
FWUP
JOLT
...BUT I'M SORRY I MADE YOU CRY.

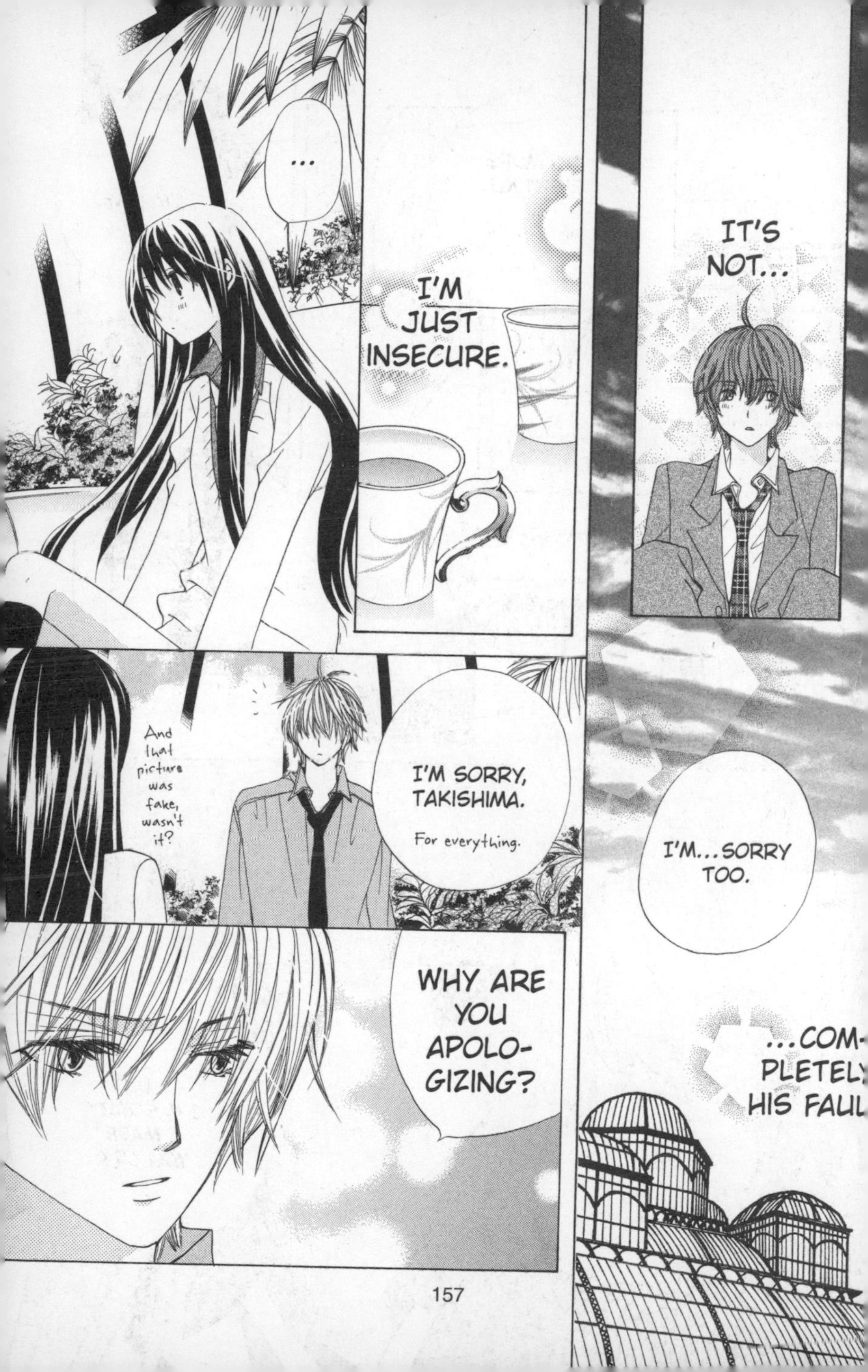
IT'S NOT...
I'M JUST INSECURE.
...
I'M... SORRY TOO.
...COM- PLETEL HIS FAUL
I'M SORRY, TAKISHIMA.
For everything.
And that picture was fake, wasn't it?
WHY ARE YOU APOLO- GIZING?

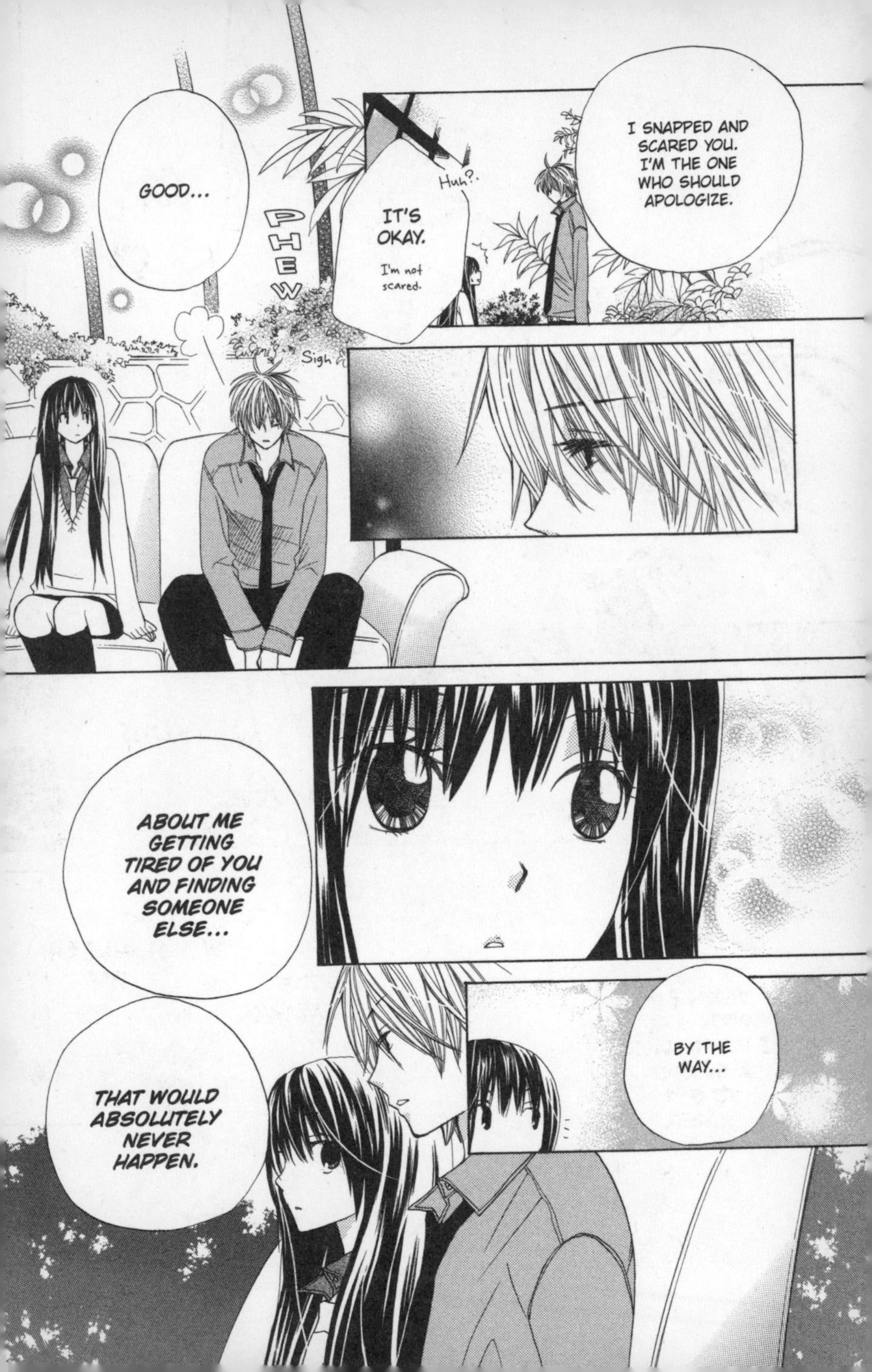
I SNAPPED AND SCARED YOU. I'M THE ONE WHO SHOULD APOLOGIZE.
Huh?
IT'S OKAY.
I'm not scared.
PHEW
Sigh
GOOD...
ABOUT ME GETTING TIRED OF YOU AND FINDING SOMEONE ELSE...
THAT WOULD ABSOLUTELY NEVER HAPPEN.
BY THE WAY...

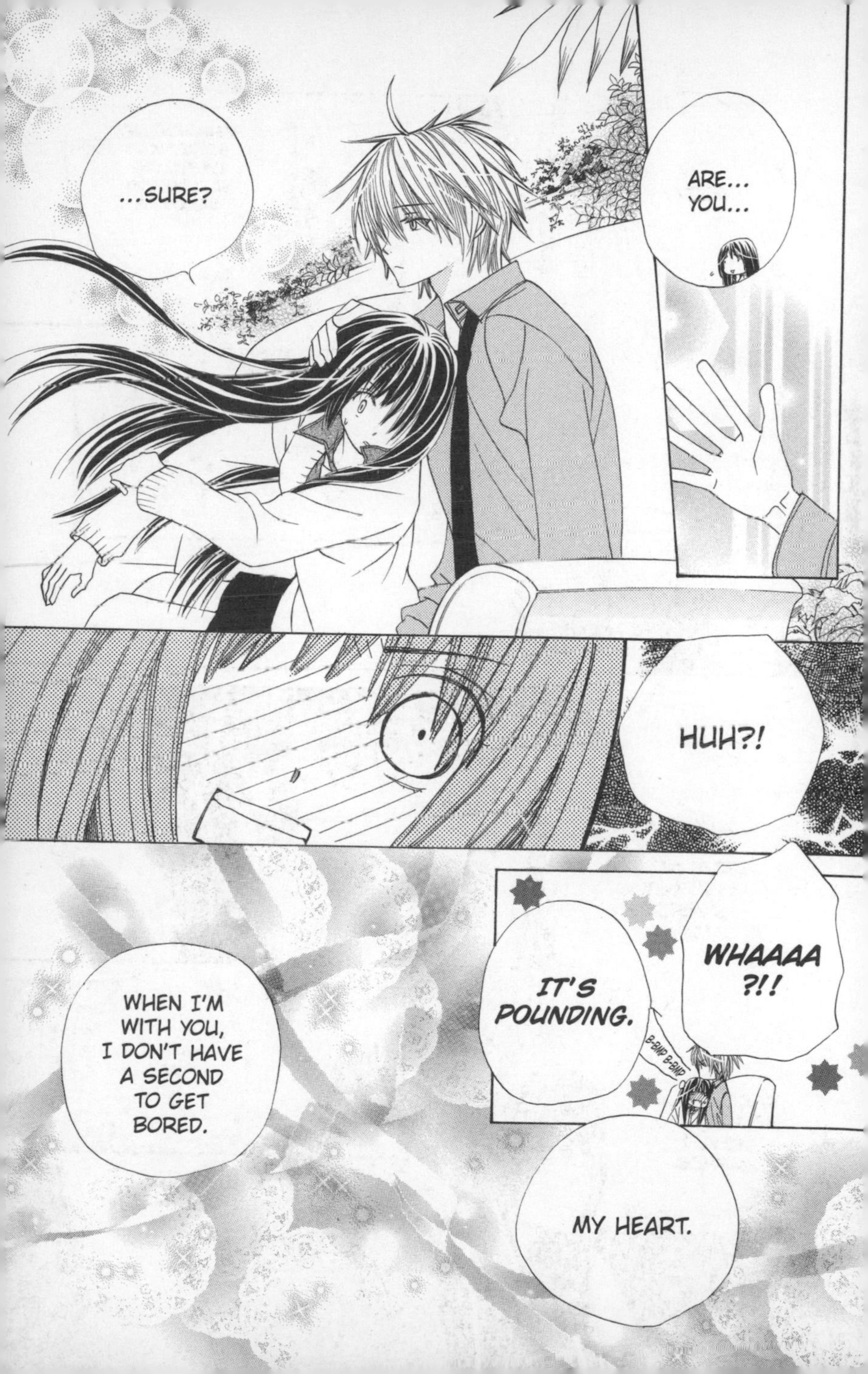
ARE... YOU...
...SURE?
HUH?!
WHAAAA ?!!
IT'S POUNDING.
B-BMP B-BMP
MY HEART.
WHEN I'M WITH YOU, I DON'T HAVE A SECOND TO GET BORED.

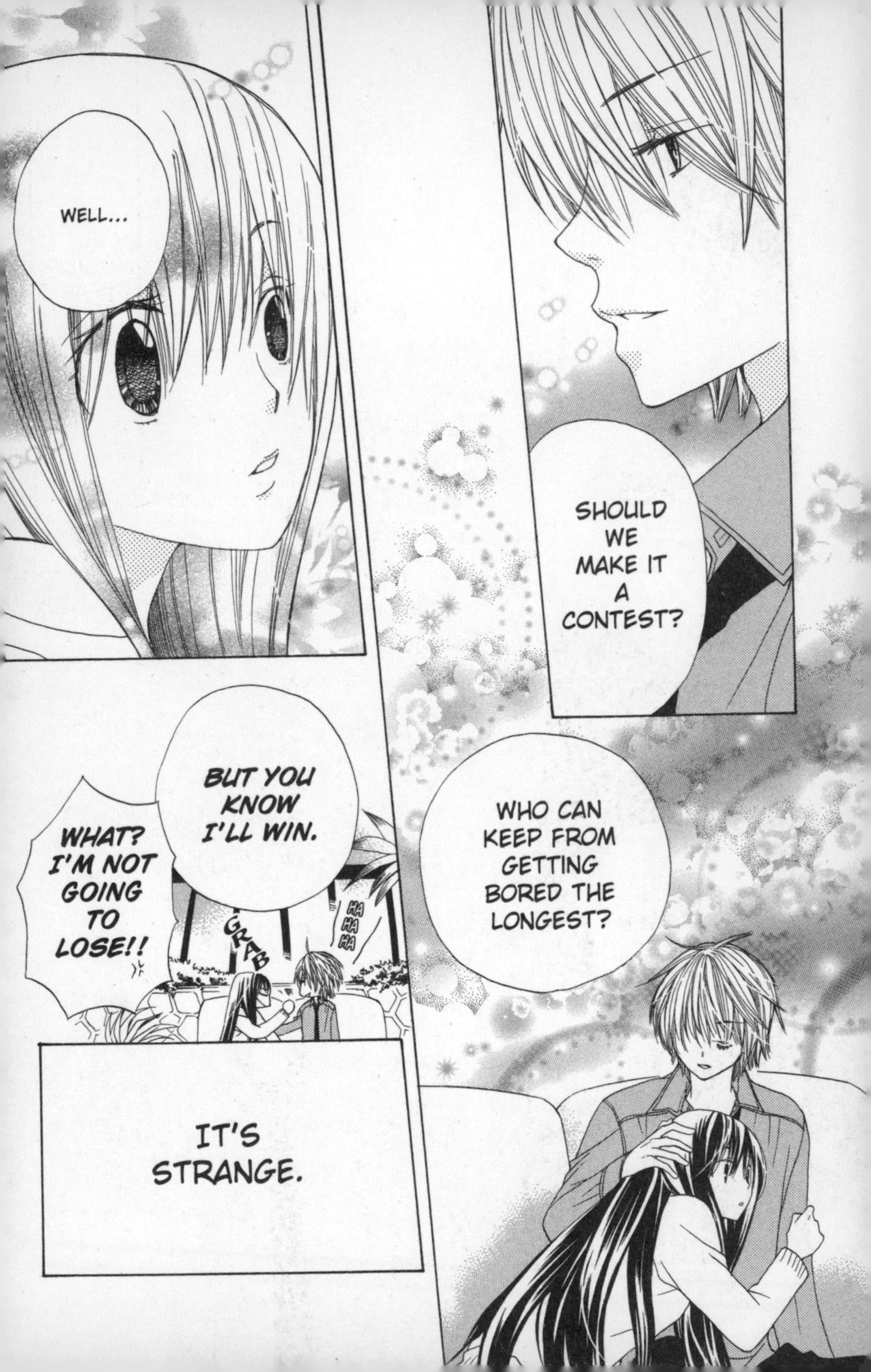
SHOULD WE MAKE IT A CONTEST?
WELL...
WHO CAN KEEP FROM GETTING BORED THE LONGEST?
BUT YOU KNOW I'LL WIN.
WHAT? I'M NOT GOING TO LOSE!!
HA HA HA HA
GRAB
IT'S STRANGE.

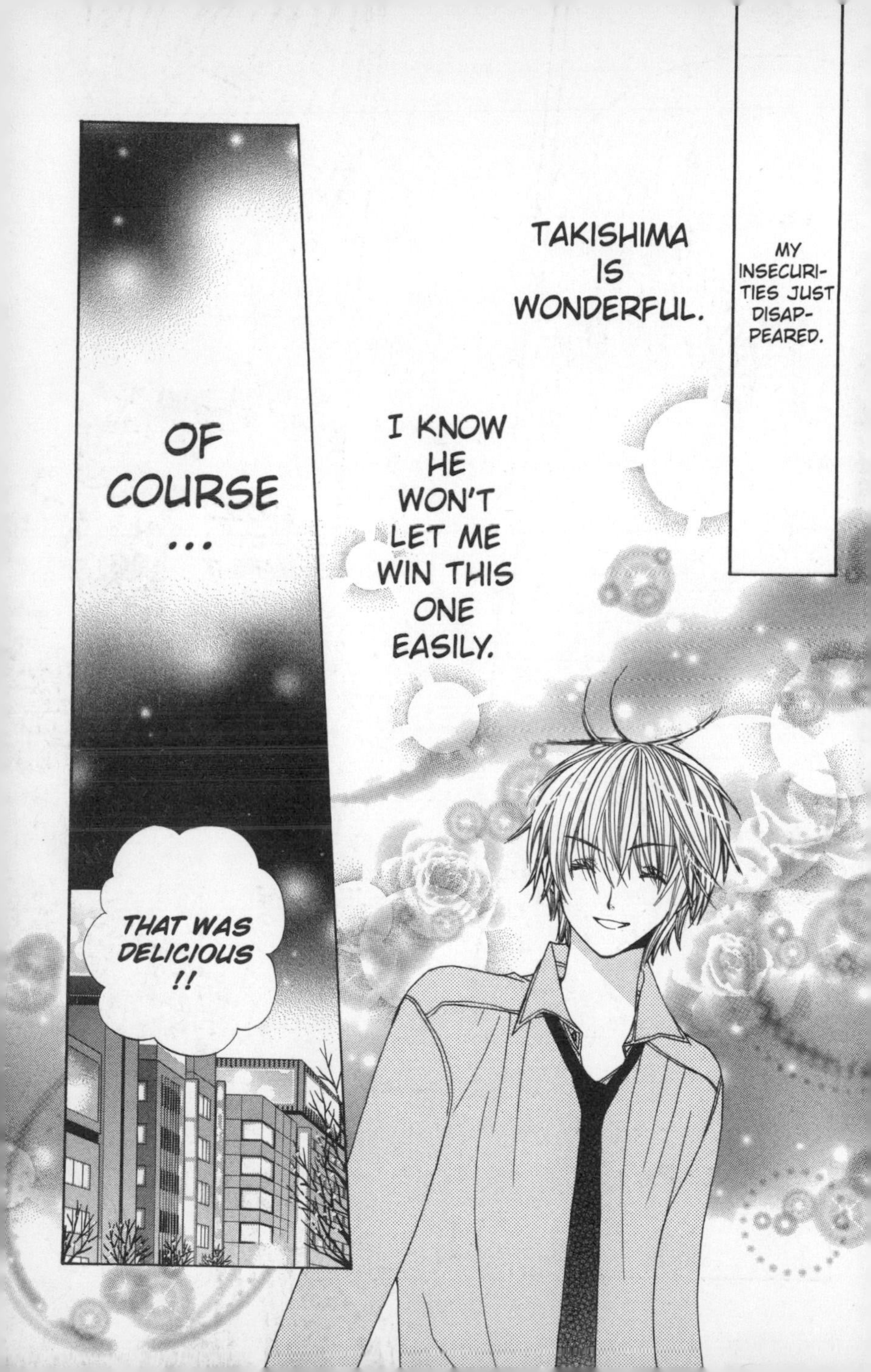

MY INSECURITIES JUST DISAPPEARED.
TAKISHIMA IS WONDERFUL.
I KNOW HE WON'T LET ME WIN THIS ONE EASILY.
OF COURSE ...
THAT WAS DELICIOUS !!

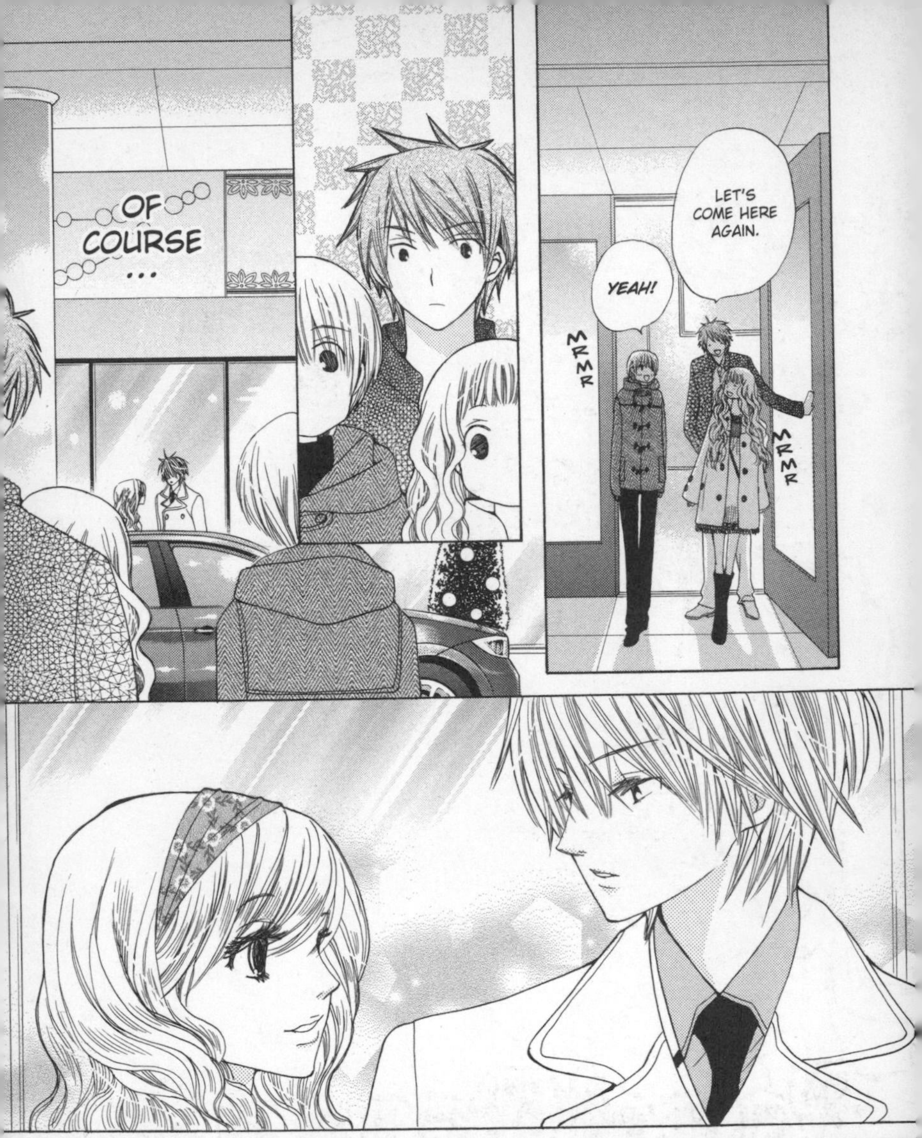
LET'S COME HERE AGAIN.
YEAH!
MRMR
MRMR
OF COURSE ...
I DON'T PLAN ON LOSING.
...
Oh?
KEI!?! BUT WHO'S SHE?

S·A VOLUME 11 / END

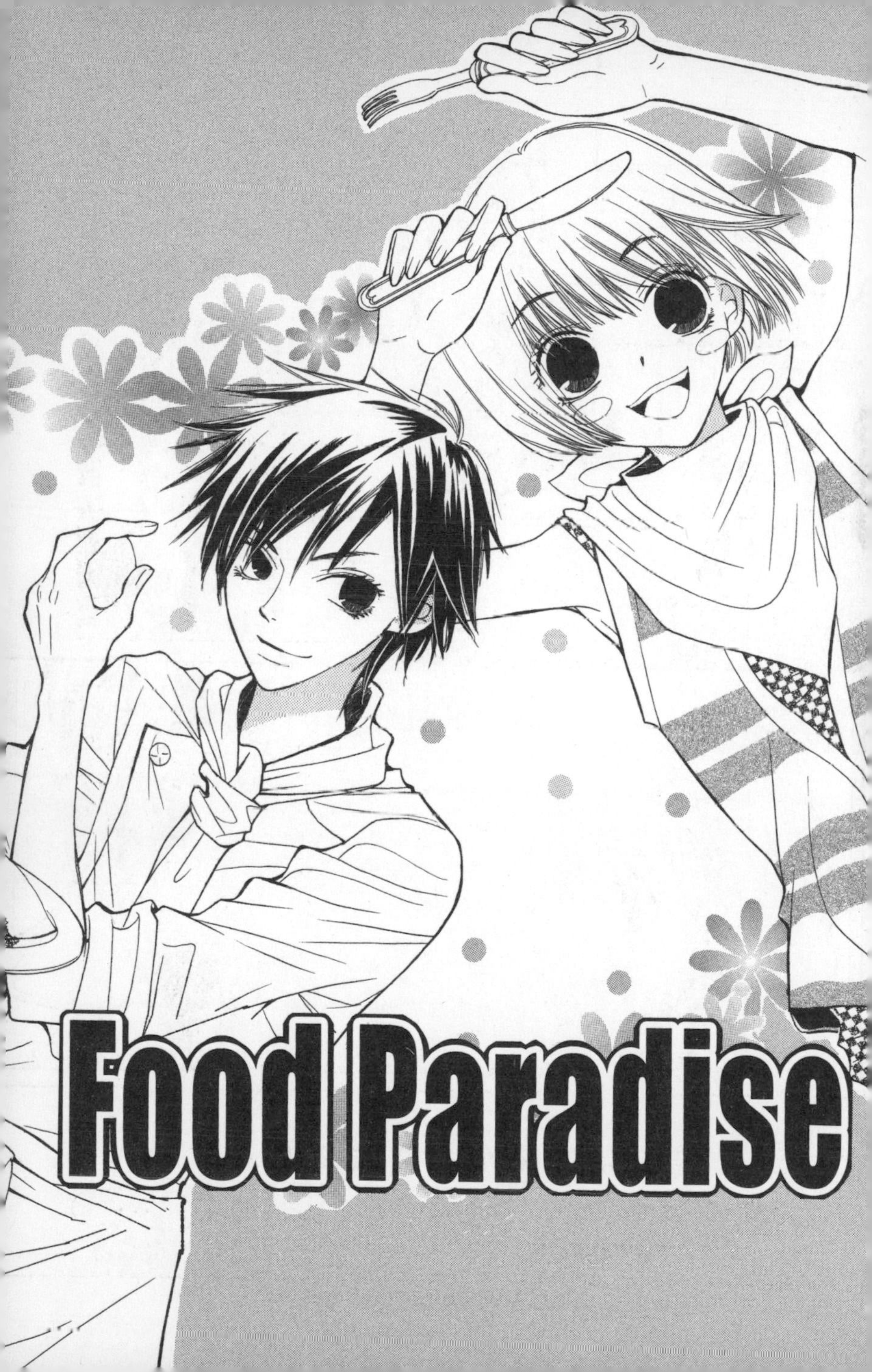
Food Paradise

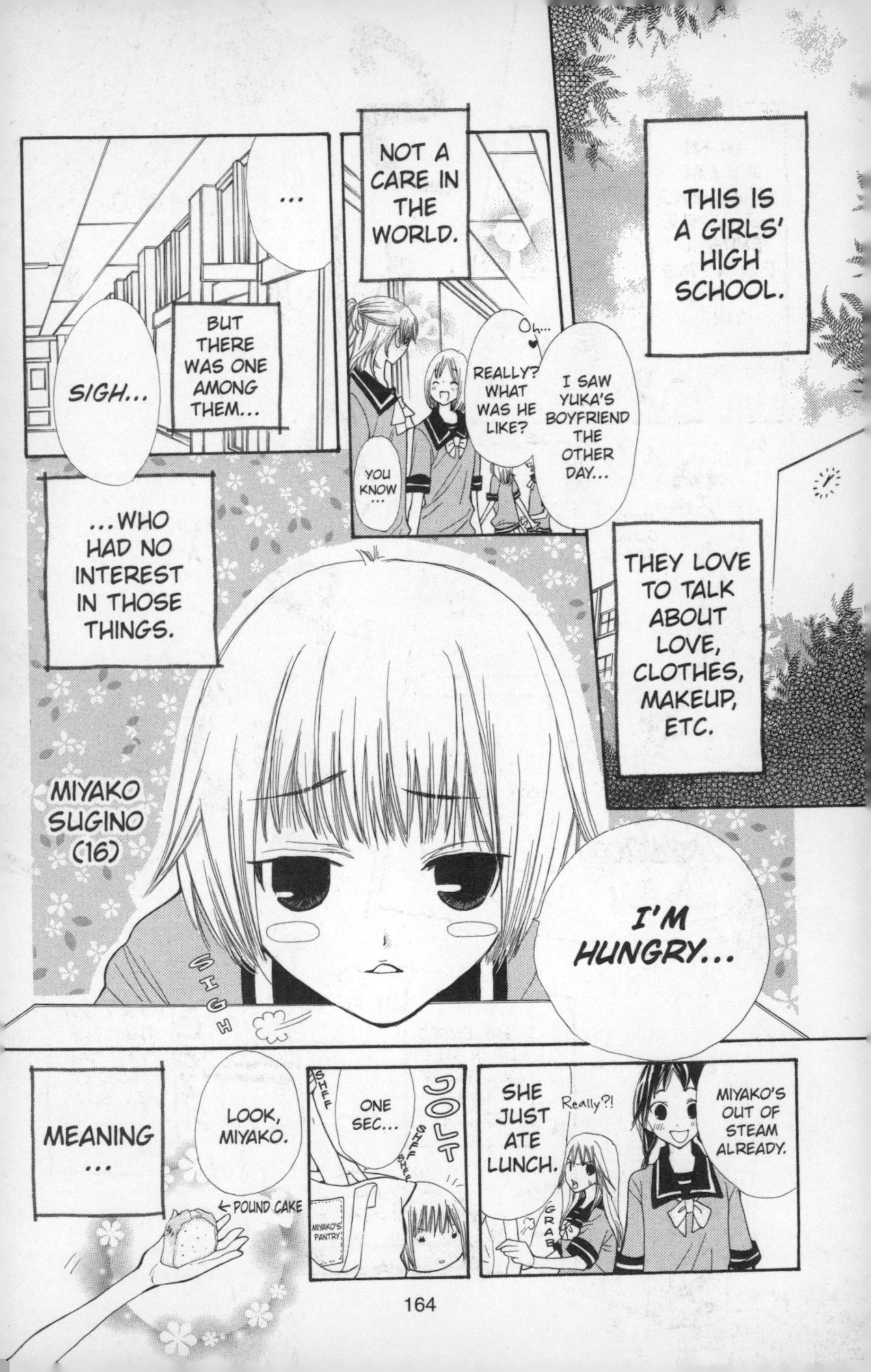
THIS IS A GIRLS' HIGH SCHOOL.
NOT A CARE IN THE WORLD.
Oh...♥
I SAW YUKA'S BOYFRIEND THE OTHER DAY...
REALLY? WHAT WAS HE LIKE?
YOU KNOW...
THEY LOVE TO TALK ABOUT LOVE, CLOTHES, MAKEUP, ETC.
...
BUT THERE WAS ONE AMONG THEM...
SIGH...
...WHO HAD NO INTEREST IN THOSE THINGS.
MIYAKO SUGINO (16)
I'M HUNGRY...
SIGH
MIYAKO'S OUT OF STEAM ALREADY.
Really?!
SHE JUST ATE LUNCH.
GRAB
JOLT
ONE SEC...
SHFF
SHFF SHFF
MIYAKO'S PANTRY
LOOK, MIYAKO.
← POUND CAKE
MEANING...

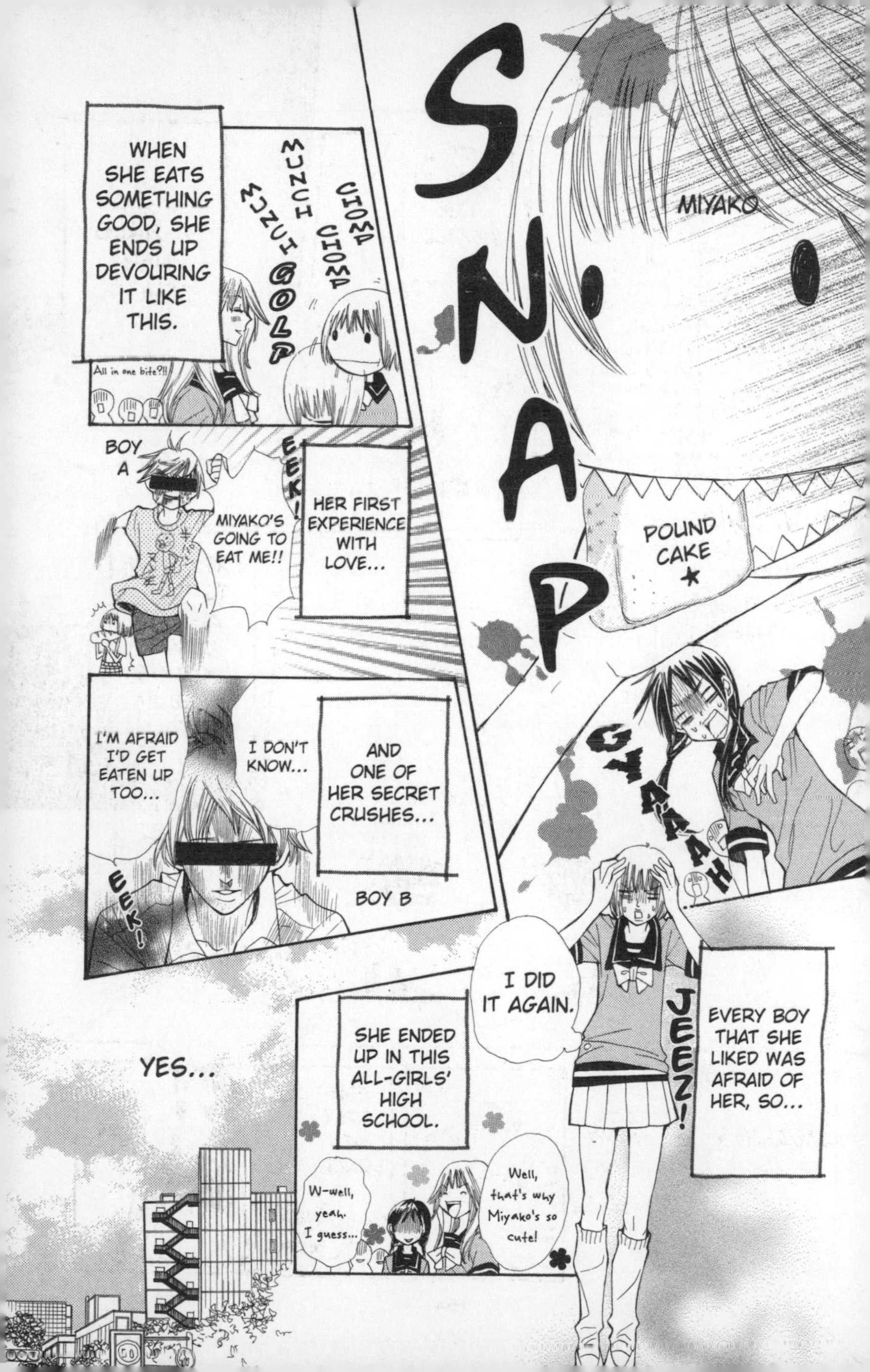

SNAP
MIYAKO
POUND CAKE ★
GYAAAAH
WHEN SHE EATS SOMETHING GOOD, SHE ENDS UP DEVOURING IT LIKE THIS.
CHOMP CHOMP
MUNCH MUNCH
GOLP
All in one bite?!!
HER FIRST EXPERIENCE WITH LOVE...
EEK!
MIYAKO'S GOING TO EAT ME!!
BOY A
AND ONE OF HER SECRET CRUSHES...
I DON'T KNOW...
I'M AFRAID I'D GET EATEN UP TOO...
EEK!
BOY B
EVERY BOY THAT SHE LIKED WAS AFRAID OF HER, SO...
JEEZ!
I DID IT AGAIN.
SHE ENDED UP IN THIS ALL-GIRLS' HIGH SCHOOL.
YES...
Well, that's why Miyako's so cute!
W-well, yeah. I guess...

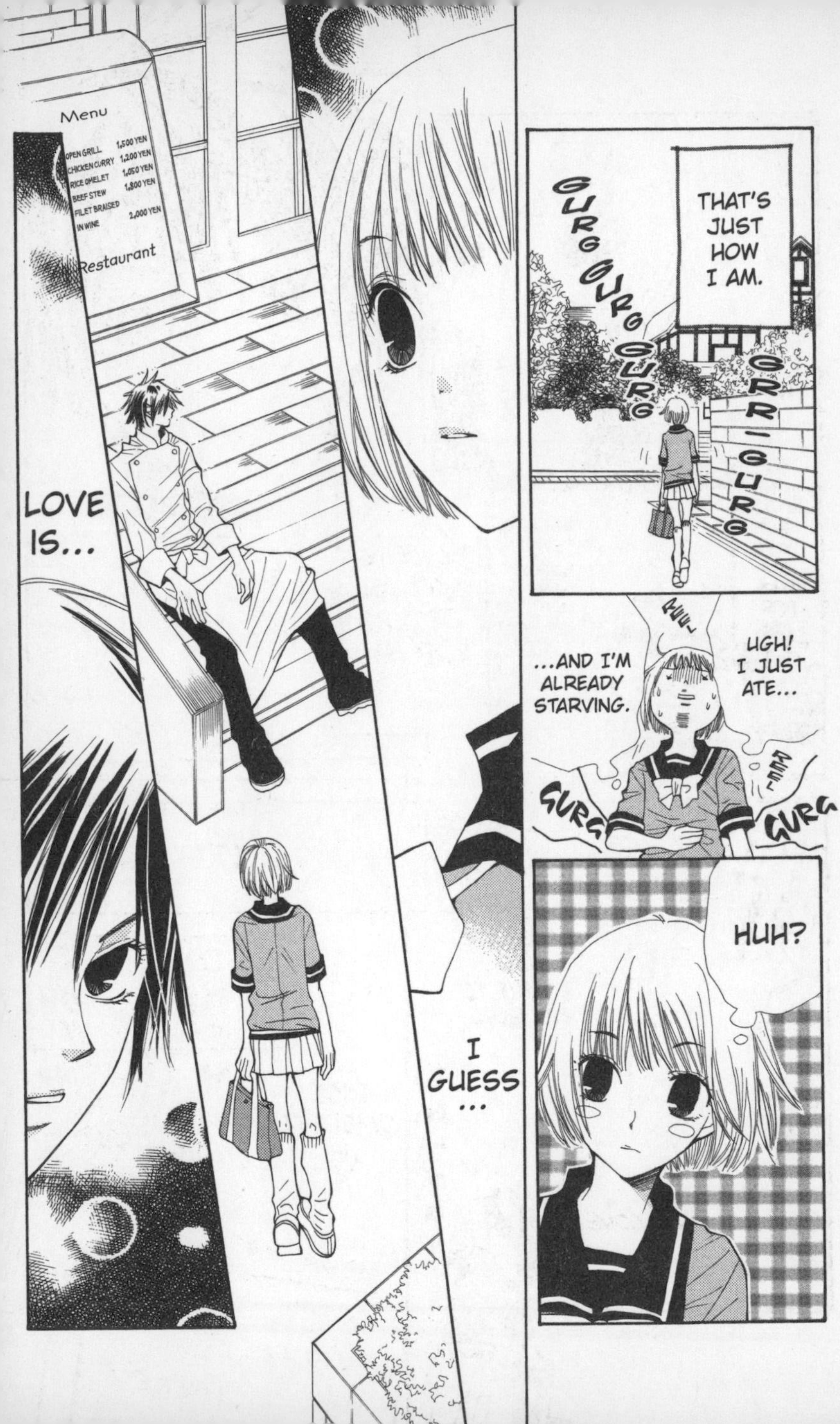
THAT'S JUST HOW I AM.
GURG GURG GURG GURG
GRR-GURG
UGH! I JUST ATE...
...AND I'M ALREADY STARVING.
REEL
GURG
GURG
HUH?
Menu
OPEN GRILL 1,500 YEN
CHICKEN CURRY 1,200 YEN
RICE OMELET 1,050 YEN
BEEF STEW 1,800 YEN
FILET BRAISED IN WINE 2,000 YEN
Restaurant
LOVE IS...
I GUESS...

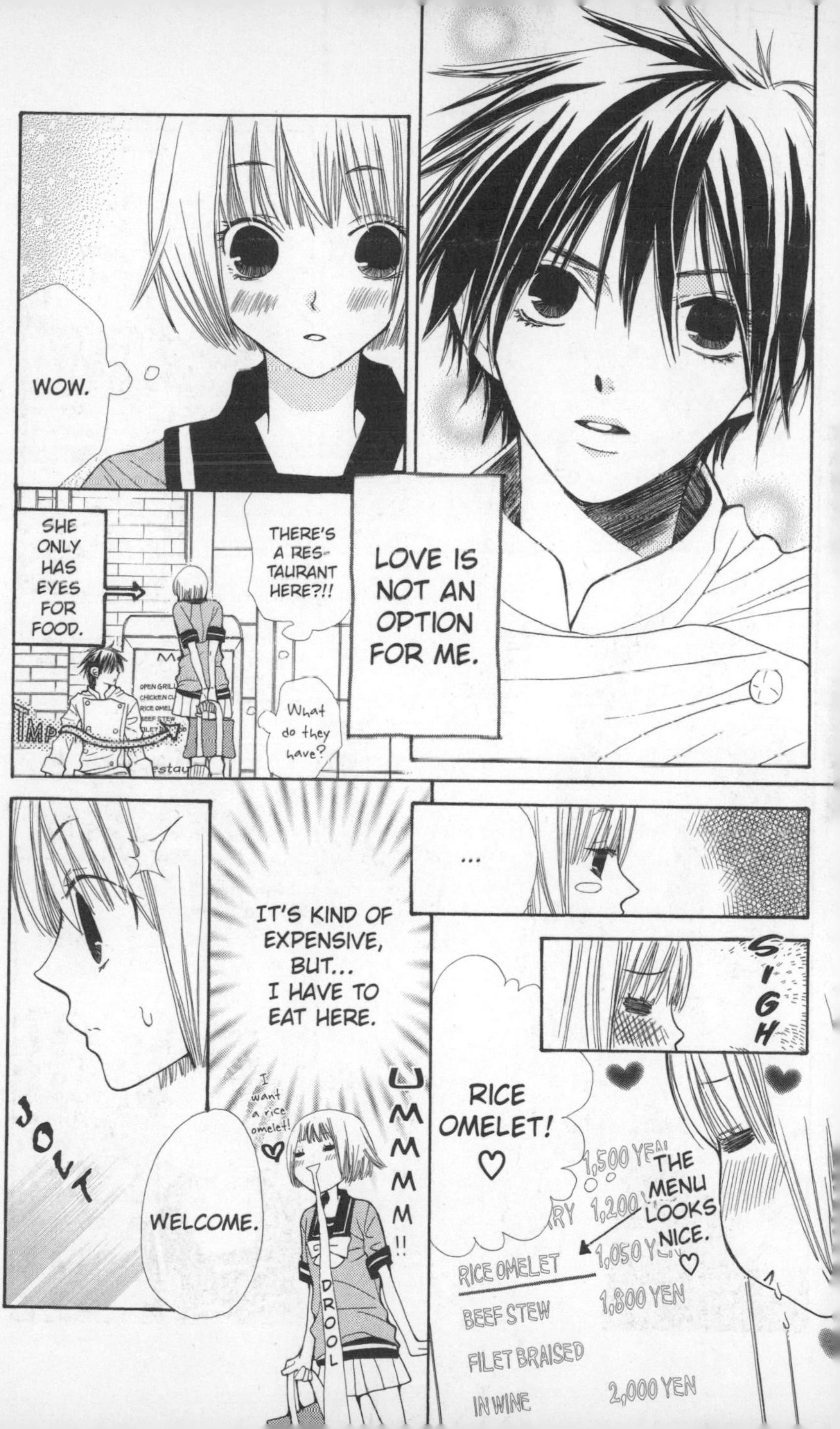
LOVE IS NOT AN OPTION FOR ME.
WOW.
THERE'S A RES-TAURANT HERE?!!
What do they have?
SHE ONLY HAS EYES FOR FOOD.
...
SIGH
RICE OMELET! ♡
THE MENU LOOKS NICE. ♡
RICE OMELET 1,050 YEN
BEEF STEW 1,800 YEN
FILET BRAISED IN WINE 2,000 YEN
IT'S KIND OF EXPENSIVE, BUT... I HAVE TO EAT HERE.
UMMMMM!!
I want a rice omelet! ♡
DROOL
JOLT
WELCOME.

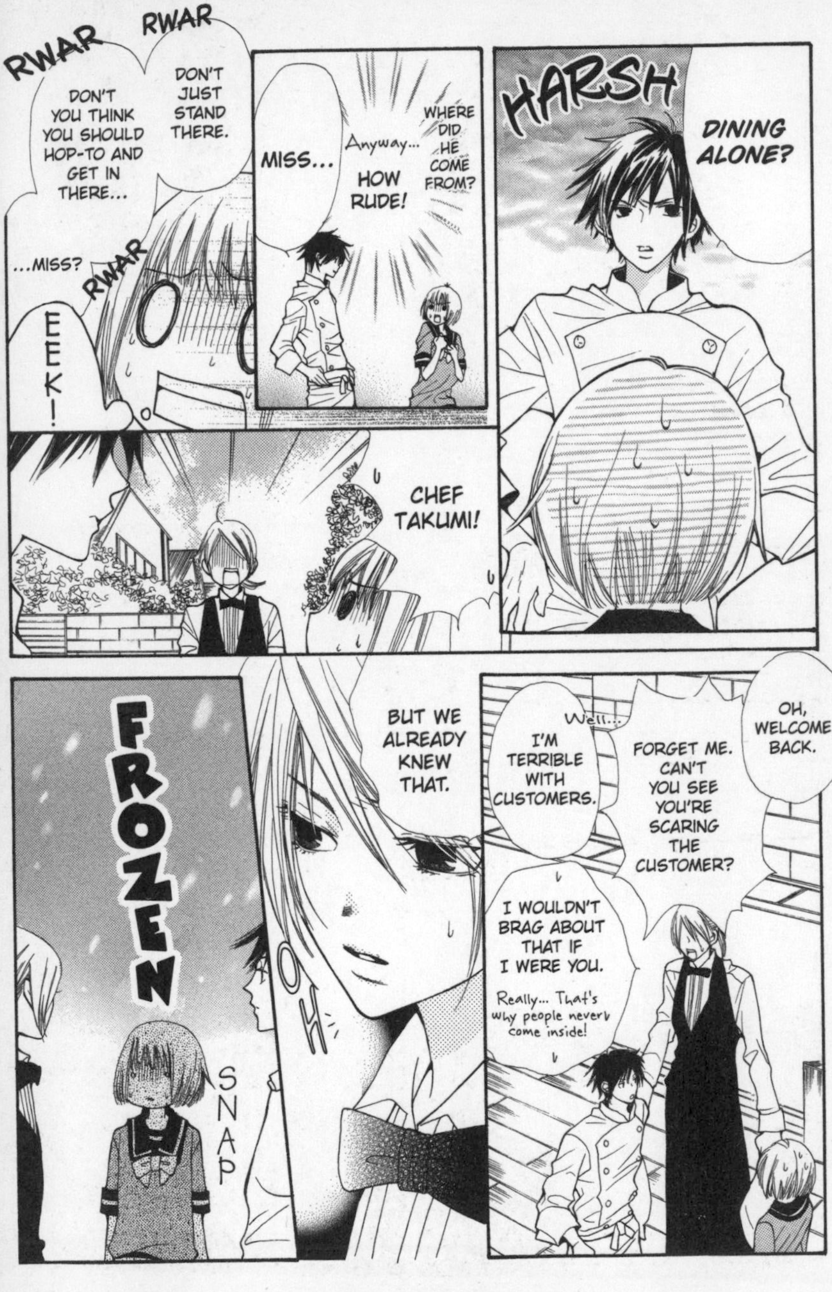
HARSH
DINING ALONE?
MISS...
Anyway... HOW RUDE!
WHERE DID HE COME FROM?
RWAR RWAR
DON'T JUST STAND THERE.
DON'T YOU THINK YOU SHOULD HOP-TO AND GET IN THERE...
...MISS?
RWAR
EEK!
CHEF TAKUMI!
OH, WELCOME BACK.
FORGET ME. CAN'T YOU SEE YOU'RE SCARING THE CUSTOMER?
Well... I'M TERRIBLE WITH CUSTOMERS.
I WOULDN'T BRAG ABOUT THAT IF I WERE YOU.
Really... That's why people never come inside!
BUT WE ALREADY KNEW THAT.
OH
FROZEN
SNAP

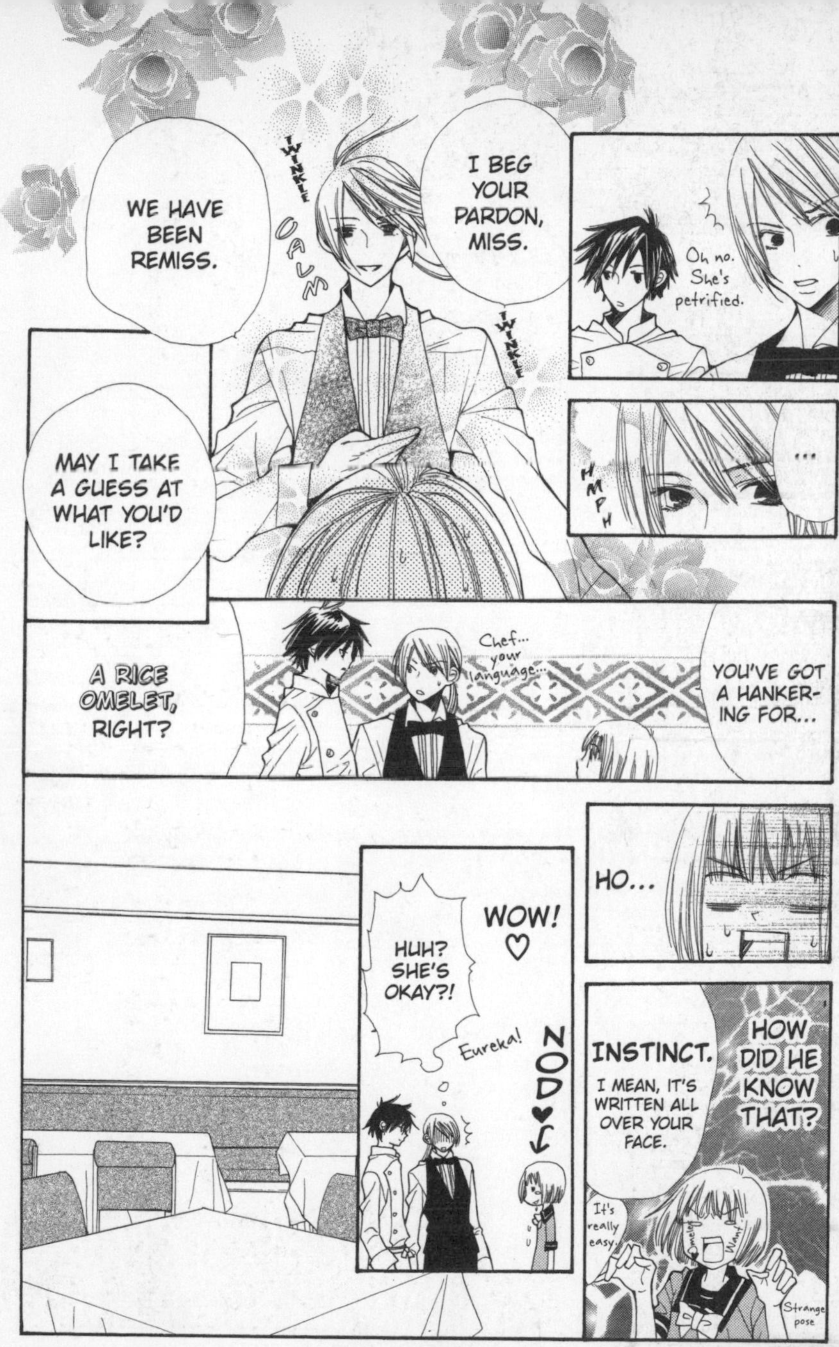
Oh no. She's petrified.
HMPH
...
I BEG YOUR PARDON, MISS.
TWINKLE
TWINKLE
WE HAVE BEEN REMISS.
MAY I TAKE A GUESS AT WHAT YOU'D LIKE?
YOU'VE GOT A HANKERING FOR...
Chef... your language...
A RICE OMELET, RIGHT?
HO...
HOW DID HE KNOW THAT?
INSTINCT.
I MEAN, IT'S WRITTEN ALL OVER YOUR FACE.
It's really easy.
Omelet
Want
Strange pose
WOW! ♡
NOD ♥
HUH? SHE'S OKAY?!
Eureka!

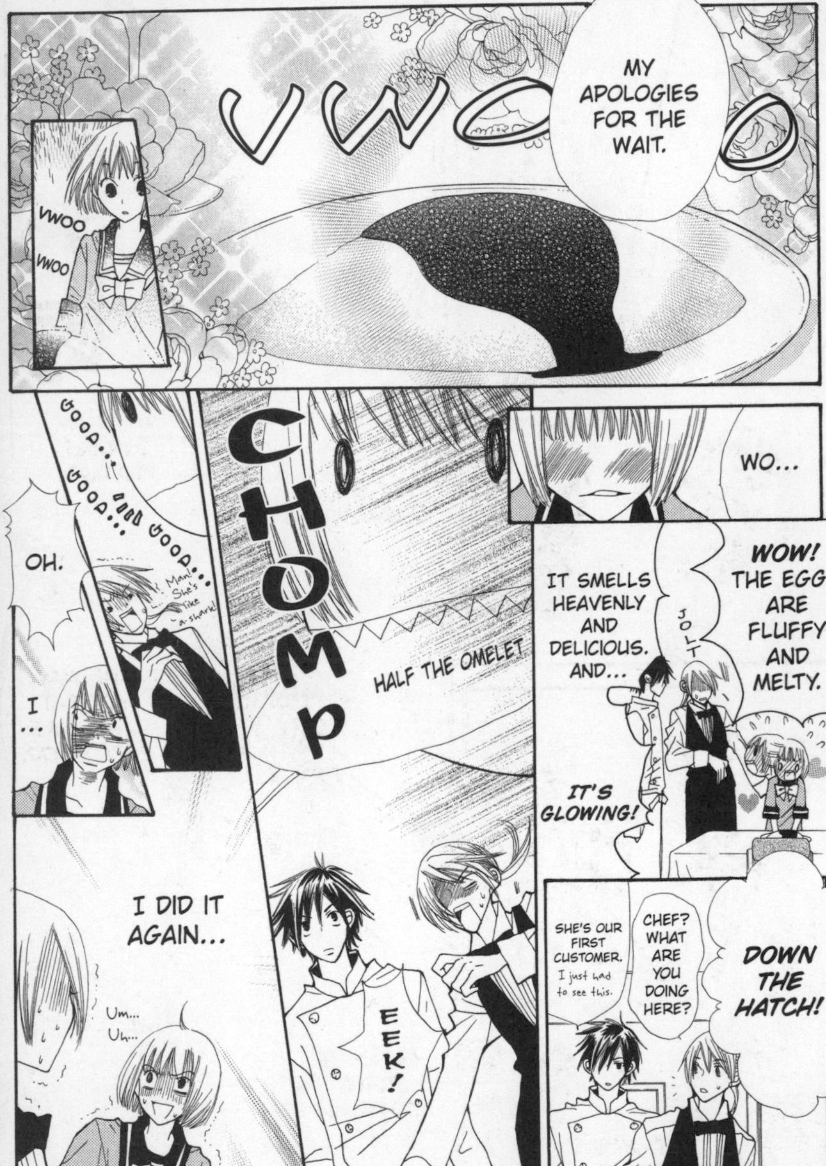
VWOO
MY APOLOGIES FOR THE WAIT.
VWOO
VWOO
WO...
WOW! THE EGGS ARE FLUFFY AND MELTY.
JOLT
IT SMELLS HEAVENLY AND DELICIOUS. AND...
IT'S GLOWING!
CHOMP
HALF THE OMELET
GOOD... GOOD... GOOD... GOOD GOOD...
Man! She's like a shark!
OH.
I...
DOWN THE HATCH!
CHEF? WHAT ARE YOU DOING HERE?
SHE'S OUR FIRST CUSTOMER.
I just had to see this.
EEK!
I DID IT AGAIN...
Um... Uh...

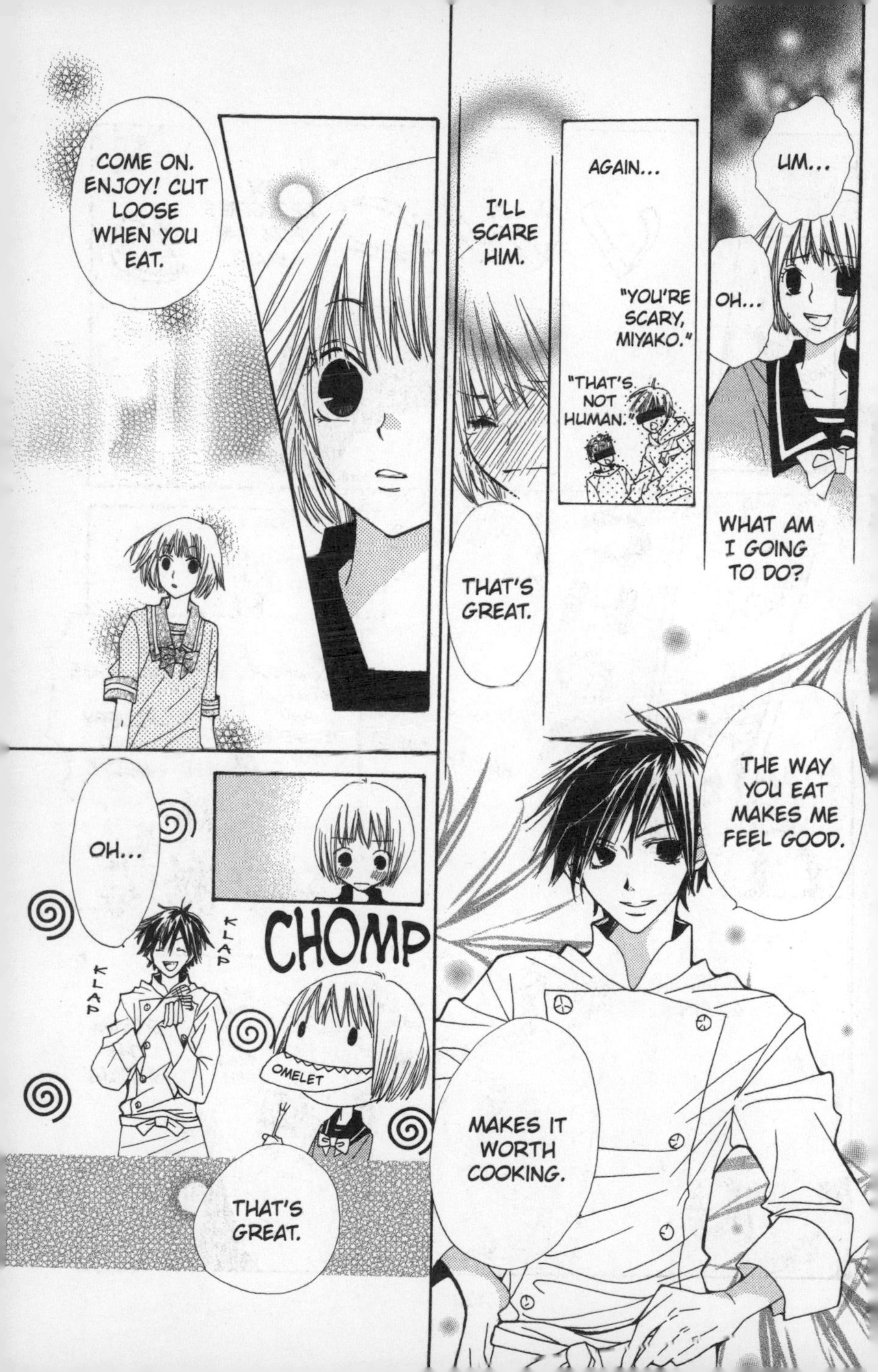
UM...
OH...
WHAT AM I GOING TO DO?
AGAIN...
"YOU'RE SCARY, MIYAKO."
"THAT'S NOT HUMAN."
I'LL SCARE HIM.
THAT'S GREAT.
THE WAY YOU EAT MAKES ME FEEL GOOD.
MAKES IT WORTH COOKING.
COME ON. ENJOY! CUT LOOSE WHEN YOU EAT.
CHOMP
OMELET
KLAP
KLAP
OH...
THAT'S GREAT.

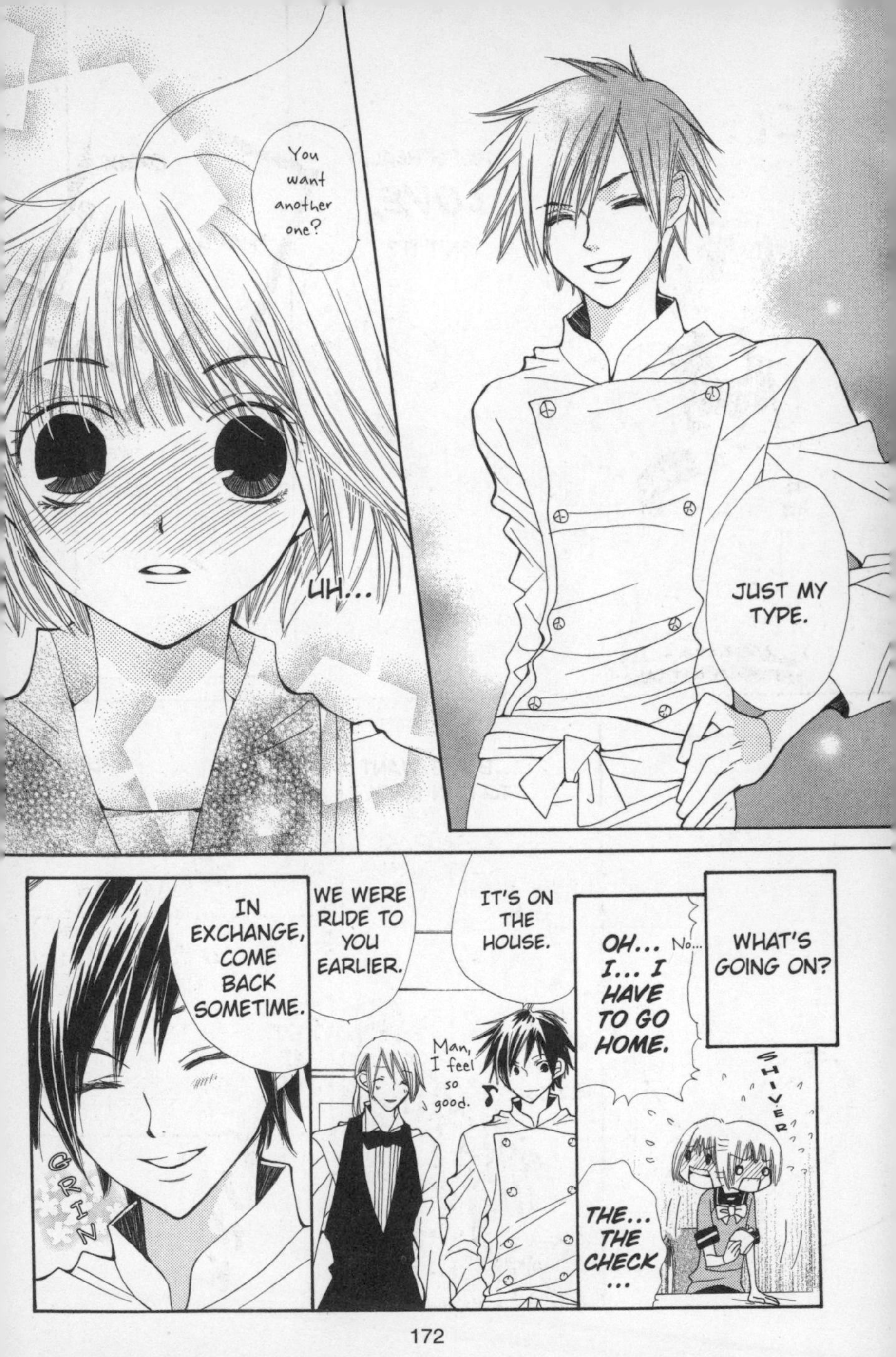
JUST MY TYPE.
You want another one?
UH...
WHAT'S GOING ON?
No...
OH... I... I HAVE TO GO HOME.
SHIVER
THE... THE CHECK ...
IT'S ON THE HOUSE.
WE WERE RUDE TO YOU EARLIER.
Man, I feel so good.
IN EXCHANGE, COME BACK SOMETIME.
GRIN

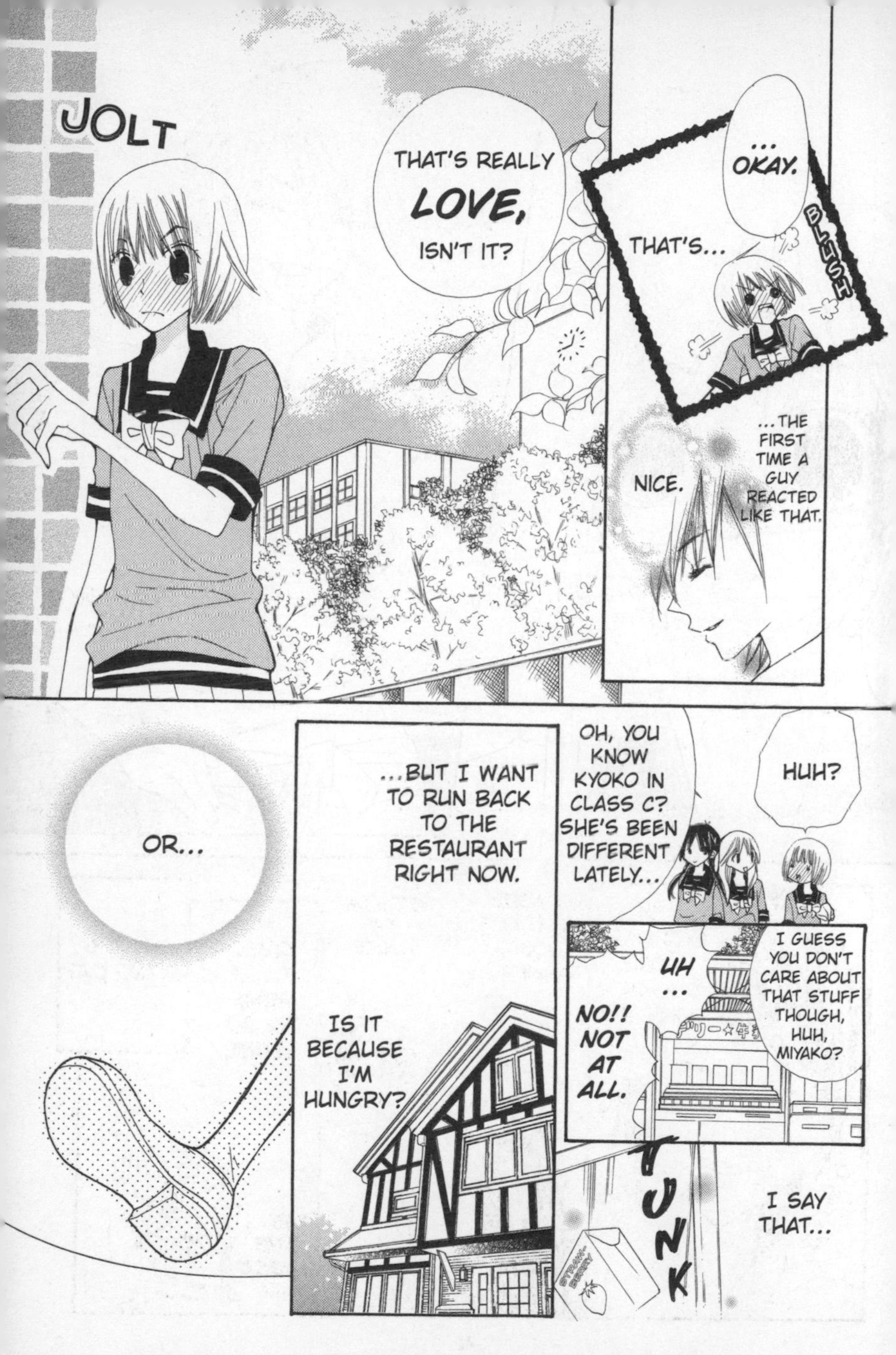
...OKAY.
THAT'S...
BLUSH
...THE FIRST TIME A GUY REACTED LIKE THAT.
NICE.
THAT'S REALLY LOVE, ISN'T IT?
JOLT
HUH?
OH, YOU KNOW KYOKO IN CLASS C? SHE'S BEEN DIFFERENT LATELY...
I GUESS YOU DON'T CARE ABOUT THAT STUFF THOUGH, HUH, MIYAKO?
UH...
NO!! NOT AT ALL.
I SAY THAT...
TUNK
STRAW-BERRY
...BUT I WANT TO RUN BACK TO THE RESTAURANT RIGHT NOW.
IS IT BECAUSE I'M HUNGRY?
OR...

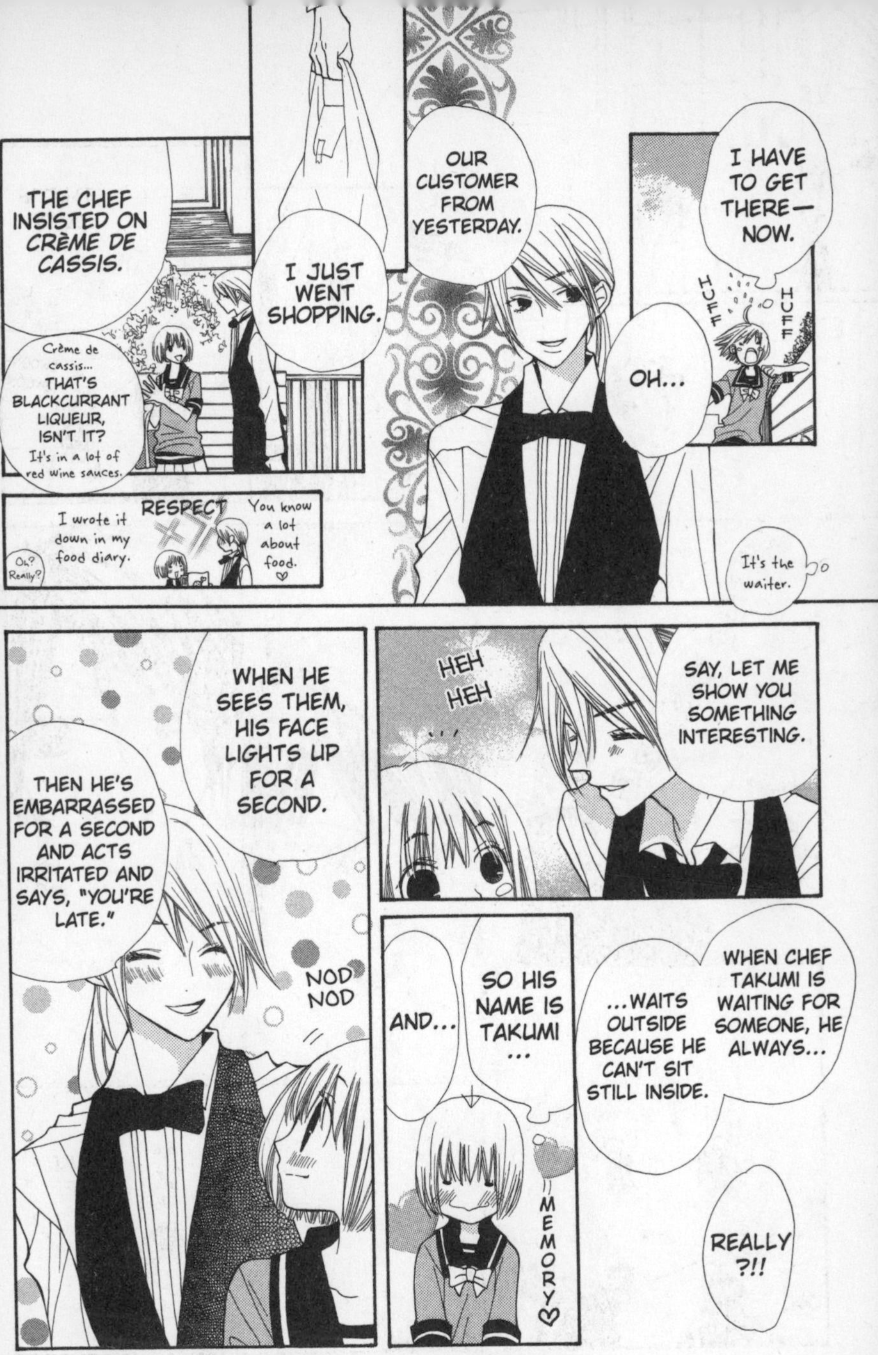
I HAVE TO GET THERE—NOW.
HUFF
HUFF
OH...
It's the waiter.
OUR CUSTOMER FROM YESTERDAY.
I JUST WENT SHOPPING.
THE CHEF INSISTED ON CRÈME DE CASSIS.
Crème de cassis... THAT'S BLACKCURRANT LIQUEUR, ISN'T IT? It's in a lot of red wine sauces.
You know a lot about food. ♡
RESPECT
I wrote it down in my food diary.
Oh? Really?
SAY, LET ME SHOW YOU SOMETHING INTERESTING.
HEH HEH
WHEN CHEF TAKUMI IS WAITING FOR SOMEONE, HE ALWAYS...
...WAITS OUTSIDE BECAUSE HE CAN'T SIT STILL INSIDE.
SO HIS NAME IS TAKUMI...
AND...
MEMORY♡
REALLY?!!
WHEN HE SEES THEM, HIS FACE LIGHTS UP FOR A SECOND.
THEN HE'S EMBARRASSED FOR A SECOND AND ACTS IRRITATED AND SAYS, "YOU'RE LATE."
NOD NOD

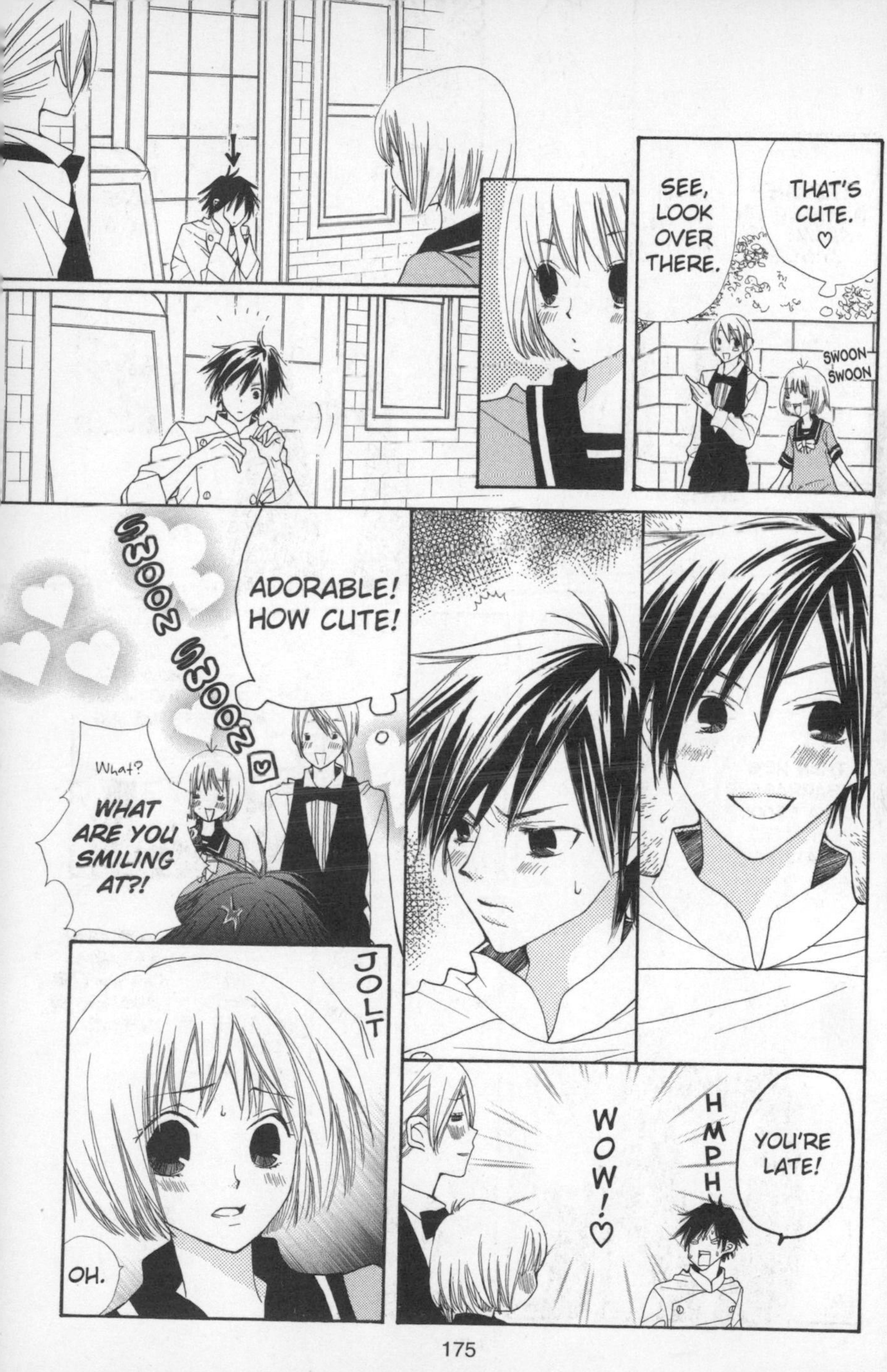
THAT'S CUTE. ♡
SEE, LOOK OVER THERE.
SWOON SWOON
ADORABLE! HOW CUTE!
SWOON SWOON ♡
What?
WHAT ARE YOU SMILING AT?!
YOU'RE LATE!
HMPH
WOW! ♡
JOLT
OH.

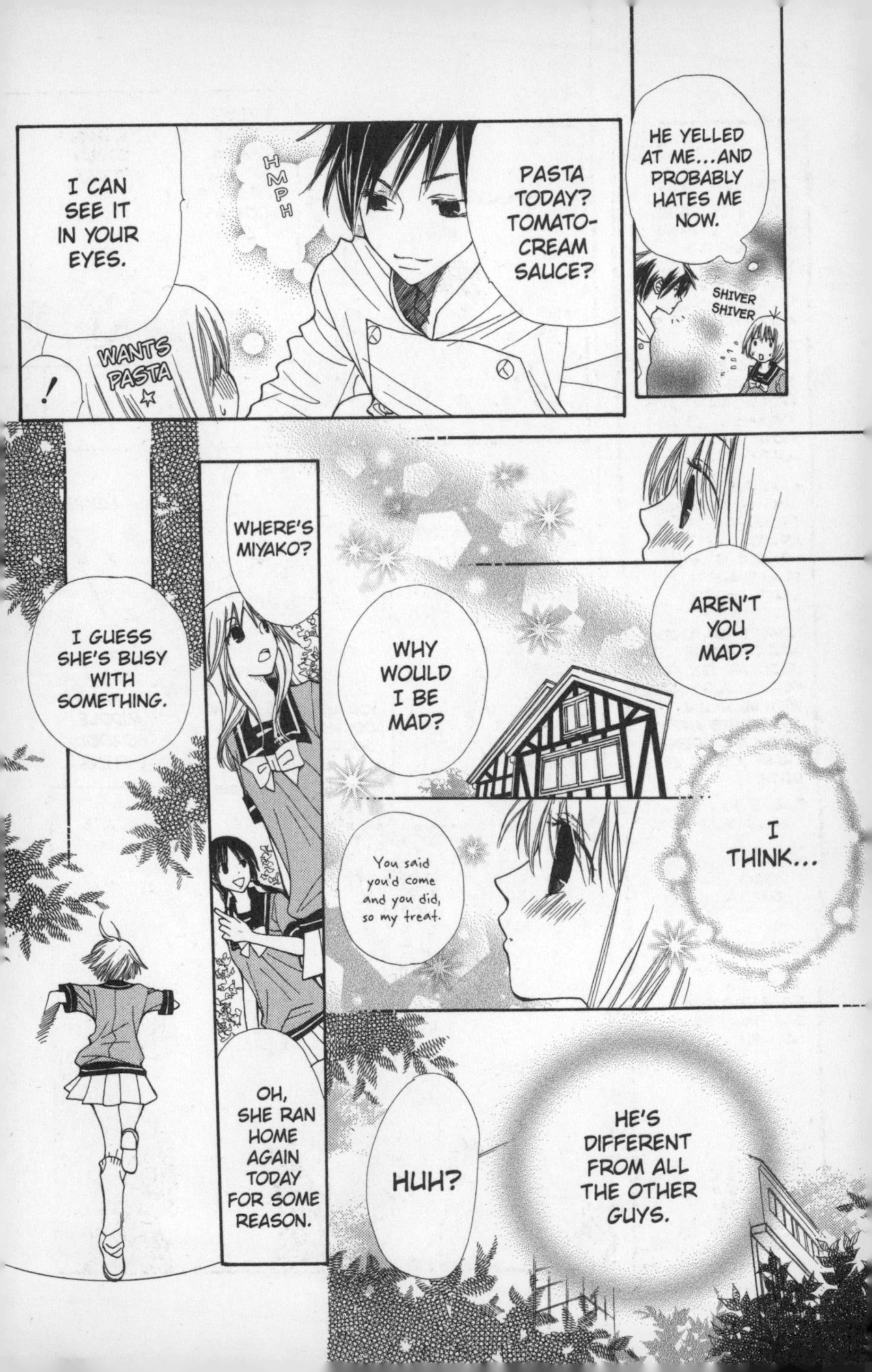
HE YELLED AT ME...AND PROBABLY HATES ME NOW.
SHIVER SHIVER
PASTA TODAY? TOMATO-CREAM SAUCE?
HMPH
I CAN SEE IT IN YOUR EYES.
WANTS PASTA
!
AREN'T YOU MAD?
WHY WOULD I BE MAD?
I THINK...
You said you'd come and you did, so my treat.
HE'S DIFFERENT FROM ALL THE OTHER GUYS.
HUH?
WHERE'S MIYAKO?
OH, SHE RAN HOME AGAIN TODAY FOR SOME REASON.
I GUESS SHE'S BUSY WITH SOMETHING.

6

∘THIS AND THAT∘

• THANK YOU FOR STICKING WITH ME THROUGH THE WHOLE BOOK AND ALL THE QUARTER PAGES. SOMEONE ASKED ME ONCE IN A LETTER:

"IS THE STUFF IN THE QUARTER PAGES TRUE?" IT'S TRUE—ALL OF IT. MANY THINGS HAPPEN IN LIFE...

• THE THEME THIS TIME IS FAIRY-TALE DRESS-UP. I TRIED DRAWING PETER PAN AND IT WAS FUN! THANK YOU VERY MUCH!!

NOW, TO ALL THOSE WHO READ THE BOOK, MY EDITOR WHO COLLABORATES WITH ME AND MY ASSISTANTS AND FAMILY AND FRIENDS, THANK YOU SO VERY MUCH!

I HOPE WE MEET AGAIN IN VOLUME 12!!

IF YOU'D LIKE TO, PLEASE SEND US YOUR THOUGHTS.

MAKI MINAMI
C/O VIZ MEDIA
SA EDITOR
P.O. BOX 77010
SAN FRANCISCO,
CA 94107

WITH ALL MY HEART.

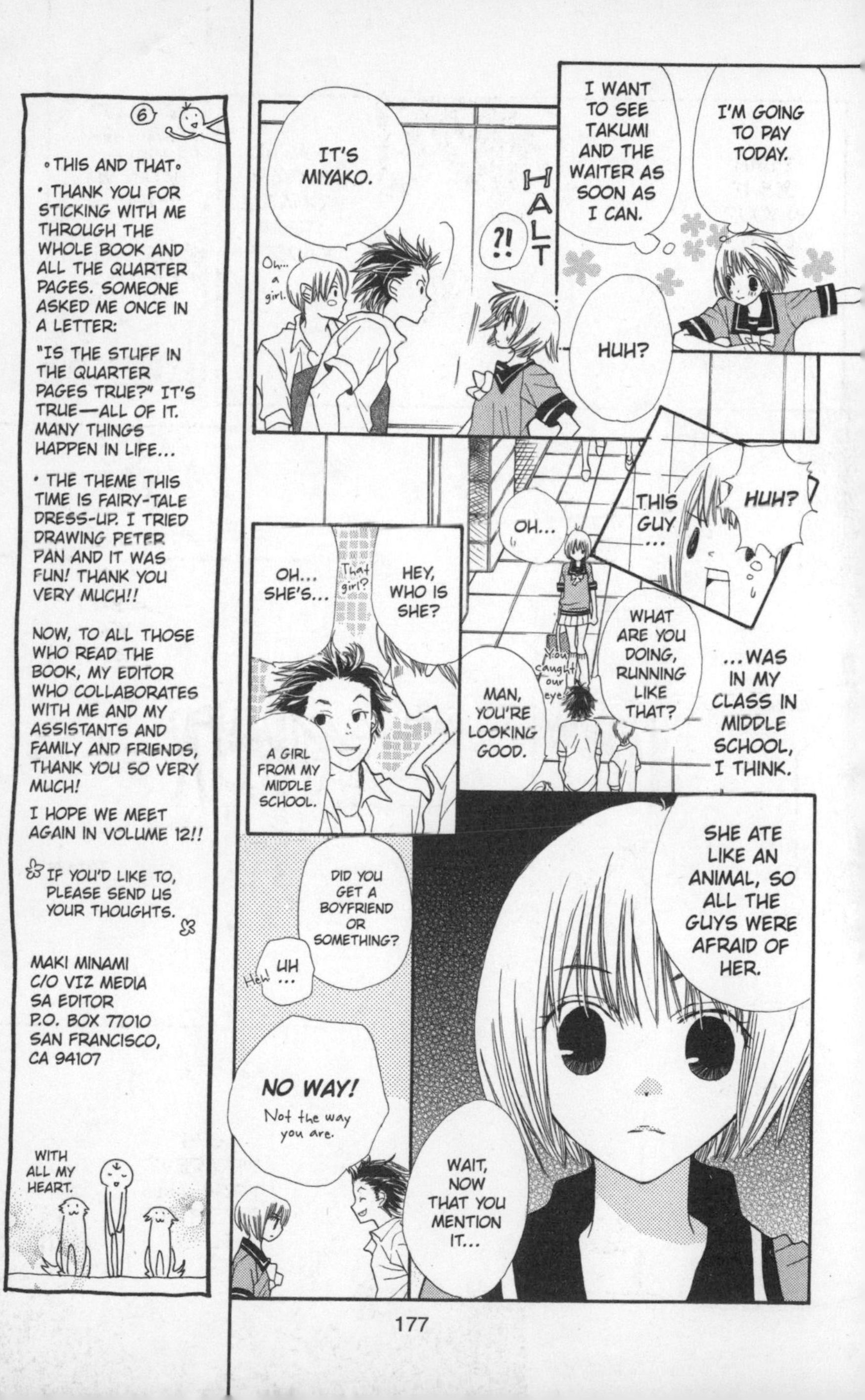

I'M GOING TO PAY TODAY.
I WANT TO SEE TAKUMI AND THE WAITER AS SOON AS I CAN.
HALT
?!
HUH?
IT'S MIYAKO.
Oh... a girl.
HUH?
THIS GUY...
...WAS IN MY CLASS IN MIDDLE SCHOOL, I THINK.
OH...
WHAT ARE YOU DOING, RUNNING LIKE THAT?
You caught our eye.
MAN, YOU'RE LOOKING GOOD.
HEY, WHO IS SHE?
That girl?
OH... SHE'S...
A GIRL FROM MY MIDDLE SCHOOL.
SHE ATE LIKE AN ANIMAL, SO ALL THE GUYS WERE AFRAID OF HER.
DID YOU GET A BOYFRIEND OR SOMETHING?
UH...
Heh!
NO WAY!
Not the way you are.
WAIT, NOW THAT YOU MENTION IT...

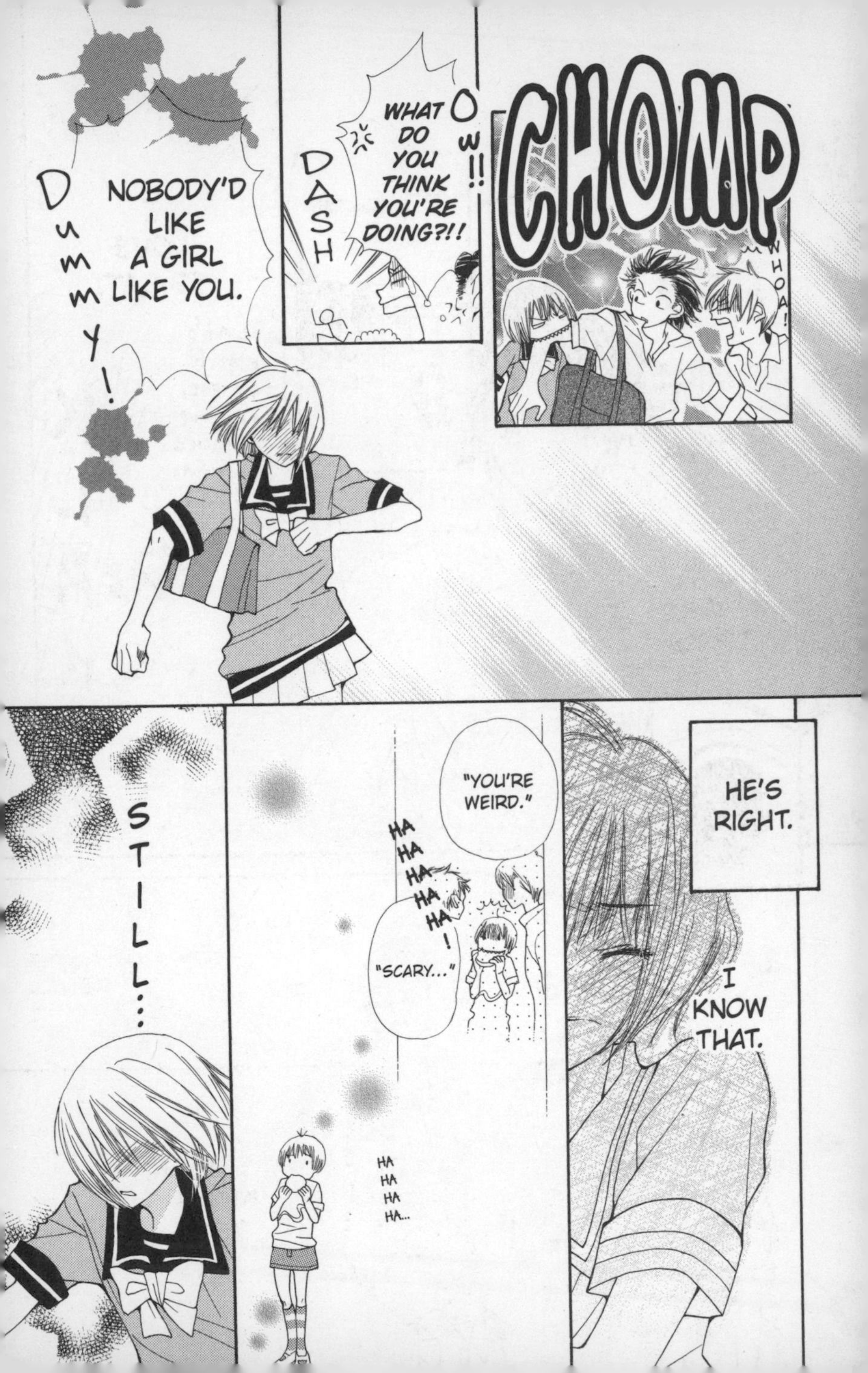
CHOMP
WHOA!
OW!!
WHAT DO YOU THINK YOU'RE DOING?!!
DASH
NOBODY'D LIKE A GIRL LIKE YOU.
Dummy!
HE'S RIGHT.
I KNOW THAT.
"YOU'RE WEIRD."
HA HA HA HA HA!
"SCARY..."
HA HA HA HA...
STILL...

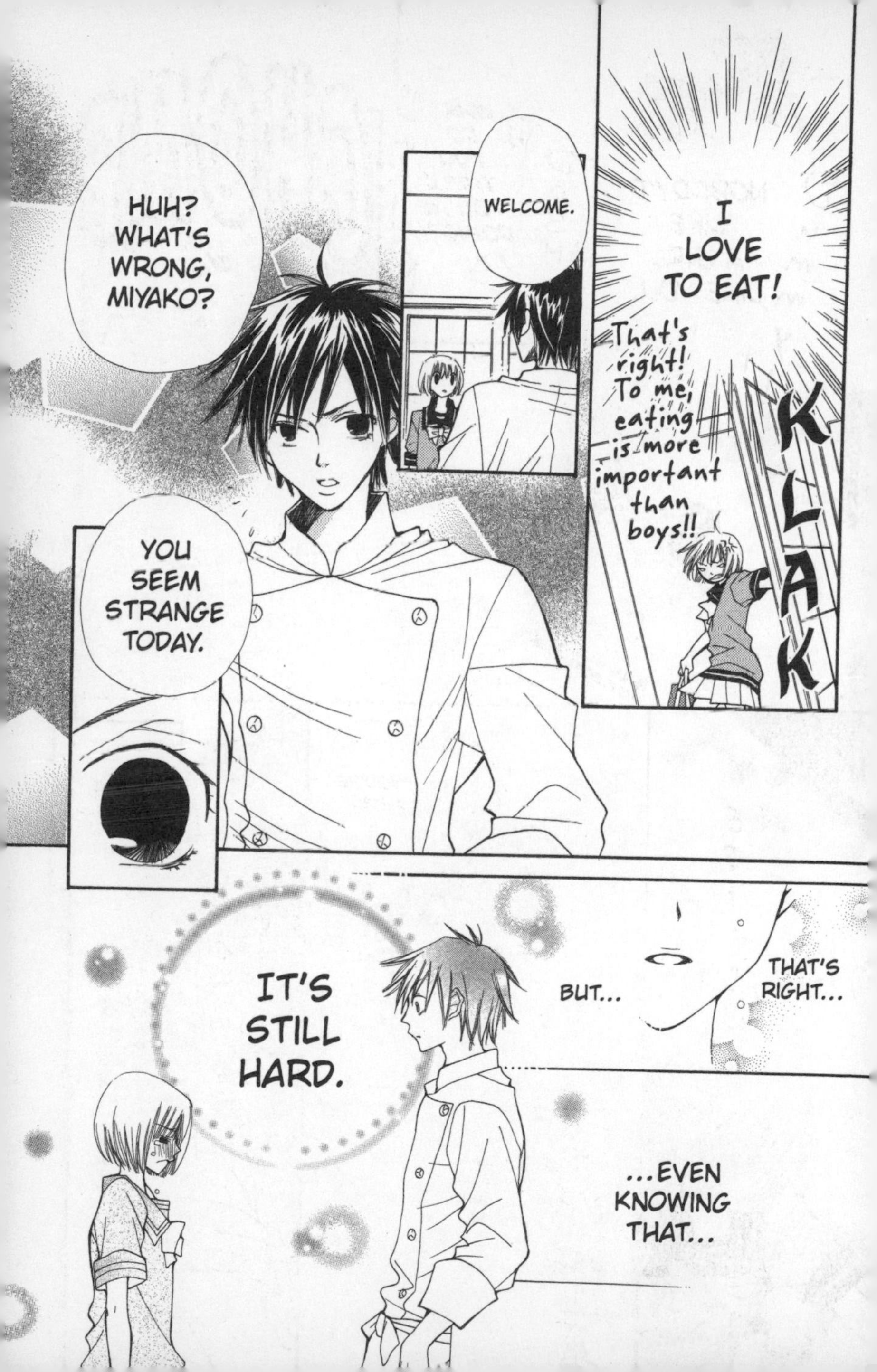
I LOVE TO EAT!
That's right! To me, eating is more important than boys!!
KLAK
WELCOME.
HUH? WHAT'S WRONG, MIYAKO?
YOU SEEM STRANGE TODAY.
THAT'S RIGHT...
BUT...
...EVEN KNOWING THAT...
IT'S STILL HARD.

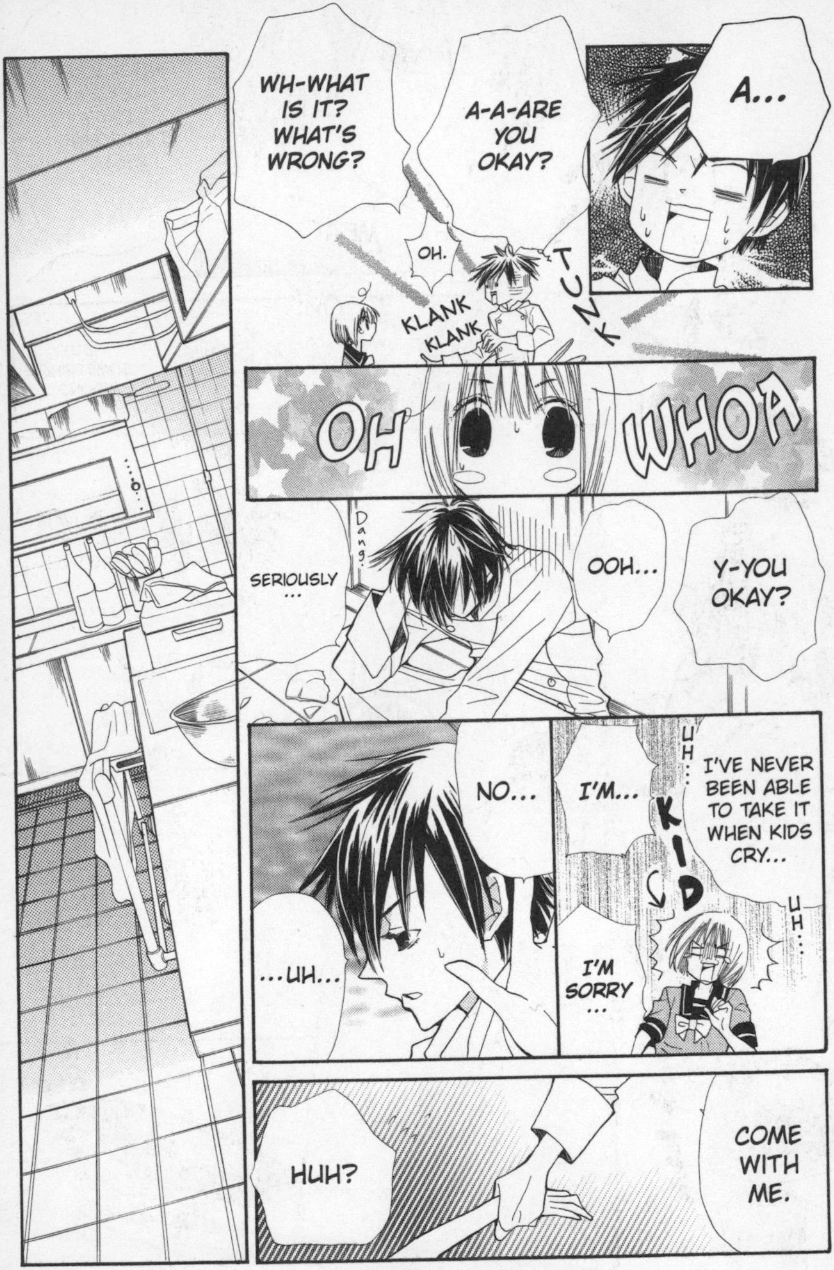
A...
TUNK
A-A-ARE YOU OKAY?
WH-WHAT IS IT? WHAT'S WRONG?
OH.
KLANK KLANK
WHOA
OH
Y-YOU OKAY?
OOH...
Dang.
SERIOUSLY...
UH...
I'VE NEVER BEEN ABLE TO TAKE IT WHEN KIDS CRY...
UH...
KID
I'M...
I'M SORRY...
NO...
...UH...
COME WITH ME.
HUH?

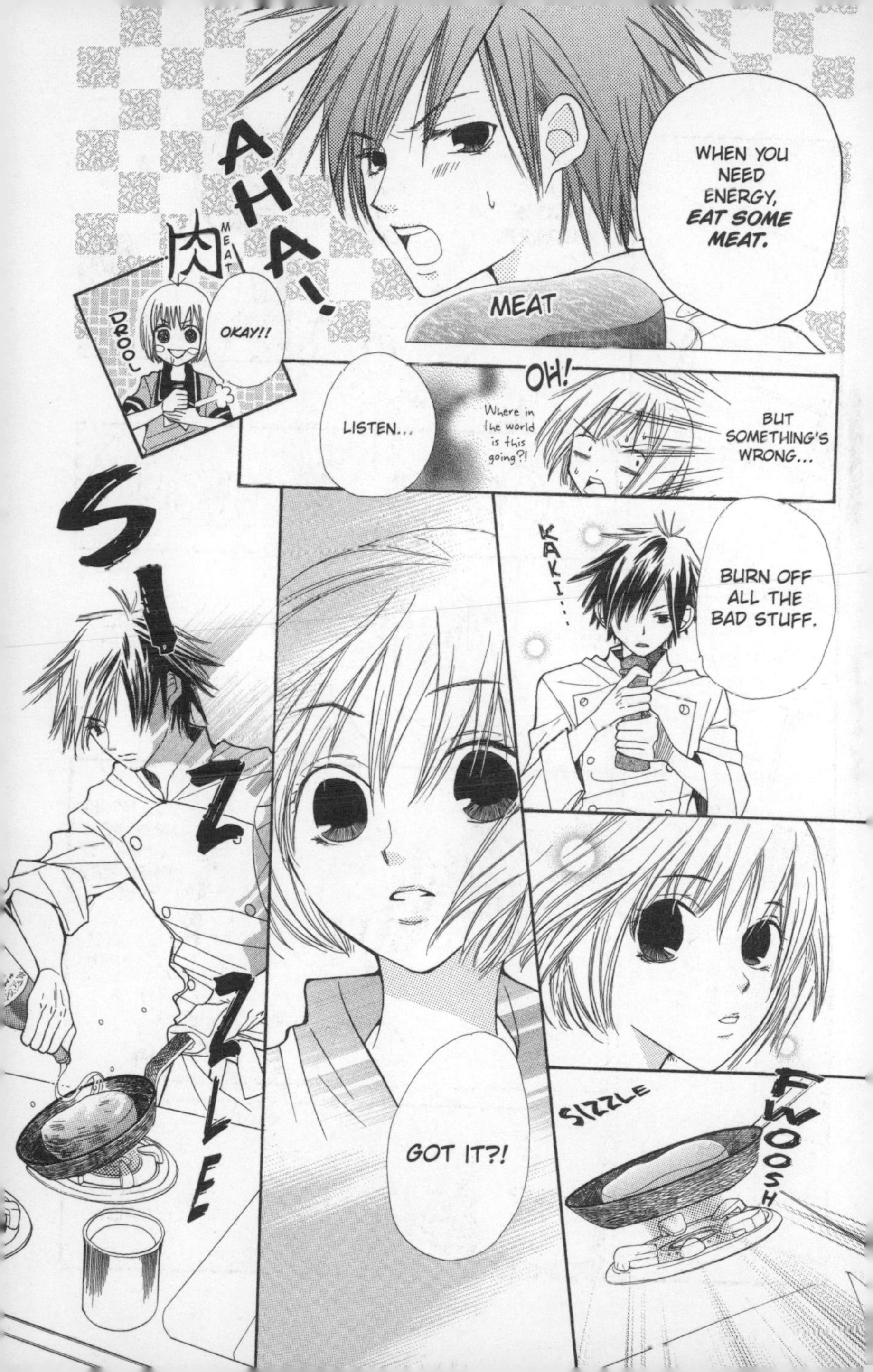
AHA!
WHEN YOU NEED ENERGY, EAT SOME MEAT.
MEAT
肉 MEAT
OKAY!!
DROOL
OH!
BUT SOMETHING'S WRONG...
Where in the world is this going?!
LISTEN...
KAKI...
BURN OFF ALL THE BAD STUFF.
FWOOSH
SIZZLE
GOT IT?!
SIZZLE

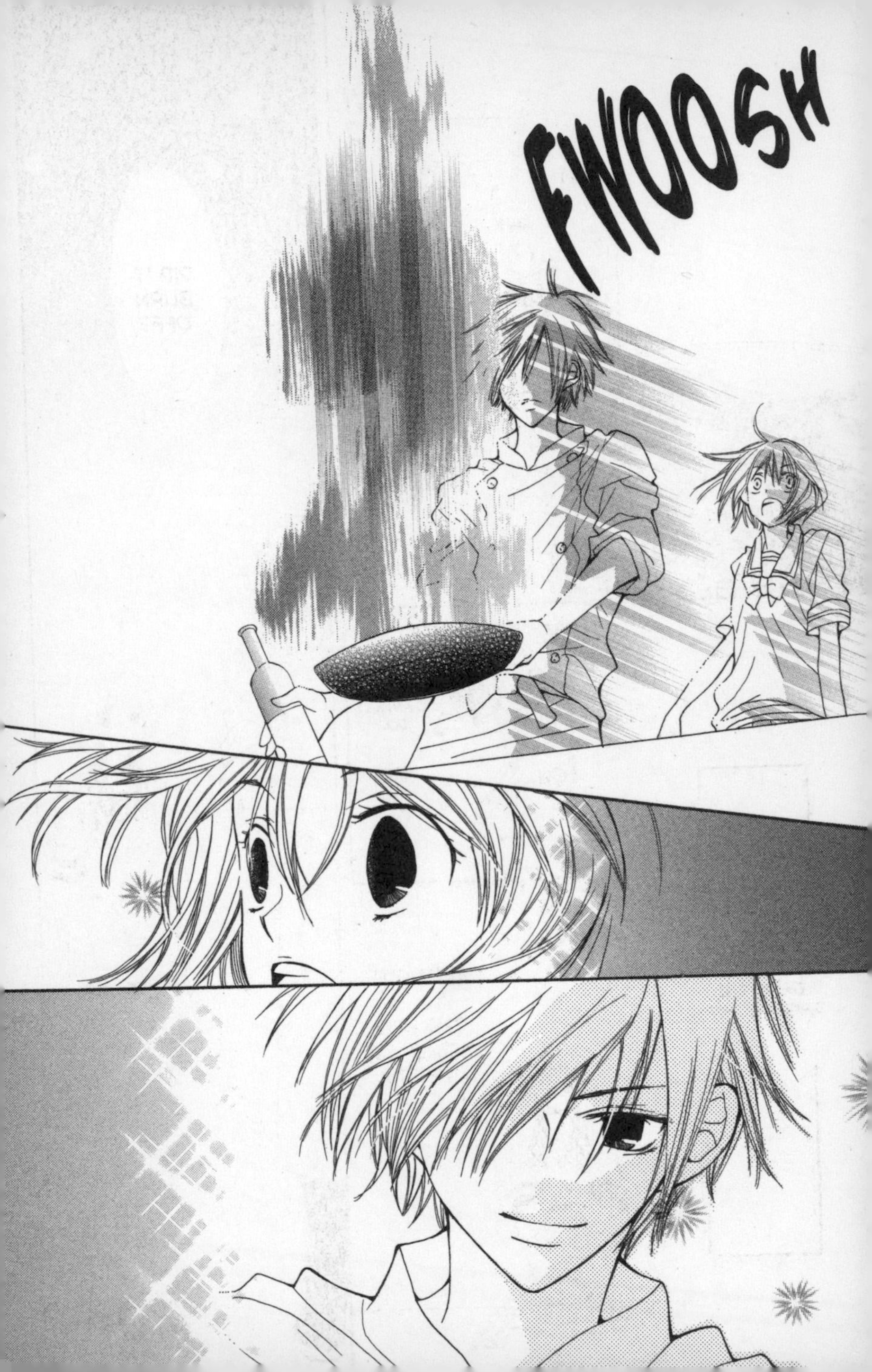
FWOOSH

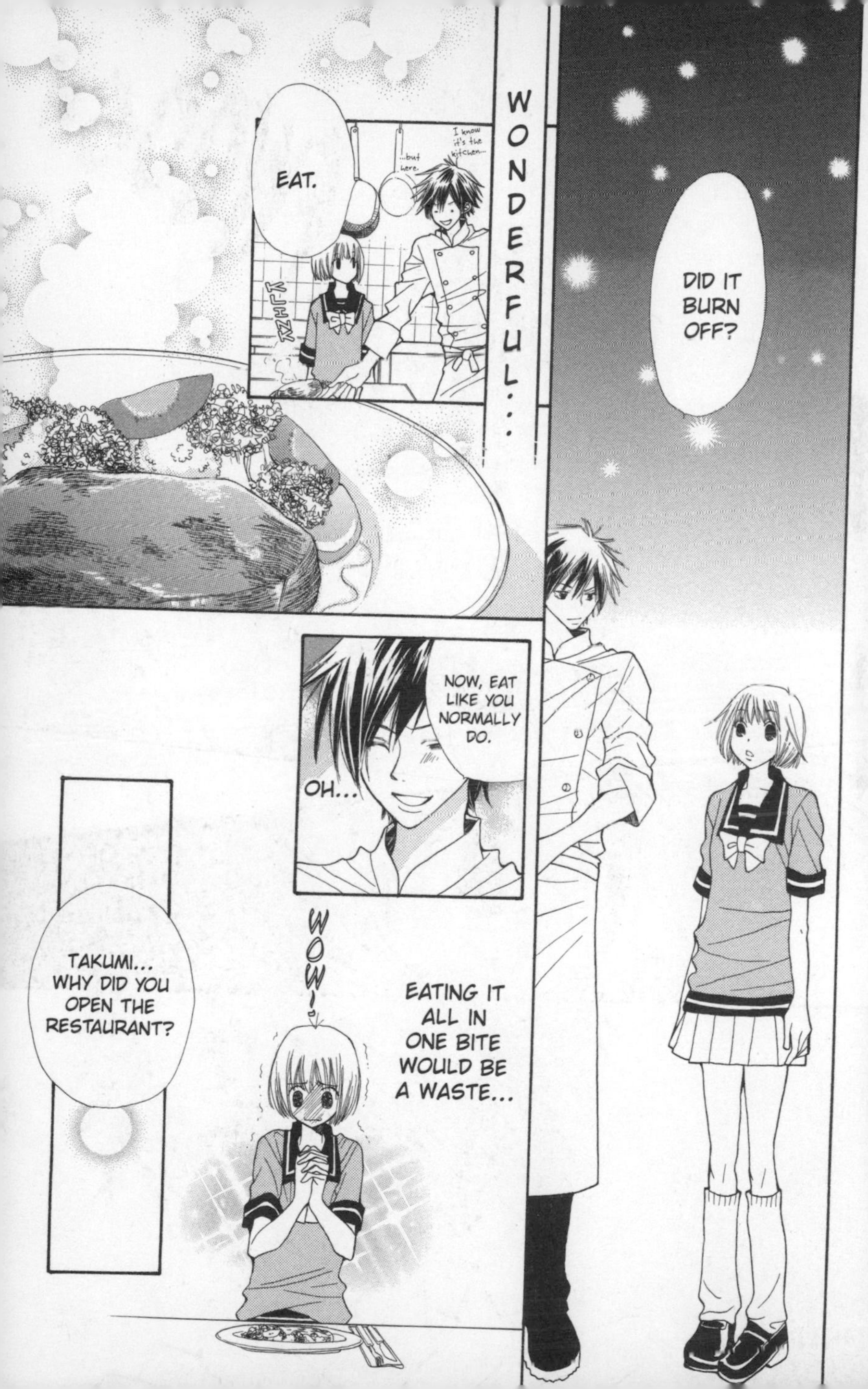
DID IT BURN OFF?
WONDERFUL...
I know it's the kitchen...
...but here.
EAT.
NOW, EAT LIKE YOU NORMALLY DO.
OH...
EATING IT ALL IN ONE BITE WOULD BE A WASTE...
WOW!
TAKUMI... WHY DID YOU OPEN THE RESTAURANT?

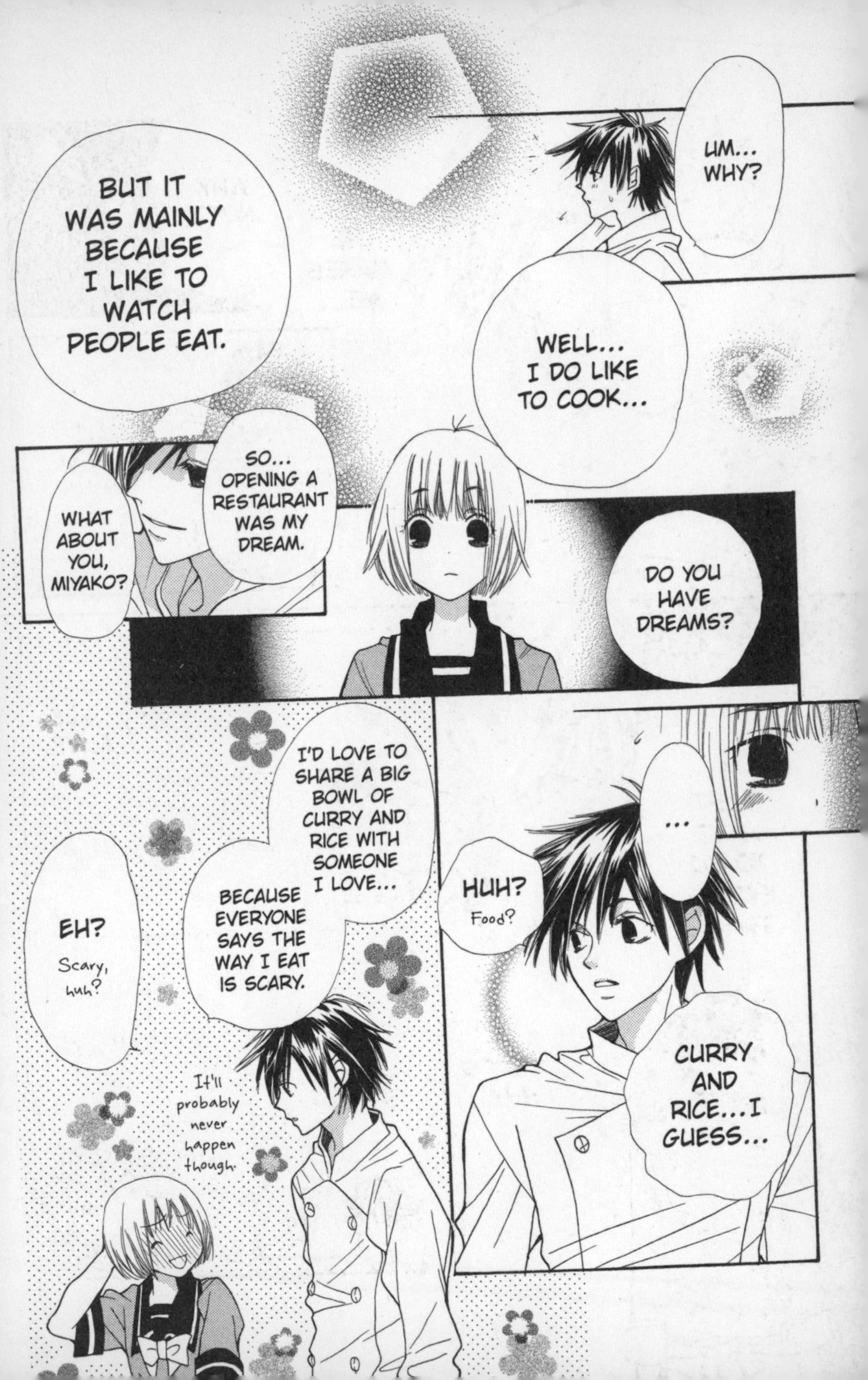
UM... WHY?
WELL... I DO LIKE TO COOK...
BUT IT WAS MAINLY BECAUSE I LIKE TO WATCH PEOPLE EAT.
SO... OPENING A RESTAURANT WAS MY DREAM.
WHAT ABOUT YOU, MIYAKO?
DO YOU HAVE DREAMS?
...
CURRY AND RICE...I GUESS...
HUH? Food?
I'D LOVE TO SHARE A BIG BOWL OF CURRY AND RICE WITH SOMEONE I LOVE...
BECAUSE EVERYONE SAYS THE WAY I EAT IS SCARY.
EH? Scary, huh?
It'll probably never happen though.

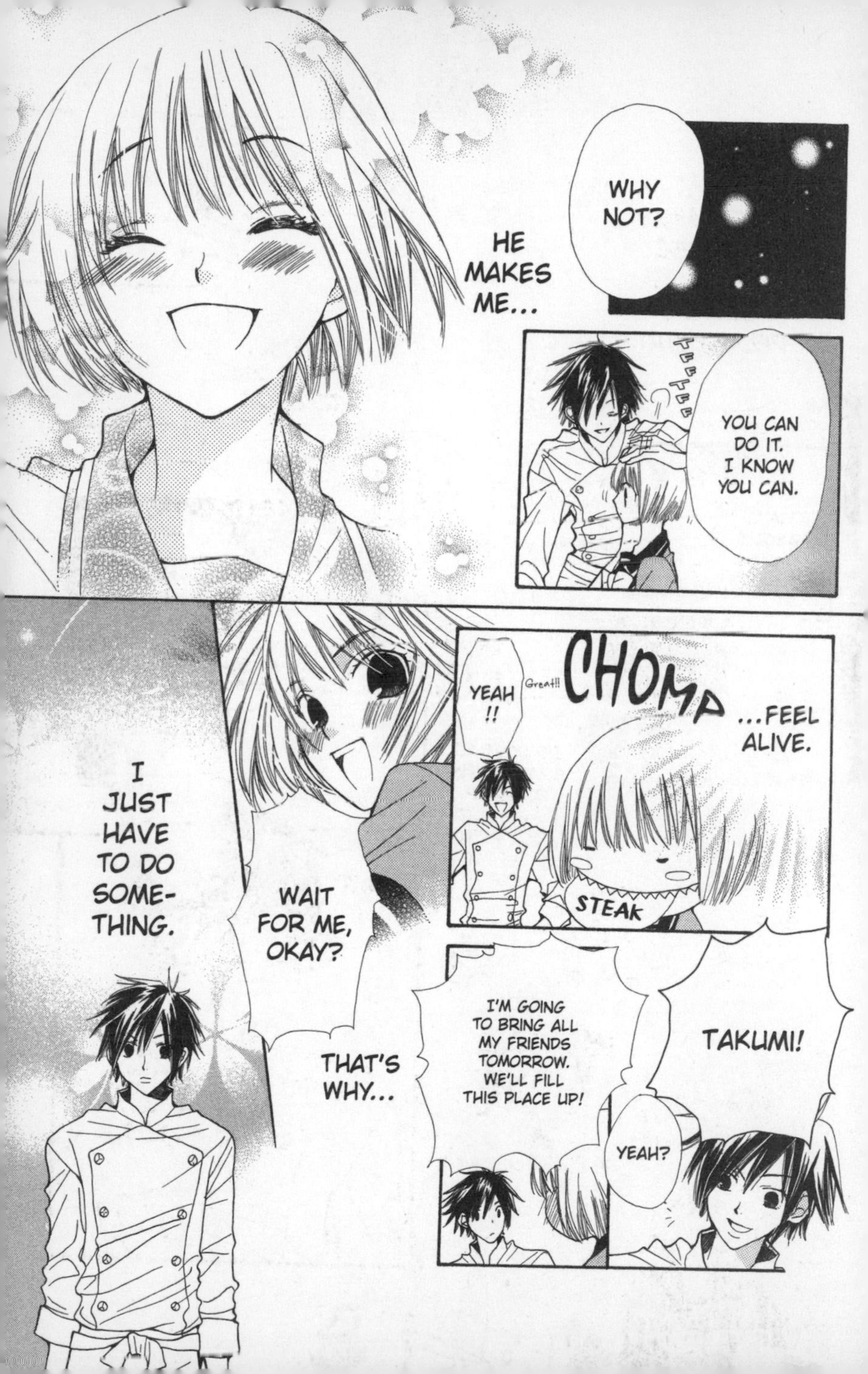
WHY NOT?
TFFTFF
YOU CAN DO IT. I KNOW YOU CAN.
HE MAKES ME...
CHOMP
...FEEL ALIVE.
YEAH !!
Great!!
STEAK
TAKUMI!
YEAH?
I'M GOING TO BRING ALL MY FRIENDS TOMORROW. WE'LL FILL THIS PLACE UP!
THAT'S WHY...
I JUST HAVE TO DO SOME-THING.
WAIT FOR ME, OKAY?

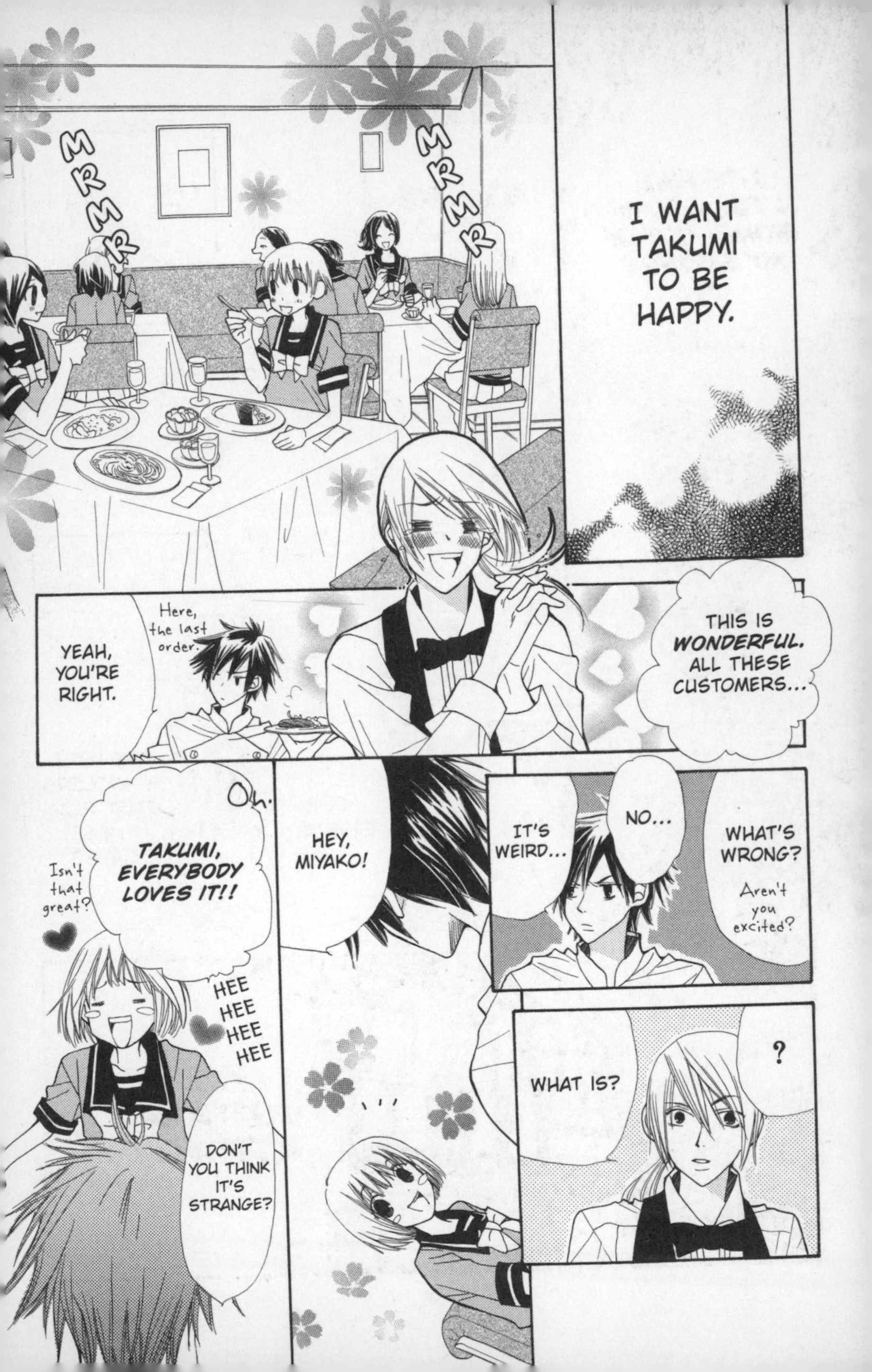
I WANT TAKUMI TO BE HAPPY.
MRMMR
MRMMR
THIS IS WONDERFUL. ALL THESE CUSTOMERS...
Here, the last order.
YEAH, YOU'RE RIGHT.
WHAT'S WRONG?
Aren't you excited?
NO...
IT'S WEIRD...
?
WHAT IS?
HEY, MIYAKO!
DON'T YOU THINK IT'S STRANGE?
Oh.
TAKUMI, EVERYBODY LOVES IT!!
Isn't that great?
HEE HEE HEE HEE

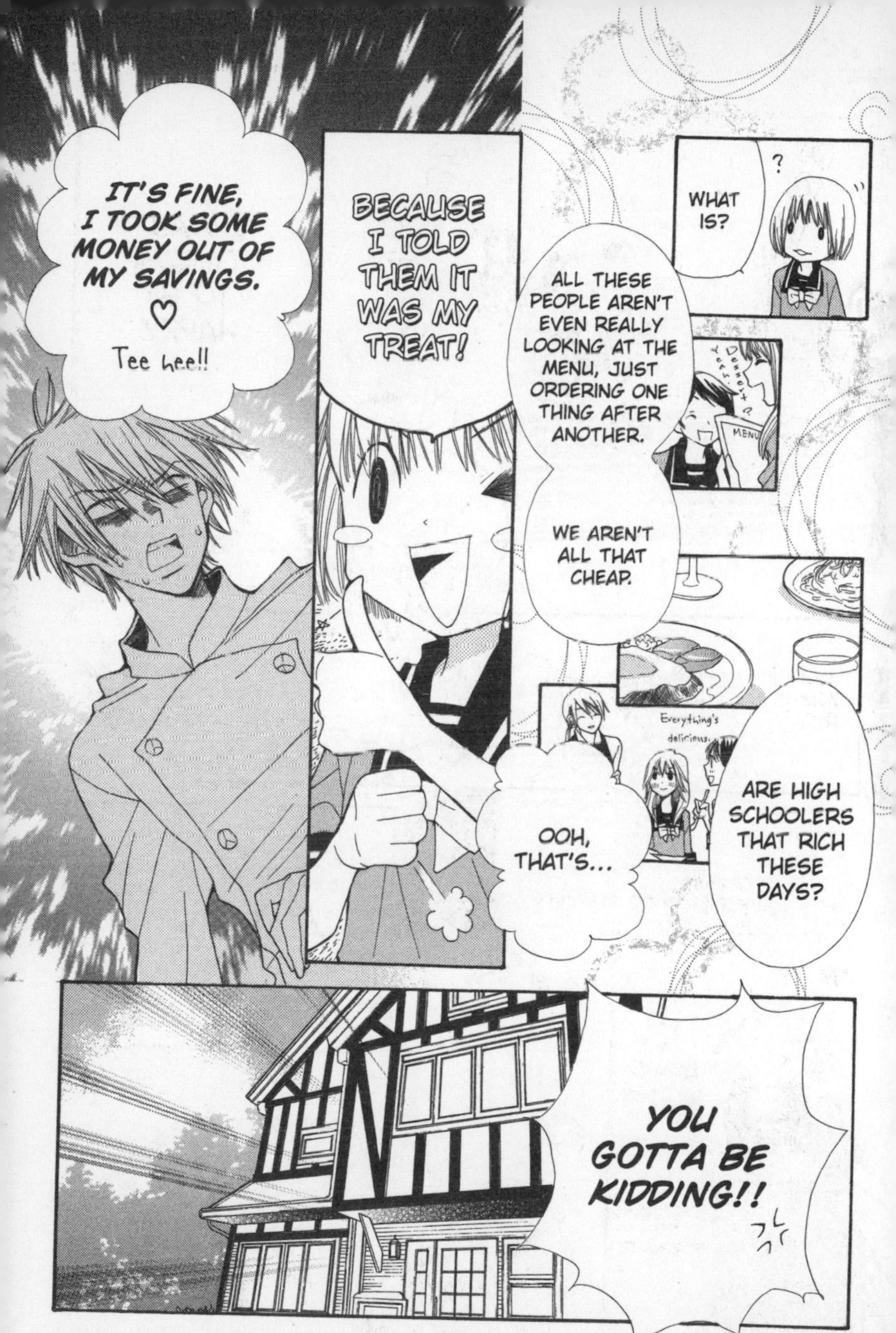
?
WHAT IS?
Dessert? Yeah.
MENU
ALL THESE PEOPLE AREN'T EVEN REALLY LOOKING AT THE MENU, JUST ORDERING ONE THING AFTER ANOTHER.
WE AREN'T ALL THAT CHEAP.
Everything's delicious.
ARE HIGH SCHOOLERS THAT RICH THESE DAYS?
OOH, THAT'S...
BECAUSE I TOLD THEM IT WAS MY TREAT!
IT'S FINE, I TOOK SOME MONEY OUT OF MY SAVINGS. ♡
Tee hee!!
YOU GOTTA BE KIDDING!!

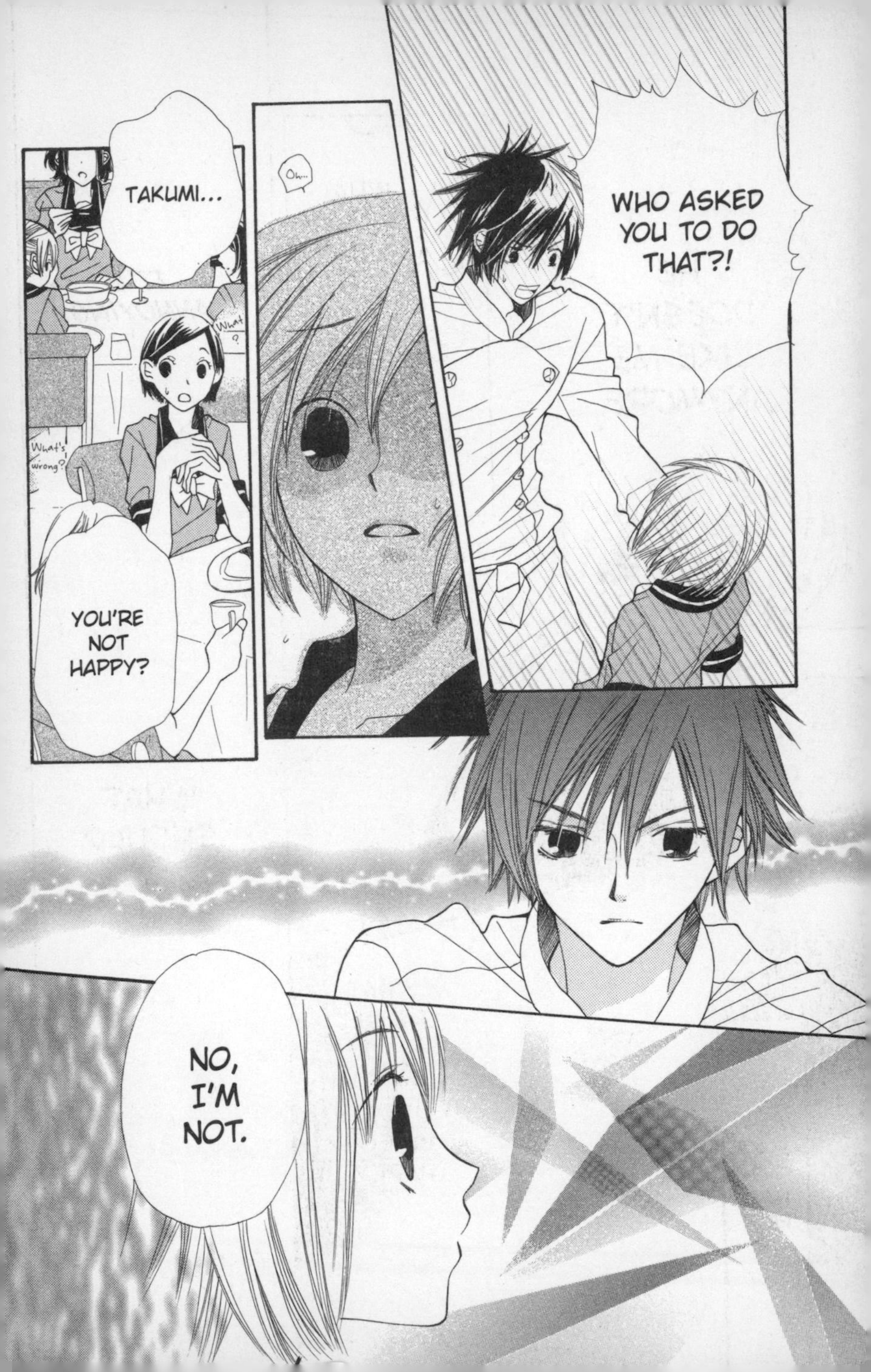
WHO ASKED YOU TO DO THAT?!
Oh...
TAKUMI...
What?
What's wrong?
YOU'RE NOT HAPPY?
NO, I'M NOT.

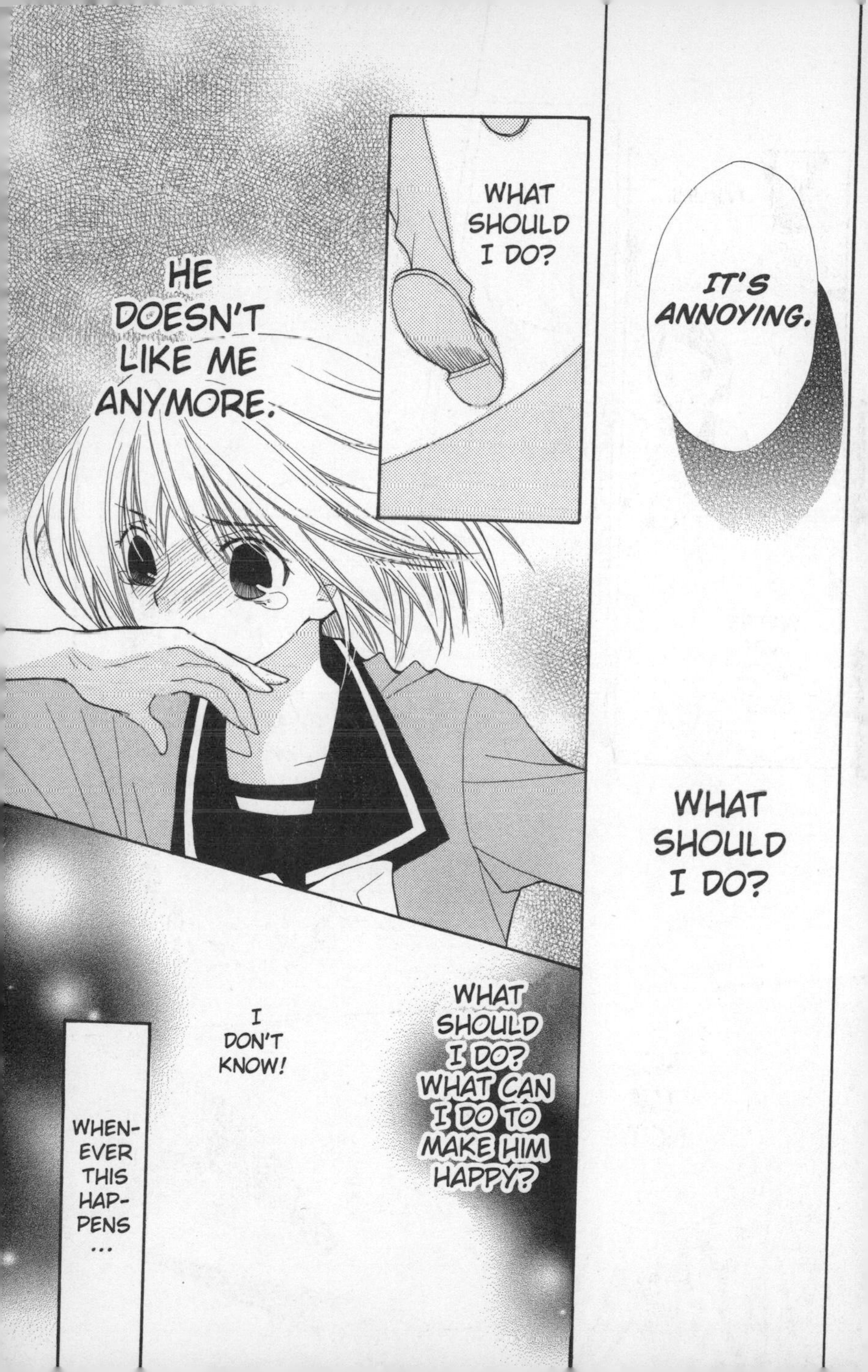
IT'S ANNOYING.
WHAT SHOULD I DO?
WHAT SHOULD I DO?
HE DOESN'T LIKE ME ANYMORE.
WHAT SHOULD I DO? WHAT CAN I DO TO MAKE HIM HAPPY?
I DON'T KNOW!
WHEN-EVER THIS HAP-PENS...

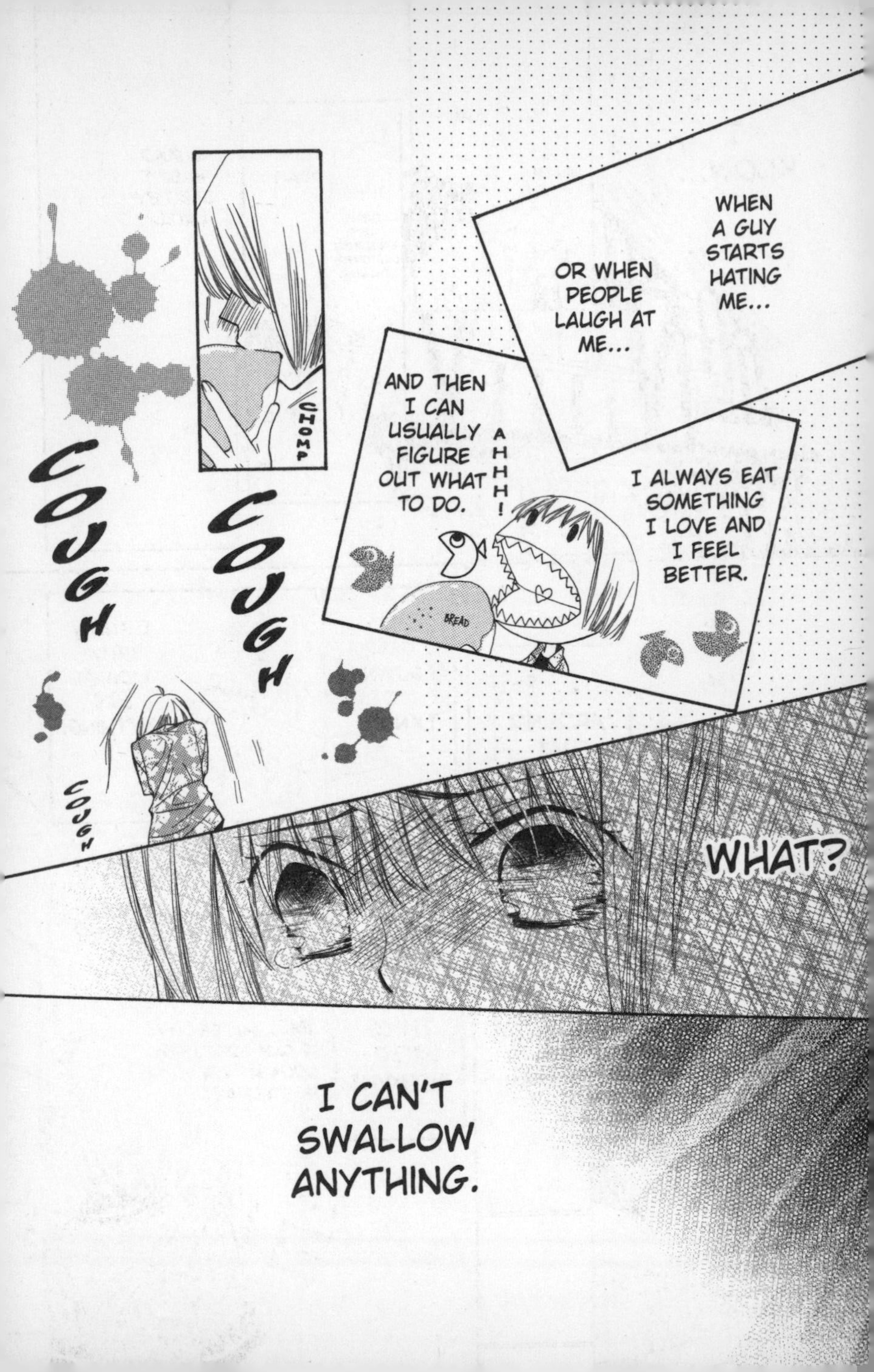
WHEN A GUY STARTS HATING ME...
OR WHEN PEOPLE LAUGH AT ME...
I ALWAYS EAT SOMETHING I LOVE AND I FEEL BETTER.
AHHHH!
BREAD
AND THEN I CAN USUALLY FIGURE OUT WHAT TO DO.
CHOMP
COUGH
COUGH
COUGH
WHAT?
I CAN'T SWALLOW ANYTHING.

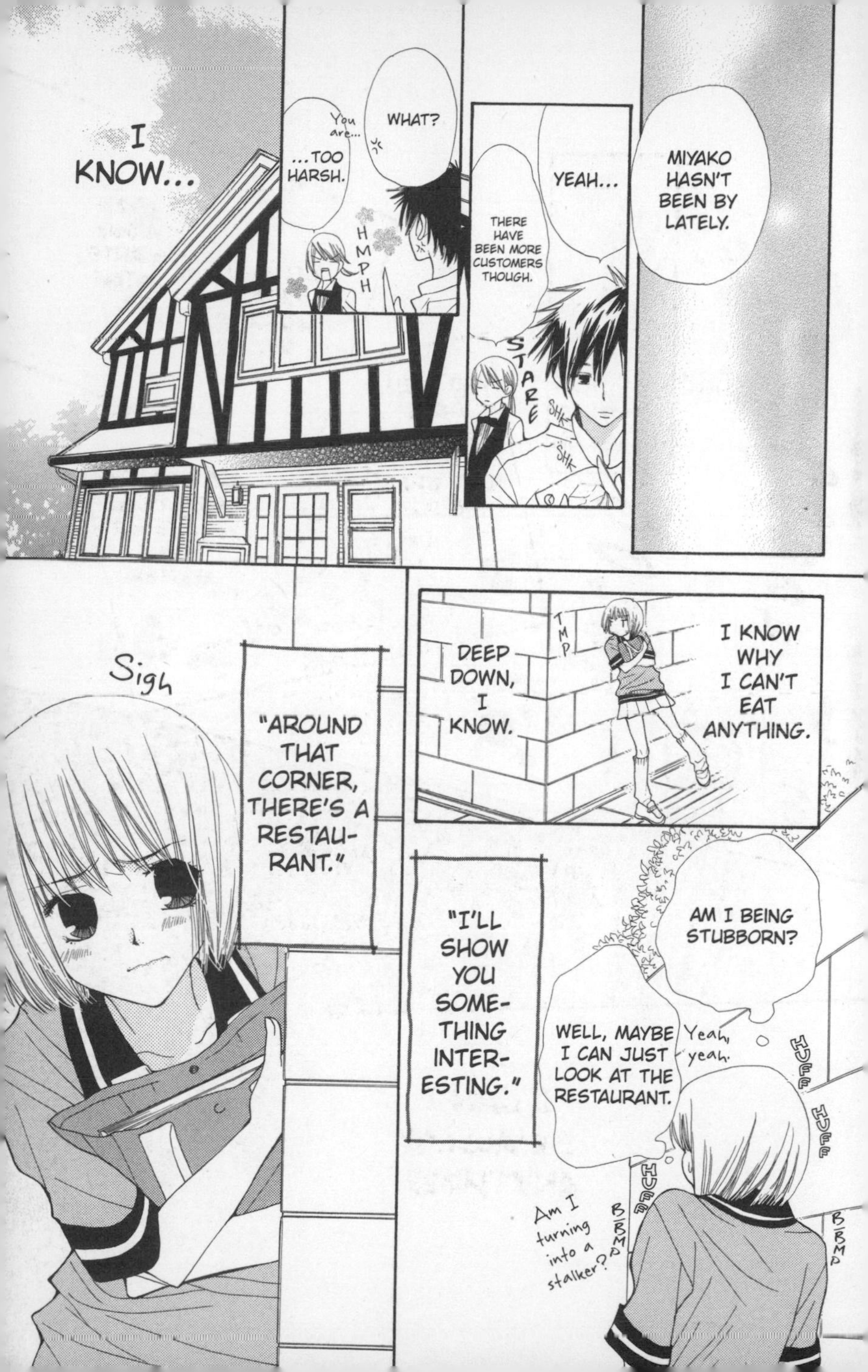
MIYAKO HASN'T BEEN BY LATELY.
YEAH...
THERE HAVE BEEN MORE CUSTOMERS THOUGH.
STARE
SHK
SHK
WHAT?
You are...
...TOO HARSH.
HMPH
I KNOW...
I KNOW WHY I CAN'T EAT ANYTHING.
DEEP DOWN, I KNOW.
TMP
Sigh
"AROUND THAT CORNER, THERE'S A RESTAURANT."
"I'LL SHOW YOU SOMETHING INTERESTING."
AM I BEING STUBBORN?
WELL, MAYBE I CAN JUST LOOK AT THE RESTAURANT.
Yeah, yeah.
HUFF
HUFF
HUFF
Am I turning into a stalker?
B-BMP
B-BMP

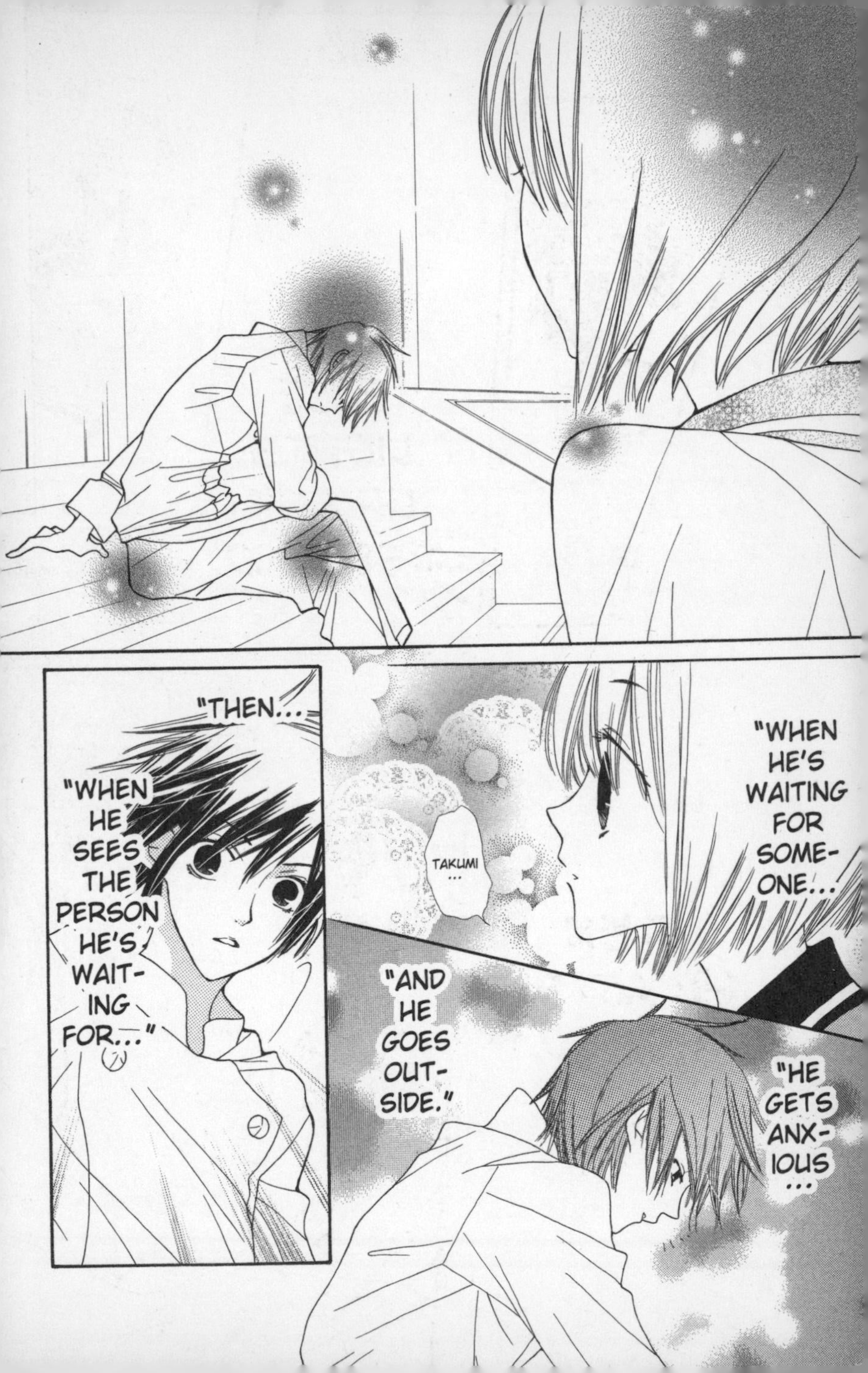
"WHEN HE'S WAITING FOR SOMEONE...
TAKUMI...
"HE GETS ANXIOUS...
"AND HE GOES OUTSIDE."
"THEN...
"WHEN HE SEES THE PERSON HE'S WAITING FOR..."

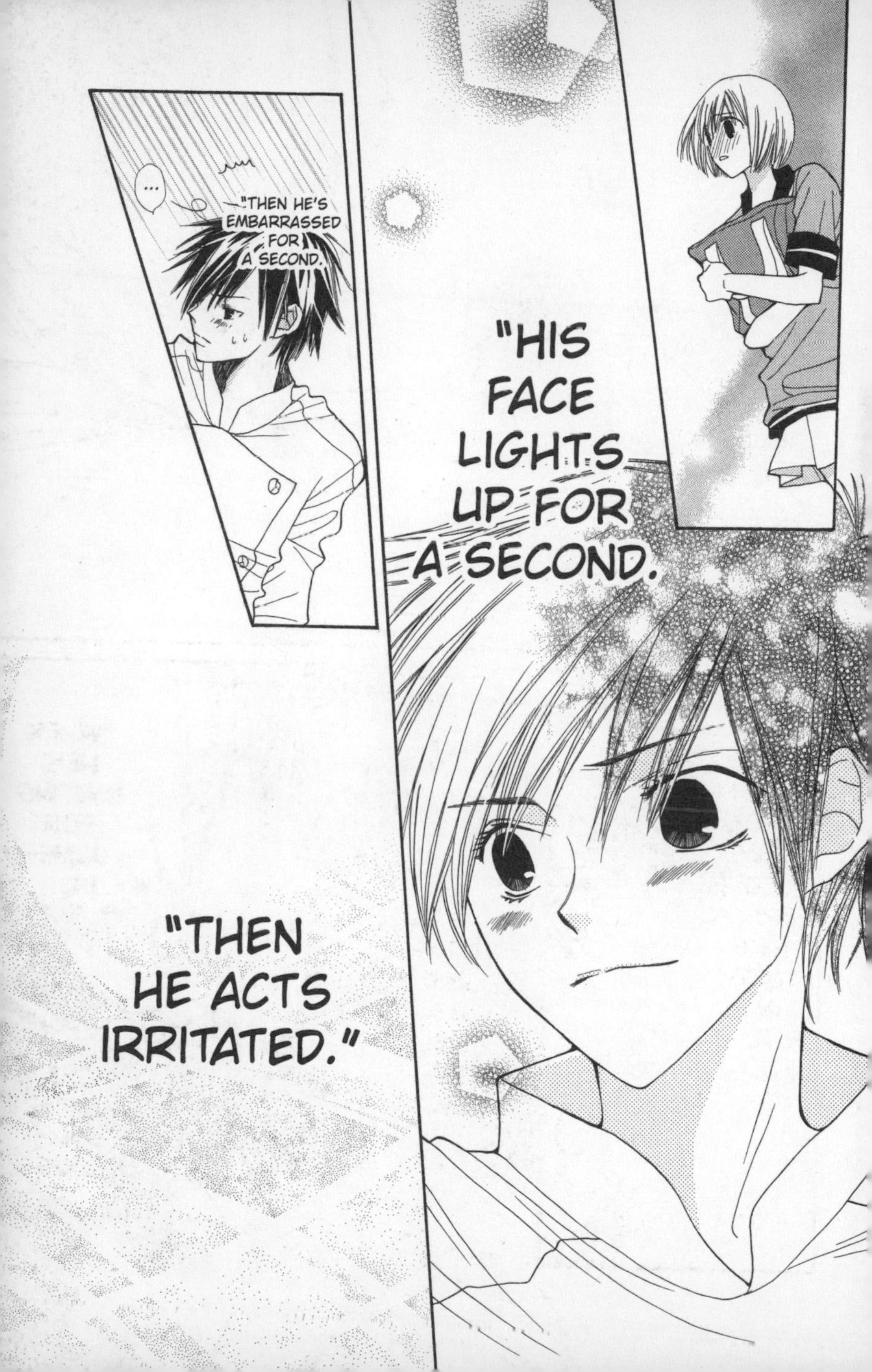
"HIS FACE LIGHTS UP FOR A SECOND.
...
"THEN HE'S EMBARRASSED FOR A SECOND.
"THEN HE ACTS IRRITATED."

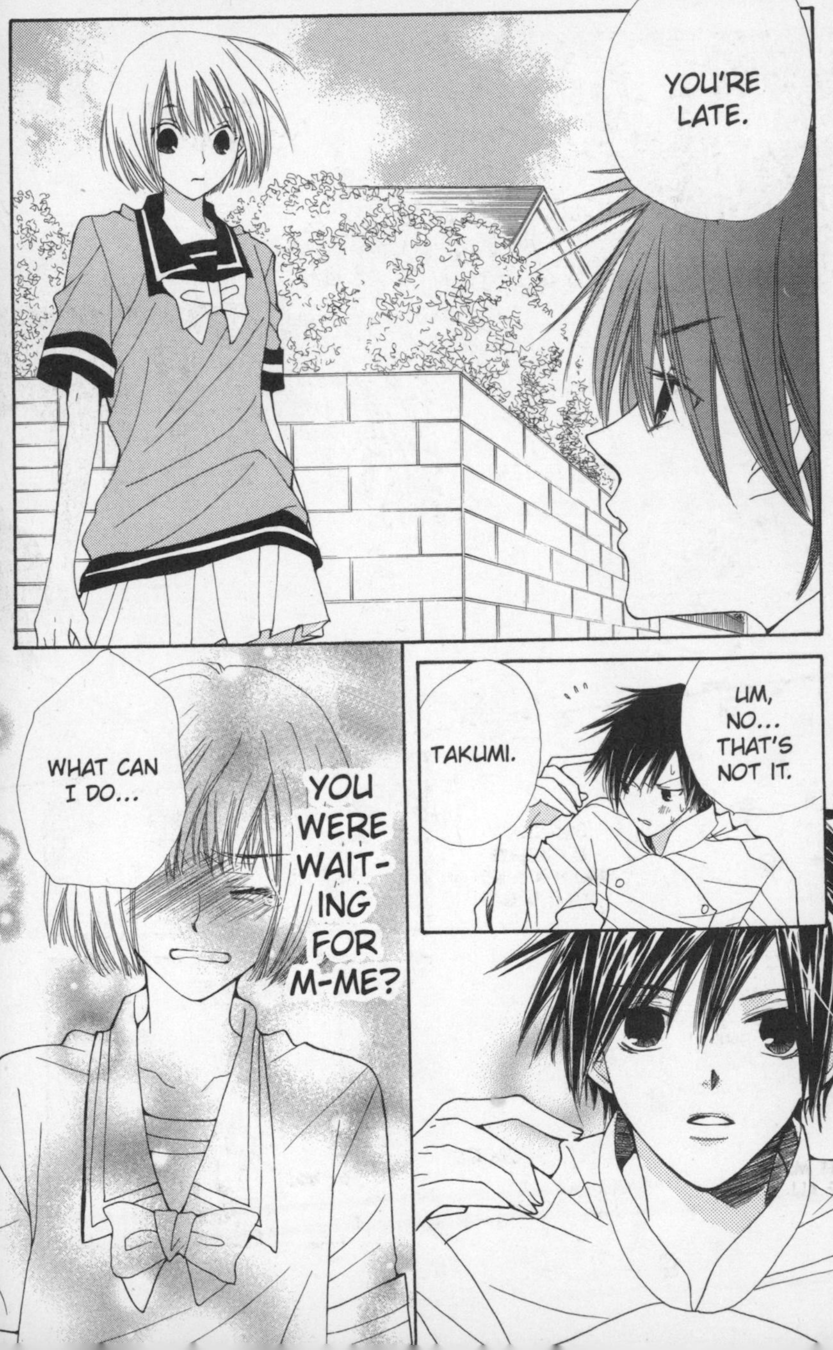
YOU'RE LATE.
UM, NO... THAT'S NOT IT.
TAKUMI.
YOU WERE WAIT-ING FOR M-ME?
WHAT CAN I DO...

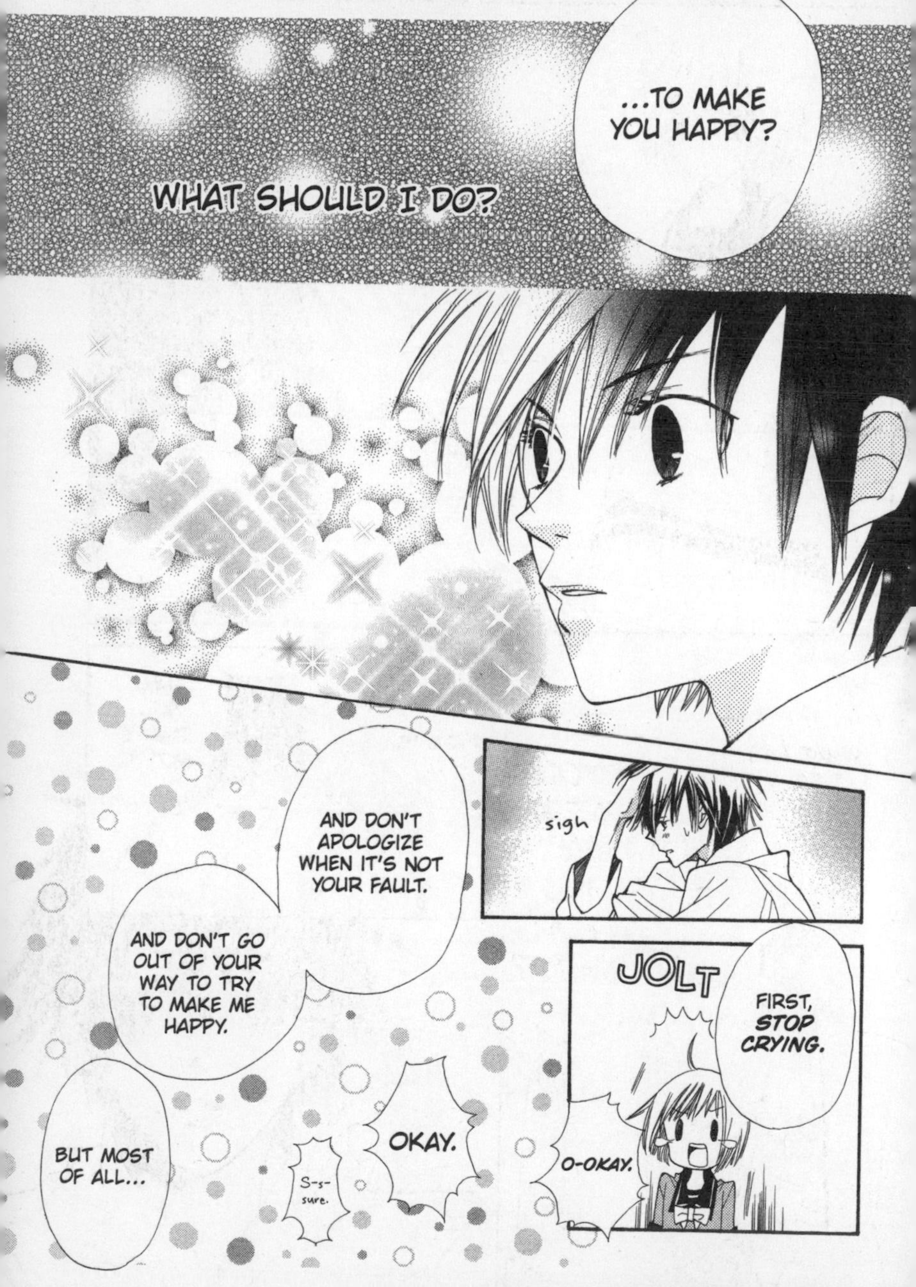
...TO MAKE YOU HAPPY?
WHAT SHOULD I DO?
sigh
JOLT
FIRST, STOP CRYING.
O-OKAY.
AND DON'T APOLOGIZE WHEN IT'S NOT YOUR FAULT.
OKAY.
AND DON'T GO OUT OF YOUR WAY TO TRY TO MAKE ME HAPPY.
S-s-sure.
BUT MOST OF ALL...

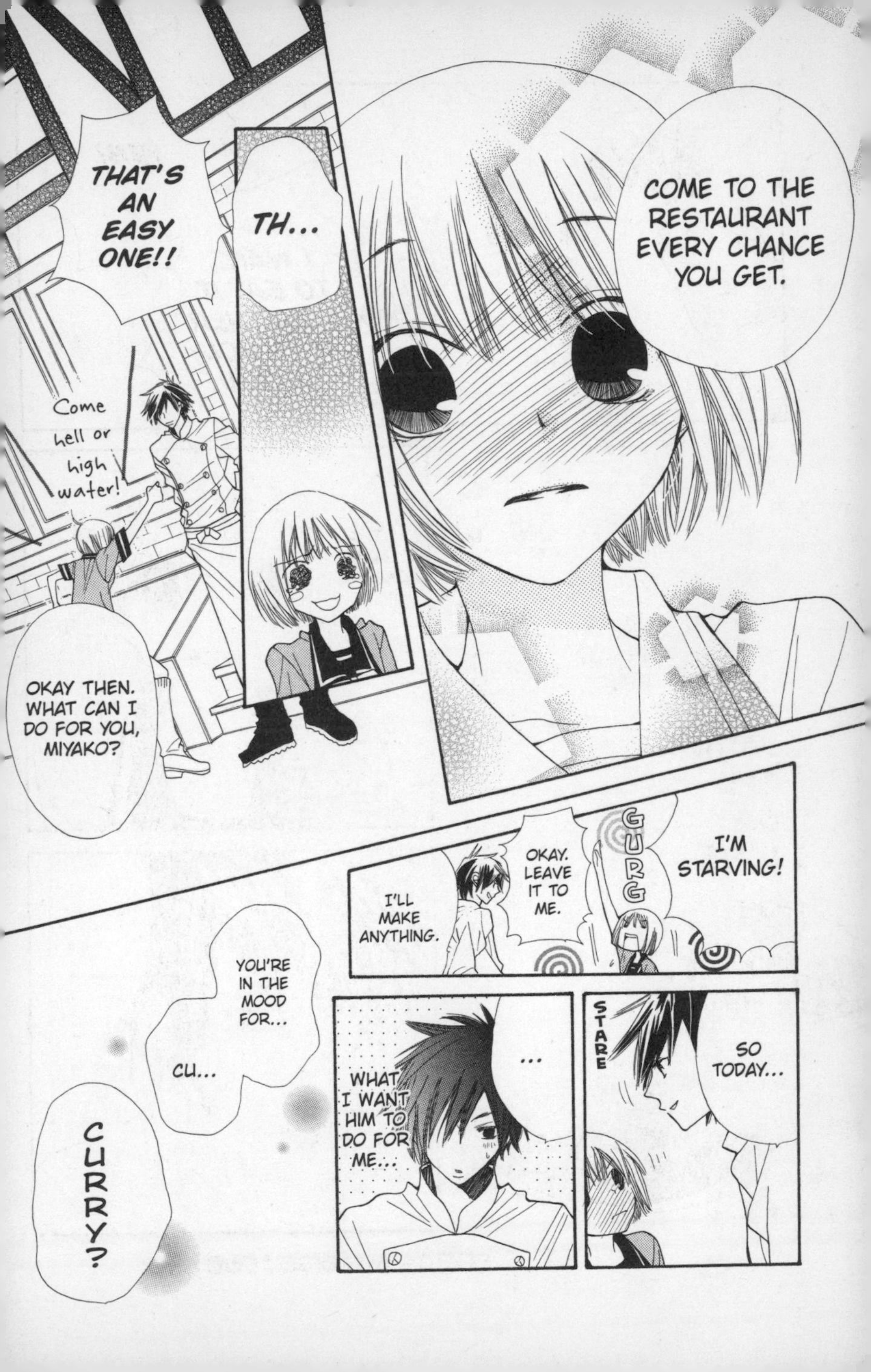

COME TO THE RESTAURANT EVERY CHANCE YOU GET.
TH...
THAT'S AN EASY ONE!!
Come hell or high water!
OKAY THEN. WHAT CAN I DO FOR YOU, MIYAKO?
I'M STARVING!
GURG
OKAY. LEAVE IT TO ME.
I'LL MAKE ANYTHING.
STARE
SO TODAY...
...
WHAT I WANT HIM TO DO FOR ME...
YOU'RE IN THE MOOD FOR...
CU...
CURRY?

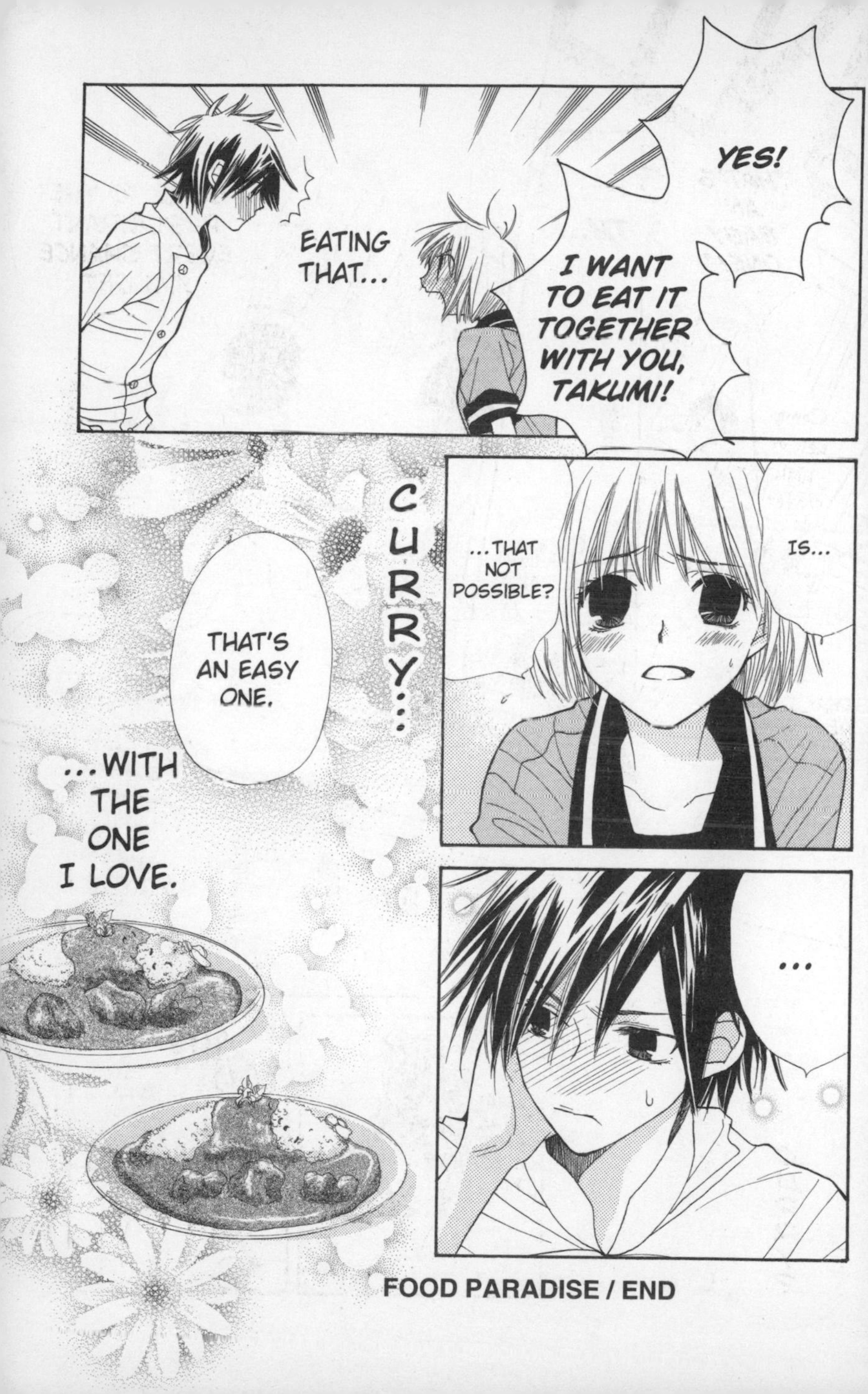
YES!
I WANT TO EAT IT TOGETHER WITH YOU, TAKUMI!
EATING THAT...
IS...
...THAT NOT POSSIBLE?
...
CURRY...
THAT'S AN EASY ONE.
...WITH THE ONE I LOVE.

FOOD PARADISE / END

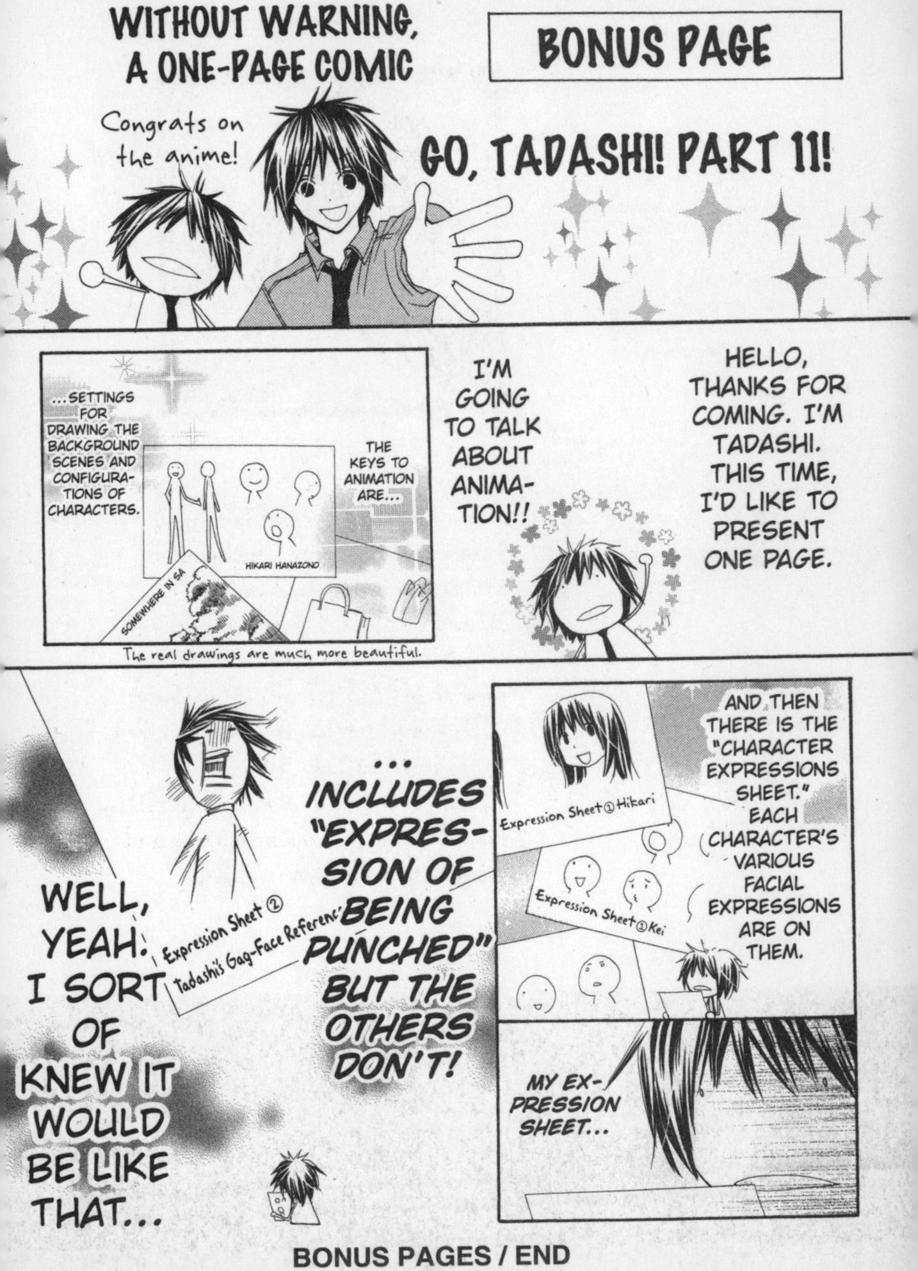
BONUS PAGE
WITHOUT WARNING, A ONE-PAGE COMIC
GO, TADASHI! PART 11!
Congrats on the anime!
HELLO, THANKS FOR COMING. I'M TADASHI. THIS TIME, I'D LIKE TO PRESENT ONE PAGE.
I'M GOING TO TALK ABOUT ANIMATION!!
THE KEYS TO ANIMATION ARE...
...SETTINGS FOR DRAWING THE BACKGROUND SCENES AND CONFIGURATIONS OF CHARACTERS.
HIKARI HANAZONO
SOMEWHERE IN SA
The real drawings are much more beautiful.
AND THEN THERE IS THE "CHARACTER EXPRESSIONS SHEET." EACH CHARACTER'S VARIOUS FACIAL EXPRESSIONS ARE ON THEM.
Expression Sheet ① Hikari
Expression Sheet ① Kei
MY EXPRESSION SHEET...
...INCLUDES "EXPRESSION OF BEING PUNCHED" BUT THE OTHERS DON'T!
Expression Sheet ②
Tadashi's Gag-Face Referenc
WELL, YEAH. I SORT OF KNEW IT WOULD BE LIKE THAT...

BONUS PAGES / END

Maki Minami is from Saitama Prefecture in Japan. She debuted in 2001 with *Kanata no Ao* (Faraway Blue). Her other works include *Kimi wa Girlfriend* (You're My Girlfriend), *Mainichi ga Takaramono* (Every Day Is a Treasure) and *Yuki Atataka* (Warm Winter). *S•A* was serialized in Japan's *Hana to Yume* magazine and made into an anime in 2008.

S·A

Vol. 11

The Shojo Beat Manga Edition

STORY & ART BY

MAKI MINAMI

English Adaptation/Amanda Hubbard
Translation/JN Productions
Touch-up Art & Lettering/Hudson Yards
Design/Deirdre Shiozawa
Editor/Jonathan Tarbox

Editor in Chief, Books/Alvin Lu
Editor in Chief, Magazines/Marc Weidenbaum
VP, Publishing Licensing/Rika Inouye
VP, Sales & Product Marketing/Gonzalo Ferreyra
VP, Creative/Linda Espinosa
Publisher/Hyoe Narita

Published by VIZ Media, LLC
P.O. Box 77010
San Francisco, CA 94107

Shojo Beat Manga Edition
10 9 8 7 6 5 4 3 2 1
First printing, July 2009

www.viz.com   store.viz.com